THE LANGUAGE ENCOUNTER IN THE AMERICAS, 1492–1800

EUROPEAN EXPANSION AND GLOBAL INTERACTION

GENERAL EDITORS
Pieter Emmer, Institute for the History of European Expansion,
   Leiden University
Karen Ordahl Kupperman, New York University
H. G. Roeber, Penn State University

Published in association with the Forum on European Expansion and Global Interaction

IN THIS SERIES:

The Language Encounter in the Americas, 1492–1800
Edited by Edward G. Gray and Norman Fiering

The Jews and the Expansion of Europe to the West, 1400–1800
Edited by Paolo Bernardini and Norman Fiering

THE LANGUAGE ENCOUNTER IN THE AMERICAS, 1492–1800

A Collection of Essays

Edited by
Edward G. Gray
and
Norman Fiering

Berghahn Books
NEW YORK · OXFORD

Published in 2000 by **Berghahn Books**

© 2000 The John Carter Brown Library

All rights reserved.
No part of this publication may be reproduced in any form or by any means without the written permission of Berghahn Books.

Library of Congress Cataloging-in-Publication Data

The language encounter in the Americas, 1492–1800 : a collection of essays / edited by Edward G. Gray and Norman Fiering.
      p. cm. — (European expansion and global interaction ; v. 1)
      Papers presented at a conference entitled "Communicating with the Indians: aspects of the language encounter with the indigenous peoples of the Americas, 1492–1800," held Oct. 18–20, 1996, John Carter Brown Library, Providence, R.I.
      Includes bibliographical references and index.
      ISBN 1-57181-160-5 (alk. paper)
      1. Languages in contact—America—History—Congresses. 2. Indians—Languages—Congresses. 3. Communication—America—History—Congresses. I. Gray, Edward G., 1964– . II. Fiering, Norman. III. Series.
P130.52.A45 L36 2000   99–034723
409'.7 21—dc21

This collection of essays originated at a conference at the John Carter Brown Library, 18-20 October 1996, entitled: "Communicating with the Indians: Aspects of the Language Encounter with the Indigenous Peoples of the Americas, 1492 to 1800." The conference was partially supported by a grant from the Rhode Island Committee for the Humanities and was sponsored by the Center for New World Comparative Studies at the Library.

The John Carter Brown Library is an independently funded and administered institution for advanced research in history and the humanities at Brown University. Inquiries may be addressed to: Box 1894, Providence, RI 02912 or to JCBL_information@brown.edu.

British Library Cataloguing in Publication Data

A catalogue record for this book is available from the British Library

Printed in the United States on acid-free paper

CONTENTS

Preface *by Norman Fiering*   vii

Introduction *by Edward G. Gray*   1

I. Terms of Contact

1. Babel of Tongues: Communicating with the Indians in Eastern North America   15
   James Axtell

2. The Use of Pidgins and Jargons on the East Coast of North America   61
   Ives Goddard

II. Signs and Symbols

3. Pictures, Gestures, Hieroglyphs: "Mute Eloquence" in Sixteenth-Century Mexico   81
   Pauline Moffitt Watts

4. Iconic Discourse: The Language of Images in Seventeenth-Century New France   102
   Margaret J. Leahey

5. Mapping after the Letter: Graphology and Indigenous Cartography in New Spain   119
   Dana Leibsohn

III. The Literate and the Nonliterate

6. Continuity vs. Acculturation: Aztec and Inca Cases of Alphabetic Literacy   155
   José Antonio Mazzotti

7. Native Languages as Spoken and Written: Views from Southern New England   173
   Kathleen J. Bragdon

8. The Mi'kmaq Hieroglyphic Prayer Book: Writing   189
and Christianity in Maritime Canada, 1675–1921
Bruce Greenfield

IV. Intermediaries

9. Interpreters Snatched from the Shore: 215
The Successful and the Others
Frances Karttunen

10. Mohawk Schoolmasters and Catechists in   230
Mid-Eighteenth-Century Iroquoia: An Experiment
in Fostering Literacy and Religious Change
William B. Hart

11. The Making of Logan, the Mingo Orator   258
Edward G. Gray

V. Theory

12. Spanish Colonization and the Indigenous   281
Languages of America
Isaías Lerner

13. Descriptions of American Indian Word Forms in   293
Colonial Missionary Grammars
Lieve Jooken

14. "Savage" Languages in Eighteenth-Century   310
Theoretical History of Language
Rüdiger Schreyer

Select Bibliography   327
List of Contributors   332
Index   334

Preface

IDEALLY, THE WORLD OF THE MIND ought to be seamless; thought should circulate around the globe like the waters of the sea. But as we know, even the sea has currents and divisions within it, and within the world of the intellect divisions are rampant. Not only do the various disciplines often not talk to each other—at least not routinely—but much useful scholarly work within a single discipline, work that is only slightly differentiated in method and content, may proceed for decades on widely separated parallel tracks. One wishes for a non-Euclidian geometry in such matters, in which parallel lines do ultimately converge.

This collection of essays is a direct reaction to my personal frustration with such artificial segmentation within academe. The John Carter Brown Library has been for 150 years a completely hemispheric collection. It acquires books printed before ca. 1830 relating to the entire area from Hudson Bay to Tierra del Fuego. This policy is not arbitrary. For although the space is vast, for the period between Columbus and Bolívar there are many commonalties in human experience. It is true, *diverse* Europeans—largely, Spanish, Portuguese, French, Dutch, and English—encountered *diverse* indigenous peoples, and forcibly imported *diverse* Africans; but everywhere broad conditions were similar and comparable basic ingredients were present—in peoples, geography, and resources—to the extent that we have now come to characterize the area as a single Atlantic world.

Looking particularly at the encounter of person with person in this era, hardly any factor was as universal as the problem of communication, given the incredible—perhaps even unique—language density of the pre-Columbian Americas. The burden of overcoming language barriers was a problem faced by all peoples of the New World in the early modern era: African slaves and native peoples in the Lower Mississippi Valley; Jesuit missionaries and Huron-speaking peoples in New France; Spanish conquistadors and the

Aztec rulers. All of these groups confronted America's complex linguistic environment, and all of them had to devise ways of transcending that environment—a problem that sometimes arose with life or death implications.

Yet despite these facts, Latin Americanists engaged in studying sixteenth-century Franciscan and Dominican missionaries to the Indians often know nothing of Anglo-American Protestant missionaries to the Indians in seventeenth-century New England, and reciprocally, Anglo-Americanists are equally ignorant of the work of Catholic missionaries in colonial Mexico and Peru, although in both cases the European confrontation with indigenous languages may be a major factor in the research of these scholars.

Such a situation can lead to evident absurdities. The New England specialists might innocently claim that John Eliot's translation of the Bible into Massachusett, in the middle of the seventeenth century, was the first printed book in an Indian language, or that Eliot was the first European to write in an Indian language. At the same time, the Latin American colonial specialists will marvel at the linguistic feats of Spanish priests who, more than a century before Eliot, had mastered sometimes two or three of the native languages of Mexico and published in these tongues, without these scholars realizing that Eliot had, in sheer bulk, outdone them all by translating the entirety of the Scriptures into a native tongue.

Finding this Euclidean world intolerable, we decided to enter the realm of advanced mathematics by organizing a conference that would lure into the same room scholars who, hitherto in isolation, were studying French, Spanish, or English encounters with Indian languages. (We wished also to include scholars studying Dutch, Portuguese, or German encounters but were unable to cast the net that wide in a single gathering.) The John Carter Brown Library owns about six hundred books with Indian language content printed before ca. 1800—a collection that may be unequalled anywhere—and maintains among its programs a Center for New World Comparative Studies, the mandate of which is "to help to counterbalance the particular affliction of parochialism in the study of the early American past." So the conference, and this book, emerged easily from this setting.

Comparison in the study of the past adds precision to historical generalization and is fruitful of insight, in accordance with the principle that one can gain a better understanding of any one culture through using another as a foil. The history of the European conquest of the Americas offers unusual opportunities for comparative study, since it is a history that for the entire hemisphere begins de novo, creating a gigantic laboratory for the investigation of human interaction and social, political, economic, and cultural development.

Following the conference, which was in October 1996, Professor Gray and I, who had worked closely together in planning the event, felt that what we had assembled was good enough to justify publication of a selection of the essays. We were fortunate to link up with Berghahn Books, which is launching a series of titles on the history of European expansion in the early-modern period—a vast and unprecedented process in which the language encounter worldwide was clearly a major component.

It is a pleasure to acknowledge here that we were assisted financially by a generous grant from the Rhode Island Committee for the Humanities, as well as by private gifts donated on the occasion of the celebration of the 150th anniversary of the Library's founding in 1846.

In the preparation of the volume, Professor Gray and I were ably reinforced by a John Carter Brown Library volunteer, Mrs. Breffny Walsh of Providence, and at all levels the Library staff played an essential part.

This book deals in good part with the *problems* that arose as a result of the impenetrability of the thousands of different forms of human speech. In the European conquest of the Americas, we face an era—one of the worst in the entire history of mankind in this respect—when the curse of the Tower of Babel caused enormous suffering. How different it might have been if, as Columbus had hoped, the Native Americans had only one language rather than hundreds and hundreds, and it was a language intelligible to Europeans, perhaps the supposed *ur*-language in the theory of the time, Hebrew. Instead, decent levels of communication had to be painstakingly established in order to bridge the language divide, such bridges being almost a precondition of social and political peace. Even before Europeans arrived, tribal warfare in the Americas appears to have been endemic, which no doubt was hugely facilitated, if that's the right word, by the simple fact of the multitude of mutually unintelligible languages.

Yet following George Steiner, the great cultural critic of our day, need we only bemoan this diversity? The positive element should not be altogether neglected, and indeed, it occasionally shines through in this book. "Babel was the contrary of a curse," Steiner writes in *Errata* (1997). "The gift of tongues is precisely that: a gift and benediction beyond reckoning. The riches of experience, the creativities of thought and of feeling, the penetrative and delicate singularities of conception made possible by the polyglot condition are the preeminent adaptive agency and advantage of the human spirit."

Norman Fiering

Introduction

⸙

Edward G. Gray

THE ESSAYS IN THIS BOOK deal with two subjects that are often equated but not necessarily related: language—defined narrowly as spoken and written utterance—and communication. While language is a medium of communication, one can communicate without language—as one might with smoke signals or Morse code—and one can use language without communicating, as one might in prayer or song. Similarly, one can speak but communicate something wholly unrelated to what one intended. These facts, we might say, make it possible to speak of a "language encounter." When people speak or write to each other, their interaction is often as much an "encounter"—as between two resilient objects—as it is a meshing, mingling, or interface of like minds. And while the concept might be applied to any social or historical situation, the focus of this volume is its application to the meetings of native peoples and Europeans in the early modern Americas.

This application is particularly fitting in light of the growing sense among historians of the colonial Americas that, far from being passive victims of historical developments, native peoples were instrumental and autonomous historical actors. Given this increased sensitivity to the dynamic place of Indians in early American history, it has made sense to describe the meetings of Native Americans and Europeans not in terms of "conquest" and "domination" but in more neutral terms, or at least terms that do not imply that Indians were mere victims. To this end, perhaps the most widely used term—initially suggested by the Mexican Nahua scholar, Miguel León-Portilla, among others—has been "encounter." The term suggests a more balanced historical meeting, in which both Indians and Europeans negotiated difficult and unfamiliar cultural practices. In keeping with the spirit of this term, the essays in this collection thus seek not simply to explore the forces that shaped communication between Indians and Europeans but also to illuminate some of the ways in which those forces produced shared experience.

In a certain sense, the subject of this volume is not new. Sixteenth- and seventeenth-century missionaries to the Americas devoted much attention to the study and use of local languages; but few of them labored under the illusion that a capacity to speak or write Nahuatl, Quechua, Huron, Mahican, or any of the hundreds of other American Indian languages and dialects would alone afford ready and easy access to Indians souls. Jean de Léry, a Huguenot pastor (and a member of the first Protestant mission to the New World) who resided in Brazil between 1556 and 1558, recounted the difficulty of saying something so simple as his own name to the Tupinamba people:

> The interpreter had warned me that [the Indians] wanted above all to know my name; but if I had said to them Pierre, Guillaume, or Jean, they would have been able neither to retain it nor to pronounce it (in fact, instead of saying "Jean," they would say "Nian"). So I had to accommodate by naming something that was known to them. Since by a lucky chance my surname, "Léry," means "oyster" in their language, I told them that my name was "Léry-oussou," that is, a big oyster.[1]

It was one thing to say something so simple as a name, altogether another to convey the abstract, metaphysical knowledge that would lead to an understanding of Christianity. Father Pierre Biard, a French Jesuit missionary active among the Micmac peoples in what is now Nova Scotia, explained to his superior in 1612 that one of his fellow missionaries understood the Indians' language "better than anyone else here, is filled with earnest zeal, and every day takes a great deal of trouble to serve as our interpreter. But, somehow, as soon as we begin to talk about God, he feels as Moses did—his mind is bewildered, his throat dry, his tongue tied." In what was destined to become a common explanation for this problem, Biard claimed that "the reason for this is that, as the savages have no definite religion, magistracy or government, liberal or mechanical arts, commercial or civil life, they have consequently no words to describe things which they have never seen or even conceived."[2]

One should not mistake this assessment for a meaningful assertion about the nature of Indians themselves. That is, there is no reason to equate the absence of certain terms or parts of speech with a lack of mental or social development. Indeed, one need only reiterate the dicta that there are many ways to say something, and that the division of words into various parts of speech is actually a fairly random gesture, constituting what the twentieth-century American linguist Edward Sapir called "a vague, wavering approximation to a constantly worked out inventory of experience." The simple absence of a word, that is, indicates nothing at all about a person's capacity to grasp or even to express a certain idea. Consider the case of Borges's imaginary language of Tlön, a language with no nouns. While one cannot say "The moon rose over the sea," one *can* say, "upward, behind the onstreaming, it mooned."[3]

This is not to say that missionaries and others engaged in the arduous process of learning American languages did not face very real difficulties. Indeed, there is much that makes these tongues particularly difficult for speakers of European languages. We might begin with the simple fact that parts of speech familiar to Europeans—nouns, verbs, adjectives, adverbs, and so forth—are often difficult to identify. For example, there might be no single word for the infinitive "to plow." This does not mean that the idea does not exist. One might, as is done in Kiowa (spoken in what is now south-central Kansas and central Oklahoma), express the idea by combining the verb for "shatter" with the noun for "earth." The resulting term, however, constitutes not so much a distinct word but rather a root word or verb stem that, when combined with other words, constitutes a single, meaningful word—and, as spoken, this word might include information that an English speaker would convey in separate words. Hence, a Mohawk speaker would use a single word—roughly transcribed as "sahuwanhotukwahse"—to say "She opened the door for him again."[4] Linguists refer to the Indian tendency to combine many words to create a single word as "polysynthesis," and it is widespread—although not universal—among the language families of the Americas. The Iroquoian and Algonquian language families in the North-American Northeast—among which the Jesuits worked extensively—are polysynthetic, as is Nahuatl and Quechua. The Mayan languages, however, constitute notable exceptions to this rule.

Given the difficulties Europeans and Indians faced when communicating their thoughts, one might ask: how did they respond to the perceived limits of the spoken word? How, that is, did they explain and remedy the seeming failures of utterance as a communications medium? These questions, more than any other, unify the essays in this collection. Hence, there is much here about gesture, material symbols, and various graphic systems for displaying information—of which writing is only one. What this diversity of subject matter reflects is the contributors' shared assumption that to understand the language encounter in its fullest sense is to understand this historical phenomenon to be about much more than simply face-to-face oral exchange. For Indians and Europeans to communicate with each other, both had to employ a range of media.

Surely the most common of these was gesture, or hand signals. However, exactly what was communicated in this way is often difficult to determine. In an account of La Salle's fateful search for the mouth of the Mississippi in the late 1680s, Henri Joutel described an encounter with Indians somewhere on the Gulf coast of what is now Texas. "Monsieur de la Sale was very well pleas'd to see them, imagining they might give him some account of the river he sought after," Joutel wrote, "but to no purpose, for he spoke to them in several of the languages of the savages, which he knew, and made many signs to them, but still they understood not what he meant, or if they did comprehend anything, they made signs, that they knew nothing of what he ask'd."[5] To the frustration of missionaries, gesture also became in integral part of language-learning in early America. Father Biard observed that,

> as [the Indians] neither know our language nor we theirs, except a very little which pertains to daily and commercial life, we are compelled to make a thousand gesticulations and signs to express to [the Indians] our ideas, and thus to draw from them the names of some of the things which cannot be pointed out to them. For example, to think, to forget, to remember, to doubt; to know these four words, you will be obliged to amuse our gentlemen for a whole afternoon at least by playing the clown; and then, after all that, you will find yourself deceived, and mocked anew.[6]

In this case, the use of gesture and theatrics is closely tied to perceived barriers to translation, barriers resulting in part, at least, from the Jesuits' failure to accept the possibility that infinitives, much like other parts of speech, do not constitute universal and unvarying units of speech.

While speech and gesture were the most common media through which Europeans and Indians communicated, neither has been the subject of as much scholarly discussion as another medium: writing. Europeans and Indians possessed distinct systems for displaying information, and while alphabetic writing has come to be the prevailing system in the Americas, it has only recently existed to the exclusion of indigenous systems. In the early modern era, not only did Indians and Europeans often resort to different systems for the visual communication of information, they also frequently shared those systems. So, for instance, in early colonial Mexico, Spanish missionaries employed Nahua pictograph painters in their efforts to Christianize Indians. The Jesuit José de Acosta described the way these Indian painters rendered the Paternoster:

> For to signifie these words, I, a sinner, do confesse my self, they painted an Indian upon his knees at a religious mans feete, as one that confesseth himselfe: and for this, to God most mighty, they painted three faces, with their crownes, like to the Trinitie; and to the glorious Virgine Marie, they painted the face of our Lady, and halfe the body of a little childe.[7]

What is perhaps most important about Acosta's remarks is that they describe a collaboration—a collaboration between European missionaries and Aztec painters. This was an almost universal feature of Indian-European communication in the early modern Americas. Indeed, most of the best known sixteenth- and seventeenth-century Indian-language writings are the result of collaborations of some kind. Whether one is speaking of the famous Massachusett Bible (1663), or the *Florentine Codex* (1559–1569), the origins of the works are similar: both resulted from a collaboration between European missionaries and American Indians. In the case of the Massachusett Bible, the Puritan missionary John Eliot employed Indian students to verify the phonetics of his translations—translations written in a modified Roman alphabet. In the case of the *Florentine Codex*, the collaboration is even more readily apparent. The work consists of a combination of Aztec pictographs and alphabetic writings—the latter being commentaries, written initially in a phonetic Nahuatl and later translated into Spanish by Indians and the Franciscan missionary, Bernardino de Sahagún (1499–1590). These collaborations are indicative of the give-and-take that was everywhere a part of the language encounter. Rarely do we find an instance in which one mode of communication—written or oral; indigenous or European—is used to the exclusion of another. Even in cases in which Indians wrote in European languages using the Roman alphabet, scholars have identified (as José Mazzotti does in his essay included here) vestiges of Indian oral traditions.

Although there were a number of indigenous American writing systems—including Aztec pictographic writing and assorted hieroglyphic systems—a more purely phonetic alphabet was not to be found in the Americas. This is not to say that phonetic writing of any kind was absent from the New World. Nahua pictographs contain "glyphs," or symbols that correspond to distinct sounds, and Mayan writing has an even more prominent phonetic component. Furthermore, writing was only one of several indigenous methods for displaying information. A number of mnemonic devices have been used throughout the Americas—including wampum belts and quipus, the latter being color-coded, knotted cords—that might have served their purpose better than written text. Nonetheless, the sorts of phonetic alphabets used by Europeans were unknown in the Americas, and the ways in which Indians responded to this novel technology, while widely varied, rarely included indifference.

Among certain Nahuas, for example, the transition from their own largely pictographic system to a more purely phonetic European system seems to have been fairly rapid. Sahagún observed that after scarcely two or three years, sons of the indigenous Mexican nobility grasped all that "which concerns grammar, and speaking, understanding and writing in Latin, even to the point of composing heroic verses."[8] Sahagún himself, it should be said, probably did much to accelerate the assimilation of alphabetic writing in central Mexico. The first major example of written Nahuatl was his own *Historia general de las cosas de Nueva España* (1547–62).

Outside of Mexico, particularly north of the Rio Grande, the indigenous experience with alphabetic writing seems to have been very different. European observers repeatedly remarked on the astonishment and awe with which Indians greeted the seemingly magical qualities of Western script. One such account comes from the explorer and founder of the Russian Northeastern America Company, Grigorii Shelikhov, who between 1784 and 1786 established a series of Russian trading posts on Kodiak and several adjoining islands off the southern coast of Alaska. Shelikhov recalled that when he would send one of the Kodiak Island Eskimos with a letter to

> my arteshiks, or workmen, in other parts of the islands, they fell into the utmost astonishment, that they [the workmen] should send me back exactly what they knew I wanted from what I had said to them a day or two before, though they had not spoke a word of it. I sent one of them ... with a letter to one of my under-traffickers, desiring him to send me some plums and other dried fruits. My messenger, unable to resist the temptation, ate up half of them by the way, as I found by comparing the quantity he brought me with that mentioned in the letter. For this, I chid [sic] him.... On this he expressed the most extreme surprise, persuaded as he was that the letter had seen him eat [the fruit].

This incident, Shelikhov continued, was followed by another, in which the same messenger ate some of the fruit he had been sent for. When confronted with this misdeed, the Indian "was struck with still greater amazement than before; as this time he had the precaution to keep the letter buried in the sand all the while he was eating the fruit."[9]

Precisely how this event—and many similar instances recorded by Europeans—should be interpreted is difficult to know.[10] What is clear is that reading and writing are best understood as cultural practices whose meaning and purpose vary widely among peoples. There is good reason to believe, for instance, that literate Indians in early New England viewed legal documents written in their own language as mnemonic devices, useful for recovering the broad social significance of a given transaction—this in contrast to their literate English neighbors who understood them to be literal and binding transcriptions of those transactions.[11]

The fact that the language encounter in the Americas resulted in much confusion, not to mention creative adaptation, might lead one to conclude that the experience of communicating with the peoples of the New World—in addition to those of Asia and Africa—inspired novel thinking about language and communication. And, indeed, as the essays here by Isaías Lerner, Lieve Jooken, and Rüdiger Schreyer all suggest, the study of American languages did result in a re-evaluation of European assumptions about language. The nature of that re-evaluation, though, was slow and generally consistent with Sir John Elliott's suggestion that, far from razing the fundamental and sustaining truths of their universe, sixteenth- and seventeenth-century European intellectuals generally worked to reinforce those truths.[12]

By the late seventeenth century, however, it is clear that the intellectual climate of Europe—at least with respect to the wider non-European world—was changing. Consider just one example. Among the more far-reaching and influential European scientific projects of the seventeenth and eighteenth centuries was the search for a perfect language. Such a language, so its proponents assumed, would be to general thought and communication what numbers were to mathematics. It would eliminate from philosophy any debate over the meaning of terms and it would be intelligible to speakers of all languages. Such a language, so its advocates assumed, would allow truths to reveal themselves (much like the solution to an arithmetic problem) without being obscured by the various failings of human speech or differences of human culture. For the most part, the search for a perfect language centered on a quest for a universal writing system rather than for a wholly new spoken and written tongue. The idea was that such a system, much like Roman or Arabic numerals, could eliminate the need for translation, at least in written discourse.

A series of English and Continental natural philosophers set out to discover this system—either among existing languages or through invention. And it seems clear that in this pursuit, they became increasingly aware of the varying forms of the world's writing systems. None received more attention, in this light, than Chinese writing—introduced to Europeans by the sixteenth-century Jesuit missionary, Matteo Ricci (1552–1610). As Ricci illustrated in his posthumous *De Christiana expeditione apud Sinas suscepta ab Societate Jesu* (1615), Chinese writing is largely semantic. For, unlike the phonetic Roman alphabet, in which letters represent sounds, Chinese characters all represent things or ideas (although they can also represent sounds). The result of this is that speakers of widely varying Chinese dialects understand written Chinese perfectly well. As such, it seemed a promising foundation for a new universal language.[13]

If Ricci's readers saw in Chinese a promising basis for a purely "ideographic" language (or a language that conveys only meaning), readers of another overseas missionary, Father Acosta, may have had a different response. Acosta devoted two chapters of his *Historia natural y moral de las Indias* (1590) to Chinese writing and Chinese education, all as part of an effort to establish the limits of the sort of pictographic or nonphonetic writing he found in Mexico. In Acosta's view, far from offering a solution to the universal language problem, this kind of writing was distinctly inferior to phonetic alphabetic writing. As he explained, "with all their knowledge, an Indian of Peru or Mexico that hath learned to read and write knowes more than the wisest Mandarin that is amongst them: for that the Indian with foure and twentie letters which he hath learned will write all the wordes in the world, and a Mandarin with a hundred thousand letters will be troubled to write some proper names ... and with greater reason he shall be lesse able to write the names of things he knowes not."[14] Although Acosta presumed the inferiority of both Chinese and Meso-American writing systems, his premise is nonetheless the same as defenders of these systems. Both assumed that such writing possessed a literalness—a logical, readily grasped connection between its symbols and the things they symbolized—that made them at once nearly perfect in their capacity to represent ideas and objects and yet constrained by an inability to represent ideas with no clear correlates in ordinary experience.

Another implication of the European assimilation of linguistic knowledge about the non-European world involved the prevailing explanation for the diversity of the world's tongues. According to the Book of Genesis, with the fall of the Tower of Babel there arose numerous distinct, mutually unintelligible languages. The dominant late medieval and Renaissance view was that seventy-two such tongues emerged out of the Tower's wreckage. But the discovery of literally thousands of new languages in the Americas, Asia, and Africa rendered this number nearly impossible to justify. Nonetheless, Europeans did seek ways to make new knowledge consistent with the Biblical story. The most common way of doing this involved an extension of the basic reasoning behind the Biblical account. In much the way that Genesis explained the diversity of tongues, commentators generally assumed that in America and other non-Christian regions, the abundance of languages was an indication of social decay and human delinquency. In their failure to become Christians, and to pursue the divine mandate of uniting all of humanity in Christianity, inhabitants of these areas had simply perpetuated the sort of hubris and moral decay that made the Tower of Babel possible. According to this reasoning, the results of such delinquency were plain to see in the confused linguistic landscape.[15]

It should be said that much of this volume necessarily deals with European interpretations and impressions of the language encounter. In part, this emphasis reflects the simple fact that the vast bulk of remaining written historical evidence was produced by Europeans. Nonetheless, where possible, the contributors have worked to bring out the Indian side of the language encounter. For instance, of the themes that link the essays (particularly those of James Axtell, Ives Goddard, and myself) one is the suggestion that Indians used language much as one might a family crest: as a mark of tribal or kin identity. Among the indications of this was the tendency among Indians to resist speaking the languages of others—both Europeans and other Indian groups—during diplomatic meetings. This suggests that at least some Indian communities used language as a barrier to protect local knowledge and that the crucial marker of clan or tribal affiliation was not pedigree or property but language. Indeed, it would appear that among American Indians there has long been a sense that language and politics are intertwined. None of this is to say that Indians are distinct because they regard language as an important identity marker. For most of known history, Europeans too have employed language to similar ends. What one might conclude, instead, is that the native peoples of the Americas were as sensitive as Europeans to the fact that, as Tzvetan Todorov has put it, "Language has always been the companion of Empire."[16] One fact that the essays collected here make clear is that language, as a functional social and political mechanism, was as integral to the overseas extension of European societies as it was to the ongoing efforts of American Indians to resist and adapt to that extension.

Among our ambitions for this book, and for the series of which it is the inaugural volume, is to promote the comparative study of history and culture in the early modern Americas. To this end, we have divided the volume into five thematic parts, each containing essays that, though similar in subject matter, differ in regional, chronological, or methodological emphasis. The first, "Terms of Contact," contains two essays that explore the use of pidgins, trade jargons, and other media in North America. The second part, "Signs and Symbols," consists of three essays that explore the use of images and gestures by Indians and Europeans in North and Central America. Part three, "The Literate and the Nonliterate," includes three essays that explore Indians' experience of alphabetic literacy in Peru, New England, and Maritime Canada, respectively. The fourth part, "Intermediaries," focuses on figures who in one way or another served as go-betweens, or agents of Indian-White communications. Last, part five, "Theory," is comprised of three essays addressing various aspects of the European response to the languages of the New World.

Notes

1. Jean de Léry, *History of a Voyage to the Land of Brazil, Otherwise Called America*, ed. and trans. Janet Whatley (Berkeley, 1990), 162.
2. *The Jesuit Relations and Allied Documents*, ed. Reuben Gold Thwaites (Cleveland, 1896), 2:9–11.
3. Edward Sapir, *Language: An Introduction to the Study of Speech* (New York, 1921), 117; Jorge Louis Borges, *Ficciones* (New York, 1962), 23.
4. These specific examples are from Marianne Mithun, "Overview of General Characteristics," in *Handbook of North American Indians*, vol. 17, *Languages*, ed. Ives Goddard (Washington, DC, 1996), 141, 138.
5. Henri Joutel, *The Last Voyage Perform'd by de la Sale* (London, 1714), 22.
6. Thwaites, *The Jesuit Relations*, 2:11.
7. José de Acosta, *The Natural and Moral History of the Indies*, ed. Edward Grimston (London, 1880), 2:405.
8. Quoted in Tzvetan Todorov, *The Conquest of America: The Question of the Other* (New York, 1984), 220.
9. Gregory Shelekhof, *The Voyage of Gregory Shelekhof ... to the Coast of America, in the Years 1783, 1784, 1785, 1786, 1787 ...* (1795; reprint, Washington, DC, 1941), 19–20.
10. For other contemporary remarks on Indians and print, see Thwaites, *The Jesuit Relations*, 8:113; and Fr. Louis Hennepin, *A New Discovery of a Vast Country in America ...*, ed. Reuben Gold Thwaites (1698; reprint, Chicago, 1903), 1:260. For two differing interpretations of Indians' reactions to print, see James Axtell's seminal "The Power of Print in the Eastern Woodlands," in *After Columbus: Essays in the Ethnohistory of Colonial North America* (New York, 1988), 86–99; and, Peter Wogan, "Perceptions of European Literacy in Early Contact Situations," in *Ethnohistory* 41(Summer 1994), 407–29.
11. Ives Goddard and Kathleen J. Bragdon, *Native Writings in Massachusett* (Philadelphia, 1988), 1:19. More generally, see Jonathan Boyarin, ed., *The Ethnography of Reading* (Berkeley, 1993), esp. Boyarin's introduction and Brian Stock's afterword.
12. J.H. Elliott, *The Old World and the New 1492–1650* (1970; paperback ed., Cambridge, England, 1992), 14.
13. See Paul Cornelius, *Languages in Seventeenth- and Eighteenth-Century Imaginary Voyages* (Geneva, 1965), 25–38; and Rüdiger Schreyer, *The European Discovery of Chinese (1550–1615) or The Mystery of Chinese Unveiled* (Amsterdam, 1992).
14. De Acosta, *The Natural and Moral History of the Indies*, 2:402.
15. On this argument, see Edward G. Gray, *New World Babel: Languages and Nations in Early America* (Princeton, NJ, 1999), 21–23.
16. Todorov, *The Conquest of America*, 221.

Part I

Terms of Contact

– Chapter 1 –

BABEL OF TONGUES: COMMUNICATING WITH THE INDIANS IN EASTERN NORTH AMERICA

James Axtell

> If I know not the meaning of the voice, I shall be unto him that speaketh a barbarian, and he that speaketh shall be a barbarian unto me.
>
> I Corinthians 14:10–11

WHILE EUROPEAN SHIPS and the trade winds could bring the people of the "Old World" face to face with those of the "New," they could not guarantee that the newcomers would gain more than a wet toehold on the margins of North America. If the native "others" remained hidden, like Mardi Gras mummers, behind gaudy face paint, bizarre behavior, and the manifest mime of trade, the Europeans had no hope of discovering the value of the country or of sizing up—much less neutralizing or eliminating—their indigenous rivals for it. The key to the continent was information—reliable, unambiguous, and digestible—and the quickest and best source of it was the Indians. Rumor simply would not do in the long run, though it had its motivational uses early on; nor would guesswork, which was expensive and often dangerous.

Only natives could tell novices where to find assayable gold and silver (not just the dazzling promise of iron pyrite), how to get around or through the Appalachians, when and what to plant when Atlantic storms or privateers claimed supply ships, how to recognize the log-choked mouth of the Mississippi, and where to obtain the plushest beaver pelts. Only natives knew how to navigate the narrow moccasin trails that crisscrossed the landscape, to draw maps of the next terra incognita on birchbark, deerskin, or borrowed paper, to pilot flimsy canoes through dangerous defiles and trackless chains of evergreen lakes, and to kill enough game en route to keep the travelers alive. Certainly only natives could teach the strangers to wage effective war against, and to avoid the lethal ambushes of, other Indians, in short, to think—temporarily and with malice aforethought—like the enemy in order to win the new high-stakes game for the continent.

But extracting these vital pieces of information from the natives was no easy matter. In the face of iconoclastic missionaries and gold-digging prospectors, the Indians were understandably reticent: why invite sacred customs to be maligned and ridiculed and favorite mountain hunting spoiled?[1] But in less threatening circumstances, the natives were notably forthcoming and eager to share their knowledge. What was needed was a mode of communication, a language, common to both parties.

Finding a common tongue was vastly complicated by the linguistic complexion of Europe and America. Both, as the white man's Bible put it, were Babels, cursed for the overweening pride of Noah's descendants with a profusion and confusion of tongues.[2] Native North America spoke at least 221 mutually unintelligible languages, each fractured into myriad dialects that were themselves confounding even to native ears. East of the Mississippi, four major language families covered most of the map: Algonquian (named after the speech of the Algonquin tribe west of Montreal), Iroquoian (after the five Iroquois nations of New York), Siouan (after the Dakota or Sioux tribes initially found around the western Great Lakes), and Muskogean (after the Creek or Muskogee tribes of Alabama and Georgia).[3] Happily for newcomers, the members of each family shared common parentage and some resemblance. All the Algonquian tongues of eastern Canada, thought the practiced Baron de Lahontan, came as near to Algonquin as Portuguese or Italian did to Spanish. Likewise, the difference between Huron and the other Iroquois languages was "not greater than that between the Norman and the French." Even early in his linguistic acculturation, a French Jesuit found Algonquin and Montagnais (another Algonquian tongue) as close as Provençal and Norman.[4]

But family resemblances did not always make it possible for the speakers of one language to make themselves understood by their conversing cousins. Just as in Europe, dialects and patois muted exchanges between countrymen. Among the Algonquian-speakers of New England, noticed Roger Williams, "the varietie of their Dialects and proper speech within thirtie or fortie miles each of other, is very great." Neighboring tribes, for example, favored different consonants. When the Nipmucks spoke of a *dog*, they said *alum*; their Quinnipiak brethren in Connecticut said *arum*.[5] The Carolina backcountry was even more polyglot. To one experienced traveler, "the Difference of Languages, that is found amongst these Heathens, seems altogether strange. For it often appears, that every dozen Miles, you meet with an *Indian* Town, that is quite different from the others you last parted withal." In that part of the country, villages speaking radically different Iroquoian, Siouan, Muskogean, and even Algonquian tongues might stand within short walks of each other. The peripatetic John Lawson was amazed that the core vocabularies he collected of the Tuscarora, Pamptico, and Woccon tribes—located "not above ten Leagues distant" from each other—differed in literally every word save one.[6] A newly landed European seeking to learn to speak "Indian" clearly had his work cut out for him.

By the same token, native Americans hoping to fathom or tap into the mysterious power of the immigrant strangers were equally nonplused by the verbal variety behind the newcomers' "European" persona. Even sorting them into "Frenchmen," "Englishmen," and "Spaniards" would not help a great deal. A "French" sailor was likely to speak a northwestern Breton or Norman dialect or the ancient and still-mysterious tongue of the Basques, rather than the "proper" French of Paris and the court. *Troupes de la marine* and *habitants* from the Midi who spoke the soft southern *langue d'oc* had as much trouble parleying with the crew and fellow passengers partial to the northern *langue d'oeil* as they did with new world *sauvages*. As late as the French Revolution, France was still deeply divided by regional patois, which differed almost from parish to parish.[7] English immigrants, largely from East Anglia and the Home Counties, spoke somewhat more congruent tongues, homogenized by London and the King James Bible. Spanish sailors, conquistadors, and settlers from the former Moorish region of Andalusia had some difficulty with the harder sounds of the central tablelands of Castile, but even more with Galician, the ancestor of Portuguese, and Catalan, which is still radically different from nationalized *Español*.

But when Indians and Europeans met for the first time, as they continued to do in many different places over three centuries, it was obvious that they would initially have to communicate not through a common tongue but by some shared syntax of signs, motions, and gestures. Relying on limbs rather than larynx carried a number of serious liabilities and forced each "speaker" upon the resources of his imagination. The first drawback of sign language was that the Indians of North America had no single system of accepted signs except perhaps on the Plains, and the Europeans had no experience in reading or making signs unless they had traveled or traded in Africa.[8] Since body languages, no less than verbal ones, are culturally variable, the opportunities on both sides for ambiguity and misinterpretation were legion.

A second liability was that signs could not convey abstractions well. Concrete objects and basic human emotions were relatively easy to "talk" about, but concepts of religion, time, and law were less reducible to gesture. Finally, signs, unlike voices, were not "audible" at night or beyond a modest distance, a considerable hazard in unfamiliar territory where the intentions of "others" were equally unknown.

While the new world of mute discourse was fraught with some danger, much frustration, and no little humor, natives and strangers found some room for mutual understanding in signs from the heart and messages from the face, the telltale "mirror of the soul." Unlike the "wild Irish," who camouflaged their eyes behind thick bangs or "glibs," the Indians, while notoriously taciturn among Europeans, did not dissemble their true feelings on their own turf.[9] When they held their hands over their hearts or broke out in toothy grins, the Europeans could take them at their "word" and trust their sincerity.

Unhappily, the reverse was not always possible, because Europeans who had learned to thread their way through the Old World maze of social hierarchy, religious war, and court intrigue were adepts at dissimulation. The two-faced approach was used most by European officers whose task was not to honor native integrity or to safeguard native interests but to accomplish their own imperial goals. Humbler folks and followers, and even some bigwigs in a bind, felt freer to speak with unforked "tongues" at the onset of intercultural relations in a strange land.

When the very first Europeans and obdurate ethnocentrics even later tried to "have speech" with the natives they met, both sides quickly slammed into a wall of incomprehension. Before picking their pride up and dusting it off, they may have resorted to the old tactic of simply speaking their ethnic tongue louder, as if their audience consisted of deaf or disobedient children largely impervious to the voice of right reason. We know that even when

Europeans and Indians learned to speak a common language, white men usually spoke too fast and too loudly for native ears, so it is likely that they increased the volume of their initial utterances when confronted with blank stares. Some Indians may have done the same. When Captain George Waymouth's ship approached the Maine coast in 1605, it was intercepted by a canoe whose leader "spake in his language very lowd and very boldly, seeming as though he would know why we were there, and by pointing with his oare [paddle] towards the sea, we conjectured he meant we should be gone."[10]

As soon as it dawned on the participants that dialogue would have to take a nonverbal form, they launched into the search for mutually intelligible signs and gestures to ask questions, return answers, and express feelings. Traders had a relatively easy time of it because the universal context of trade was peace, and the relative value of goods in barter could be established simply by adding or subtracting items, holding up fingers, and nodding or shaking the head. But explorers seeking fabled lands, merchant-adventurers chasing gold or the Northwest Passage, and missionaries yearning to bathe savage souls in the "swete and lively liquor of the gospell" faced more daunting obstacles.[11]

Since the Europeans were always outnumbered and in strange surroundings, their first obstacle was to establish the peaceful intent of the natives. This was accomplished fairly quickly through the readable, if novel, nomenclature of native etiquette. The laying down of bows and arrows was perhaps the best sign of the Indians' good intentions, especially if followed by a traditional native greeting. On the Gaspé Peninsula, both the local Micmacs and the visiting Stadaconans who met Jacques Cartier "rubbed his arms and his breast with their hands" in welcome. Fifty years later, Arthur Barlowe was greeted at Roanoke by Granganimeo, the local chief's brother, who struck his head and chest and then Barlowe's "to shewe [they] were all one." Several hundred miles away, on the icy coasts of Baffin Island, Eskimo traders were initiating relations with John Davis and his crew by pointing to the sun, striking their chests "so hard that [the sailors] might heare the blow," and crying "Iliaoute" in a loud voice. When Davis stuck out his hand to greet one of them English-style, the man kissed it instead.[12]

The customary greeting in South Carolina, as the English noted in the late 1660s, was the "stroaking of our shoulders with their palmes and sucking in theire breath the whilst." In Louisiana the French experienced a variation on the same theme. At their first camp near Biloxi in 1699, Pierre Le Moyne d'Iberville and his officers had their faces rubbed with white clay before being saluted in friendly fashion, which was, he wrote, to "pass their hands over their faces and breasts, and then pass their hands over yours, after which they raise them toward the sky, rubbing them together again and embracing again." Antoine de Sauvole, the fort commander, found one party of Pascagoulas almost too much for his Gallic sensibilities. "I have never seen natives [*sauvages*] less inhibited," he confided to his journal. "They have embraced us, something that I have never seen the others do." The most sensual treatment, however, was reserved for Europeans who had hiked into Indian country: their hosts massaged their feet, legs, joints, and even eyelids with soothing bear oil.[13]

Caressing and touching were reassuring signs of acceptance, but they were only the first of several "words" in elaborate rites of welcome. The visitors were next seated on fresh skins or reed mats, "harangued" (as they put it) with unintelligible speeches, entertained with dancing, singing, and games, and feasted to surfeit on such native delicacies as *sagamité* (corn meal mush seasoned with fat) and roasted dog. By the seventeenth century the natives also offered their guests a belt or string of wampum, painstakingly made from tiny purple and white marine-shell beads, or a calumet, a two-to-four-foot-long wood-stemmed redstone pipe richly decorated with paint, bird heads, and a fan of long white feathers.

Wampum was the major medium of alliance and peace in the Northeast; the calumet rapidly spread from the northern Plains and Great Lakes down the Mississippi and all through the Southeast in the late seventeenth century, often in the canoes of French explorers and colonizers. Among the tribes of the Great Lakes and Illinois, the French had quickly learned that possession of a calumet was a passport through even hostile Indian country and that sharing its consecrated smoke was the major ticket to diplomatic success. In America the white-feathered calumet signaled peaceful intentions as clearly as the flag of truce did on a European battlefield, and thereby lent a measure of predictability to social situations whose codes had yet to be cast. Having seen the calumet's power in Canada, Iberville sought to harness it by taking his own ersatz model to Louisiana, an iron one "made in the shape of a ship with the white flag adorned with fleur-de-lis and ornamented with glass beads."[14]

As early as the sixteenth century, smoke played another key role in welcoming the bearded strangers from Europe. In native America tobacco was sacred, and on its smoke prayers were lifted to heaven. The best way to honor any novel or great-spirited being, therefore, was to offer it tobacco or smoke. When Father Claude Allouez advised a Fox man to have his dangerously ill parents bled, the man poured powdered tobacco all over the priest's gown and said, "Thou art a spirit; come now, restore these sick people to health; I offer thee this tobacco in sacrifice." A dusty gown was small enough price to pay for such status, but other Frenchmen paid more dearly. In another part of the Great Lakes, Nicolas Perrot had smoke blown directly into his face "as the greatest honor that they could render him; he saw himself smoked like meat," but gamely "said not a word."[15]

With Iberville on the Mississippi, Father Paul du Ru reported that after puffing two or three times on a calumet, one of the Indians "came and blew smoke from his pipe into my nose as though to incense me." Du Ru may have come off better than the first French captain who sailed to the Menominees on Lake Michigan: he had tobacco ground into his forehead. One of the earliest Europeans to be honored with smoke was too ethnocentric to recognize his good fortune. When some Baffin Island Inuits tried to place John Davis in the consecrating smoke of their fire, he pushed one of them into the smoke instead and testily had the fire stomped out and kicked into the sea.[16]

Thanks largely to the natives' pronounced sense of hospitality, most European newcomers were able to get a foot in the native door without much linguistic effort. But once they gained entry, they were brought up short by their urgent need but excruciating inability to speak with their hosts—to make their purposes and wants known, to convey what they had to offer in return for continued cooperation, and to establish their character as men whose word could be trusted. By the same token, the natives sought to probe the strange tickings of mind behind the foreign faces of their guests, half-hidden behind hair, while assuring those bearers of murderous new weapons of their own benignity and honor.

One way to flatter and reassure the "other" in his own wordless dialect was to imitate his introductory and apparently bona fide behavior. When *La Dauphine* was greeted by twenty canoes of apprehensive natives in Newport harbor, Verrazzano and his crew "reassured them somewhat by imitating their gestures" and throwing them "trinkets." During the next two weeks, the local sachem often visited the ship, "discussing by signs and gestures various fanciful [because unintelligible?] notions" and asking about the ship's equipment. And because he was out of his own element aboard ship, he "imitated our manners," wrote the captain, and "tasted our food" before courteously taking his leave. The French, accordingly, felt free to hobnob with the natives on shore without fear of ambush or betrayal.[17]

Less than sixty years later, not far away in Buzzard's Bay, Gabriel Archer defused a tense situation with some fast and formidable signing. When the local sachem and fifty bowmen advanced hastily toward him and only eight men, he wrote, "I mooved my selfe towards him seven or eight steps, and clapt my hands first on the sides of mine head, then on my breast, and after presented my Musket with a threatening countenance, thereby to signifie unto them, either a choice of Peace or Warre." Perhaps daunted by the Englishman's audacity, the chief returned Archer's "owne signes of Peace" and received a relieved bearhug in reply.[18]

Reassurance was one thing, information-gathering and sharing quite another. When each party's hackles had fallen, it was time for charades. In antic pantomimes that perhaps only children could fully fathom, white and brown folks postured and pranced, wiggled and wagged, gesticulating to noteless scores of imagined song. But unlike charades, this game had few rules to govern play, no spoken words to declare winners and losers, and stakes as high as survival. The work was embarrassing, frustrating, and, more often than the participants would or could admit, wildly ridiculous, but it had to be done if they hoped to actually *speak* the same language in the foreseeable future. Before they could pun, they had to learn to drawl.

On both sides, signing gave rise to prodigious feats of guesswork and wishful thinking, but our evidence, unfortunately, comes from only one side. Columbus was the first but not last European to raise the art of imaginative "listening" to new heights. Transfixed by his dream of reaching the gold-rich provinces of "Catay" and "Cipangu" (China and Japan), the admiral "heard" in the signs of his kidnapped Taino "interpreters" (who, of course, knew no Spanish at first and precious little after three months) mostly what he wanted to hear. As he neared home, Columbus assured his royal sponsors that his interpreters had "soon understood us, and we them, either by speech or signs," a claim totally belied by his daily log.[19]

The self-delusion began as early as his third day in the "Indies." While exploring the eastern part of Guanahaní island, several natives swam to the ship's boat, from which, said the admiral, "we understood that they asked us if we had come from heaven." Two weeks later in a Cuban harbor, local natives allegedly "said by signs that within three days many merchants would come from the interior to buy the things which the Christians brought there, and that they would give news of the king of that land, who, as far as [Columbus] could understand from the signs which they made, was four days' journey from there, because they had sent many men through the whole land to tell of the admiral"—a flattering but extremely "long-winded" and complex piece of signing. Another gilded bit of news allegedly came from the interpreters on 12 November. On "Babeque" (Great Inagua Island), "they said, according to the signs which they made,... the people of the place gather gold on the shore at night with candles, and afterwards ... with a mallet they make bars of it." A month later, Columbus had "heard" enough to convince himself that the Grand Khan of China lived not far away and periodically sent ships to enslave the timorous natives of the islands the Spanish had been visiting. This gave Columbus renewed hope that people speaking an "intelligent" language would soon be found and that he could, at long last, employ his Hebrew-Chaldee-Arabic-speaking interpreter, Luis de Torres.[20]

But it was not to be, on the first or any other of the master sailor's voyages. Geography was the great impediment, of course—Asia was a whole ocean away—but even if the East had been reachable, the initial linguistic barrier was too great to overcome. Columbus had confessed as much to his log in late November. He was confident that "innumerable things of value" could be found in the new lands, but he never discovered what they were because of the shortness of his stays in port, caused largely by his failure to communicate. "I do not know the language," he admitted after six weeks, "and the people of these lands do not understand me, nor do I or anyone I have with me understand them." Moreover, his captive interpreters "I often misunderstand, taking one thing for the contrary, and I have no great confidence in them, because many times they have attempted to escape."[21]

Columbus's many successors in North America had no more cause for smugness in the language department, despite the advantage of hindsight, for neither he nor anyone else left a manual of signing, an anthology of American gestures for tongue-tied invaders. Each explorer had to invent a "silent rhetorick" from scratch, out of scraps of childhood playfulness and the brazen confidence of cultural "superiority." Verrazzano's fifteen-week cruise up the east coast in 1524 allowed the French precious little insight into the inner lives of the native inhabitants. Relying solely on sight rather than speech, the explorers were shocked, for example, to find people in Maine "so barbarous that we could never make any communication with them, however many signs we made to them." Yet this deficiency gave the Christians no pause when it came to ethnography. "Due to the lack of language," they confessed, "we were unable to find out by signs or gestures how much religious faith these people we found possess." So they simply assumed the worst: "We *think* they have neither religion nor laws, that they do not know of a First Cause or Author ... nor do they even practice any kind of idolatry."[22]

Ten years later, Cartier was equally at sea among the Stadaconans on the Gaspé. Upon spotting the thirty-foot cross the French erected, chief Donnacona pointed to it from his canoe, made a crosslike sign with two fingers, and launched into a "long harangue," sweeping his hand over the surrounding land "as *if* he wished to say that all this region belonged to him, and that we ought not to have set up this cross without his permission." After Cartier explained by signs that the cross was a mere landmark for his eventual return with more substantial trade goods, the Stadaconans "made signs to us that they would not pull down the cross, delivering at the same time several harangues which we did not understand."[23]

The earliest French explorers, in search of temporary trading partners rather than permanent colonies, were positively humble in their interpretation of native signs and sounds compared with the English planters of earliest Virginia. Whether due to national character, inexperience, circumstance, or goals, the Jamestown colonists in 1607 were so confident they could communicate by signs with the inhabitants of the Powhatan (renamed James) River that they placed the most favorable interpretation possible on every native speech they heard—or saw—during their initial exploration to the falls and back. One necessary but not sufficient reason for their confidence was the unusual ability of their Arrohattoc guide Nauirans, whose tribesmen also "would shew us anything we Demaunded, and laboured very much by signes to make us understand their Languadg." After drawing an accurate map of the river with pen and ink upon "being shewn their use," Nauirans successfully mediated the English visit to Powhatan's village near the falls. After only five days out, Gabriel Archer, the trip's scribe, boasted how the Indian "had learned me so much of the Languadg, & was so excellently ingenious in signing out his meaning, that I could make him understand me, and perceive him also wellny [-nigh] in any thing." When some local natives "murmured" at the large cross the English planted near the falls to claim the country as their own, it was Nauirans who signed the allegedly "wise" reply of the friendly Arrohattoc chief who had followed them upriver: "Why should you bee offended with them as long as they hurt you not, nor take any thing away by force, they take but a little waste ground"—an apt description of swampy Jamestown Island—"which doth you nor any of us any good."[24]

Nauirans' skill notwithstanding, there is some reason to suspect that the English had fallen prey to wishful thinking. For on 18 May, three days before the start of the upriver journey, the Paspahegh chief and a hundred warriors approached the colonists who were in the process of erecting James Fort on his land and signaled two messages. The first—"to lay our Armes away"—was unambiguous and under the circumstances clearly not to be implemented. The second obviously received a thoroughly English interpretation: the chief, they understood, "at length made signes that he would give us as much land as we would desire to take." What the English probably saw was the chief's possessive sweep of arm over his birthright, not unlike Donnacona's. To judge by their fierce attacks in subsequent weeks, the Paspaheghs had most likely issued a strongly "worded" warning against trespass.[25]

The Jamestown English were not alone in thinking they had enjoyed some success in chatting up the natives by signs. On his voyage up the St. Lawrence in 1535, Cartier had the effective help of several signing natives. The chief of Achelacy above modern Quebec City pointed out to the French "clearly by signs and in other ways that the river was extremely dangerous a little higher up" and warned them to be on their guard. At the end of Lac St. Pierre, Cartier asked some Indian fishermen "by signs if this was the way to Hochelaga," their destination on Montreal Island. "They made clear to us that it was," wrote the grateful captain, "and that we had still a three days' journey thither," which proved to be correct.[26]

Álvar Núñez Cabeza de Vaca and his fellow survivors of the disastrous Narváez expedition to Florida elicited even more aid as they walked from the East Texas coast to Mexico in the nine years after 1527. Even before leaving Florida, they sent one tenderhearted group of natives into a half-hour howling lamentation by explaining "by signs that our boat had sunk and three of our number had been drowned." By the time they reached the Texas interior, Cabeza de Vaca's party had been reduced to a handful of men and had acquired reputations as shamans and facility in six native languages after many months in captivity. "We passed through many and dissimilar tongues," the leader remembered, but "Our Lord granted us favor with the people who spoke them, for they always understood us, and we them. We questioned them, and received their answers by signs, just as if they spoke our language and we theirs."[27]

Few Europeans enjoyed the kind of wholesale success the Cabeza de Vaca party seems to have had. More often, the victories were small, practical, few, and far between. On Bartholomew Gosnold's expedition to Cape Cod in 1602, a gentleman-passenger inquired by signs about the source of the copper from which the natives made drinking cups for trade. An Indian acquaintance answered simply by taking a piece of copper in his hand, making "a hole with his finger in the ground," and pointing to the mainland from which he and his tribesmen had just come. Three years later on the coast of Maine, Captain Waymouth's crew wanted to barter tobacco from the local Indians. But since it was only early June, the natives signed that "it was growen yet but a foot above ground, and [eventually] would be above a yard high, with a leafe as broad as both their hands."[28]

In 1673 the Virginia trader Gabriel Arthur used signs to teach a village of Ohio Shawnees the trading value of beaverskins. When the Shawnees skidded a fat beaver into the compound and proceeded to singe its hair off for roasting, Arthur "made signes to them that those skins were good amongst the white people toward the riseing sun." They in turn wanted to know "by signes" how many skins the English would take for such a knife as Arthur had given to the chief. The trader told them four, and eight for a hatchet, "and made signes that if they would lett him return"—he was a recent captive—"he would bring many things amongst them."[29] And so they did. If Arthur never returned to them with his promised bounty (we have no evidence one way or the other), they may have chalked it up as much to his fumbling fingers as to his forked tongue.

Europeans used sign language to get themselves out of all kinds of sticky situations, not all of which were as potentially life-threatening as Arthur's. Indeed, the enlisted men in Iberville's exploring party up the Mississippi in 1700 no doubt regretted their leader's finesse in the American art of gesture and grimace. When the French bateaux pulled up at a friendly Bayogoula village for the night, the chief asked if the strangers would like a warm woman for every man in the company. Apparently Iberville was alarmed by this traditional token of native hospitality and "by showing his hand to them ... made them understand that their skin—red and tanned—should not come close to that of the French, which was white."[30] The grumbling of the men was not recorded for posterity but is plainly audible even at this remove.

So, too, are the extreme disgruntlement and frustration of those Europeans who were force-fed a steady diet of signs during their initial errands into the wilderness. To hear their complaints is to understand just how inadequate sign language was in eastern America, and how much both sides needed to establish some sort of verbal rapprochement in order to achieve their respective ends. Henri Joutel, the literate but humble chronicler of La Salle's ill-fated colony in Texas in the late 1680s, was anything but a grumbler, yet even he had to give frequent vent to the utter failure of the French survivors to converse intelligibly by signs with the natives they encountered on their slow trek to the Mississippi and eventually to the linguistic familiarity of New France.

Although La Salle had picked up some facility in several Indian tongues on his descent of the Mississippi in 1682, it proved useless when his second expedition two years later overshot the mouth of the great river and grounded in Matagorda Bay on the east coast of Texas. The local natives were initially friendly, "but to no Purpose, for [La Salle] spoke to them in several Languages ... and made many Signs to them, but still they understood not what he meant." When the French commandeered some of their canoes, however, relations soured and the fragile colony was reduced by attack and forced inland.[31]

In a futile search for the Mississippi, La Salle made several sorties before he was assassinated by some of his men in March 1687. Joutel then was left to live with the Cenis to prepare stores for an all-out search for home. After a week among them, the most useful word he had learned was *Coussica*, "I do not understand you," for most conversation was conducted in signs. Despite the solicitude of the village elders, Joutel spent most of his talks "nodding my Head, tho' very often," he admitted, "I knew not what they meant." When his loneliness without anyone to talk to grew "very irksome," the offer of a young wife brought no consolation. How he must have yearned for some semblance of the diversion that greeted him, in which "all the old Men lifted up their Right Hands above their Heads, crying out in a most ridiculous Manner." Only a politic regard for his own skin had prevented him from laughing aloud.[32]

A return stay in the Cenis village two months later gave the French, including two Catholic priests, an opportunity to explain the nature of their daily devotions to the inquisitive villagers. "Pointing to Heaven," the French proclaimed that they paid duty to one God, "the only Supreme Sovereign" and Creator of all things. "But this being only by Signs," Joutel confessed, "they did not understand us, and we labour'd in vain." The rest of their journey to the Mississippi was conducted in "dumb Show" only marginally more productive.³³

La Salle's men had several years' experience in native America before finally realizing that sign language was an impossibly blunt instrument for building a French empire. Colonel Henry Norwood, cast away with other Royalist refugees on the coast of Maryland in 1649 and having no overt interest in empire, had to wait less than two weeks to discover that he was deaf and dumb in the "common dialect of signs and motions" that developed between the English and their native rescuers. Forced to abandon ship on a small island in early January, the English saw no Indians for ten days until a small party visited the secluded women's cabin at night and gave them food. Then the guessing games began. According to the women, the natives had "pointed to the south-east with their hands, which they knew not how to interpret, but did imagine by their several gestures, they would be with them again tomorrow." The bookish Norwood concluded that their pointing southeast "was like to be the time they would come, meaning nine o'clock to be their hour, where the sun will be at that time." He was dead wrong: they showed up in mid-afternoon, as they no doubt had planned. Fortunately, their first communications were encouragingly benevolent: they flashed "most chearful smiles," shook hands all around, and kept intoning "Ny Top" (*nétop*), the common Algonquian word for "friend." Then began the English, particularly Norwood's, descent into befuddlement, for they parleyed in signs, he remembered, "more confounded and unintelligible than any other conversation I ever met withal; as hard to be interpreted as if they had expres'd their thoughts in the *Hebrew* or *Chaldean* tongues."³⁴

The next day the Indians returned with an older leader, who tried by signs to pump Norwood for information about his country and the occasion of the English predicament. "I made return to him in many vain words," said the colonel, "and in as many insignificant signs as himself had made to me, and neither of us one jot the wiser. The several nonplus's we both were at in striving to be better understood, afforded so little of edification to either party, that our time was almost spent in vain." Then Norwood remembered a single word from his reading of John Smith's history of Virginia—*werowance*, "chief"—and that word, he thought (probably wrongly), saved their lives because they were immediately ferried by canoe and conducted to the chief of Kickotank, on whose shores they had washed up. En route they were fed royally at the lodge of a "queen," which they left—in a telling phrase—

"with all the shews of gratitude that silence of each other's tongues knew how to utter."[35]

Warmly ensconced in the chief's lodge, Norwood was asked by his host, with "many gestures of his body, his arms display'd in various postures," for details of their mishap. "By all which motions," Norwood despaired, "I was not edify'd in the least, nor could imagine what return to make by voice or sign.... In fine, I admired their patient sufferance of my dulness to comprehend what they meant, and shew'd myself to be troubled at it." The chief laughed it off and got Norwood to do the same. But the English remained pampered prisoners of silence until one of the chief's councilors scratched a map of the region in the dirt and Norwood recognized "Achomack" on Virginia's Eastern Shore as his destination. Yet even then the English could not move until an English trader and his Indian guide arrived to enlighten the chief in a frontier patois of "broken *Indian*" with "some sprinklings of *English*."[36]

When Norwood reached the "civilized" settlements of Northampton County, he gladly honored the chief's request to have his camblet coat, glittering with gold and silver lace, because, the resolute Royalist quipped, "he was the first king I could call to mind that ever shew'd any inclination to wear my old cloaths." His humor does nothing to conceal from us his profound gratitude to the Kickotank chief for his inexhaustible hospitality and, perhaps equally important, his laughing patience with a stranger's tortured failure to speak or hear by signs.[37]

* * * *

THE ESSENTIAL PROBLEM REMAINED: how could the adult speakers of totally foreign languages learn the myriad rules and nuances of each other's tongues fast enough and well enough to begin reliable communication? And if one party sought to dictate the verbal terms of engagement, which would it be? Who would accommodate whom, and how? Human ingenuity being what it is, the new partners-in-contact invented two basic solutions. One was to fashion from shards of a European and one or more Indian languages a *jargon* to facilitate the simpler needs of sporadic trade and treaty. The other, more prevalent option was for one party to create a *pidgin* by reducing its native speech to its simplest elements and suppressing most of the features that made it distinctive and therefore difficult for strangers to learn.

Both solutions were predicated on treating the "others" not as capable adults but as young children just learning to wrap their tongues around polysyllabic words and to tease out of usage the imperfect regularities of grammar and syntax. Pidgins and jargons (which are technically pidgins) were designed specially for neophytes in the difficult art of speaking a new language. If these amateur argots seemed to native linguists like so much "baby talk," the analogy was not inapt.[38]

In addition to simplicity, America's versions of verbal shorthand had three other attractive features. The first was that pidgins were flexible tools capable of growing in sophistication and complexity with the speakers, until they either closely approximated the mature language from which they were chipped or were totally superseded by a rival tongue. The latter was the eventual fate of the four major Indian-based pidgins east of the Mississippi: the Mohawk, Delaware, and Powhatan pidgins succumbed to the mother tongue of the English colonists who swarmed over New York, Pennsylvania, New Jersey, and Virginia; and French supplanted the Mobilian trade language in the Lower Mississippi Valley. The English-based pidgin spoken largely by Indians in colonial New England was "elevated," predictably if slowly, to more standard English, particularly in the anglicized "praying towns" established by Protestant missionaries.

The second feature of the jargons and of any pidgin that served several ethnic groups was their normative neutrality. Since they were no one's proper language, they lent a measure of verbal impartiality and social stability to fragile frontiers where ethnic pride was easily bruised and often inflamed. Accessible and useful to all parties, they were stigmatized by none as inferior or preferential. This quality entailed a third value: Indian groups who used pidgins were able to preserve their proper language and its cultural secrets from the prying ears and mocking mouths of white men.[39]

The oldest pidgin in eastern North America and one of the most durable was born on the hard coasts of the Gulf of St. Lawrence early in the sixteenth century when Basque fishermen and whalers worked, traded, and ate with local Micmacs and Montagnais and possibly visiting Inuits. "Since their languages were completely different," testified a group of Basque fishermen in 1710, "they created a form of *lingua franca* composed of Basque and two different languages of the Indians, by means of which they could understand each other quite well." When the codfishers greeted their Montagnais helpers each year, they asked them in Basque *"Nola zaude?"* (How are you?), to which the natives replied politely, *"Apaizak hobeto"* (The priests [shamans] are better). The cod, of course, were called *bacaillos* or *bakalaos* even by the local Micmacs, whose own name for them was *apegé*. Four hundred years later, two words of Basque origin are still used by Micmac-speakers: *atlai*, "shirt" (from Basque *atorra*; modern Micmac has no "r") and *elege*, "king" (from Basque *errege*).[40]

When French colonists arrived in Acadia in 1604 and founded Quebec four years later, the language of the coastal tribes, noted one observer, with only small exaggeration, was "half Basque" and had been for a long time. Depending upon how they were treated, natives uttered such Basque phrases as *"Endia chave normandia"* (The French know many things) and *"Maloes mercateria"* (Those from Saint-Malo are unfair traders). They even referred to their own moose as *orignac* (Basque for "deer"), their shamans as *pilotoua* (pilots), and their celebratory feasts as *tabaquia* (shelter, indicating the place where they were held). Although in the 1540s the Indians of the St. Lawrence Gulf palavered with foreign fishermen in "any language," French, English, Gascon, or Basque, by the seventeenth century, a French lawyer said, they traded with the French only in Basque.[41]

This was a slight stretch, because it overlooked the solid substratum of Algonquian words and features that underlay the jargon. According to Marc Lescarbot, a keen-eyed lawyer-historian who spent a year in nascent Acadia, the native Micmacs for "convenience" spoke to the French a simple, "familiar" version of their own language with which "much Basque is *mixed*," although they also had a fuller, proper tongue "known only to themselves." Around early Quebec it was equally easy to miss the multilingual origins of the jargon used by the Montagnais. In 1633 a Jesuit linguist noticed "a certain jargon ... which is neither French nor Indian; and yet when the French use it, they think they are speaking the Indian Tongue, and the Indians, in using it, think they are speaking good French." When the Montagnais and French addressed each other, for example, they always used *ania*, "my brother." But Father Le Jeune already knew that *nichtais* was Montagnais for "my eldest brother" and *nichim* for "my youngest," which led him to declare *ania* "an alien word." It was, predictably, the Basque word for "brother," *anaia*, brought from the Gulf with the rest of the jargon.[42]

In the opening years of the seventeenth century, the "Basque" jargon also drifted down the Maine coast, perhaps into Massachusetts. Micmacs and Etchemins sailing hefty Basque shallops were a frequent sight as they plied the middleman's trade between Maine's native trappers and the Laurentian Gulf's European traders. When

Bartholomew Gosnold's ship reached the northern New England coast in mid-May 1602, it was met by eight Indians aboard a "Baske-shallop." The leader wore shoes, stockings, and a black serge seaman's suit; the rest were largely "naked" save for white-painted eyebrows. "It seemed by some words and signes they made," the English surmised, "that some Basks or of S. John de Luz [St.-Jean-de-Luz, a major French Basque port], have fished or traded in this place." The tardy English were right, but they would have been chagrined to learn how long ago those Basque or (as they called them) "Christian" words had entered the working vocabulary of the coast's inhabitants.[43]

The rough equality between the native Americans and the European, particularly Basque, mariners on the Atlantic frontier fostered the growth and maintenance of a bi- or tri-lingual trade jargon for at least a century. Similar conditions and needs gave rise to a near-copy in the Carolinas. Not long after the arrival of the Basques in northern waters, Spain began to explore, claim, and fortify the southern coasts between Florida and Chesapeake Bay. Except for its capital at Santa Elena, however, their hold on the coast and its natives was exceedingly tenuous. But in maintaining even a minor military and missionary presence, the Spanish had frequent contact with the coastal tribes, with whom they gradually learned to communicate. In 1564 Spanish coastal squadrons were able to track down French interlopers with the help of only native "signs and some intelligible words."[44] During the next century, however, the Spanish and the Indians fashioned a usable jargon for their sporadic interchanges. By the time the English began to make serious inroads in Carolina in the 1660s and 1670s, they were greeted by numerous natives wagging hispanicized tongues.

The crew on William Hilton's exploratory voyage in 1663 quickly learned that *bonny* meant "good" and *skerry* its opposite and were so taken with their new vocabulary that they named two landmarks "Mount-Skerry" and "Mount-Bonny." Another native group from Santa Elena greeted the English with what Hilton recognized as "many Spanish words, [such] as, *Cappitan [capitan], Commarado [camarado],* and *Adeus [adios]*." Seven years later, the first settlers on the newly renamed Ashley River were delighted to be stroked in welcome and greeted with "*Bony Conraro Angles*" (Good friend English). Shortly after, another party laid on them "*Hiddy doddy Comorado Angles Westoe Skorrye*," which was to say, "English very good friends, Westoes"—pugnacious inland enemies—"are nought." Picking up the drift of conversation quickly, the newcomers determined that the natives "hoped by our arrival to be protected from the Westoes."[45]

As the English inundated the Carolina coast, the Spanish-inspired jargon ebbed. Supremely confident of their own cultural superiority and bent on sovereignty, the English settlers, many from the inegalitarian slave society of Barbados, saw no need to perpetuate a bastardized jargon of alien, indeed enemy, tongues. At least on the coast, English would be the lingua franca. For many of the same reasons, the colonists of southern New England sought to replace the indigenous tongues with an English pidgin, scaled down and "juvenilized" for native consumption. In the gruesome wake of plague and smallpox epidemics, the often decimated tribes of the Massachusetts and Plymouth coast were rapidly overwhelmed by the popular success of the Great Migration of the 1630s. In such circumstances, they had little choice but to forge their survival largely in the white man's words, however ridiculous he found them to be on Algonquian tongues.

The first English settlers in New England—as distinguished from fishermen, explorers, and slavers—found conversation with the first Indians they actually met so easy that they must have seen no reason to learn a native tongue. On 16 March 1620, after two-and-a-half months of cold, hard labor building houses and a fort on abandoned Indian land, the Plymouth pilgrims were boldly approached by a nearly naked "savage" who spoke to them in "broken English, which they could well understand but marveled at." Before asking for some beer, an eyewitness said, Samoset "saluted us in English, and bade us welcome, for he had learned some broken English among the Englishmen that came to fish" at Monhegan Island off the coast of his native Maine, from which he had recently come to visit the local Wampanoags. He was so chatty, in fact, that the English spent all afternoon talking with him and could not persuade him to leave the fort for the night.[46]

Far from being a threat to security, Samoset introduced the foreign seekers to another loquacious Indian whose unusual facility in their own tongue would give them a crucial advantage in an uncertain, at times hostile, New World. Squanto turned out to be a native of the site where Plymouth sat. He had been kidnapped by an English slaver six years earlier, sold in Spain, redeemed, taken to London, where he lived with an officer of the Newfoundland Company, and eventually returned to his birthplace, which in his absence had been depopulated by a shipborne plague in 1616. Understandably, he spoke better English than did Samoset, whose Abenaki accent and fisherman's jargon were not equal to the demands of tricky negotiations between the pushy Pilgrims and a variety of divided Indian polities.[47]

The "broken" English spoken by Samoset and Squanto, liberally spiced with native words and locutions, was to remain the standard language of intercourse between natives and newcomers in southern New England for most of the colonial period. Only missionaries trying to woo native converts were obliged to operate in aboriginal languages. Even in Algonquian mouths, the earliest versions of the pidgin bore little resemblance to the proper native tongues that many Indians continued to speak well into the eighteenth century. Captain Miles Standish discovered the distinction in early March 1623 when he ran into Wituwamat, a caustic character from Massachusetts Bay who was trying to foment a conspiracy against the English on Cape Cod. The Indian made a long speech in an "audacious manner," wrote Edward Winslow, not in the still heavily native pidgin but in a pure Massachusett dialect, "framing it in such sort as the Captain, though he be the best linguist amongst us, could not gather anything from it."[48]

For conversation that sought to include Englishmen, the natives resorted to the increasingly anglicized pidgin. By 1634 an English visitor noticed that although the natives loved anyone who could "utter his mind in their words," they were "not a little proud that they can speak the English tongue, using it as much as their own when they meet with such as can understand it." Indeed, they loved to confound "stranger Indians" with their novel lingo. On occasion, the pidgin even served as a lingua franca between strangers. In 1624 the governor of Maine brought an Abenaki warrior seventy miles to confer with a local native of the same tribe. "They were glad to use broken English to express their mind each to other," said a witness, "not being able to understand one another in their Language" because of dialectical differences.[49]

The first thing the Abenakis may have said to each other, as Samoset probably greeted the Pilgrims, was "What cheare *Nétop*? (How are things, friend?)," the general salutation in New English-Indian relations. But since the pressure of English population, land-grabbing, and missionaries soon soured relations, our best examples of pidgin come freighted with fear and hostility. A native memory of their first encounter with a European ship yielded a characteristic line. When the Indians saw this great "walking island" approach, they paddled out to pick strawberries on it. But the ship saluted them with a broadside of "lightning and thunder," which so astonished them that they cried out (as recaptured in 1630s jargon) "What much hoggery, so big walk, and so big speak, and by and by kill." A few years later, the Pequots of southern Connecticut echoed those sentiments when a Massachusetts invasion force coasted along their territory in search of a landing place: "What, Englishmen, what cheer, what cheer, are you hoggery, will you cram us?" An English captain interpreted this to mean "Are you angry, will you kill us, and do you come to fight?"[50]

In a lighter moment forty years later, an English captain, preparing to lead sixty men against three hundred allies of King Philip (Metacomet), plucked off his precious wig and stuffed it into his pants for safekeeping. Having witnessed this bizarre act from a distance, the enemy warriors howled "hideously" and their leader allegedly yelled, "Umh, umh me no stawmerre [understand?] fight Engismon, Engismon got two Hed, Engismon got two Hed; if me cut off un Hed, he got noder, a put on beder as dis." Upon which they fled into the consoling forest.[51]

To English ears, much of the Indian jargon was laughable. The popular trader Christopher Levett obviously relished reporting Abenaki attempts to wield their new-found English words with grace and effect, and he was not a little proud to jabber in broken Algonquian. When two sagamores returned to trade with Levett after a brief flirtation with a rival English captain, they asked if he was angry. He said he was not, but he warned them that "if they were MATCHETT, that is, naughtie men, and rebellious," he would be MOUCHICK HOGGERY, that is very angry, and would CRAM, that is, kill them all." Whereupon they branded the rival trader a "Jacknape," "the most disgraceful word that may be in their conceite," and told Levett that he was, by contrast, a "foure fathom" sagamore, borrowing a metaphor from their wampum strings to indicate his worth. When he explained that he was returning to England to fetch his wife, who would not make the crossing alone, "they bid a pox on her hounds, (a phrase they have learned and doe use when they doe curse) and wished me to beat her," Indian-style. With a more gracious eye to the future, one sagamore predicted "muchicke legamatch, (that is friendship)" between his and Levett's sons "untill TANTO"—an Abenaki deity—"carried them to his wigwam, (that is untill ... they died)."[52]

In other North American colonies, the initial surge of settlement was nothing like that in New England, and the natives retained the upper hand long enough to concoct the dominant pidgins that would be used by the early colonists. Early Dutch Reformed ministers in New Netherland were particularly stymied by their inability to get past simple trade jargons to more sophisticated concepts of cosmology and religion. Jonas Michaëlius, the first minister in New Amsterdam, thought he knew something about the "savage mind" after brief tours of duty in Brazil and West Africa. To his thinking, the Indians around Manhattan in 1628 were "uncivil and stupid as garden poles, proficient in all wickedness and godlessness,... [and] thievish and treacherous as they are tall." Imagine his chagrin, then, when he deduced that the natives designed to "conceal their language from us than to properly communicate it, except in things which happen in daily trade; saying that it is sufficient for us to understand them in that." But the trade jargon—much to his disgust—was nothing but "a made-up, childish language" in which the Indians spoke only "half sentences" made up of "shortened words" that frequently lumped together a dozen or more objects. The Dutch traders who did business in it clearly were fools to think of themselves as "wonderful" linguists, because they badly botched the pronunciation of its "difficult aspirants and many gutteral[s]" and were "wholly in the dark and bewildered when they hear[d] the savages talking among themselves."[53]

If the misanthropic Michaëlius was frustrated by an Algonquian jargon in New Amsterdam, the Reverend Johannes Megapolensis suffered even greater pains in the 1640s learning the Iroquoian Mohawk tongue in order to preach in it. The dominie of Rensselaerswyck's biggest problem was lack of competent instructors. The local Dutch experts knew only "a kind of jargon just sufficient to carry on trade with it" but were ignorant of "the fundamentals of the language." The Mohawks themselves were even less helpful, probably by design. When he asked them for the names of things, he complained, "one tells me the word in the infinitive mood, another in the indicative; one in the first, another in the second person; one in the present, another in the preterit [past]. So I stand oftentimes and look, but do not know how to put it down." The fault, of course, was not his: "As *they* are very stupid," he explained, "I sometimes cannot make them understand what *I* want." To pour salt in his wounds, "they pronounced their words so differently." So Megapolensis asked an eighteen-year veteran of the area for an explanation; the man's best guess was that "they changed their language every two or three years," which seemed a stupid answer even to the ethnocentric evangelist.[54]

At the same time the Dutch founded New Amsterdam and built Fort Orange, however, they had settled briefly on the Delaware River, from 1624 to 1628. There, in pitifully small numbers, they established relations with the powerful and numerous Delaware Indians. Understandably, the natives saw no reason to learn

Dutch to be able to communicate with the strangers in their midst. But they did cut their southern Unami dialect down to European size in order to make their own needs and prerogatives known in pidgin form. The resulting Delaware jargon (as it is known) served not only the Dutch, who carried it northward when they moved, but successive colonies of Swedes and English.

In 1683 William Penn characterized the native language of Pennsylvania as "lofty, yet narrow ...; in Signification full, like Short-hand in writing; one word serveth in the place of three, and the rest are supplied by the Understanding of the Hearer: Imperfect in their Tenses, Wanting in their Moods, Participles, Adverbs, Conjunctions, [and] Interjections." What he described so well was not full and proper Delaware but the jargon used, as an early colonist noted, between natives and "Christians" who traded with them "or when they meet one another in the Woods accidentally, one a looking for his Cattel, and the other a Hunting the Wild Deer, or other Game."[55] Yet the jargon was not entirely useless in other realms. In the 1640s the Swedish minister Johannes Campanius managed to translate Luther's little catechism for children into the Delaware "shorthand." Although it was not published until 1696 in Sweden, it was reimported and saw limited use among the Indians who had inspired it.[56]

The best examples of the Delaware jargon come from a promotional book published in 1698 by Gabriel Thomas, an early Pennsylvanian, and a lengthy word-and-phrase list from the 1680s called "The Indian Interpreter," found in the Salem, New Jersey, land records. Thomas's short dialogue between an Indian hunter and an English woodsman featured practical lines such as "When wilt thou bring me Skins and Venison, with Turkeys?" and "I have good Powder, and very good Shot, with red and blue Machcots [matchcoats]." The native phrases in the "Interpreter" also tended to be "almost grammarless and based chiefly on an English construction," for the convenience of the colonists, but most of the vocabulary was distinctly Delaware, with a spare sprinkling of New England Natick, English, Dutch, and onomatopoetic words. Jargon-speakers called a duck *quing quing*, a lead bullet *alunse* (from *alluns*, the Delaware word for "arrow"), and rum *brandywyne* (a famous Pennsylvania place-name today, thanks to the artistic Wyeths). Sometime in the seventeenth century, the Natick words *squaw* and *papouse* had migrated from eastern Massachusetts to the mid-Atlantic interior. And number and gender, so important in proper Delaware, were ignored in the jargon (except for a distinction between "I" and "we"). As in most pidgins, *me* replaced the first-person singular "I," as in *Me mauholumi* (I will buy it).⁵⁷

Like its New York counterparts, the Delaware jargon eventually was replaced by pidgin English and standard English, but not until the eighteenth century. The Powhatan and Occaneechi pidgins that arose to accommodate and incorporate the English settlers of early Virginia died much faster, the victim of rapid English immigration after the development of saleable tobacco, interracial warfare, and a system of rigid apartheid.⁵⁸

Between 1607 and 1611, Captain John Smith and William Strachey, the first secretary of the Virginia colony, compiled native vocabularies that consisted largely of single terms for trade goods, anatomical parts, natural phenomena, native relationships, numbers, flora, and fauna. One version of Strachey's manuscript was entitled "A Short Dictionary ... By which, such who shall be Imployed thether may know the readyer how to confer, and how to truck and Trade with the People." Traders would indeed have found it useful, but officials bent on holding conferences with the touchy Powhatans also would have needed a few principles of pidgin grammar, for the list of nearly 750 words contains no guide to sentence construction, perhaps assuming—probably correctly—that English syntax would work most of the time. Smith's much shorter list of 137 words at least gave some examples of pidgin sentences, as well as some insight into the psychology of Indian-white relations. One native speaker asked with obvious concern, "In how many daies will there come hether any more English ships?" And we can just hear the gruff captain ordering native messengers to "Bid Pokahontas bring two little Baskets, and I wil give her white beads to make her a chaine."⁵⁹

Another pidgin flourished in south-central Virginia to serve the interests of native and English traders who operated between the Tidewater and the Carolina Piedmont. The Occaneechis, who lived on an island in the Roanoke River astride the main north-south route, created a lucrative business as middlemen and brokers. They also fashioned "a sort of general Language ... which is understood by the Chief men of many Nations, as *Latin* is in most parts of Europe, and *Lingua Franca* quite thro the *Levant*." Their wealth in furs and key position proved too tempting to the Virginians under rebel Nathaniel Bacon, and they were robbed and eliminated in 1676. But their trade jargon may have persisted in the region well into the eighteenth century. When the Huguenot settler John Fontaine visited Fort Christanna on the Meherrin River in 1716, he jotted down a sample of native words in use by the polyglot remnants of mostly Siouan-speaking tribes, including Occaneechis, who lived around the fort. The vocabulary consisted of almost equal parts Siouan and Algonquian words with a smattering of Iroquoian terms, which probably indicates the character of the original "Occaneechi" pidgin.[60]

The southernmost Indian pidgin enjoyed a much longer life and held sway over a much wider area than did the Powhatan or other southern pidgins. The so-called Mobilian or Chickasaw trade jargon was fashioned in the Lower Mississippi Valley at least by 1700 in response to French explorers and traders from Illinois and the Gulf of Mexico. It soon spread as far as East Texas, the Ohio River, Alabama, and the northwestern Gulf coast of Florida. Formed on a Western Muskogean lexical base, primarily Choctaw and Chickasaw, it incorporated elements from Alabama and Koasati (Eastern Muskogean tongues) and a very few words from Spanish, French, and Algonquian, and evolved a grammar very different from those of its constituent languages. Since children were never taught the jargon, it remained a secondary contact language that adults learned "by practice rather than by rules" for purposes of trade and diplomacy. It was, testified a French engineer, "a kind of mother tongue which is general for all, and which is understood everywhere.... When one knows it, one can travel through all this province [Louisiana] without needing an interpreter."[61]

According to Antoine Le Page du Pratz, an early settler and historian of Louisiana, the Cadodaquioux and the Nachitoches living on the Red River some three hundred miles west of the Mississippi were no strangers to *la langue mobilienne*. Although both spoke their own "peculiar" languages, "there is not a village in either of the nations, nor indeed in any nation of Louisiana, where there are not some who can speak the Chicasaw language, which is called the vulgar [common] tongue, and is the same here as the Lingua Franca is in the Levant."[62]

Nearly as far east of the great river, in Alabama territory, three Frenchmen saved their own necks by their competence in Mobilian. In 1708 two French hunters were sent by their commander to hunt game for the ill-supplied Spanish governor of Passacol (Pensacola). During the chase they were captured by a party of "Alibamons" and asked what they were doing so close to Passacol. The two hunters, "who had a good understanding of the Mobilian tongue in which the Alibamons had addressed them," told them about their hunting assignment. To test the truth of what the Frenchmen said, two chiefs the next day returned their guns and took them hunting. A herd of buffalo appeared, the two natives "in their eagerness fired at once," the hunters shot the natives and returned home with both their and the Indians' scalps.[63]

Three decades later, fluency in Mobilian enabled another Frenchman to escape captivity and possible death. In November 1741, Antoine Bonnefoy was taken from a river convoy bound for Illinois by a war party of Cherokees. After more than five months in captivity, he escaped and made his way to the northernmost Alabama town, Conchabaka, three days' journey from French Fort Toulouse. Since he looked like a Cherokee, the Alabamas were reluctant to take him in for fear that he was an enemy decoy. But after two hours of questions, which he answered "in French and in Mobillian," the natives were assured of his identity and recent origins. The trouble came when six Carolina traders and fifteen Chickasaw escorts sought his release into their hands. In the council house the English even gladhanded him and, "in the Chicachas language," promised him a good job if he would follow them to Carolina. Choosing the flag over trade, he put them off in Mobilian, "which they understood," and declared his preference for remaining with the Alabama warrior who had first "captured" him, who concurred. The next day, with his "captor's" blessing, he set off for Fort Toulouse and freedom.[64]

In the vast, polyglot Lower Mississippi, Mobilian retained its usefulness as a lingua franca well into the eighteenth century and perhaps even the next. On the proliferating plantations of the whites, the jargon was heard less and less frequently, except in occasional orders to Indian hunters and servants. Inevitably, French—perhaps in pidgin form initially—and American English became the masters' languages of preference. But in the region's innumerable native communities, especially when they fractured, moved, and amalgamated, a common tongue was still needed to bridge Babel's fissures. Mobilian served that need perfectly. And it continued to find uses all over the Southeast, apparently, for less than twenty years ago linguists collected more than 150 Mobilian words and phrases in native communities in Louisiana and Texas.[65]

* * * *

As SHORT-TERM SOLUTIONS to the New World's language problem, signs, pidgins, and jargons served their modest purpose. But when the Europeans got down to the serious business of moving inland from their narrow beachheads—opened as often by disease as by words and gifts—they could no longer depend on truncated thoughts, juvenile jabber, and half-baked notions about "savage" culture and institutions. With the exception of the Powhatan chiefdom in tidewater Virginia, the native polities of coastal America were too small, too divided, or too curious to put up much resistance to the explorers, traders, and colonial advance men who scudded in on the flood tides of the sixteenth and seventeenth centuries. Not so the large tribes who dominated the interior, its land, and its resources. The Hurons and Iroquois, Cherokees and Creeks were simply too fit, too proud, and too dangerous to push around or out of the way. If they were to be cajoled into cooperation rather than stampeded into resistance, the invaders had to learn what motivated them and how their social institutions worked. Most of all, they had to learn the characteristic idioms of native thought, for unless they could appeal to the Indians' self-interest—in their own tongues—they hadn't a prayer of converting, conquering, or removing them to open the way for the wagon ruts of progress.

Certainly the vast majority of colonists and officials had no aptitude for or interest in learning to think and speak like Indians. So they searched for reliable surrogates—interpreters whose closeness to native culture gave them an intimate knowledge not only of native tongues but of the mental and moral codes for deciphering native acts, hopes, and fears. An obvious source of experts was, as Columbus discerned, the Indians themselves. Who knew the enemy and his tongue better than the enemy? Early in the colonial process, natives were kidnapped, enticed, or otherwise sent to Europe to pick up enough French, English, or Spanish to be able to translate native words and concepts and to impress their fellow tribesmen with the invaders' homegrown numbers and wonders. In 1534, Cartier purloined two of chief Donnacona's sons from the Gaspé for this purpose and received fair return the following year when they piloted and palavered him up the St. Lawrence. Manteo and Wanchese served the same end fifty years later when they accompanied Ralegh's colonists back to Roanoke. Even earlier in the Chesapeake, a young, possibly York River, Indian was picked up by the Spanish, educated in Mexico, Spain, and Havana, baptized, and returned to Virginia in 1570 as interpreter and guide to a party of Jesuits. Rather than lead his people to the bruited glories of Christian salvation, however, he promptly ran away, took several wives Indian-style, and led the slaughter of the deceived blackrobes.[66]

The earliest Jesuits and Recollects in Canada also were fond of sending native boys, and occasionally girls, to European schools and convents for religious and linguistic acculturation. But their pupils often died en route or in the disease capitals of Europe, reverted to typecast "savagery" on return, or, perhaps most frustrating of all, lost much of their native fluency during the total immersion of their junior years abroad. The Recollects' best hope, Pierre-Antoine Pastedechouen, a Montagnais, was thoroughly ruined by his six years in France. When he returned to Canada in 1626, he certainly knew his French (not to mention Latin) and reveled in Gallic culture, but he had so thoroughly forgotten his own language that he had to be forced to return to his former district around Tadoussac to learn it. Having lost any forest skills he may have had, he earned only contempt from his tribesmen, took to drink, and went through four or five wives before dying of starvation in the woods. The French, who badly needed his skills as an interpreter and missionary language instructor, had to reconsider their options.[67]

One of their solutions was also employed by the English over the next two centuries: sending likely native boys to colonial Indian schools to acquire the invaders' tongue. In the seventeenth century, these stiffly formal institutions proved unequal to the task of endowing aspiring warriors with European minds, manners, and mouths. Both the Recollect and Jesuit *séminaires* (largely for Hurons) folded within five years. The proposed Indian school at Henrico in Virginia came to naught in the Powhatan uprising of 1622. Harvard graduated exactly two Indians, one of whom was killed by native traditionalists, the other by the white man's tuberculosis.[68]

The French learned from their mistakes and never tried again, but the English suffered the selective amnesia of arrogance and periodically dusted off their scheme to anglicize the natives for future deployment as interpreters. In the eighteenth century, a wide variety of New England and Middle Atlantic tribesmen were schooled in English words and ways in Philadelphia, Stockbridge, Massachusetts, New Haven, and Lebanon, Connecticut. Almost the sole accomplishment of Eleazar Wheelock's famous charity school in Lebanon was training up a number of Indian boys as interpreters (and schoolmasters) for the frontiers of New York and New England; after a short but bitter run at the business, Wheelock gave up his founding hope of producing native missionaries and settled for the lesser but still important goal.[69]

The basic problem facing Wheelock and all European officials seeking interpreters was that, at bottom, Indians lacked full credibility. While they certainly could be counted on to know what made their brethren tick, they were much less in tune with European modes of thinking and codes of conduct, into which the native views were somehow to be translated. This cultural deficiency was not insurmountable in trade or even day-to-day diplomacy, but in the delicate minuets of treaty-making and in the sacred precincts of religion it was a distinct liability. And as the racial climate in America darkened, no Indian—no matter how fluent, able, or experienced—could ever be fully trusted with the white man's business. The natives' "national" reputation for secrecy, subterfuge, and revenge was too well known to allow the Europeans, the English especially, the luxury of putting their complete faith in native interpreters.

If natives were ultimately unacceptable, then fellow colonists themselves must somehow gain the fluency and understanding of natives. Although their loyalty to their employers could not always be taken for granted, given the normal seductions of party, interest, and greed, at least they began on the right side of the cultural and linguistic divide.

Most European interpreters—and the best—acquired their skills by living among the Indians as teenagers or in their early twenties, when learning is an unstudied and often pleasurable pastime. Their native domicile could be either voluntary or forced, as long as they chose to return to colonial society to earn their living and to own their primary allegiance. The three main groups who followed this course were war captives or adoptees, traders, and boys or young men placed in friendly villages by their parents or colonial officials for total immersion in native words and ways.

Europeans who had been forcibly acculturated by Indians made perhaps the most trustworthy interpreters because, although they might remain sympathetic to their adopted cultures, they were usually happy to be repatriated by their countrymen; their loyalties to their rescuers were reliable. Moreover, their linguistic skills were often pronounced because they had acquired them quickly and in isolation from their natal tongues in order to survive, not from duty or for mere pleasure. Hernando de Soto's entrada through the Southeast after 1539 would never have left the coast of Florida had he not redeemed Juan Ortiz, a survivor of the Narváez debacle in 1528 who had lived with the natives for twelve years. Fortunately, although he closely resembled the Indians, down to his arm tattoos and breechclout, Ortiz had not forgotten the Spanish he had learned in Seville. When he died somewhere west of the Mississippi in March 1542, the expedition began to unravel, for the only interpreter left was a young Indian enslaved in northeastern Georgia, where different languages were spoken. "So great a misfortune was the death of ... Ortiz ... that to learn from the Indians what he stated in four words, with the youth the whole day was needed; and most of the time he understood just the opposite of what was asked."[70]

In the late seventeenth and early eighteenth centuries, some of the best interpreters were schooled by northeastern tribes after being captured during Euro-Indian conflicts or intercolonial wars. Louis-Thomas Chabert de Joncaire became a formidable agent and interpreter for New France among the Iroquois after he was captured by the Senecas in the 1680s, adopted, and married. He helped broker the major Franco-Iroquois peace treaty of 1701 and fathered (by a French wife) two sons who succeeded him as accomplished interpreters, forest diplomats, and thorns in the sides of British officials.[71] Two of the Joncaires' ablest rivals for Iroquois loyalties were Lawrence Claessen van der Volgen and Jan Baptist van Eps, who worked for the English in New York colony. Both Dutchmen had been captured by French-allied Iroquois in the daring nighttime raid on Schnectady in 1690—Claessen at thirteen, Van Eps at seventeen—and raised among the Caughnawagas across the river from Montreal. Having had native tutoring for only three years, van Eps was quickly supplanted as New York's chief interpreter when Claessen returned after ten years of cultural reconditioning.[72]

The three-way contest for New England also bred its share of adept "linguisters." John Gyles was in great demand by English officials for peace negotiations and prisoner exchanges in Maine because he spoke fluent French, Micmac, and Maliseet after nine years of captivity. Taken at the age of nine by a Maliseet war party in 1689, he spent six years with the Indians and another three with a French trader in Acadia before returning to an effective military career on the Maine frontier.[73] Joseph Kellogg and his sister Rebecca were equally effective as hired tongues after they returned from captivity in Canada. At the age of twelve and eight, respectively, they had been seized with the rest of their family from Deerfield, Massachusetts, by a French and Indian war party in 1704. Joseph stayed with the natives only a year but then traveled widely with French traders in Indian country as far as the Mississippi. When he returned to New England, he drew a substantial salary for serving as captain at Fort Dummer, head of its trading post, sometime teacher at the Hollis Indian school in Stockbridge, and the best male interpreter in New England. After twenty-five years among the Caughnawagas, his sister was even better, but, being a woman, she was seldom used for public diplomacy. Instead, she employed her "extraordinary" fluency in the Hollis school (which boarded mostly Iroquois children) and for the Oneida mission of the Reverend Gideon Hawley at Oquaga, New York.[74]

While the captive experience was invaluable training for potential interpreters, it was not always reliable. Most young captives—literally hundreds—never returned to their colonial homes at all or were compelled by peace treaties and prisoner exchanges to do so against their will.[75] A safer way to produce interpreters was to place "likely lads" in allied Indian villages, usually in the families of headmen, for at least a year of cultural and linguistic immersion. During their years abroad, the boys served not only as vulnerable sureties for the good behavior of their colonial sponsors but as unwitting participants in a venerable native ritual, in which trading partners and allies exchanged children as tokens of good faith. Only occasionally did the Europeans reciprocate by requesting or accepting Indian children; when they did, the political need for hostages or brown bodies to fill philanthropic Indian schools was uppermost in their minds, not bowing to "savage" custom.[76]

In the Americas, the French initiated the practice of placing student interpreters in native villages.[77] In the sixteenth century, French sea captains in the brazilwood trade sent young sailors to native villages along the Brazilian coast to recruit woodcutters while learning the local languages. Many of these blond *"truchements de Normandie"* went quite native, going relatively "naked," painting themselves, taking native wives, and even dining on Indian enemies with their new tribespeople. Protestant French missionaries and rival Portuguese settlers alike were appalled at the extent of the interpreters' acculturation but profited immeasurably from their linguistic skills and knowledge of the land and its peoples.[78]

One of the veterans of the Brazil run was Jacques Cartier of Saint-Malo. On his third voyage to Canada in 1541, he left with the cooperative chief of Achelacy "two yong boyes ... to learne their language." On his previous reconnaissance of the St. Lawrence six years earlier, the chief had sought to ally himself with the patently powerful strangers by giving Cartier his own eight-or nine-year-old daughter, whom Cartier took to France the following spring. Since Cartier had not returned her to her homeland (she had probably died of an unfamiliar urban disease), he was taking a calculated risk with the lives of his two student interpreters. Perhaps the chief had swallowed a version of the tale Cartier had manufactured for the new chief of Stadacona, that Donnacona, the former chief, had died in France but that the other four headmen the French had shanghaied upon departing remained there "as great Lords, and were maried, and would not returne backe into their Countrey."[79]

The French need to prepare their own interpreters was all the more urgent because two of their latest hostages were the same two sons of Donnacona whom Cartier had plucked from the mouth of the river on his first voyage in 1534 and taken to France to learn enough French to serve as his guides and tongues the following year. But the results were mixed: one, Dom Agaya, was only partially accommodating in French dealings with his wary and politically embroiled father. The other, Taignoagny, used his newfound knowledge of the French to counteract their ploys and policies in his homeland—a scene that would be re-enacted when the English repatriated their two Indian interpreters at Roanoke a half century later.[80]

After the French resumed their colonizing efforts on the St. Lawrence in 1608, officials soon planted young Frenchmen in the distant villages of all their potential trading partners and allies. Between 1610 and 1629, they sent a dozen to winter *"chez les Sauvages."* Most stayed two or three years, but several served as the eyes, ears, and tongues of the fur trade monopolists and civil governors much longer. Étienne Brulé lived with the Hurons for eighteen years; Jean Nicollet followed the nomadic Algonquins and Nipissings for ten years; Jean Richer worked the camps of the Montagnais and Algonquins for seven years, half as many as Nicolas Marsolet. When the Recollects and Jesuits launched their different and often rival missions in the same native cantons, they often assailed the morality and loyalty of the acculturated *truchements*, but they usually had no way to get a purchase on the native tongues without their begrudging assistance. Marsolet protected his employer's trading interests by vowing never to teach anyone a word of the native languages he commanded. He relented only to teach an importunate Recollect the Montagnais phrase for "No, I do not understand you." Fortunately for the missionaries, other interpreters were more forthcoming.[81]

When the French (many of them Canadians) extended their geopolitical reach to Louisiana after 1699, they transferred their effective mode of interpreter training as well. Since the southern mission was more military than mercantile, the students sent among the Houmas, Bayogoulas, Natchez, and other Mississippi tribes were either cabin boys on naval ships or young cadets in the French army, all under martial command to perform their linguistic duties. In the first three years alone, six boys aged fourteen or fifteen were sent to tribes upriver while another dozen operated out of the Mobile command post. For strategic reasons, the policy continued throughout the colonial period. Promising or experienced young linguists either were put on the military payroll as cadets or were selected by the governor, who was ordered by the Minister of Marine to "choose from the number of young cadets ... those whom he thinks most intelligent in order to learn the Indian languages so that they may be able some day to serve as interpreters and to win the confidence of the Indians." French officials thought that official interpreters of "rank" could command the Indians' respect better than mercenary and dissolute *coureurs de bois* and traders.[82]

The manifest superiority of Indian-trained interpreters was not lost even on English colonizers. Having no opportunity to commandeer natives for language indoctrination in England before they arrived in 1607, as their Roanoke predecessors had done, the Jamestown settlers were obliged to entrust their own boys to the Powhatans to acquire double tongues. After only one month in Virginia, thirteen-year-old Thomas Savage was exchanged for "Emperor" Powhatan's trusty and probably older servant Namontack. Within a short time, Savage was fluent and trusted enough to carry messages from the chief to the Jamestown fort. In 1614 he helped broker the end of armed hostilities between the English and the Powhatans, even though he had angered and perhaps saddened his adopted father by abandoning him four years earlier when the fighting got too hot.[83]

In 1609 Savage was joined by fourteen-year-old Henry Spelman, who initially was given to one of Powhatan's sons and "made very much of." Eventually, he lived in Powhatan's capital and dined at his "Table" with Thomas Savage, until he stole away with a visiting chief from the Potomac, where he lived for a year or more. Other students soon joined them on the native side of the frontier. Captain John Smith left his page Samuel Collier with the Pamunkeys "to learne the Language." By the time he was killed accidentally during the Powhatan uprising in 1622, Collier was considered "very well acquainted with [the Indians'] language and habitation, humors and conditions." Two days before the surprise attack, the Powhatans "sent home to his Master" a young man named Browne, who had lived among them as a language apprentice and apparently had earned enough of their regard to save his life.[84]

Like their French rivals, English officials and merchants continued to educate their own interpreters in native communities throughout the colonial period, not exclusively but often enough to demonstrate their faith in the efficiency and reliability of the method. Up and down the Atlantic seaboard, from post-Conquest Canada to South Carolina, English sons, nephews, and employees were entrusted to native villagers to be raised as complete Indians without forsaking their civic mission or forgetting their natal tongue. Some of the best Indian diplomats in the war-torn eighteenth century—Conrad Weiser and Daniel Claus among them—had their ethnological tutelage at the hands of native experts, thanks to the timely and politically astute sponsorship of English officials and relatives.[85]

The third class of interpreters—traders—also acquired nativized tongues in smoky wigwams and longhouses but usually did so less thoroughly and with less finesse while seeking customers for their beads, guns, and blankets. In pursuit of profits from native deerskins and beaver pelts, most traders regarded native languages pragmatically as relatively crude tools to do a job for their employers or creditors. It is no coincidence that the great majority of Indian-speakers in colonial North America were involved in the Indian trade, either as hired employees—packhorsemen in the Southeast, *engagés* in the Great Lakes and *pays d'en haut*, truckhouse clerks in New England and Hudson Bay country—or as the "master traders" who put together conglomerates in and ran outfits out of Albany and Philadelphia, Charles Town and Augusta, Montreal and New Orleans. While being able to haggle and attend to the ritual niceties of exchange with their native customers was essential, trade did not require a highly sophisticated vocabulary or a punctilious command of treaty council protocol to make a living. Only when colonial officials were forced to rely on traders as their sole sources of political and military intelligence—and the traders were forced to conduct the colonies' official business in addition to their own—did the traders have to hone their linguistic and cultural skills. Early and prolonged residence in native villages often qualified traders for these demanding tasks of interpreting and explaining the radically different cultures to each other.[86] Often they were assisted by native wives, and not a few were the *métis* products of similar unions themselves.[87]

No matter how adequate the preparation and credentials of the interpreters, they still had to perform their roles consistently and with the utmost accuracy and sensitivity to cultural nuance and norms if the Europeans hoped to obtain their economic, military, and religious ends without bloodshed and undue expense. How well they succeeded is not easy to determine. The quality of interpreters' performances is inherently difficult to judge. Unless critics command the interpreters' double linguistic skills, they can never fully measure the accuracy and spirit of their dialogic translations. Fortunately, in the colonial period several observers, European and Indian, did have these special skills, or at least enough of the second language to detect weaknesses. Together, their judgments give us some understanding of the high art of interpreting and cultural brokering and of how many contemporaries managed to meet its standards.

After verbal dexterity, the main desideratum in any interpretation was trust. Did the interpreter convey faithfully and fully the messages that each side of the cultural conversation intended to send? Or did he, in the privacy of the others' language, tell them what they wanted to hear or what he wanted them to hear? As the mouthpiece for both sides, was he strictly neutral? Or did he allow birth, greed, or party to warp his words? Although the Indians had the most to lose in the contest for North America, especially by using colonial interpreters, as peoples without writing they believed in the inviolability of the spoken word, particularly in public councils and treaties. "As they are honest themselves," Cadwallader Colden noted after long experience in New York Indian affairs, "they naturally think others to be so, until they find themselves abused by them."[88]

They did not have long to wait, at which point they took extra measures to check the performance of the interpreters chosen largely by the colonists from their own ranks. The most telling way was to assign someone they trusted implicitly to monitor the translations as they occurred. After the Pequot War ended in 1637, the Narragansetts of Rhode Island were reluctant to attend any council with the English unless Roger Williams, the exiled Puritan minister who lived among them and was fluent in their tongue, went along. Chief Miantonomo was not confident of the "faithfullnes" of Connecticut's Thomas Stanton "in point of interpretation" nor, in Boston, of interpreters in general, "whom he feares to trust." No doubt he had learned his lesson at a treaty council during the war, when Massachusetts officials "could not well make [the natives] understand the articles perfectly" by one of their own interpreters and had to send a copy to Williams, who everyone agreed "could best interpret them to them." Ten years later, Stanton stood in no better odor. The governor of Connecticut hoped that, at the next meeting of the Commissioners of the United Colonies, an honorable Benedict Arnold might supplement Stanton as interpreter, "wherby all suspitions of mistake may be removed, wherto I doubt wee are very subject in our transactions with Indyans."[89]

A century later, Moravian missionary David Zeisberger, an adopted Onondaga as well as a fluent speaker of Delaware, was entrusted by both tribes to tell them the truth about the colonists' statements in councils. "In what he said they placed full confidence; and when he was absent from treaties held with the white people, they could not be easily reconciled, believing that his presence served as a check upon the interpreters, who (as the Indians were apt to say) would suffer themselves to be bribed—especially when purchases of land were about being made from them." At a council at Onondaga in 1753 to hear a message from the governor of Virginia, the Iroquois politely listened to métis Andrew Montour interpret the letter and then asked Zeisberger to translate it again for them, "no doubt," his Moravian companion wrote, "in order to find out whether it agreed with what Andres [Montour] had said." Even though Zeisberger modestly excused himself as being insufficiently qualified, the Moravians "noticed that Andres would not have been much pleased to have him do so."[90]

Six years later, a group of Ohio Indians placed their full confidence in Montour when they asked Pennsylvania authorities that he interpret the written minutes of a conference they had had with Colonel Hugh Mercer at Pittsburgh. "If it be wrong," they suggested mildly, "it might be set right." "We had very bad interpreters."[91] Their problem was common, given the disparity between a rigorously sanctioned oral culture, where accurate collective memories preserved words verbatim, and the corrasable freedom of a written one, where ink was cheap, hands easy to copy, and sheets of paper virtually indistinguishable. When even white men complained of colonial "faithlessness in Treatys" and testified that they had been "present when an Article of the Peace has run in one sense in the English, and quite contrarie in the Indian, by the Governour's express orders," the natives were understandably anxious to ensure the veracity of their words, agreements, and cessions on the "talking papers" the white men regarded—in their own courts—as enforceable "law."[92]

If only one interpreter (usually a white one) could be engaged to conduct a council meeting or treaty, the natives had three other ways to protect themselves from forked tongues. First, their established council protocol, which Europeans were forced to adopt early in their relationship, mandated that any proposal be recapitulated before offering an answer. Thus repetition opened the interpreter's translations to regular scrutiny on both sides of the fire. Second, by the eighteenth century, growing numbers of settlers, officials, and natives were functionally bilingual, thus enabling more council participants to kibbitz on the official work of the linguists. Moreover, although many Indians understood English or French, they often refused to speak it in public settings, a habit that allowed them to overhear the opposing side as well as to test the quality of the interpreter's version in "Indian."[93] And, finally, if the natives suspected that their thoughts and words had been misrepresented either orally or in writing, they might, as a Maine Penobscot village did after the Casco Bay treaty in 1727, issue their own written rejoinder and clarification, thus hoisting the scribbling white men on their own petard. The Penobscots' interlocutor, Laurence Sagouarrab, wrote that he wished to broadcast in his "own Tongue" to "you who are spread all over the earth," he wrote, because of "the diversity and contrariety of the interpretations I receive of the English writing in which the articles of Peace are drawn up." "These writings appear to contain things that are not, so that the Englishman [interpreter] himself disavows them in my presence, when he reads and interprets them to me himself." There followed a long recital of what he (on behalf of his village) did *not* do or say at the conference and a much shorter one of what he did.[94]

Given the vulnerability of their fields, farms, and populations, the colonists, too, had to be concerned with the conduct and quality of their interpreters. According to European lights, Indian notions of "Freedom, property, and independence" were "extravagant" and their brand of warfare terrifyingly effective. A slip of the tongue or an insulting breach of etiquette was often enough to unleash stealthy forces of native revenge on unsuspecting frontier settlements. Unfaithful, corrupt, or simply careless interpreters were well known throughout the colonial period for their ability to cause "frequent mischeifes and mistakes," "disputes and Misunderstandings," "serious mishap[s]," and even bloody wars.[95]

Both the English and the French sought to reduce these risks by professionalizing their interpreter corps. The best linguists were given public or military rank and salaries and expense accounts that allowed them to forgo their usual involvement in the Indian trade.[96] In several English colonies, they were also obliged to swear an oath of fidelity, promising to "faithfully & truly Execute" their office, not to conceal anything they might learn in the course of their duties, and to do all in their power to promote "the good of the province" in Indian affairs.[97] Many official interpreters accumulated long records of service, and the competence in conducting delicate negotiations between two different, proud, and often prickly cultures that only practice could bring.

One group of invaders who seldom had access to the best or most obliging interpreters was missionaries, Protestant and Catholic. In many ways, the missionaries' task was more difficult than that of colonial officials, fur traders, and land speculators. In attempting to conquer native souls as well as bodies for the "work of Christ," they had to translate the ancient history and mixed precepts of the Bible for people who knew nothing of Israel, books, sheep, churches, or even candles, much less Heaven, Hell, and Purgatory, and whose languages made it impossible to speak non-possessively of a triune Father-Son-and-Holy-Ghost. Moreover, an interpreter whose own life made a mockery of the morality he propagated, who had no "experimental" (as opposed to doctrinal) knowledge of religion, or who had been raised in the tenets of a rival or, worse yet, no denomination was clearly a liability to devout proselytizers. In the Northeast, missionaries who had yet to master a native dialect seemed to find only mercenary Dutch traders and other "low-lived, ignorant, & commonly Vitious Persons," such as semi-acculturated Indians and former captives, for hire.[98] Such people typically made the kind of mistake Sir William Johnson detected in an interpreter for a Boston missionary, "the best in that Country," who tried to translate "For God is no Respector of persons" for a native assembly and came out with "God had no Love for such people as them," which cannot have engendered much for him, his employer, or their religion.[99]

For most of the colonial period, the colonists' best interests were served by avoiding conflict with the American natives and cultivating their friendship and cooperation. Discerning the natives' ways and wants was never easy for the confident newcomers from the self-proclaimed center of "civilization," but many people on both sides of the cultural divide made bona fide efforts to clarify and communicate native positions to colonial movers and shakers. Despite seemingly insurmountable differences in thought, values, and language, the two sides managed, for the most part, to understand one another, at least for practical purposes. How, then, do we explain the horrible armed conflicts that periodically shattered the three centuries of colonial coexistence?

Wars broke out not because the colonists failed to understand their Indian neighbors, but because they usually did and chose—or their distant European leaders chose—to ignore the natives' needs and wishes. Backed by healthier, proliferating populations of humans and animals, technological superiority, and other forms of social power, Europeans could simply impose their will if the native complaints and concerns they heard through their interpreters and other sensitive observers did not move them to care or caution. Colonial officials who, after decades of determined listening, knew the meaning of the Indians' voice unleashed the dogs of war not upon inscrutable "barbarians" but upon articulate human beings like themselves.

Notes

1. John Lawson, *A New Voyage to Carolina*, ed. Hugh Talmage Lefler (Chapel Hill, 1967 [1709]), 214, 219, 239.
2. Genesis 11:1–9
3. Harold E. Driver, *Indians of North America*, 2d rev. ed. (Chicago, 1969), ch. 3.
4. Baron de Lahontan, *New Voyages to North-America*, ed. Reuben Gold Thwaites, 2 vols. (New York, 1970 [1703]), 1:47, 2:733–34; Thwaites, ed., *The Jesuit Relations and Allied Documents* (hereafter cited as *JR*), 73 vols. (Cleveland, 1896–1901), 5:115 (Paul Le Jeune, 1633).
5. Roger Williams, *A Key into the Language of America* (London, 1643), A2v–3r, 104–105.
6. Lawson, *New Voyage to Carolina*, 233, 239.
7. Fernand Braudel, *The Identity of France*, Vol. l, *History and Environment*, trans. Siân Reynolds (New York, 1988), 85–96; Robert Mandrou, *Introduction to Modern France, 1500–1640: An Essay in Historical Psychology*, trans. R.E. Hallmark (New York, 1977), 62–65; Patrice L.-R. Higonnet, "The Politics of Linguistic Terrorism and Grammatical Hegemony during the French Revolution," *Social History* 5 (1980): 41–69.
8. W.P. Clark, *The Indian Sign Language* (Philadelphia, 1885; repr. Lincoln, NE, 1982); Garrick Mallery, *Sign Language among North American Indians* (Washington, DC, 1881; repr. The Hague, 1972); D. Jean Umiker-Sebeok and Thomas A. Sebeok, eds., *Aboriginal Sign Languages of the Americas and Australia*, 2 vols. (New York, 1978).
9. David Beers Quinn, *The Elizabethans and the Irish* (Ithaca, 1966), 92, 126, 151, 169.
10. David B. Quinn and Alison M. Quinn, eds., *English New England Voyages, 1602–1608*, Hakluyt Society Publications, 2d ser. 161 (London, 1983), 267.
11. Richard Hakluyt the Younger, "Discourse of Western Planting" (1584), in *The Original Writings and Correspondence of the Two Richard Hakluyts*, ed. E.G.R. Taylor, Hakluyt Society Publications., 2d ser. 76–77 (London, 1935), 215 (continuous pagination).
12. H.P. Biggar, ed. and trans., *The Voyages of Jacques Cartier*, Publications of the Public Archives of Canada [hereafter PAC] 11 (Ottawa, 1924), 56, 62, 162; David B. Quinn and Alison M. Quinn, eds., *Virginia Voyages from Hakluyt* (London, 1973), 4 (Barlowe); David B.Quinn, ed., *New American World : A Documentary History of North America to 1612*, 5 vols. (New York, 1979), 1:235, 236, 240, 242 (Davis).
13. Alexander S. Salley, Jr., ed., *Narratives of Early Carolina, 1650–1708*, Original Narratives of Early American History [hereafter ONEAH] (New York, 1911),

91, 117,132 (bear oil); Richebourg Gaillard McWilliams, ed. and trans., *Fleur de Lys and Calumet: Being the Pénicaut Narrative of French Adventure in Louisiana* (Baton Rouge, 1953), 5 (clay); McWilliams, ed. and trans., *Iberville's Gulf Journals* (University, AL., 1981), 46; Jay Higginbotham, ed. and trans., *The Journal of Sauvole* (Mobile, 1969), 31; Louise Phelps Kellogg, ed., *Early Narratives of the Northwest, 1634–1699*, ONEAH (New York, 1917), 85, 155 (bear oil).
14. Lynn Ceci, "The Value of Wampum among the New York Iroquois: A Case Study in Artifact Analysis," *Journal of Anthropological Research* 38 (1982): 97–107; Ian W. Brown, "The Calumet Ceremony in the Southeast and Its Archaeological Manifestations" *American Antiquity* 54 (1989): 311–31; McWilliams, *Iberville's Gulf Journals*, 46.
15. Kellogg, *Early Narratives of the Northwest*, 85 (Perrot), 129 (Allouez).
16. Ruth Lapham Butler, ed. and trans., *Journal of Paul Du Ru: Missionary Priest to Louisiana* (Chicago, 1934 [1700]), 18; Walter James Hoffman, "The Menomini Indians," Bureau of American Ethnology, 14th *Annual Report* (Washington, DC, 1896), pt. 1:214–16 at 215; Quinn, *New American World*, 1:240.
17. Lawrence C. Wroth, *The Voyages of Giovanni da Verrazzano, 1524–1528* (New Haven, 1970), 138–39.
18. Quinn and Quinn, *English New England Voyages*, 134 (1602).
19. *The Journal of Christopher Columbus*, trans. Cecil Jane, ed. L. A. Vigneras (New York, 1960), 196.
20. Ibid., 27, 50, 51, 57.
21. Ibid., 76.
22. Henry Norwood, "*A Voyage to Virginia. By Colonel Norwood*" [1649], in *Tracts and Other Papers Relating Principally to the Origin, Settlement, and Progress of the Colonies in North America* ..., Peter Force, comp., 4 vols. (Washington, DC, 1836–1847), vol. 3, no. 10: 38; Wroth, *Voyages of Verrazzano*, 140, 141 (my emphasis).
23. Biggar, *Voyages of Cartier*, 65, 67 (my emphasis). For a similarly guilty interpretation of Indian speech by a seagoing European trader, see Quinn and Quinn, *English New England Voyages*, 267.
24. Philip L. Barbour, ed., *The Jamestown Voyages under the First Charter, 1606–1609*, Hakluyt Society Publications., 2d ser. 136–37 (Cambridge, 1969), 90, 94, 141 (continuous pagination).
25. Barbour, *Jamestown Voyages*, 139.
26. Biggar, *Voyages of Cartier*, 143, 147.
27. Quinn, *New American World*, 2: 29, 51.
28. Quinn and Quinn, *English New England Voyages*, 156, 280.
29. Clarence W. Alvord and Lee Bidgood, eds., *The First Explorations of the Trans-Allegheny Region by the Virginians, 1650–1674* (Cleveland, 1912), 222–23.
30. McWilliams, *Iberville's Gulf Journals*, 24.
31. [Henri] *Joutel's Journal of La Salle's Last Voyage, 1684–7*, ed. Henry Reed Stiles (Albany, N.Y., 1906), 71. A reprint edition published in 1962 by Corinth Books is a photo-duplicate of the Stiles edition; but because it lacks Stiles's historical introduction, its pagination begins thirty-two pages earlier.
32. *Joutel's Journal*, 139, 140, 148.
33. *Joutel's Journal*, 156–57, 168.
34. Norwood, "*Voyage to Virginia*," in Force, *Tracts*, vol. 3, no. 10: 29, 39.
35. Ibid., 30, 35.
36. Ibid., 36, 39, 43.
37. Ibid., 44.

38. Robert A. Hall, *Pidgin and Creole Languages* (Ithaca, 1966); Dell Hymes, ed., *Pidginization and Creolization of Languages* (Cambridge, 1971); Emanuel J. Drechsel, "'Ha, Now Me Stomany That': A Summary of Pidginization and Creolization of North American Indian Languages," *International Journal of the Sociology of Language* 7 (1976): 63–81; Albert Valdman, ed., *Pidgin and Creole Linguistics* (Bloomington, IN, 1979); Michael Silverstein, "Dynamics of Linguistic Contact," in *Handbook of North American Indians*, vol. 17, *Language*, ed. Ives Goddard (Washington, DC, 1996), 117–36; Silverstein, "Encountering Language and Languages of Encounter in North American Ethnohistory," *Journal of Linguistic Anthropology* 6 (Dec. 1996): 126–44.
39. Emanuel J. Drechsel, "Towards an Ethnohistory of Speaking: The Case of Mobilian Jargon: An American Indian Pidgin of the Lower Mississippi Valley," *Ethnohistory* 30 (1983): 165–76 at 168.
40. Francisque Michel, *Le pays Basque* (Paris, 1857), 159, quoted in Peter Bakker, "Two Basque Loanwords in Micmac," *International Journal of American Linguistics* 55 (1989): 258–61 at 259; René Bélanger, *Les Basques dans l'Estuaire du Saint-Laurent, 1535–1635* (Montreal, 1971), 86 (quoting a Basque chronicle of 1625); Marc Lescarbot, *The History of New France*, ed. and trans. W.L. Grant, intro. H.P. Biggar, 3 vols. (Toronto, Champlain Society, 1911 [1609]), 2:24.
41. Lescarbot, *History of New France*, 2:24; Peter Bakker, "Basque Pidgin Vocabulary in European-Algonquian Trade Contacts," in *Papers of the Nineteenth Algonquian Conference*, ed. William Cowan (Ottawa: Carleton University, 1988), 7–15 at 10–11; H.P. Biggar, ed. and trans., *A Collection of Documents Relating to Jacques Cartier and the Sieur de Roberval*, Publications of the PAC 14 (Ottawa, 1930), 453–54; Pierre de Lancre, *Tableau de l'inconstance des mauvais anges et démons* (Paris, 1613), quoted in Bakker, "Basque Pidgin Vocabulary," 9.
42. Lescarbot, *History of New France*, 3:125 (my emphasis); *JR* 5:113, 115 (Paul Le Jeune, 1633). See also Peter Bakker, "A Basque Nautical Pidgin: A Missing Link in the History of FU?," *Journal of Pidgin and Creole Languages* 2 (1987): 1–30; Bakker, "'The Language of the Coast Tribes is Half Basque': A Basque-Amerindian Pidgin in Use between Europeans and Native Americans in North America, ca. 1540–ca. 1640," *Anthropological Linguistics* 31 (1989): 117–47.
43. Quinn and Quinn, *English New England Voyages*, 117, 145–46. See Bruce J. Bourque and Ruth Holmes Whitehead, "Tarrentines and the Introduction of European Trade Goods in the Gulf of Maine," *Ethnohistory* 32 (1985): 327–41, and Laurier Turgeon, "La traite Française dans le Saint-Laurent au XVIe siècle," *Saguenayensia* 27 (1985): 190–92.
44. Quinn, *New American World*, 2:311–13.
45. Salley, *Narratives of Early Carolina*, 39, 50–51, 117, 119.
46. William Bradford, *Of Plymouth Plantation, 1620–1647*, ed. Samuel Eliot Morison (New York, 1952), 79; *A Journal of the Pilgrims at Plymouth: Mourt's Relation*, ed. Dwight B. Heath (New York, 1963 [1622]), 51.
47. Bradford, *Of Plymouth Plantation*, 80; *Mourt's Relation*, 55: Neal Salisbury, "Squanto: Last of the Patuxets," in *Struggle and Survival in Colonial America*, ed. David G. Sweet and Gary B. Nash (Berkeley, 1981), 228–46.
48. Edward Winslow, *Good News from New England* (London, 1624), reprinted in Edward Arber, ed., *The Story of the Pilgrim Fathers, 1606–1623* (London and Boston, 1897), 544–45.
49. William Wood, *New England's Prospect*, ed. Alden T. Vaughan (Amherst, Mass., 1977 [1634]), 110; Christopher Levett, *A Voyage into New England* (London, 1628),

reprinted in *Forerunners and Competitors of the Pilgrims and Puritans*, ed. Charles H. Levermore, 2 vols. (Brooklyn, 1912), 2:629.
50. Williams, *Key into the Language*, 2; Wood, *New England's Prospect*, 95–96; Captain John Underhill, *Newes from America* (London,1638), reprinted in *History of the Pequot War*, ed. Charles Orr (Cleveland, 1897), 7.
51. Charles H. Lincoln, ed., *Narratives of the Indian Wars, 1675–1699*, ONEAH (New York, 1913), 39.
52. Levett, *Voyage into New England*, 2:622–24. For more on the New England pidgin, see Douglas Leechman and Robert A. Hall, "American Indian Pidgin English: Attestations and Grammatical Peculiarities," *American Speech* 30 (1955): 163–71; Ives Goddard, "Some Early Examples of American Indian Pidgin English from New England," *Int. J. of Amer. Linguistics* 43 (1977): 37–41; Goddard "A Further Note on Pidgin English," ibid., 44 (1978): 73.
53. J. Franklin Jameson, ed., *Narratives of New Netherland, 1609–1664*, ONEAH (New York, 1909), 126–27, 128.
54. Ibid., 172–73 (my emphasis). See also Lois M. Feister, "Linguistic Communication between the Dutch and Indians in New Netherland, 1609–1664," *Ethnohistory* 20 (1973): 25–38.
55. Albert Cook Myers, ed., *Narratives of Early Pennsylvania, West New Jersey, and Delaware., 1630–1707*, ONEAH (New York, 1912), 230 (Penn), 342 (Gabriel Thomas, 1698).
56. *Martin Luther's Little Catechism Translated into Algonquian Indian by Johannes Campanius*, notes by Isak Collijn, New Sweden Tercentenary Publications (New York, 1937).
57. Myers, *Narratives of Early Pennsylvania*, 342–43; J. Dyneley Prince, "An Ancient New Jersey Indian Jargon," *American Anthropologist*, n.s. 14 (1912): 508–24; Ives Goddard, "The Delaware Jargon," in *New Sweden in America*, ed. Carol E. Hoffecker et al. (Newark, DE, 1995), ch. 1 (thanks to Dr. Goddard for an advance copy of his essay). See also his "The Ethnohistorical Implications of Early Delaware Linguistic Materials," *Man in the Northeast* 1 (1971): 14–26.
58. James Axtell, "The Rise and Fall of the Powhatan Empire," *After Columbus: Essays in the Ethnohistory of Colonial North America* (New York, 1988), ch. 10.
59. John Smith, *A Map of Virginia* (Oxford, 1612), reprinted in *The Complete Works of Captain John Smith (1980–1631)*, ed. Philip L. Barbour, 3 vols. (Chapel Hill, 1986), 1:136–39; William Strachey, *The Historie of Travell into Virginia Britania (1612)*, ed. Louis B. Wright and Virginia Freund, Hakluyt Society Publications., 2d ser. 53 (London, 1953), 174–207 at 174. For linguistic analyses of these word-lists that fail to recognize their pidginization, see Barbour, "The Earliest Reconnaissance of the Chesapeake Bay Area: Captain John Smith's Map and Indian Vocabulary," pt. 2, *Virginia Magazine of History and Biography* 80 (1972): 21–51; and Frank T. Siebert, Jr., "Resurrecting Virginia Algonquian from the Dead: The Reconstituted and Historical Phonology of Powhatan," in *Studies in Southeastern Indian Languages*, ed. James B. Crawford (Athens, GA, 1975), 285–453.
60. Robert Beverley, *The History and Present State of Virginia*, ed. Louis B. Wright (Chapel Hill, 1947 [1705]), 19; Wilcomb E. Washburn, *The Governor and the Rebel: A History of Bacon's Rebellion in Virginia* (Chapel Hill, 1957), ch. 3; *The Journal of John Fontaine: An Irish Huguenot Son in Spain and Virginia, 1710–1719*, ed. Edward Porter Alexander (Williamsburg, 1972), 12–13.
61. Antoine Simon Le Page du Pratz, *Histoire de la Louisiana*, 3 vols. (Paris, 1758), 2:323; Louis François Benjamin Dumont de Montigny, *Mémoires historiques sur la Louisiane*, 2 vols. (Paris, 1753), 1:181–82.

62. M. Le Page du Pratz, *The History of Louisiana* (London, 1774), 318.
63. McWilliams, *Fleur de Lys and Calumet*, 126–27.
64. "Journal of Antoine Bonnefoy's Captivity among the Cherokee Indians, 1741–1742," in *Travels in the American Colonies*, ed. Newton D. Mereness (New York, 1961), 253–55.
65. James M. Crawford, *The Mobilian Trade Language* (Knoxville, 1978); Mary R. Haas, "What Is Mobilian?" in Crawford, *Studies in Southeastern Indian Languages*, 257–63; Emanuel J. Drechsel, "An Integrated Vocabulary of Mobilian Jargon, a Native American Pidgin of the Mississippi Valley,"*Anthropological Linguistics* 38 (Summer 1996): 248–354; Drechsel, *Mobilian Jargon: Linguistic and Sociohistorical Aspects of a Native American Pidgin*, Oxford Studies in Language Contact (Oxford, 1997).
66. Biggar, *Voyages of Cartier*, 66–67, 102–3, 106, 120–24, 127–28; Quinn and Quinn, *Virginia Voyages from Hakluyt*, 12, 32, 99, 101, 109; Clifford M. Lewis and Albert J. Loomie, *The Spanish Jesuit Mission in Virginia, 1570–72* (Chapel Hill, 1953), 15–18, 36–55, 89, 92, 108–12.
67. James Axtell, *The Invasion Within: The Contest of Cultures in Colonial North America* (New York, 1985), 56.
68. Ibid., ch. 8; Margaret Connell Szasz, *Indian Education in the American Colonies, 1607–1783* (Albuquerque, NM, 1989); Samuel Eliot Morison, *Harvard College in the Seventeenth Century*, 2 vols. (Cambridge, MA, 1936), 1:ch. 17.
69. Axtell, *The Invasion Within*, 204–15; Axtell, "Dr. Wheelock and the Iroquois," in *Extending the Rafters: Interdisciplinary Approaches to Iroquoian Studies*, ed. Michael K. Foster, Jack Campisi, and Marianne Mithun (Albany, 1984), ch. 3.
70. Quinn, *New American World*, 2:104, 137; Lawrence A. Clayton, Vernon James Knight, Jr., and Edward C. Moore, eds., *The De Soto Chronicles: The Expedition of Hernando de Soto to North America in 1539–1543.*, 2 vols. (Tuscaloosa, 1993), 1:59–62, 76, 130. For Spanish interpreters in other parts of the Americas, see Francisco de Solano, "El intérprete: uno de los ejes de la aculturación," *Estudios sobre la politica indigenista española en América. Terceras Jornadas Americanistas de la Universidad de Valladolid* (1975): 265–78; Solano, ed., *Documentos sobre politica lingüística en Hispanoamérica (1492–1800)*, Coleccion tierra nueva e cielo nuevo 32 (Madrid, 1991); Emma Martinell Gifre, *Aspectos lingüísticos de descubrimiento y de la conquista* (Madrid, 1988), 60–99; Carroll L. Riley, "Early Spanish-Indian Communication in the Greater Southwest," *New Mexico Historical Review* 46 (1971): 285–314.
71. *Dictionary of Canadian Biography* [hereafter *DCB*], 2:125–27; 3:101–102; 4:137–38.
72. Nancy L. Hagedorn, "Brokers of Understanding: Interpreters as Agents of Cultural Exchange in Colonial New York," *New York History* 76 (Oct. 1995): 379–408 at 383–85. On the Potomac, Henry Fleet served as interpreter for Virginians and Marylanders after living four years with the Nacotchtanks, who had seized him from a canoe brigade in 1623. J. Frederick Fausz, "Middlemen in Peace and War: Virginia's Earliest Indian Interpreters, 1608–1632," *Virginia Magazine of History and Biography* 95 (Jan. 1987): 41–64 at 60.
73. Richard VanDerBeets, ed., *Held Captive by Indians: Selected Narratives, 1642–1836* (Knoxville, 1973), 91–129; *DCB*, 3:272–73. Stuart Trueman, *The Ordeal of John Gyles* (Toronto, 1966) is semi-fictional. Gyles's written English was never equal to his speech.
74. Hagedorn, "Brokers of Understanding," 393–94. For the Hollis school, see James Axtell, "The Rise and Fall of the Stockbridge Indian Schools," *Massachusetts Review* 27 (Summer 1986): 367–78.

75. James Axtell, "The White Indians of Colonial America," *The European and the Indian: Essays in the Ethnohistory of Colonial North America* (New York, 1981), ch. 7; also Axtell, *The Invasion Within*, ch. 11. See also Alden T. Vaughan and Daniel K. Richter, "Crossing the Cultural Divide: Indians and New Englanders, 1605–1763," *Proceedings of the American Antiquarian Society* 90 (April 1980): 23–99.
76. Axtell, *The Invasion Within*, 55–59, 179–217; Szasz, *Indian Education in the American Colonies*.
77. In the fifteenth century, Portuguese explorers employed a progression of local slaves educated in Portugal to traverse the linguistic Babel of coastal Africa. For his final approach to India, however, Vasco Da Gama shipped out ten Portuguese *degradados* (convicts) to scout unknown shores and to acquire local languages. Jeanne Hein, "Portuguese Communication with Africans on the Searoute to India," *Terrae Incognitae* 25 (1993), 41–51.
78. Jean de Léry, *History of a Voyage to the Land of Brazil*, ed. and trans. Janet Whatley (Berkeley, 1990), xix, 43, 128, 153, 170; John Hemming, *Red Gold: The Conquest of the Brazilian Indians, 1500–1760* (Cambridge, MA, 1978), 8–13.
79. Biggar, *Voyages of Cartier*, 143–44, 252, 257.
80. Ibid., 66–67, 120, 128, 129, 133, 187–88, 212–13, 227, 249. To lure the suspicious Stadaconans into his grasp, Cartier assured the two brothers that his master, King Francis I, "had forbidden him to carry off to France any man or woman but only two or three boys to learn the language," a plausible lie (idem, 224).
81. Marcel Trudel, *Histoire de la Nouvelle-France*, II, *Le Comptoir, 1604–1627* (Montreal, 1966), 390–91; Trudel, "Discours du President: Les premiers balbutiements du bilinguisme, 1524–1634," Canadian Historical Association, *Report 1964*: 1–8; Benjamin Sulte, "Les interprètes du temps de Champlain," *Transactions of the Royal Society of Canada* (1882): 47–56; Philippe Jacquin, *Les Indiens blancs: Francais et Indiens en Amérique du Nord (XVIe–XVIIIe siècle)* (Paris, 1987), 37–67 at 45; *DCB*, 1:130–31, 341, 493–95, 516–18; H.P. Biggar, ed. and trans., *The Works of Samuel de Champlain*, 6 vols. (Toronto, 1922–1936), 2:138–42, 188, 201, 205–206, 307; 5:100–101, 108, 132; F. Gabriel Sagard Théodat, *Histoire du Canada*, 4 vols. (Paris, 1865 [1636]), 2:334 (quotation), 335–36.
82. Patricia Galloway, "Talking with Indians: Interpreters and Diplomacy in French Louisiana," in *Race and Family in the Colonial South*, ed. Winthrop D. Jordan and Sheila L. Skemp (Jackson, MS, 1987), 109–29, 161–64; Dunbar Rowland, Albert Godfrey Sanders, and Patricia Kay Galloway, ed. and trans., *Mississippi Provincial Archives: French Dominion*, 5 vols. (Jackson and Baton Rouge, 1927–1984), 3:128–29, 585–86 (quotation); 4:100; McWilliams, *Fleur de Lys and Calumet*, 25, 30, 67–68, 73, 78, 79: McWilliams, *Iberville's Gulf Journals*, 137, 176–77.
83. Fausz, "Middlemen in Peace and War," 41–64; Martha Bennett Stiles, "Hostage to the Indians," *Virginia Cavalcade* 12 (Summer 1962): 5–11.
84. Henry Spelman, "Relation of Virginea," in Capt. John Smith, *Works, 1608–1631*, ed. Edward Arber (Birmingham, Eng., 1884), ci–civ; Barbour, *Complete Works of Captain John Smith*, 2:193, 294, 315; Susan Myra Kingsbury, ed., *The Records of the Virginia Company of London*, 4 vols. (Washington, DC, 1906–35), 3:129.
85. See, for example, Paul A.W. Wallace, *Conrad Weiser (1696–1760): Friend of Colonist and Mohawk* (Philadelphia, 1945), 17–18, 24–25, 326, 330–31, 332, 337–39; William H. Beauchamp, *The Life of Conrad Weiser as It Relates to His Services as Official Interpreter between New York and Pennsylvania* (Syracuse, 1925);

Milton W. Hamilton, *Sir William Johnson: Colonial American, 1715–1763* (Port Washington, NY 1976), 82–84; Salley, *Narratives of Early Carolina*, 104–105; *John Long's Voyages and Travels in the Years 1768–1788*, ed. Milo Milton Quaife, Lakeside Classics (Chicago, 1922), 8, 45–46; Fausz, "Middlemen in Peace and War," 62.

86. See, for example, Hagedorn, "Brokers of Understanding," 386–88; Nicholas B. Wainwright, *George Croghan, Wilderness Diplomat* (Chapel Hill, 1959); Wallace, *Conrad Weiser*; Hamilton, *Sir William Johnson*; Dunbar, Sanders, and Galloway, *Mississippi Provincial Archives*, 4:100; Wilbur R. Jacobs, ed., *The Appalachian Indian Frontier: The Edmund Atkin Report and Plan of 1755* (Lincoln, NE, 1967 [1954]), 12, 29, 81; Feister, "Linguistic Communication between the Dutch and Indians," 35–36; Peter Wraxall, *An Abridgement of Indian Affairs ... in the Colony of New York [1678–1751]*, ed. Charles Howard McIlwain, Harvard Historical Studies, no. 21 (Cambridge, MA, 1915), 155; William L. McDowell, Jr., ed., *Documents Relating to Indian Affairs, 1750–1765*, 2 vols., Colonial Records of South Carolina, series 2 (Columbia, 1958–70), 1:23, 75, 148; 2:55, 192–93, 196–97, 334–35, 437, 485 (hereafter cited as *South Carolina Indian Records)*; Eirlys M. Barker, "Much Blood and Treasure: South Carolina's Indian Traders, 1670– 1775" (Ph.D.Thesis, College of William and Mary, Dept. of History, 1993); Francis Jennings, "Jacob Young: Indian Trader and Interpreter," in *Struggle and Survival in Colonial America*, ed. Sweet and Nash, 347–61.

87. Hagedorn, "Brokers of Understanding," 381, 382, 388; James Sullivan et al., eds., *The Papers of Sir William Johnson*, 14 vols. (Albany, 1921–65), 13:631; Howard Lewin, "A Frontier Diplomat: Andrew Montour," *Pennsylvania History* 33 (April 1966): 153–86; Nancy L. Hagedorn, "'Faithful, Knowing, and Prudent': Andrew Montour as Interpreter and Cultural Broker, 1740–1772," in *Between Indian and White Worlds: The Cultural Broker*, ed. Margaret Connell Szasz (Norman, 1994), 44–60, 308–12; James H. Merrell, "'The Cast of His Countenance': Reading Andrew Montour," in *Through a Glass Darkly: Reflections on Personal Identity in Early America*, ed. Ronald Hoffman, Mechal Sobel, and Fredricka J. Teute (Chapel Hill, 1997), 13–39; *DCB*, 3;147–48 (Elizabeth Couc); Raphael Semmes, *Captains and Mariners of Early Maryland* (Baltimore, 1937), 539–60, 724–26, 803–804 at 550, 552; Milo Milton Quaife, ed., *The Siege of Detroit in 1763*, Lakeside Classics (Chicago, 1958), 18–19n., 50n., 88n.

88. *The Letters and Papers of Cadwallader Colden*, 9 vols., Collections of the New York Historical Society, vols. 50–56, 67–68 (New York, 1917–35), 9:106 (1751).

89. Collections of the Massachusetts Historical Society, 4th ser. 6 (1863): 224 (1638), 263 (1640), 335 (1647); *[John] Winthrop's Journal "History of New England," 1630–1649*, ed. James Kendall Hosmer, 2 vols., ONEAH (New York, 1908), 1:193 (21 Oct. 1636). Williams published his *Key into the Language of America*, a sophisticated guide to Narragansett language and culture, in 1643. See the critical edition by John J. Teunissen and Evelyn J. Hinz (Detroit, 1973).

90. Paul A.W. Wallace, ed., *Thirty Thousand Miles with John Heckewelder* (Pittsburgh, 1958), 86; William M. Beauchamp, ed., *Moravian Journals Relating to Central New York, 1745–66* (Syracuse, 1916), 175. In 1754 Conrad Weiser was asked to play the same role at a meeting with the Iroquois in Albany. He declined to be the principal interpreter for Pennsylvania, allegedly because he was out of practice, but he allowed that his understanding of the spoken language was unimpaired and he would "Use his Endeavour that whatever is said by the Indians be truly interpreted to the Gentlemen" (*Minutes of the*

Provincial Council of Pennsylvania, ed. Samuel Hazard, 16 vols. [Philadelphia and Harrisburg, 1838–53], 6:49 [2 June 1754]).
91. Minutes of conference with Indian messengers, Philadelphia, 8 Feb. 1759, Historical Society of Pennsylvania, Penn MSS., Official Correspondence, vol. 3 (reproduced in *Iroquois Indians: A Documentary History of the Diplomacy of the Six Nations and Their League*, ed. Francis Jennings et al., microfilm [Woodbridge, CT, 1984], reel 23, 1759, 8–9 Feb.). Thanks to Nancy Hagedorn for this and other references. See her "'A Friend to Go between Them': Interpreters Among the Iroquois, 1664–1775" (Ph.D. Thesis, College of William and Mary, Dept. of History, 1995); "'A Friend to Go between Them': The Intepreter as Cultural Broker during Anglo-Iroquois Councils, 1740–70," *Ethnohistory*, 35 (Winter 1988): 60–80; and "'A Great Deal Depends upon the Interpreters: Anglo-Iroquois Relations and Imperial Diplomacy in the Colonial Northeast, 1664–1774," International Seminar on the History of the Atlantic World, 1500–1800, Harvard University, *Working Paper* no. 97–23 (Cambridge, MA, 1997), 1–43.
92. W. Noel Sainsbury et al., eds., *Calendar of State Papers, Colonial Series, America and the West Indies* (London, 1860—), 28:233–35 (no. 521, 15 July 1715).
93. Hagedorn, "'A Great Deal Depends upon the Interpreters,'" 20–21.
94. E.B. O'Callaghan and Berthold Fernow, eds., *Documents Relative to the Colonial History of the State of New-York*, 15 vols. (Albany, 1856–87), 9:966–67 (4 Aug. 1727) (hereafter cited as *NYCD*).
95. Sullivan, *Papers of William Johnson*, 3:915 (24 Oct. 1762); E.B. O'Callaghan, ed., *Documentary History of the State of New York*, 4 vols. (Albany, 1846–51), 2:946 (21 Aug. 1769); *Virginia Magazine of History and Biography*, 14 (1906):294 (1677); Sagard, *Histoire du Canada*, 2:444.
96. The traders who resided among the several Creek and Cherokee towns and served as sworn interpreters for South Carolina were the major exceptions.
97. Minutes of the [New York] Indian Commissioners, 6 Jan. 1739, quoted in Hagedorn, "'A Great Deal Depends upon the Interpreters,'" 21. See also Semmes, *Captains and Mariners of Early Maryland*, 544; Wraxall, *An Abridgement of Indian Affairs*, 212; Jacobs, *The Appalachian Indian Frontier*, 12, 81; McDowell, *South Carolina Indian Records*, 1:290, 298; 2:336–37.
98. Eleazar Wheelock to George Whitefield, 4 July 1761, Papers of Eleazar Wheelock, Dartmouth College Library, Hanover, NH (microfilm), no. 761404. Two prominent exceptions who assisted roving missionaries in western Pennsylvania and the Ohio country were Joseph Peepy and Moses Tatamy, both Delaware converts. See the favorable accounts in *Diary of David McClure ... 1748–1820*, ed. Franklin B. Dexter (New York, 1899), 46–47, 72, 81,86; and *David Brainerd: His Life and Diary*, ed. Jonathan Edwards (Chicago, 1949 [1817]), 208–12, 247–48, 324–25.
99. *NYCD*, 7:970 (22 Sept. 1767).

– *Chapter 2* –

The Use of Pidgins and Jargons on the East Coast of North America

Ives Goddard

In any attempt to understand the encounter between the natives of America and the European immigrants, the languages they used merit attention. The specific characteristics of the means of communication can be expected to have had an effect on the content and quality of the communication and to reflect aspects of the encounter, yet scholars have typically shown little interest in exploring this topic.[1] It seems to be generally assumed that some individuals would have learned the language of the other group and served as interpreters. The matter deserves to be reopened, however, in the light of recent research in the field of linguistics that has brought into focus the widespread existence of certain types of conventionalized, simplified languages, known as trade jargons and pidgins. It has become increasingly clear that the use of pidgins and jargons between speakers of different languages has been and is extremely common around the world.[2] In North America the best documented and most familiar pidgin is Chinook Jargon, spoken in the Pacific Northwest, where it is only now passing out of memory. Less well known is the fact that a number of local pidgins and jargons were spoken on the East Coast, in the Northeast and the Mid-Atlantic region. It is these that are the topic of this paper.

Pidgins and Jargons

Pidgins and jargons are types of contact languages. A trade jargon (or traders' jargon) is the simplest type, and developmentally the earliest stage. It may consist of only the absolute minimum of vocabulary necessary to carry on the basic activities of interest to the two or more parties that use it, especially trade. A pidgin is the next, more complex stage, with a small but filled-out vocabulary and enough established grammatical patterns to permit speakers to communicate about essentially any topic. Typically a pidgin develops out of what was earlier a jargon and draws its vocabulary overwhelmingly from a single language, but there are other possibilities. The next stage after a pidgin is a creole language, which is a pidgin that has become the native language of at least some members of the speech community. The creole stage is not known to have been reached by any pidgin based on a Native North American language.

For a long time pidgins and creoles were neglected in linguistics, except perhaps for purely descriptive accounts. Since they were considered not to be the product of normal linguistic transmission and therefore not to be subject to, or illustrative of, the general principles of historical linguistic change, they had generally an uncertain status in linguistic theory. Arguments that the unusual nature of pidgins and creoles provided important evidence for general linguistic theory found little favor. In recent years, though, the study of pidgins and creoles has burgeoned. The phenomenon they represent is extremely common, not confined to encounters with colonialist Europeans as was sometimes thought. The typology of the various kinds of language-contact phenomena is highly developed, and criteria for recognizing the different types of contact languages are widely agreed on. These developments within the field of linguistics deserve to be more widely known, and in particular we have reached the point where their significance for the understanding of broader historical questions needs to be examined.[3]

Given our current understanding of the general phenomenon of contact languages, we can now make sense of some of the linguistic data from the East Coast of North America in the early contact period in the seventeenth century. The most important means of communication between Native Americans and Europeans in that period was pidgin languages of varying degrees of development. The attestation of these languages is uneven; but the generality of the phenomenon seems clear, and the consistency of the data that do exist permits extrapolation from the better known cases to the less well known ones.

The northernmost of the pidgins spoken on the East Coast was a Basque-Algonquian pidgin attested among the Micmacs of Nova Scotia and the Montagnais of Quebec in the early seventeenth century. (Micmac and Montagnais are two members of the Algonquian family of languages, spoken in northeastern North America.) The documentation of this pidgin has been discussed by Peter Bakker.[4] It was apparently of a type attested for trade jargons and their pidgin outgrowths elsewhere, which combined words from two or more languages. An example is: ⟨endia chave normandia⟩ 'the French know many things'.[5] Here ⟨endia⟩ is Basque *andia* 'big'; ⟨normandia⟩ is the Basque word for 'Normandy', used to mean 'Frenchman'; ⟨chave⟩ is the Romance word for 'know' that is nearly universal in European-derived pidgins and creoles, perhaps in this case specifically from Portuguese. Another example is: ⟨ania kir capitana⟩ 'brother, are you a captain (war leader)?' Here ⟨ania⟩ is Basque *anaia* 'brother' and ⟨capitana⟩ is the word for captain in a Basque guise (cf. Basque *capitaina* 'captain'), but ⟨kir⟩ is the early seventeenth-century Montagnais or Micmac word for 'you'.[6]

Further south there were pidgin Algonquian languages; these drew almost all their words from the local Indian languages and consequently existed in several regional varieties. There was also Pidgin English.

Pidgin Delaware

The best attested of the East Coast pidgins is Pidgin Delaware.[7] The Delaware comprised several peoples, distinct but similar in culture and language, who lived in the lower Hudson and Delaware river valleys and the area between.[8] They spoke dialects of two Eastern Algonquian languages, Munsee and Unami.[9] Munsee was the language of the central and lower Hudson River Valley, westernmost Long Island, the upper Delaware River Valley, and the northern third of New Jersey; Unami was spoken to the south of Munsee in the Delaware River Valley and the southern two-thirds of New Jersey. Pidgin Delaware was a pidginized form of Unami that first came into use on the middle Delaware River, where the first permanent Dutch settlements were attempted in 1624, on Burlington Island (at Burlington, New Jersey, some distance below Trenton), and at Ft. Nassau (on the site of Gloucester). It arose between Dutch settlers and traders and the Indians of the area, who were speakers of the Unami language. Within a few years the settlers were removed to Manhattan, bringing their knowledge of the pidgin with them. We know this because the first attestation of the pidgin, published by Johannes de Laet in 1633, is a short vocabulary specifically ascribed to the Sankhikans, a local band living at the falls of the Delaware at Trenton.[10] Also, although the local Indian language of Manhattan and the surrounding area was Munsee, it was the Unami-based pidgin that was used by Dutch and Indians in the lower Hudson Valley. This explains the otherwise puzzling fact that distinctively Unami rather than Munsee words are recorded by the Dutch as having been used by Indians on Staten Island, Manhattan, and western Long Island and on the Hudson River as far north as Esopus Creek near Kingston. The Munsee speakers communicated with the Dutch in Pidgin Unami. This is a very significant fact for our understanding of the use of these pidgins. It is part of the evidence that we are not dealing simply with the imperfect learning and recording of Indian languages by Europeans but with a distinct, conventionalized contact language, a language that all speakers had to learn.

Besides the Dutch in New Netherland, the European users of Pidgin Delaware included the Swedes in New Sweden (now the state of Delaware) and the English in Pennsylvania, New Jersey, and New York. The most extensive source for Pidgin Delaware is the Swedish minister Johannes Campanius's vocabulary and translation of Martin Luther's "Small Catechism," which stemmed from Campanius's service in New Sweden in the years 1642–1648 and was published in 1696 (see Fig. 2.1).[11] The second major source is an anonymous vocabulary titled "The Indian Interpreter" compiled in West New Jersey in the late seventeenth century and surviving in a book of land records from Salem County, New Jersey.[12] Other sources for Pidgin Delaware include a few lines of dialogue and some numbers published by the New Jersey settler Gabriel Thomas, a few words and phrases noted by the Swedish engineer Peter Lindeström and by William Penn, and scattered words in various other early records and reports.[13]

There is evidence that Europeans sometimes learned the pidgin from each other. The English manuscript of "The Indian Interpreter" shows clear traces of a written Swedish source for some words, although it was compiled more than a decade before Campanius's book was published.[14] In fact, there are known cases in which the Swedes used Dutch interpreters and the English of Pennsylvania used Swedish interpreters.[15] But what these interpreters

CATECHESIS,

Hátte Pæmyy ſuhwijvan chínti-
cha mamaræckhíckan.

**Catechiſmus LUTHERI, ſom
innehåller Summan och
kiärnan af then Hel. Skrift.**

Enáckát chirǫ̃na Nisſiaa-
nus, Pináættæt ock Àquæt-
tæt, ock pyri Renáppi,
chéko mátta nitáto chin-
tika mamaræckhíckan,
Thæǽræn chíſbo Simoác-
kan, mâchǽærick, mâchijrick Sacchee-
mans, nirǫ̃na hœtítt MANÉTTOS.

**Sålunda ſkole edre barn/ Söner
och Döttrar / vnga dränger och pij-
gor / ſamt flere andre Menniſkior /
ſnartigen befſita ſig om at lära the
Tijo Buden / then mächta ſtora
HERrans wår Gudz.**

A   Hu-

Verſio.

FIGURE 2.1 A page in Swedish and Pidgin Delaware from Martin Luther, *Lutheri Catechismus, Öfwersatt på American-Virginiske Språket* (Stockholm, 1696). The text of Luther's small catechism, first published in 1529, was translated into Pidgin Delaware by Johannes Campanius. (Courtesy of the John Carter Brown Library at Brown University)

could speak was not the real, full-blown Indian languages but the pidgin. This explains why some Europeans, for instance William Penn,[16] ascribed the sparseness and simplicities of the pidgin to the language of the Indians, apparently oblivious of the existence of real Delaware, which is unmistakably grammatically complex and lexically rich. It is noteworthy, though, that as early as 1628, in the first published reference to Pidgin Delaware, Jonas Michaëlius clearly and somewhat acerbically described the language used between the New Netherland Dutch and the Indians as a "made-up, childish language" greatly simplified, by the conscious design of the Indians, from what the Indians spoke among themselves.[17] Michaëlius's observation that Pidgin Delaware was "made up" by the Indians is another significant fact for us; but to see why, we must look at some of the features of the pidgin. The technical details of Algonquian grammar turn out to be directly germane to understanding what is significant about the pidgin for the larger picture.

The grammatical complexities of Delaware, which include inflecting verbs for subject and object as well as for mode, negation, and other features, are not used in the pidgin. Pidgin sentences are strings of grammatically invariant words that leave many things unexpressed. The differing forms of words that do exist in the pidgin seem never to be meaningfully distinct. They are mostly the frozen relics of Delaware inflectional forms that are used in the pidgin without regard to their distinct grammatical meanings in real Delaware. Concomitantly, there is a massive reduction in the number of grammatical categories that are actively distinguished in Pidgin Delaware. In order to understand the extent and significance of this reduction we must naturally start by surveying the grammar of real Delaware, particularly the grammatical categories.[18]

Delaware ordinarily indicates pronouns as part of the inflection of verbs or the possessive inflection of nouns. The verbal inflections differ in the various modes. The usual three persons, first, second, and third, singular and plural, are distinguished. As in many languages, there are two first-person plural categories, one meaning 'we (including you)' and one meaning 'we (not including you)'. There is also a set of independent emphatic pronouns, used for emphasis and contrast and to indicate what linguists call focus and topic (e.g., *ní·* 'I, me, mine', *kí·* 'you (sing.), your', *né·k·a* 'he, she, him, her, his, hers').[19] A second set of independent pronouns is used for certain kinds of verbal objects that cannot be indicated by inflection, such as reflexive objects, and in nominal (or equational) sentences (e.g., *nhák·ay* 'me', *khák·ay* 'you (sing.)', *hɔ́kaya* 'him, her').

Delaware also has two sets of demonstrative pronouns ('this' and 'that'). These have different forms to mark the various nominal categories of the language, the categories distinguished in the inflection of nouns. Singular and plural are differentiated, as is the special obviative category of Algonquian that marks secondary third persons, and there are also sets of absentative forms (indicating 'absent, former, or deceased'), as well as emphatic forms. Also marked by the demonstratives, and of central significance for the grammar of any Algonquian language, is a distinction between two grammatical genders, called animate and inanimate.

The terms *animate* and *inanimate* for the Algonquian genders were first used in English by John Eliot over three centuries ago and were earlier used in French.[20] Every noun is classified as of one gender or the other, and the gender of a noun is not always predictable. All living things are animate, but also animate are miscellaneous other things, including skins, tobacco pipes, bows, nails, potatoes, raspberries, and snow. Demonstrative pronouns used with a noun or substituting for it always match the gender of the noun. Thus *wá* (emphatic form *wán* or *wáni*) is 'this' referring to a man, a peach, a kettle, or a wagon, but *yú* (emphatic form *yó·n* or *yó·ni*) is 'this' referring to a stone, a pumpkin, or a boat. Furthermore, verbs show agreement with the gender of their subjects and objects. To say 'it is red' in Delaware (which is a verb), the animate form *máxksu* has to be used if it is a pipe, a skin, or a raspberry, just as if it were, for example, a bird, but the inanimate *máxke·* must be used if it is a stone, a piece of cloth, or a strawberry. To say 'I saw it' one says *nné·mən* if it is a knife, a pumpkin, or water, but one has to use the animate form *nné·yɔ* if it is ball, an apple, or snow, just as if it were an animal or a person.

Corresponding to all these grammatical categories of Delaware, and all the pronominal inflections and the various sets of independent emphatic and demonstrative pronouns, Pidgin Delaware generally has just three pronouns: first person [ní·r] (spelled ⟨nijr⟩ by Campanius) and [ní·] (⟨nee⟩ in English sources), second person [kí·r], [kí·] (⟨kijr⟩, ⟨kee⟩), and third person [yó·ni], [yó·n] (⟨jȭni⟩, ⟨une⟩), which is used as both a personal pronoun and a demonstrative. The first- and second-person pronouns are from the corresponding emphatic singular pronouns of Delaware,[21] and the third-person pronoun is from the emphatic inanimate singular demonstrative for 'this'. Singular and plural are not distinguished; the first-person pronoun is used both for 'I' and 'me' and for 'we' and 'us'. And gender is not distinguished. The pronoun *yó·n*, which in Delaware means only 'this (emphatic inanimate singular)', is used in the pidgin for singular or plural, animate or inanimate, near and far; its English equivalents would be 'he', 'she', 'it', 'they', 'this', 'that', 'these', and 'those'.

Gender is also not distinguished in the pidgin in the interrogative-indefinite pronoun. Delaware differentiates between *awé·n* 'who?; someone' and *kéku* 'what?; something', but the pidgin has only the Delaware inanimate form *kéku*, used for 'someone' as well as 'something' (⟨kéko⟩, ⟨chéko⟩, ⟨cacko⟩); it was probably also used for 'who?', but this use is not attested.

The gender differentiation of Delaware verbs also completely disappears in the pidgin. Here things get particularly interesting. Just as it is the Delaware inanimate demonstrative and inanimate interrogative-indefinite that are used in the pidgin, it tends to be the inanimate verb that the pidgin uses for both genders. Delaware has animate *wələ́s·u* 'he, she, or it (animate) is good or pretty' and inanimate *wələ́t*, but Pidgin Delaware has only [wərə́t], [wələ́t] (⟨orit⟩, ⟨olet⟩), from the Delaware inanimate form.[22] Thus the expression for 'good friend' in the pidgin was ⟨orit nietap⟩, with the inanimate word for 'good' and ⟨nietap⟩, the pidgin word for 'friend' (discussed below). In the case of verbs that take an object, transitive verbs, it is the form used with an inanimate object in Delaware that is used with any object in the pidgin. In Delaware, to tell a person to hit someone or something animate one says *pahkám*; to tell someone to hit something inanimate one says *pahkánta*. In the pidgin only the Delaware inanimate form is used, and *pahkánta kéku*, which can only mean 'hit something' in Delaware, is attested for the pidgin as the way to say 'hit someone' (Campanius ⟨bakanta chéko⟩). Even in the case of verbs that most commonly take living creatures as objects, it is only the Delaware form used with inanimate objects that appears in Pidgin Delaware. For example, in the pidgin, 'hunt' is [məš·ó·t·amən mó·s] (Campanius ⟨mosiuttamen MWS⟩), literally 'bring down animals'. In Delaware *nəməš·ó·t·amən* means 'I shoot at it (something inanimate) and hit it', and *mó·s*, which refers to any large animal in the pidgin, means specifically 'elk, wapiti (*Cervus canadensis*)'.

The pattern is consistent. Pidgin Delaware uses the inanimate forms of Delaware rather than the animate forms. It uses the Delaware word for 'this (inanimate)' for 'he', 'she', or 'it', 'this' or 'that', referring to what would be animates in Delaware as well as to what would be inanimates. It uses the Delaware word for 'something' also to mean 'someone'. Where Delaware verbs have distinct forms for the two genders, Pidgin Delaware has the forms that are used in Delaware only with inanimates. In the case of verbs that have only primary animate forms in Delaware, the pidgin necessarily has an originally animate form. These are intransitives that are ordinarily used only about living things, like 'sleep' and 'fear', and transitives that take only animate objects, notably 'give to', and perhaps a few others, like 'understand', that are also typically used of actions between the speaker and the addressee. The only true exception to this general pattern appears to be the pidgin word [me·(x)kí·rək] 'big' (⟨mâchijrick⟩, ⟨móchijrick⟩, ⟨mockerick⟩); this comes from the Delaware animate form *me·xkí·lək* 'that (animate) which is big' but is used in the pidgin with both animates and inanimates. For example, it was combined with the inanimate noun for 'river' to make the pidgin name for the Delaware, ⟨Makerick Kitton⟩, literally 'big river'.[23] This word is already present in the very first sample of the pidgin, the De Laet vocabulary of 1633, where it modifies an animal name: the word for 'mountain lion' is given as ⟨Synquoy Mackyrggh⟩, which would be in Delaware 'big wildcat'.[24] Presumably the animate form of 'big' simply became established very early in such contexts.

How can we explain this consistent generalization of inanimate forms in Pidgin Delaware? For European traders and settlers, the gender system of Delaware would have been difficult to acquire, since they would have had to refer to many common objects (such as skins, kettles, and pipes) with animate forms of demonstrative pronouns and verbs, which included the most common forms expressing adjectival meanings. In any attempt to use real Delaware for everyday purposes like trading, Europeans would constantly have been using inanimate forms for grammatically animate objects. Why, then, do we not see in Pidgin Delaware a jumble of forms of both genders used randomly? Clearly the systematic selection of the inanimate singular as the sole third-person category could not have been achieved by Europeans who were trying to speak Delaware. This selection could only have been accomplished by native speakers of Delaware, whose native-speaker competence enabled them to select the inanimate forms systematically and across the board. This selection would have been a straightforward generalization of the erroneous use of inanimate forms for grammatical animates by Europeans, which would inevitably have been a prominent feature of their Delaware, as they attempted to speak it. There is no other reasonable explanation for the use in the pidgin of the inanimate form of verbs like that for 'shoot', which are most commonly used, and most useful, with animate objects. It does not seem possible that Europeans would have consistently learned the inanimate forms in such cases and adopted them in the pidgin.

It is also a striking feature of the pidgin that it attests the collapsing of some distinctions that were common to all the native languages of those who used Pidgin Delaware, both Germanic and Algonquian, such as the distinction between singular and plural personal pronouns and the distinction between animate and inanimate interrogative-indefinite pronouns. This is also most likely to reflect the systematic reduction of grammatical categories by speakers who controlled those categories natively. The conclusion that at least some aspects of Pidgin Delaware resulted from the conscious simplification of Delaware by native speakers in talking to Europeans corresponds exactly to the description of the pidgin by Michaëlius:

> They rather design to conceal their language from us than to properly communicate it, except in things which happen in daily trade; saying that it is sufficient for us to understand them in that; and then they speak only in half sentences, shortened words,... and all things which have only a rude resemblance to each other, they frequently call by the same name. In truth it is a made-up, childish language.[25]

The great reduction in the number of words in the pidgin was made up for by the use of descriptive compounds.[26] The Delaware word 'to have eaten one's fill' is used in the pidgin to mean 'full' or 'complete' in general, and Campanius's word for 'commandment' is 'full statement'. A mountain lion is 'big wildcat' or 'angry big wildcat'. A plum tree was 'dice or game wood', because Indian dice were plum pits. God might be referred to as 'sits above' or 'good spirit'. Many expressions were formed with the basic pidgin verbs for 'have' and 'make'. (The pidgin word for 'have' is actually from a Delaware word meaning 'be there' or 'exist'.) The Delaware word for 'be afraid' is borrowed as the pidgin word for 'fear'; to say 'be afraid', the pidgin said 'have fear'. 'To abuse' was 'make bad', the word for 'bad' being from the Delaware word for 'angry'. The Delaware word for 'dance' was used in pidgin for 'pray', and effectively 'holy', and appears in many compounds in Campanius's materials; for example, the pidgin expression for 'priest' is 'pray chief', in Delaware terms 'dance' plus 'chief'. A clipped form of the Delaware word element for 'fathom', the unit of measure for strings of wampum, is found in the pidgin also with the meaning 'honor', referring to rank. To say 'deacon' in the pidgin, Campanius says 'half fathom pray chief'. Some Delaware low words appear in the pidgin as ordinary vocabulary.[27] It seems unlikely that Campanius appreciated that the expression he uses freely to mean 'generous' literally meant in Delaware 'not dirty-butt'. The existence of such words must reflect the milieu within which the pidgin arose.

Almost all words in Pidgin Delaware come from the Unami Delaware language. There is some variation resulting from differences in local dialects and changes that took place in Delaware in the course of the seventeenth century, such as the gradual shift from [r] to [l].[28] As is typical in pidgins, some words take on different functions; the verb [tá·n] 'go' (⟨taan⟩), from the Delaware word for 'go, go to' (e.g., *ntá·n* 'I go to (it)'), is also used as a sort of all-purpose preposition meaning 'to, of, from, until'.[29] Delaware itself has no true prepositions and ordinarily expresses the equivalent by verbal derivation and inflection.

A few words in the pidgin are from other languages.[30] For example, the word for 'money' was [sé·wan] ("Indian Interpreter" ⟨sewan⟩), taken from an otherwise unattested Munsee word apparently referring to loose wampum, which was also borrowed into New Netherland Dutch. The word for 'horse' was [kápay] (⟨copy⟩, ⟨kabay⟩), which must come ultimately from Spanish *caballo*. It was presumably introduced into the pidgin by Dutch or English speakers who felt their own words were insufficiently exotic.

It is important to stress that, although there is variation in the attestations of Pidgin Delaware, the linguistic evidence cannot be explained as simply independent instances of the imperfect learning and use of Delaware on the part of individuals. The agreements among the sources and the characteristics of what the sources document are sufficient to show that a Unami-based pidgin language was in general use in the Middle Atlantic region during, at the least, the early Colonial period.

Other East Coast Algonquian-Based Pidgins

Our rather full information on Pidgin Delaware provides a basis for identifying other East Coast Algonquian-based pidgins that are much less fully documented. There was a pidgin Massachusett in use from the very beginning in the Plymouth Colony and other English settlements in southeastern New England.[31] Edward Winslow recorded examples of this pidgin in his "Good News from New England," published in 1624. He describes a situation in which the English were able to understand certain of the local Indians, whom he refers to as "those that daily converse with us," but that when these same Indians wanted to, they could speak incomprehensibly. This sounds like the same situation that Michaëlius described for the use of Pidgin Delaware in New Netherland. The samples of the Indian language Winslow gives confirm that it is really a pidgin form of Massachusett. For example, he uses the phrase ⟨squa-sachim⟩, explaining that this is what the Indians call the sachim's wife. But in real Massachusett the word for 'sachim's wife' was ⟨sonkusq⟩, and ⟨squa-sachim⟩ can only be a pidgin expression, a compound of ⟨squa⟩ 'woman' (actually 'younger woman' in Massachusett proper) and ⟨sachim⟩ 'chief'. A Pidgin Massachusett sentence used by the Wampanoag chief Massasoit that Winslow gives is: ⟨Matta neen wonckanet namen Winsnow⟩, which he translates: "O Winslow, I shall never see thee again" (word-for-word, 'not I again see Winslow').[32] Significantly, this example attests that it was the inanimate form of the Massachusett verb 'to see' that was used in Pidgin Massachusett, just as in Pidgin Delaware.[33]

Similarly, we know that the English in Virginia used a pidginized form of the local Indian language, called Virginia Algonquian or Powhatan. The sentences in the Indian language that Captain John Smith gives in his *Map of Virginia* of 1612 consist of uninflected words strung together with pidgin syntax; for example: ⟨Kator neheigh mattagh neer uttapitchewayne⟩ "Truely he is here I doe not lie" (word-for-word, 'truly be-at not I lie').[34] Smith's sentences contain no transitive verbs, but in William Strachey's vocabulary of Virginia Algonquian the word given for 'shoot' (⟨nepomotamen⟩) is, as in Pidgin Delaware, the form used only with inanimate objects in real Algonquian languages.[35] Scraps of data suggest that there was a pidgin Mahican spoken on the upper Hudson River. There are also apparent references to a pidgin used by the Dutch that was based on Mohawk, a language of the Iroquoian family spoken west of Albany, New York.

It is likely, then, that there were local forms of Algonquian-based pidgins all along the coast, though perhaps in some areas they had developed only to the extent of rudimentary trade jargons. Europeans began to learn Algonquian words even before the first permanent settlements, in some cases. English visitors to the coast of Maine in the first years of the seventeenth century learned the word *sagamore* 'chief' from speakers of Eastern Abenaki, and it was brought as an English word to Massachusetts, where the local word is cognate but distinct. English *sagamore* is from Eastern Abenaki *sàkəma* 'chief' rather than from its Massachusett cognate [sã tʸəm] (spelled ⟨sontim⟩), which is in fact the source of English *sachem*. *Sagamore* was used in English as early as 1605 (as ⟨Sagamo⟩), and the different local words for 'chief' on the northern and southern coasts of New England were remarked by an English explorer in a document that has been dated to 1614.[36] Similarly, English *wigwam* is from Eastern Abenaki *wikəwam*, not the corresponding Massachusett word [wi·tʸəw] (⟨wetu⟩).

The word ⟨netop⟩ was used for 'friend' in southeastern New England, and every Rhode Island schoolchild learns the tradition that when Roger Williams came down the Seekonk River in 1636 to found the city of Providence, he and his party were greeted with the friendly hail: "What cheer, netop."[37] The word ⟨netop⟩ comes from ⟨netomp⟩, which means 'my friend' in Massachusett and Narragansett, and it would have been one of the Indian words that virtually everyone knew. As already noted, it is also used for 'friend' in Pidgin Delaware, though this word is not attested in either of the real Delaware languages and, moreover, seems to appear consistently in Dutch and English sources in a shape that differs from what would be expected for the regular Delaware cognate of the New England word. Since ⟨nietap⟩ is attested in Dutch sources as early as 1640, it may be that Dutch traders learned it along the Rhode Island coast and spread its use.[38] Strachey attests it for the Virginia pidgin as well, where it may be from a genuine cognate that was recorded by Smith.[39] In the later English sources for Pidgin Delaware, the southern New England words *squaw* for 'woman' and *papoose* for 'baby' appear, presumably introduced by English speakers from the pidgin of southeastern New England.[40]

Pidgin English and the Learning of Algonquian by Europeans

A remarkable fact about Pidgin Algonquian, at least in some areas, is that it existed side-by-side with Pidgin English.[41] An example of this as used by Indians in Massachusetts was given by William Wood in 1634: ⟨English man all one speake, all one heart⟩, meaning something like: 'What an Englishman says is the same as what he thinks.' Another example he gives is: ⟨What much hoggery, so bigge walke, and so bigge speake, and by and by kill.⟩ The reference is to a ship discharging its gun; perhaps the meaning is: 'How angry it is! It goes fast and makes a loud noise, and it is going to kill people.' The dual use of the two pidgins is attested in account of a court case in Killingworth, Connecticut, in 1704, in which one of the justices, in trying to explain to an Indian defendant what a hog's-head was, patted his head, saying: "tatapa you, tatapa you; all one this." ⟨Tatapa you⟩ is Massachusett (or a closely related language), presumably actually pidgin, for 'like this', and ⟨all one this⟩ is Pidgin English for the same thing. The two pidgins in use in a single trading encounter are also attested in an account from Connecticut in 1651.[42]

We should also mention that some Europeans did learn, to varying degrees, the real Indian languages in these areas. This was the case with the missionary linguists in Massachusetts, like John Eliot and John and Josiah Cotton, and some of the Moravian missionaries among the Delawares in the mid-eighteenth century and later. Roger Williams's Narragansett phrase book, *A Key into the Language of America* (1643), shows a basic control of the rudiments of Algonquian grammar, though this control tended to break down when he ventured to compose sentences not in everyday use. And we know of at least two men who were native speakers of Southern New England Algonquian languages in the eighteenth century: Experience Mayhew on Martha's Vineyard and Jonathan Edwards, Jr., among the Mahican of Stockbridge, Massachusetts.[43] Both were the sons of missionaries and grew up among Indians.

The Historical Significance of Pidgin Algonquian

What, then, is the wider significance of the pidgin languages that we now can identify as having been spoken along the East Coast? Of course, their existence has implications for many of the details of history. European interpreters in most or all cases were probably adept in the use of a pidgin, rather than the real local Indian language. Loanwords must be seen as having often passed through the medium of a pidgin on their way from Algonquian languages to English. The most important implications, though, are for our general view of the Indians in the early period and their relations with the Europeans. Pidgins based on European languages have been considered emblematic of the attitudes and power relationships of colonialism, but what of pidgins used by Europeans based on local, indigenous languages? The East Coast Algonquian-based pidgins evolved from the joint efforts of the parties involved, but we have seen that a close examination of the way the Algonquian grammatical contrasts were reduced in the pidgins shows that Algonquian speakers must have played the major formative role in selecting the forms and words used in the pidgin. Not only did they control the formation of the pidgins, but by presenting a pidgin model to the Europeans and keeping their real languages largely inaccessible they controlled the flow of information between themselves and the Europeans. This control is directly attested by their well-documented ability, and inclination, to shut Europeans out of their discourse at will by using nonpidgin Algonquian. As to their underlying motivations in this, it will be sufficient here to suggest that the formation and use of the Algonquian pidgins furnishes important insights into the attitudes of the East Coast Indians toward the Europeans as they tried to control the impact of the European encounter.

Notes

1. An exception is Lois M. Feister, "Linguistic Communication between the Dutch and Indians in New Netherland, 1609–1664," *Ethnohistory* 20 (1973): 25–38.
2. A recent survey of the use of pidgins and trade jargons and other aspects of language contact in North American, with copious references, is Michael Silverstein, "Dynamics of Linguistic Contact," in *Handbook of North American Indians* (gen. ed. William C. Sturtevant), vol. 17, *Languages*, ed. Ives Goddard (Washington, 1996 [1997]), 117–36. A comprehensive worldwide survey with historical background and extensive linguistic analysis is John Holm, *Pidgins and Creoles*, 2 vols. (Cambridge, England, 1988).
3. A valuable and highly readable survey of types of contact languages and their patterns of development is Sarah Grey Thomason and Terrence Kaufman, *Language Contact, Creolization, and Genetic Linguistics* (Berkeley 1988 [paperback 1991]). The earlier, skeptical view can be found in Antoine Meillet, "Sur le degré de précision qu'admet la définition de la parentée linguistique," and "Introduction à la classification des langues," in A. Meillet, *Linguistique historique et linguistique générale*, 2nd printing, 2 vols. (Paris, 1926, 1952), 2:47–52, 53–69.
4. Peter Bakker, "'The Language of the Coast Tribes is Half Basque': A Basque-American Indian Pidgin in Use between Europeans and Native Americans in North America, ca. 1540–ca. 1640," *Anthropological Linguistics* 31, nos. 3–4 (1989): 117–47.
5. In citing or referring to linguistic forms, single quotes mark a gloss (which may, but typically does not, quote verbatim the translation given in the source); shallow-pointed brackets indicate that the transcription is not normalized to conform to either a conventional orthography or a standard phonetic alphabet but merely reproduces the spelling of the source; and square brackets mark forms in phonetic transcription.
6. Modern Montagnais dialects have [tsi·l] and [tsi·n], with regular sound changes.
7. Ives Goddard, "The Delaware Jargon," in *New Sweden in America*, ed. Carol E. Hoffecker et al. (Newark, DE, 1995), 137–49; Goddard, "Pidgin Delaware," in

Contact Languages: A Wider Perspective, ed. Sarah G. Thomason (Amsterdam, 1997), 43–98.
8. Ives Goddard, "Delaware," in *Handbook of North American Indians* (gen. ed. William C. Sturtevant), vol. 15, *Northeast*, ed. Bruce G. Trigger (Washington, 1978), 213–39.
9. The Eastern Algonquian languages, forming a branch of the widespread Algonquian family, were spoken along the East Coast, from the Maritime provinces to North Carolina; see Ives Goddard, "Eastern Algonquian Languages," in *Handbook of North American Indians* (gen. ed. William C. Sturtevant), vol. 15, *Northeast*, ed. Bruce G. Trigger (Washington, 1978), 70–77.
10. Johannes de Laet, *Novvs Orbis: Seu descriptionis Indiæ occidentalis libri XVIII* (Leiden, 1633), 75–76; there are some copying errors in the translation: "From the 'New World,' by Johan de Laet, 1625, 1630, 1633, 1640," in *Narratives of New Netherland 1609–1664*, ed. J. Franklin Jameson (New York, 1909; reprinted 1967), 29–60, esp. 57–60.
11. Johannes Campanius, *Lutheri Catechismus Öfwersatt på American-Virginiske Språket* (Stockholm, 1696); a facsimile edition was issued as Johannes Campanius, *Martin Luther's Little Catechism Translated into Algonquian Indian* (bound with Isak Collijn, *The Swedish-Indian Catechism: Some Notes*) (Stockholm and Uppsala, 1937); translation of the Swedish text and glosses is in Johannes Campanius, *Luther's Catechism Translated into the American-Virginian Language*, trans. Daniel Nystrom and E.W. Olson (New York, 1938).
12. "The Indian Interpreter," 1684, State Archives of New Jersey, Salem Town Records, book B.64–68; William Nelson, *The Indians of New Jersey* (Paterson, NJ, 1894); J. Dyneley Prince, "An Ancient New Jersey Indian Jargon," *American Anthropologist*, n.s. 14 (1912): 508–24; Goddard, "Pidgin Delaware," 84–85 n. 3.
13. Gabriel Thomas, *An Historical and Geographical Account of the Province and Country of Pensylvania; and of West-New-Jersey in America*, 2 vols. in 1 (London, 1698; facsimile reprint: New York, 1848), 1:47, 2:7–13. Peter Lindeström, *Geographia Americae: With an account of the Delaware Indians*, trans. Amandus Johnson (Philadelphia, 1925), 203; this book was written in 1691 on the basis of notes made in 1654–56. Albert Cook Myers, ed., *William Penn His Own Account of the Lenni Lenape or Delaware Indians, 1683* (Moylan, PA, 1937), 26–28. Goddard, "Pidgin Delaware."
14. Goddard, "Pidgin Delaware," 56.
15. Goddard, "Delaware Jargon," 138.
16. Myers, *William Penn*, 26–28.
17. "Letter of Reverend Jonas Michaëlius, 1628," in *Narratives of New Netherland 1609–1664*, ed. J. Franklin Jameson (New York, 1909; reprinted 1967), 117–33, esp. 128.
18. A survey of the main features of Delaware grammar with examples is in Goddard, "Pidgin Delaware," 47–50.
19. In the phonemic transcription of Delaware, given in italics, letters are used with their usual Americanist values; č is English *ch* (as in *church*); š is English *sh* (as in *ship*); *x* is German *ch* (as in *Bach*); ə is a mid-central vowel (as in the excuse-maker's colloquial American English *But ..., but ..., but ...*); the raised dot indicates a long vowel (as in German) or a long consonant (as in Italian); the acute accent marks primary stress and raised pitch.
20. John Eliot, *The Indian Grammar Begun* (Cambridge, MA, 1666), 9; Ives Goddard, "The Description of the Native Languages of North America before Boas," in *Handbook of North American Indians* (gen. ed. William C. Sturtevant),

vol. 17, *Languages*, ed. Ives Goddard (Washington, 1996 [1997]), 17–42, esp. 21. Eventually the French missionary linguists working on Algonquian languages settled on the terms *noble* and *ignoble* for the two genders, and these terms may give a better idea of some of the more elusive aspects of the contrast. For a recent survey, see Amy Dahlstrom, "Motivation versus Predictability in Algonquian Gender," in *Papers of the Twenty-Sixth Algonquian Conference*, ed. David H. Pentland (Winnipeg, 1995), 52–66. The individual languages generally agree on the gender-assignment of common words but differ in a few cases.

21. Campanius's pronouns with final ⟨-r⟩ were taken from a dialect with older forms that preserved this segment, which is lost in the modern forms of both Delaware languages (Goddard, "Pidgin Delaware," 58, 88).

22. Within the historical period several Algonquian languages, including Montagnais, Micmac, and the Abenaki and Delaware languages, shifted [r] to [l]; Pidgin Delaware materials show both pronunciations.

23. This name is found in a 1682 deed to William Penn (Myers, *William Penn*, 77); Goddard, "Pidgin Delaware," 68, 91.

24. De Laet, *Novvs Orbis*; Goddard, "Pidgin Delaware," 72. The pidgin word for 'wildcat' substitutes [s] for the initial segment of Unami *čínkwe* (idem, 55).

25. "Letter of . . . Michaëlius," 128.

26. The following examples are summarized from Goddard, "Pidgin Delaware," 71–73.

27. Goddard, "Pidgin Delaware," 80–81.

28. See note 22.

29. Goddard, "Pidgin Delaware," 61, 73, 91.

30. Goddard, "Pidgin Delaware," 77–78.

31. Ives Goddard, "Some Early Examples of American Indian Pidgin English from New England," *International Journal of American Linguistics* 43 (1977): 37–41, esp. 41. Massachusett was the Algonquian language spoken in eastern Massachusetts.

32. Edward Arber, ed., *The Story of the Pilgrim Fathers, 1606–1623 A.D.; as Told by Themselves, their Friends, and their Enemies* (London 1897), 550. Massasoit pronounced [n] for [l], which did not exist in Massachusett.

33. Massachusett [nəna·mən] (⟨nunnamun⟩) 'I see it (inanimate)' rather than [nəna·w] (⟨nunnau⟩) 'I see him, it (animate)'.

34. Philip L. Barbour, ed., *The Jamestown Voyages under the First Charter, 1606–1609*, 2 vols. (Cambridge, England, 1969), 2:334. It is not certain that Smith was the author.

35. William Strachey, *The Historie of Travell into Virginia Britania (1612)*, ed. Louis B. Wright and Virginia Freund (London, 1953), 201 (British Library ms.). This is the fully inflected form for 'I shoot (or shot) it', hence not pidgin in form; but as with many other entries in Strachey's list, its selection and incomplete gloss must reflect the use of the local pidgin.

36. David B. Quinn and Alison M. Quinn, eds., *The English New England Voyages, 1602–1608* (London, 1983), 309, 479.

37. According to the tradition, the greeting was shouted from Slate Rock, on the former shore that is now under the filled land at the east end of Power Street, not far from the site of the conference at which this paper was given (Edward Field, *State of Rhode Island and Providence Plantations at the End of the Century: A History*, 3 vols. [Boston and Syracuse, 1902], 1:24–25); John Hutchins Cady, *The Civic and Architectural Development of Providence, 1636–1950* (Providence,

1957), 3, 14, 146–47. This greeting is the first vocabulary item in Roger Williams, *A Key into the Language of America* (London, 1643), 2.
38. Goddard, "Pidgin Delaware," 78, 94.
39. Strachey, *Historie*, 184, 194; Barbour, *Jamestown Voyages*, 2:332.
40. Goddard, "Pidgin Delaware," 78.
41. Goddard, "Some Early Examples," 37–38 (from which the examples in this paragraph are cited); Goddard, "A Further Note on Pidgin English," *International Journal of American Linguistics* 44 (1978): 73.
42. J. Hammond Trumbull, ed., *The Public Records of the Colony of Connecticut* (Boston, 1850), 218–19; John Demos, "Searching for Abbottsij van Cummingshuysen, House Carpenter in Two Worlds," in *The Impact of New Netherlands upon the Colonial Long Island Basin*, ed. Joshua W. Lane (New Haven and Washington, 1993), 13–20.
43. Ives Goddard and Kathleen J. Bragdon, *Native Writings in Massachusett*, 2 vols. (Philadelphia, 1988), 2:761; Jonathan Edwards, *Observations on the Language of the Muhhekaneew Indians* (New Haven, 1788).

Part II

Signs and Symbols

– Chapter 3 –

Pictures, Gestures, Hieroglyphs: "Mute Eloquence" in Sixteenth-Century Mexico

Pauline Moffitt Watts

IN RECENT YEARS a number of scholars have drawn attention to the role that alphabetic writing played in the forms of communication that evolved between Europeans and indigenous peoples in Mexico and Peru after 1492. Serge Gruzinski, Thomas Cummins, and James Lockhart have published works that analyze the ways in which the Nahuas and the Incas adapted their traditional media to those introduced by the Spanish missionaries. In these adaptations, indigenous oral and pictographic techniques are merged with arrangements of pictorial space and with the letters and phonetics found in European books. These studies and others consider these postconquest media to be hybrid negotiations of language through which the Nahuas and the Incas deliberately selected, adapted, preserved, and subverted meanings.[1]

Walter Mignolo has introduced a broader, darker interpretation in which indigenous languages and collective memories were vanquished by the "colonizing" power of alphabetic writing. Mignolo links the Renaissance humanists' philological and literary studies and their revival of the *studia humanitatis* of classical antiquity to the invention of the printed book in the mid-fifteenth century. The convergence of these events produced a particular Western European "ideology" of the written word built on a "complicity" between alphabetic writing and the printed book. The "Western literacy" that resulted from this "complicity," in turn, was crucial to the European conquest of the peoples of Mexico and Peru, effecting the "colonization of Amerindian languages and memories." According to Mignolo, this concatenation of events represents the "darker side of the Renaissance."[2]

Studies such as those mentioned here and the debates they stimulate raise the question of how to define fundamental terms such as "writing" and "literacy." In her important introduction to *Writing Without Words: Alternative Literacies in Mesoamerica and the Andes*, Elizabeth Hill Boone has called for an expanded definition of writing. She urges us to move beyond the common "limited" assumption that writing is simply the record or the redaction of the spoken word "referenced phonetically by visible marks," that is, by alphabetic scripts.[3] Boone proposes that we understand writing as "the communication of relatively specific ideas in a conventional manner by means of permanent, visible marks," including various "visual and tactile systems of recording information."[4] According to this definition, the pictographs and hieroglyphs used by the Mayas and Nahuas, and the texts encoded in the knotted strings of the Incan quipus, would be considered forms of writing. Boone's expanded definition of writing implies an expanded understanding of literacy as well, an understanding displayed in the essays contributed to *Writing Without Words*.

Boone's essay is focused on Mesoamerican and Andean literacy, but some of its insights can be fruitfully applied to a reconsideration of "European literacy" as well. Most people living in Europe during the period we call the Renaissance could not read or write alphabetic scripts. But this does not mean they were entirely "illiterate," although they are habitually described this way by those who study them.[5] Extrapolating from Boone's definition, I want to argue instead that these people were indeed literate, literate in various visual, tactile, *and performative* systems of recording and transmitting information.[6]

Pictures, glyphs, and gestures had been used throughout Europe since antiquity to teach, to entertain, to translate, and to impose and subvert meanings. These forms of "mute eloquence" had working vocabularies shared and transmitted by sufficient numbers of people that they can be said to have functioned as languages. Such languages did not especially rely upon the written word, either before or after the advent of printing with moveable type (though they were not entirely divorced from it). They were built instead out of the interaction of various types of mnemonics with the contemplation and exegesis of images. These techniques originated in deeply instilled patterns of public speech and behavior.[7] If we take into account this broader range of what historian Peter Burke has called "communicative events, " it is reasonable to suppose that Renaissance people were literate in a variety of vernaculars knit together from the rituals, spectacles, and sounds that were part of their lives.[8]

Scholars working with such expanded notions of "European literacy" have begun to reappraise the ways in which Europeans communicated and "excommunicated" within and without their own cultures.[9] For example, the essays edited by Claire Farago in *Reframing The Renaissance: Visual Culture in Europe and Latin America 1450–1650* purposively invoke a "broad range of communicative events" in their explorations of cultural exchanges between the Old World and the New in the early modern period. In taking this expansive approach, they complement the essays gathered by Boone and Mignolo in *Writing Without Words* in fascinating ways.[10]

Both collections invite us into a difficult world cohabited by peoples with no prior history of contiguity. Their halting, improvised, irrupted communications (and miscommunications and excommunications) defy easy analysis and sweeping conclusions.[11] The Europeans who first lived in this world, which actually was always many worlds at once, were the mendicant missionaries who began to arrive in Mexico in the 1520s. They came to know its difficulties and dangers only too well.

In a letter addressed to the Emperor Charles V from Mexico on 6 May 1532, the Franciscan provincial, Jacopo da Testera, spoke of the "wall" that separated the Indians of New Spain from himself and his confreres. It was a wall that could be penetrated only through the arduous task of learning indigenous languages. Without such fluency, Testera asserted, the door by which the Europeans could pass through this wall and begin to contemplate "the secrets of this people ... the sentiments of their souls," would remain closed. The tongues of those Europeans who did not undertake this task would stay "locked in their mouths"; they would remain "sleeping witnesses of that which they will never see," like the soldiers who guarded Christ's tomb at the Resurrection.[12]

Lacking polyglots or an established lingua franca, lacking a long history of cross-cultural exchanges and translations such as had marked the interactions of Christians, Muslims, and Jews in Iberia for centuries, how did these first Franciscans and their fellow mendicants, who were committed to conversion by persuasion rather than coercion, go about the task of evangelizing?[13] There is evidence to indicate that, initially at least, Testera and his brothers relied heavily upon "languages" built primarily out of mixtures of images and gestures, languages in which written, and often spoken, words were ancillary to the "mute eloquence" of these other media.

This evidence is not abundant, nor is it easy to recover. It is something of an irony that information regarding these languages of images and gestures descends to us entirely in manuscripts and printed materials—that is, encased in the adumbrated medium of the written word. There are a number of ways to account for the paucity of such materials. The transient and precarious nature of missionary work in the early decades of the evangelization of Mexico meant that the importation, distribution, transportation, and preservation of books was irregular and hazardous. For example, Diego Valadés and his teacher, Juan Focher, two important early Franciscan missionaries and scholars, lost all their books in flight from an attack by the Chichimecas. Only gradually did significant repositories of books appear and were printing presses imported as the secular and ecclesiastical institutions of Spanish colonialism became established.[14]

There is another factor, a second "wall," as it were. It is a wall constructed by reformers and Inquisitors in both Iberia and the Americas in the course of the sixteenth century. Behind this wall certain texts representative of the beliefs and techniques that underlay the early decades of Franciscan missionary activity lay long concealed, in effect "excommunicated" by their own order. A manuscript that contains a version of the colloquies exchanged between the Aztec caciques and the famous "Twelve" when they arrived to undertake the spiritual conquest of Mexico in the wake of Cortés's conquest of Monteczuma's "empire" was recovered only in this century in the Archivio Segreto Vaticano. Gerónimo de Mendieta's *Historia eclesiástica indiana*, an important chronicle of Franciscan missionary work in sixteenth-century New Spain, was "forgotten" by the Franciscan Order for several hundred years, resurfacing in the nineteenth century when it was discovered and published by the great Mexican scholar Joaquín García Icazbalceta.[15]

At least one other text that contains important information regarding the techniques of the first Franciscan missionaries was disguised or mitigated in various ways to meet the demands of post-Tridentine orthodoxy: Diego Valadés's *Rhetorica Christiana*, published in Perugia in 1579. It is not coincidental that these texts and others that are keys to the hidden history of the spiritual conquest of Mexico are also essential sources for the recovery of the techniques of "mute eloquence."[16]

The languages of gesture and gesticulation used by the Franciscans drew upon repositories of significations that can be traced back to the rhetorical arts of Greco-Roman antiquity. These arts did not merely ornament communication; they were the engine that drove it. The manuals of famous orators such as Cicero and Quintilian indicate that the language of gestures used by the rhetorician, the establishment of a space or a "theater" in the political forum or law court, and the developments of his movements within that theater, were as crucial to his effectiveness as the content and syntax of his speech.[17]

The rhetorician, like the mime, was a servant of Mnemosyne, the goddess of Memory. Through the *ars memorativa,* he stored and recalled an extensive knowledge of myth and history, of literature and philosophy. His speeches would be constructed from this repertoire of unwritten "texts." Through his mastery of the mimetic vocabularies of natural and conventional gestures, he could enhance (or subvert) his words in ways that appropriately accommodated the audience and the issues at hand. In addition to its dramatic, political, and forensic functions, the language of gestures played a significant role as an indicator of rank and status in the imperial court circles of the late antique world.

Ceremonies such as that of *adventus,* the triumphal arrival of a victorious commander or a ruler into a city, unfolded themselves in a carefully choreographed sequence of actions and gestures designed to commemorate and transmit certain meanings to the spectators. The adventus thus established or renewed hierarchies of political and military power, of social order, and admitted those present into them. It was rooted in the foundations of the rhetorical tradition as they are described by Cicero in *De inventione.* That is, it was a wordless ritual that nonetheless shaped and protected the body politic, that promised to introduce and preserve communal welfare, peace, and prosperity. Such formal, enduring applications of the language of gestures were the marks of a civilized people, setting them off from men who wandered in the fields and forests like beasts, sustaining life by eating seeds.[18]

But there was a disturbing counterpart to, an inversion of, the dramatic, forensic, and deliberative languages of gesture cultivated in ancient rhetoric. These were exaggerated, uncontrolled, or inappropriate gestures. In public settings where gestures were highly conventionalized, encoding precise, nuanced meanings, such excesses could have powerful, unpredictable effects upon the audience. By virtue of their unconventionality, they passed over into the marginal, unorthodox realm of *gesticulation.* They were morally, socially, politically subversive, redolent of bestial, uncultivated human origins.

As with many elements of Greco-Roman public culture, these languages of gesture and gesticulation were variously received and adapted by their medieval heirs. Though their ancient frameworks can still be discerned, the medieval codifications of gesture were suffused with other significations derived from the emergent, later dominant, symbols and rituals of Christianity as well as more latent meanings of obscure, archaic European origin. Both gesture and gesticulation are represented in certain lineages of manuscript illuminations, for example those accompanying texts of the plays of Terence, Prudentius's *Psychomachia*, and *Sachenspiegel*—a thirteenth-century German work describing and illustrating regional legal practices and court procedures.[19]

The mutant languages of gesticulation persisted throughout the medieval period as well. These were the languages of jesters, actors, prostitutes, and heretics. Vagrant creatures they were—lascivious, grotesque, yet seductive and necessary. Peripheral to society but inseparable from it, they adorn the margins of maps and manuscripts, entwined in the patterns and tendrils of border motifs, engraved in stone on the columns that support ecclesiastical edifices and the facades that introduce them.[20]

The Franciscans became particularly skilled in the manipulation of these curious hybrid languages; there is no better example of what Carlo Ginzburg has called the "carnivalesque" quality of primitive Franciscanism than its founder. Through deliberately incongruent acts, if not gesticulations, such as stripping himself naked before the Bishop of Assisi, or smearing his head with ashes and walking away from his audience without speaking, Francis ruptured and involuted conventions and established himself as a holy man living in a sacred space apart from society. And through his empathetic, transmogrified attachments to animals—his sermons to the birds, the taming of the wolf of Gubbio, the incantatory metamorphosis of his body into that of a donkey—he occupied a threshold between the human and the bestial worlds, always testing and blurring the boundaries between gesture and gesticulation, madness and civilization.[21]

I have spent time developing this sketch because I think that in order to fathom the curious sixteenth-century afterlife of ancient and medieval languages of gesture and their inversions, we must also understand them as antecedent to the historical moment of contact between monks and Nahuas. I now turn to several examples of transmutations of such antecedents. These seem to me to reveal the historical substrata of singular aspects of Franciscan missionary techniques and demonstrate the potential of these techniques to broadcast deeply ambivalent, even intentionally subversive, meanings.

The "spiritual conquest" of Mexico commenced in 1524 when Hérnan Cortés greeted the famous "Twelve" Franciscans led by Martin of Valencia at the edge of the recently conquered city of Tenochtitlán. This ceremonial initiation was a mnemonic and mimetic event with considerable resonance for the Europeans present. A recollection and rebirthing of the original mission of the first Apostles, it unfolded in a transmutation of the ancient Roman ceremony of adventus, but it also involved a characteristically Franciscan inversion of that ceremony, an inversion in which Cortés himself participated. The Franciscans' journey to the city from the port of Veracruz had itself been modeled after that initial phase of the ceremony of adventus known as *synantesis*—the welcome provided by the general populace as a secular or religious leader, a military victor, or a relic makes its triumphal approach to the host city.[22]

As the Twelve drew near the city, Cortés rode out to greet them. The monks approached not on horseback, as would the conqueror in the traditional adventus ceremony, but, rather, on foot; Díaz describes them as "barefoot and thin, their garments ragged, very jaundiced looking." The inversion of the ceremony continued as Cortés dismounted from his horse, divesting himself of the venerable status of equestrian conqueror, kissed the tattered fringes of Martin of Valencia's robes, and so assumed the submissive role of the vanquished.

The choreography of gestures employed by Cortés and the monks thus created a kind of universe or theater of meanings and relationships into which the Nahuas would be inducted. Without the use of words, the conquerors communicated important relationships amongst themselves to each other and to the assembled caciques. Cortes's ritual kissing of the robes of the Twelve assigned "conquerors" and "conquered" a common status vis-à-vis the monks, much as the carefully orchestrated encounters of victors and vanquished in the vanished but still vital ceremony of adventus had done centuries before.

However, the Europeans' assumption that they shared symbolic conventions with the Nahuas and that they could effectively translate rank and status through these conventions proved to be naive. This is evident in other instances of contact between monks, conquistadors, and indigenous peoples. The customs and rituals of the indigenous peoples sorely tested the Europeans' capacities to absorb and understand. Nahuatl dances were particularly disturbing. The movements of the dancers appeared to be bestial, excessive *gesticulations*, indicators of diabolical possession by the "ancient serpent" with whom the Franciscans believed they were in mortal combat.[23]

Both Spanish and indigenous sources transfix a moment in which sacred gesture and blasphemous gesticulation merge with horrifying results. It occurred in Tenochtitlán, after the initial Spanish occupation but prior to the Noche Triste and the final conquest of the city. It was the time of the annual festival of Toxcatl, perhaps the most important celebration in the Nahuatl religious calendar, and permission was granted by the Spaniards for it to be held at the main temple. An indigenous account preserved by Bernardino de Sahagún and his collaborators relates that at the very moment the Dance of The Serpent

> was loveliest and song linked to song, the Spaniards were seized with an urge to kill the celebrants.... They ran in among the dancers, forcing their way to the place where the drums were played. They attacked the man who was drumming and cut off his arms. Then they cut off his head and it rolled across the floor.[24]

A massacre of the dancers ensued.

Initial phobic responses of the Franciscans gradually gave way to more sophisticated observations and manipulations of the forms and functions of indigenous ritual dances and ceremonies. A kind of simple pantomime was devised not long after the arrival of the first Franciscans to communicate the rudiments of Christian doctrine, according to the account of Fray Juan de Torquemada in his *Monarquia Indiana*:

> These things were taught by the holy religious men in pantomime, and only in signs; in signaling to the sky and saying they ought to believe that the only God was there; and turning their eyes to the earth, they signified that there was hell, wherein walked the likeness of toads and serpents. These were the demons tormenting the condemned souls.[25]

As the monks became more aware of the parallels between the Nahua uses of song, dance, and drama as vehicles for the preservation and transmission of theogony, cosmology, and history and their own *autos sacramentales*, they began to experiment with fusions of the two theaters and the more intricate montages of gestures that various rituals employed.

These plays were intended to safely encase indigenous processions and dances within orthodox Christian parables and narratives. However, the proliferation of processions and elaborate settings featuring an abundance of topiaries, live animals, gonfalons, puppets, and Indians (costumed sometimes as animals, sometimes as hybrids of man and beast) found in plays such as those designed by Toribio de Motolinia made endemic the fear that the performances might be overly inflected by indigenous forms and content. In other words, in these plays there always remained an unresolved tension between gesture and gesticulation, between Christian and Nahua pieties, in these plays; it was a tension that Francis himself would have appreciated.[26]

Confessions as well as catechetical dramas were conducted without words. Diego Valadés, in his *Rhetorica Christiana*, described how this was done:

> In confession, by using very ingenious pictures, they show in what ways they have offended God, and they put small stones on the sign on which the vices or virtues are represented in order to indicate how many times they have relapsed back into the same sin.[27]

He also described (and depicted in an etching) how the Franciscans used images woven into tapestries to instruct indigenous peoples in the rudiments of Christian doctrine (see Fig. 3.1).[28]

The use of images, objects, and languages of gesture to instruct the Nahuas was not peculiar to missionary work in Mexico. Missionaries had used similar techniques to evangelize the "illiterate" *pagani* within Europe at least since the time of Paulinus of Nola (355–431). In fact, there is good reason to believe that there was some reciprocity between the permutations of the venerable techniques devised by the mendicants in Mexico and those adopted by the Jesuits in the contemporaneous conversion of *contadini* in mezzogiorno Italy. This reciprocity, in turn, raises an important question regarding religious, as distinct from linguistic, communities and communicants: How "Christian" was "Christian Europe" in the sixteenth century?[29]

There is still much to be learned about these forms of "mute eloquence." As I argued above, they surely were in part vestigial versions of the ancient rhetorical arts. They also may well have been adaptations of various sign languages that the monks learned as novices. These sign languages were used to communicate during

FIGURE 3.1 A Franciscan preaching to the Indians and pointing to images, from Diego Valadés, *Rhetorica Christiana* ... (Perugia, 1579). (Courtesy of the John Carter Brown Library at Brown University)

the requisite periods of silence that punctuated the daily routine of cloistered life.[30]

The catechetical pantomimes and "ingenious drawings" used to facilitate confession may also be related to a curious genre of catechisms done entirely in pictures. Named for Jacopo da Testera, who is believed to have invented them, they were used for several centuries by missionaries working in the Americas. Most scholars think it unlikely that they were entirely original, but specific European models have never been identified, if they exist. These "Testerian" catechisms may well be mélanges incorporating some of the gestures and images contained in the illustrations accompanying Prudentius' *Psychomachia* and the *Sachenspeigel*, elements of monastic sign languages, and other pictographic traditions that have not yet been identified (see Fig. 3.2).[31]

A passage from Motolinia's *History of the Indians of New Spain* indicates that initially the Franciscans made an effort to coordinate and centralize their mission and that this effort was based on directives from their Minister General in Spain.[32] Presumably the Franciscans and the other mendicant orders, the Dominicans and the Augustinians, were seeking to establish standard ways of catechizing and confessing (although Motolinia also indicates that

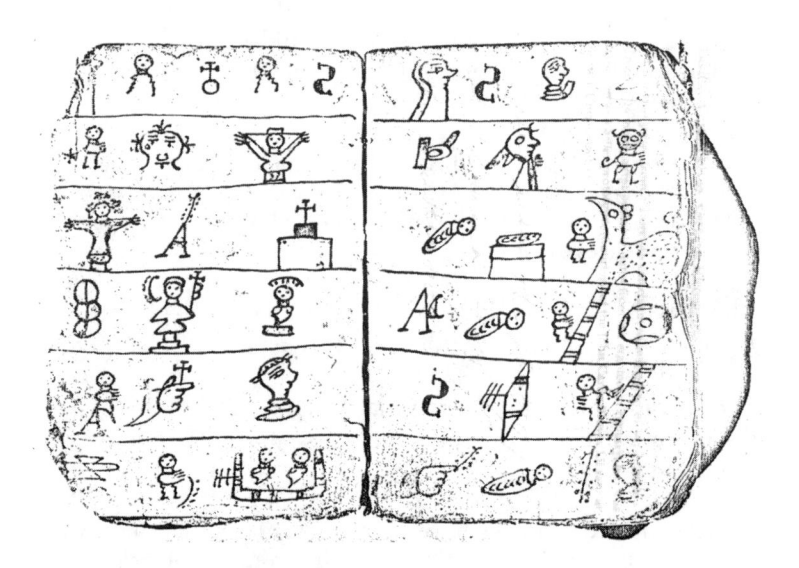

FIGURE 3.2 Two pages from a Testerian catechism showing part of the Apostle's Creed. This manuscript probably dates from the eighteenth century, but it is based on an earlier prototype. (Codex Indian 25, ff. 2v–3r). (Courtesy of the John Carter Brown Library at Brown University)

there were tensions regarding this, especially after the arrival of the secular clergy). To this end they would have wanted to consolidate their media and techniques for use throughout the territories in which they were evangelizing. This effort to standardize the media of pastoral work is borne out by the consistent vocabulary of images in surviving Testerian catechisms used by the three mendicant orders and by the Jesuits, and by the longevity of these catechisms (at least one example dates from the eighteenth century).

The effectiveness of these nonverbal techniques appears to have encouraged the Franciscans to develop other, more complicated ones derived from the systems of *loci* and *imagines* upon which the *ars memorativa* of ancient rhetoric rested. Valadés tells us the Franciscans recognised that these systems could be adapted to the task of teaching the Indians how to read and write:

> Images are certainly forms and signs and representations of those things that we wish to remember. It is necessary that we arrange these things, such as the genus of horses, lions, books, stones, in certain places. For places are like writing tablets or leaves of paper. The images are like letters, the disposition and location of the images is like writing, and speaking is like reading [the "texts" of images and places stored with the memory].[33]

To Valadés's mind, transposition would be feasible because the Indians already understood and utilized systems of loci and imagines:

> Because they are unlettered, as we have mentioned above, they make their will known to each other through certain forms and images that they are accustomed to place on panels of silk and paper sheets made from the leaves of trees.[34]

What Valadés is describing here, using the terminology of the traditional European ars memorativa, is a system of hieroglyphic writing devised by the Indians.

Valadés went on to observe that the Indians use these hieroglyphs for the full range of exchanges essential to the public life of a civilized people:

> And they used figures in the same way instead of writing in transmitting agreements with other peoples and in recording significant events and in governing themselves.... Is it not astonishing that anything in the natural universe, whether it is perceived by the senses or the intellect, can be converted to that usage [hieroglyphs] which signifies in the same way that [written] words do?[35]

In still other uses of hieroglyphs, the Indians may be compared to rulers and sages of antiquity (especially the Egyptians) who created symbolic languages in which they were able to encode and transmit secrets and arcane wisdom.[36]

These observations led Valadés to argue that although the Indians might appear "crude and uncultivated to some" they actually had developed a rather sophisticated polygraphy that makes use of objects, as well as hieroglyphs, rather than letters. Sometimes they used threads, colored differently according to the meaning they were to convey. Beans of various types and colors, small stones, and seeds were employed in this polygraphy as well. The seeds gathered by Cicero's wild men thus become morphemes in a vocabulary based on the patterns of meaning resulting from the shifting spatial arrangements of "things" rather than lines of written "words" marked on paper or vellum.[37]

For Valadés, the pinnacle of these skills was to be found in the complex calendars created by the Indians. For him at least, these calendars seemed free of the diabolic meanings that led to their systematic destruction by Europeans. Instead their intricacies conclusively revealed the Indians' humanity, their dignity, their eminent "capacity" (I use the word here in the sense that Las Casas and Sepúlveda debated it in the famous exchanges at Valladolid in 1550, for Valadés more than once in *Rhetorica Christiana* alludes to debates and related testimonies before the Council of the Indies). The penultimate chapters of Book II of *Rhetorica Christiana* explain how the Franciscans adapted their own traditional mnemonic systems and a cluster of Renaissance variants of them to their understandings of the Indians' uses of loci and imagines and so effected a transition from a hieroglyphic language to a lettered one.[38]

It was through these various innovative transmutations of the ancient rhetorical arts that the Franciscans broke through Testera's "wall." Having done this, they went on to teach the rudiments of grammar and eventually to instruct the most proficient of indigenous students in the grammar, rhetoric, and logic of the *trivium*, as at the Colegio de Santa Cruz. In 1547, Andres de Olmos, who taught at the Colegio de Santa Cruz, completed his *Arte de la lengua Mexicana*—the first grammar of Nahuatl. It is noteworthy that Olmos completed his grammar at more or less the same time that the first grammars of European vernaculars were appearing. Its principles of construction, shared by other missionary grammars that followed (and by the European vernaculars as well), were those of classical Roman Latin, themselves relatively recently codified by Renaissance philologists such as Lorenzo Valla, Erasmus, and Antonio de Nebrija.[39]

Nebrija (d. 1522), was inspired particularly by Valla's untiring efforts to recover the purity of Roman latin from the medieval "barbarisms" to which it had been subjected. Nebrija aimed to privilege Castilian by casting it within the grammatical framework of Roman latin reconstructed by Valla. In linking Castilian to Roman latin, Nebrija believed that he was contributing to the historical destiny of Ferdinand and Isabella to revive the greatest empire of antiquity in their own reign. A similar intent, to enfranchise a "barbarian" people and to locate its languages within traditions that could be traced back to antiquity, underlay the missionaries' efforts to sanction Nahuatl by framing it with the written and spoken forms of Roman Latin.[40]

Having created these grammars, the Franciscans composed sermons, catechisms, and other forms of doctrinal and devotional literature in what scholars have named "classical" or "missionary" Nahuatl. In so doing they participated in the emergent awareness of historical, linguistic, and religious vernaculars that attended Renaissance humanists' and philologists' recovery of the arcane, the forgotten texts and artifacts of antiquity. But the interpenetrations of language and culture that produced the Complutensian Bible in the Old World in 1522, and the missionary and indigenous polyglots in the New World several decades later, also deeply threatened ecclesiastical institutions and orthodoxies.

In both Iberia and Mexico, ecclesiastical resistance to these syncretisms coalesced in the office of the Inquisition. In Iberia the humanist hermeneutics inspired by Valla, Erasmus, and Nebrija and sponsored by Cardinal Jiménez de Cisneros were indexed and silenced. The heterodox pieties of the *alumbrados* and other mystics, tolerated at the beginning of the sixteenth century, were persecuted and dissolved, excommunicated by the fear of Lutheranism and by the Tridentine reforms. In Mexico, the synod of 1555, presided over by Bishop and Apostolic Inquisitor Alonso de Montúfar, established strict rules controlling works written in indigenous languages, which seemed highly vulnerable to unorthodox infiltrations from missionary and Indian alike. (The synod's suspicions were not unfounded; recent scholarly studies indicate that works written by indigenous peoples may well have encoded meanings from which Europeans were, in effect, excommunicated.) This same synod also sought to regulate the missionaries' uses of ritual dances and drama, fearful that fusions of the auto sacramentale with indigenous theater might serve as hosts to heterodox meanings and residues of diabolical possession.[41]

In such ways a second "spiritual conquest" took place within the culture of the conqueror. The missionary work inaugurated by the "Twelve" itself became foreign to the religious and political forces that prevailed in late sixteenth-century Iberia. The Franciscans' languages of conversion and the idioms that they spawned were also excommunicated, sealed off by a second wall constructed from within their own culture with such efficiency that they can now be recovered only in vestigial forms. And yet the liminal worlds negotiated by monks and Nahuas, so deeply rooted in their respective pre-contact pasts, survive today in the languages and arts, the public and private customs and ceremonies of many people living in the American Southwest and in Mexico. And so the mimetic and mnemonic power of their ancient languages of "mute eloquence" lives on as well.

Notes

Parts of this paper draw upon two previously published pieces: "Hieroglyphs of Conversion: Alien Discourses in Diego Valadés's *Rhetorica Christiana*," *Memorie Domenicane*, n.s. 22, 1991; and "Languages of Gesture in Sixteenth-Century Mexico: Antecedents and Transmutations" in *Reframing The Renaissance: Visual Culture in Europe and Latin America 1450–1650*, ed. Claire Farago (New Haven, 1995). These pieces document and develop the themes of this paper in greater detail.

1. Serge Gruzinski, *The Conquest of Mexico: The Incorporation of Indian Societies into the Western World, 16th–18th Centuries* (Cambridge, England, 1993), ch. 1."Painting and Writing"; Thomas Cummins, "From Lies to Truth: Colonial Ekphrasis and the Act of Crosscultural Translation," in *Reframing the Renaissance: Visual Culture in Europe and Latin America 1450–1650*, ed. Claire Farago (New Haven, 1995), 152–74; James Lockhart, *The Nahuas after the Conquest: A Social and Cultural History of the Indians of Central Mexico, Sixteenth Through Eighteenth Centuries* (Stanford, 1992), ch. 8, "Ways of Writing."
2. Walter Mignolo, "On the Colonization of Amerindian Languages and Memories: Renaissance Theories of Writing and the Discontinuity of the Classical Tradition," *Comparative Studies in Society and History* 34, no. 2 (1992): 301–30; "Signs and Their Transmission: The Question of the Book in the New World," in *Writing Without Words: Alternative Literacies in Mesoamerica and the Andes*, ed. Elizabeth Hill Boone and Walter Mignolo (Durham, N.C., 1994), 220–70; *The Darker Side of The Renaissance: Literacy, Territoriality, and Colonization* (Ann Arbor, 1995).
3. Elizabeth Hill Boone, "Introduction: Writing and Recording Knowledge," in Boone and Mignolo, *Writing Without Words*, 3–26, 4.

4. Boone, "Introduction: Writing and Recording Knowledge," 15, 4.
5. There is a large body of literature on literacy and illiteracy, on the relationship of oral and written traditions in Europe during the medieval and Renaissance periods. See, *inter alia*, Harry Bresslau, *Handbuch der Urkundenlehre für Deutschland und Italien*, 2 vols. (Leipzig, 1912–32); Erich Auerbach, *Literary Language and Its Public in Late Latin Antiquity and in the Middle Ages* (London, 1965); E.R. Curtius, *European Literature and the Latin Middle Ages* (Princeton, 1973); M.T. Clanchy, *From Memory to Written Record: England 1066–1307* (Cambridge, Mass., 1979); Elizabeth Eisenstein, *The Printing Press as an Agent of Change: Communications and Cultural Transformations in Early-Modern Europe* (Cambridge, England, 1979); Lucien Febvre and Henri-Jean Martin, *The Coming of the Book: The Impact of Printing 1450–1800* (London, 1984); Brian Stock, *The Implications of Literacy: Written Language and Models of Interpretation in the Eleventh and Twelfth Centuries* (Princeton, 1985); Franz H. Bäuml, "Varieties and Consequences of Medieval Literacy and Illiteracy," *Speculum* 55, no.2 (1980): 237–65; Michael Camille, "Seeing and Reading: Some Visual Implications of Medieval Literacy and Illiteracy," *Art History* 8, no. 1 (March 1985): 24–49; Mary A. Rouse and Richard H. Rouse, *Authentic Witnesses: Approaches to Medieval Texts and Manuscripts* (Notre Dame, 1991); Armando Petrucci, *Writers and Readers in Medieval Italy: Studies in the History of Written Culture* (New Haven, 1995).
6. Both Boone and Gruzinski note that performance was an important element in indigenous forms of communication in sixteenth-century Mexico. See the section entitled "Performing the Histories" in Boone's "Aztec Pictorial Histories: Records Without Words," in Boone and Mignolo, *Writing Without Words*, 50–76; Gruzinski, *The Conquest of Mexico*, 9–10.
7. Among the many pertinent studies, those which I have found useful include: George R. Kernodle, *From Art to Theater: Form and Convention in the Renaissance* (Chicago, 1944); Carla Casagrande and Silvana Vecchio, "L'interdizione dei giullare nel vocabulario clericale del XII e del XIII sècolo," *Il contributo dei giulleri alla drammaturga italiana delle origini* (Viterbo, 1977), 207–58; Rudolph Wittkower, "Hieroglyphs in the Early Renaissance," in his *Allegory and the Migration of Symbols* (Boulder, 1977), 113–28; Jean-Claude Schmitt, "Gestas-Gesticulatio: Contribution à l'étude du vocabulaire latin médiéval des gestes," *La lexicographie du latin médiéval et ses rapports avec les recherches actuelle sur la civilization du moyen âge* (Paris, 1981), 377–90; Francois Garnier, *Le language de l'image au moyen âge: Signification et symbolique* (Paris, 1982); Moshe Barasch, *Giotto and the Language of Gestures* (Cambridge, England, 1987); Paul Connerton, *How Societies Remember* (Cambridge, England, 1989); Adolf Katzenellenbogen, *Allegories of the Virtues and Vices in Medieval Art* (Toronto, 1989); Jean-Claude Schmitt, *La raison des gestes dans l'occident médiéval* (Paris, 1990); Mary Carruthers, *The Book of Memory: A Study of Memory in Medieval Culture* (Cambridge, England, 1990); Carla Casagrande and Silvana Vecchio, *Les péchés de la langue: Discipline et éthique de la parole dans la culture médiévale* (Paris, 1991); Murray Krieger, *Ekphrasis: The Illusion of the Natural Sign* (Baltimore, 1992); *The Hieroglyphs of Horapollo*, trans. by George Boas, introduction by Anthony Grafton (Princeton, 1993); Erik Iversen, *The Myth of Egypt and Its Hieroglyphs in European Tradition* (Princeton, 1993); Lina Bolzoni, *La stanza della memoria: Modelli letterari e iconografici nell'età della stampa* (Torino, 1995).
8. Peter Burke, *The Italian Renaissance: Culture and Society in Italy* (Princeton, 1987), 8–9.

9. Noteworthy examples of such work include Carlo Ginzburg, "Folklore, magia, religione," *Storia d'Italia* 1 (Turin, 1972): 603–76; James Muldoon, "The Indian as Irishman," *Essex Institute Historical Collections* 3 (1975): 267–89; Richard Trexler, *Public Life in Renaissance Florence* (Ithaca, 1980); the essays collected in *Scienze credenze occulte livelli di cultura*, ed. Giancarlo Garfagnini (Florence, 1982), especially Peter Burke, "A Question of Acculturation?" and Adriano Prosperi, "*Otras Indias*: Missionari della controriforma tra contadini e selvaggi"; Patricia Seed, *Ceremonies of Possession in Europe's Conquest of the New World 1492–1640* (Cambridge, England, 1995).
10. See Farago's introduction to *Reframing The Renaissance* and her essay "'Vision Itself Has Its History': 'Race,' Nation, and Renaissance Art History," 67–88.
11. Several decades ago, the distinguished historian of Spain, J.H. Elliott wrote an important book and article pointing to the "uncertain" or "blunted" impact that the old and new worlds had upon each other. See his *The Old World and The New 1492–1650* (Cambridge, England, 1970) and "Renaissance Europe and America: A Blunted Impact?" in *First Images of America: The Impact of the New World on the Old*, ed. Fredi Chiapelli, 2 vols. (Berkeley, 1976), I: 11–23.
12. Testera's letter to Charles V, signed by seven other mendicants, is published in *Cartas de Indias* (Madrid, 1877), carta X, 62–66. The passages excerpted and translated are on 63.
13. On the medieval origins of the idea of apocalyptic conversion, and its relations to the Franciscan missions to Jews and Muslims, see E. Randolph Daniel, "Apocalyptic Conversion: The Joachite Alternative to the Crusades," *Traditio* 25 (1969): 127–54; Daniel, *The Franciscan Concept of Mission in the High Middle Ages* (Lexington, KY, 1975); Alain Milhou, *Colón y su mentalidad mesiánica en el ambiente franciscanista español* (Valladolid, 1983). On the Franciscans' application of these traditional ideas to their missionary work in sixteenth-century Mexico, see John Leddy Phelan, *The Millennial Kingdom of the Franciscans in the New World* (Berkeley, 1970); Georges Baudot, *Utopía e historia en México: Los primeros cronistas de la civilización Mexicana (1520–1569)* (Madrid, 1983) and his *La pugna franciscana por México* (México City, 1990); Mario Cayota, *Siembra entre brumas: Utopia franciscana y humanismo renacentista: Una alternativa a la conquista* (Montevideo, 1990); P.M. Watts, "The New World and the End of the World: Evangelizing Sixteenth-Century Mexico," in *Imagining the New World: Columbian Iconography*, ed. Irma B. Jaffe et al. (Rome, 1991), 28–39.
14. Valadés' description of the loss of his books is in his introduction to his edition of Focher's *Itinerarium catholicum* (Seville, 1574). On printing in the early colonial period see José Toribio Medina, *La imprenta en México (1539–1821)* (Santiago, 1912); Francisco Fernández Del Castillo, *Libros y libreros en el siglo XVI* (Mexico, 1914); Roman Zulaica Garate, *Los franciscanos y a imprenta en México en el siglo XVI* (México, 1939); Julie Greer Johnson, *The Book in the Americas: The Role of Books and Printing in the Development of Culture and Society in Colonial Latin America* (Providence, 1988), esp. the bibliographical supplement by Susan L. Newbury; Michael Mathes, "The Press Comes to the Americas: Printing and Printers during the First Century of the Encounter of Two Worlds," in Jaffe et al., *Imagining The New World*, 41–50.
15. On the history of the manuscript of the *Coloquios*, see Miguel León-Portilla, *Coloquios y doctrina Cristiana: edición facsimilar. Introducción, Paleografía, Versión del Náhuatl y notas* (México, 1986), 20–29; on the manuscript of Mendieta's

Historia eclesiástica indiana, see Fray Geronimo Mendieta, *Historia eclesiástica indiana: Obra escrita á fines del siglo XVI,* 3d ed. (México, 1980), xvii–xxxvi.

16. On the ambiguities surrounding the provenance of Valadés' *Rhetorica Christiana,* see P.M. Watts, "Hieroglyphs of Conversion: Alien Discourses in Diego Valadés' *Rhetorica Christiana,*" *Memorie Domenicane,* n.s. 22 (1991): 405–33. On Valadés's life and work, see the references in note 11 on 408.

17. Book XI. iii. 65–136 of Quintilian's *Institutio oratoria* contains fundamental descriptions of the "languages of gesture" employed by ancient rhetoricians. Other important sources include Cicero's *De inventione, De oratore,* and the pseudo-Ciceronian work *Ad Herennium.* There is no comprehensive study of the functions of gesture in ancient rhetoric.

18. *Adventus* and related ceremonies are the subject of important studies such as Richard Brilliant, *Gesture and Rank in Roman Art: The Use of Gesture and Rank to Denote Status in Roman Sculpture and Coinage* (New Haven, 1963); Sabine MacCormack, *Art and Ceremony in Late Antiquity* (Berkeley, 1981); Michael McCormick, *Eternal Victory: Triumphal Rulership in Late Antiquity, Byzantium, and the Early Medieval West* (Cambridge, England, 1989). Cicero's remarks on rhetoric and acculturation occur in *De inventione* 1.2.

19. On illuminations of Terence, see L.W. Jones and C.R. Morey, *The Miniatures of the Manuscripts of Terence Prior to the Thirteenth Century* (Princeton, 1931); on Prudentius, see R. Stettiner, *Die illustrierten Prudentius-Handschriften* (Berlin, 1893); Adolf Katzenellenbogen, *Allegories of the Virtues and Vices in Medieval Art* (Toronto, 1989). A facsimile of the *Sachsenspiegel* now in Heidelberg has been published by W. Koschorreck, *Der Sachsenspiegel in Bildern aus der Heidelberger Bilderhandschrift* (Frankfurt am Main, 1976).

20. See G.J. Witkowski, *L'Art profane à l'église* (Paris, 1908); Rudolph Wittkower, "Marvels of the East: A Study in the History of Monsters," *Journal of the Warburg Institute* II (1938–39) (reprinted in Rudolph Wittkower, *Allegory and The Migration of Symbols* [Boulder, 1977]), 45– 74; Jurgis Baltrušaitis, *Le moyen age fantastique: Antiquités et exotismes dans l'art gothique* (Paris, 1955); H. Waddell, *The Wandering Scholars* (Garden City, 1955), especially ch. VII 'The Ordo Vagorum' and Appendix E 'Councils on the *Clericus vagus* or *Joculator*'; C. Casagrande and S. Vecchio, "L'interdizione dei giulleri nel vocabulario clericale del XII e del XIII sècolo"; John Block Friedman, *The Monstrous Races in Medieval Art and Thought* (Cambridge, MA, 1981); J.-C. Schmitt, "'Gestus-Gesticulatio'"; Michael Camille, *Image On the Edge* (Cambridge, MA, 1992).

21. For these and similar incidents, see Thomas of Celano's *First Life of St. Francis* and his *Second Life of St. Francis.* These are published in Marion A. Habig, *St. Francis of Assisi: Writings and Early Biographies: English Omnibus of the Sources for the Life of St. Francis* (Chicago, 1983), 225–609. On the ludic techniques of the early Franciscans, see C. Ginzburg, "Folklore, magia, religione," *Storia d'Italia* (Turin, 1972), I: 603–76.

22. Here I am following the account given by Bernal Díaz in his chronicle *The True History of the Things of New Spain.* For the text, see *New Iberian World: A Documentary History of the Discovery and Settlement of Latin America to the Early Seventeenth Century,* ed. John H. Parry and Robert G. Keith (New York, 1984), 3: 369. On Cortés's connections with the Observant Franciscans, see F. De Lejarza, O.F.M., "Franciscanismo de Cortés y cortesianismo de los franciscanos," *Misionalia Hispánica* (Madrid, 1948), 43–136.

23. The Twelve believed that they were playing out their providentially designated roles in a penultimate struggle with the Devil that would presage the

imminent end of postlapsarian time and space. This is manifest in the *Obediencia* and *Instrucción* given to Martin of Valencia by the Minister General of their order, Francisco de Los Angeles, upon their departure for Mexico. Observing that the world was now in its "eleventh hour," he summoned them to combat with the "ancient serpent" and assigned them the task of "snatching away from the maw of the dragon the souls ... deceived by satanic wiles, dwelling in the shadow of death, held in the vain cult of idols." Facsimiles of the Obediencia and the Instrucción are published in F. Ocaranza, *Capítulos de la historia franciscana*, 2d ser. (Mexico, 1934); the passage translated is on p. 492. On this complex subject, see Fernando Cervantes, *The Devil in the New World: The Impact of Diabolism in New Spain* (New Haven, 1994).

24. For translations of several indigenous accounts of the massacre, see M. Léon-Portilla, *The Broken Spears: The Aztec Account of the Conquest of Mexico* (Boston, 1962); the passage quoted is on 74–76.

25. Fray Juan de Torquemada, *Monarquía Indiana* (Seville, 1615), 15,13.31; the English translation is from M.E. Ravicz, *Early Colonial Religious Drama in Mexico: From Tzompantli to Golgotha* (Washington, DC, 1970), 31.

26. On theater in sixteenth-century Mexico see Ravicz, *Early Colonial Religious Drama*; José J. Rojas Garcidueñas, "El teatro franciscano en Méjico durante el siglo XVI," *Archivo Ibero-americano* 11 (1951): 129–89; Angel María Garibay Kintana, *Historia de la literatura nahuatl* (Mexico City, 1953–54) I: ch., 6; Othón Arróniz, *Teatro de evangelización en nueva españa* (México, 1979); Richard Trexler, "We Think, They Act: Clerical Readings of Missionary Theater in Sixteenth-Century New Spain," in *Understanding Popular Culture: Europe From The Middle Ages to The Nineteenth Century*, ed. Steven L. Kaplan (New York, 1984), 189–227; Louise M. Burkhart, *Holy Wednesday: A Nahua Drama from Early Colonial Mexico* (Philadelphia, 1996); on the *auto sacramentale*, see O.B. Hardison, *Christian Rite and Christian Drama in the Middle Ages* (Baltimore, 1965); R.B. Donovan, *The Liturgical Drama in Medieval Spain* (Toronto, 1958); K. Eisenbichler, *Crossing the Boundaries: Christian Piety and the Arts in Italian Medieval and Renaissance Confraternities* (Ann Arbor, 1991).

27. Diego Valadés, *Rhetorica Christiana* (Perugia, 1579), 95; for another description of this practice, see Fray Toribio Motolinía, *Historia de los indios de la Nueva España* (México, 1984), Trat. 2. cap. 6: "De cómo los indios se confiesan por figuras y carácteres y de lo que aconteció a dos mancebos indios en el artículo de la muerte," 95–96.

28. Valadés, *Rhetorica Christiana*, 95. The etching, entitled "Allegory of the Franciscan Mission in New Spain," shows one Franciscan teaching from a tapestry depicting Creation and another using a tapestry that depicts the instruments of the Passion of Christ. It is on page 207 of *Rhetorica Christiana*.

29. Both Carlo Ginzburg, "Folklore, magia, religione," 656–58 and Adriano Prosperi, "Otras Indias," 224, suggest that some of the techniques employed by Jesuits in Italy appear to have derived from those used by the mendicants in the New World. On the question of the "christianization" of Europe, see John Bossy, "The Counter-Reformation and the People of Catholic Europe," *Past and Present* 47 (May, 1970): 51–70; Jean Delumeau, *Catholicism between Luther and Voltaire: A New View of the Counter-Reformation*, introduction by John Bossy (London, 1977).

30. On monastic sign languages, see G. Van Rijnberk, *Le langage par signes chez les moines* (Amsterdam, 1953); *Monastic Sign Languages*, ed. Jean Umiker-Sebeok and Thomas A. Sebeok (Berlin, 1987).

31. On Testerian catechisms, see Narciso Sentenach, "Catecismos de la doctrina cristiana en jeroglíficos para la enseñanza de los indios Americanos," *Bibliotecas y Museos* (1900), 599–609; Donald Robertson, *Mexican Manuscript Painting of the Early Colonial Period: The Metropolitan Schools* (New Haven, 1959), ch. 3, "The Books of the Spanish World"; John N. Glass, "A Census of Middle American Testerian Manuscripts," in *Handbook of Middle American Indians*, vol. 14, pt. 3, *Guide to Ethnohistorical Sources* (Austin, 1975); Juan Guillermo Durán, *Monumenta catechetica hispanoamericana (Siglos XVI–XVIII)* (Buenos Aires, 1984), 67–186; Anne Whited Normann, *Testerian Codices: Hieroglyphic Catechisms for Native Conversion in New Spain* (Ann Arbor, 1985). Several facsimiles of Testerian catechisms have been published; see, for example, Miguel León-Portilla, *Un catecismo Náhuatl en imágenes* (México, 1979).
32. For a description of the problems and practices, see Motolinia, *Historia de los indios de la Nueva España*, trat. II, cap. 4, 86–90. For an English translation, see Francis Borgia Steck, *Motolinia's History of the Indians of New Spain* (Washington, DC, 1951), 184–91.
33. Valadés, *Rhetorica Christiana*, 90 (my interpolation in final sentence). For a discussion of the basic techniques and some of the applications of the *ars memorativa* in the European tradition, see Mary Carruthers, *The Book of Memory*: ch. 1,"Models for Memory" and ch. 3, "Elementary Memory Design." See also Frances Yates, *The Art of Memory* (Chicago, 1966); Lina Bolzoni, *La stanza della memoria* (Torino, 1995).
34. Valadés, *Rhetorica Christiana*, 93.
35. Ibid., 93–94 (my interpolation in second sentence).
36. Ibid., 94.
37. Ibid.
38. I discuss this transition in some detail in "Hieroglyphs of Conversion."
39. On Olmos's grammars and related works, see Georges Baudot, *Utopía e historia en México*, caps. 3–4; on the missionary grammars in general, see Normann A. McQuown, editor, *Handbook of Middle American Indians*, vol. 5, *Linguistics*, which includes Stanley Newman's important essay "Classical Nahuatl"; Arthur J.O. Anderson, Frances Berdan, and James Lockhart, *Beyond the Codices* (Berkeley, 1976); Frances Karttunen and James Lockhart, *Nahuatl in the Middle Years: Language Contact Phenomena in Texts of the Colonial Period* (Berkeley, 1976). The first grammar of Italian appeared in 1529, the first of French in 1550. Valla composed his great study of the Latin language, the *Elegantiae lingue latine*, in the 1440s. On the complex philological and exegetical work of this brilliant humanist, see Salvatore Camporeale, O.P., *Lorenzo Valla: Umanesimo e teologia* (Florence, 1972); Mariangela Regoliosi, *Nel cantiere del Valla: Elaborazione e montaggio delle "Elegantiae"* (Rome, 1993).
40. On Nebrija, see Marcel Bataillon, *Érasme et L'Espagne: Recherches sur l'histoire spirituelle du XVIe siècle* (Paris, 1937), 24–42; Francisco Rico, *Nebrija frente a los bárbaros: El canon de gramáticos nefastos en las polémicas del humanismo* (Salamanca, 1978); Antonio Quilis's introduction to his edition of Nebrija's *Gramática de la lengua Castellana* (Madrid, 1980).
41. On the Inquisition in Spain, see M. Bataillon, *Érasme et L'Espagne*, caps. 9–10; 13; Henry Kamen, *Inquisition and Society in Spain in the Sixteenth and Seventeenth Centuries* (Bloomington, 1985), especially ch. 5; Stephen Haliczer, ed., *Inquisition and Society in Early Modern Europe* (Totowa, 1987); William Monter, *Frontiers of Heresy: The Spanish Inquisition From the Basque Lands to Sicily* (Cambridge, England, 1990). On the Inquisition in the New World, see Richard

Greenleaf, *The Mexican Inquisition of the Sixteenth Century* (Albuquerque, 1969); Mary Elizabeth Perry and Anne J. Cruz, eds., *Cultural Encounters: The Impact of the Inquisition in Spain and the New World* (Berkeley, 1991). On the Nahuas' uses of the written form of their language and its relation to post-contact culture and society, see Lockhart, *The Nahuas After the Conquest*, esp. ch. 8, "Ways of Writing." An important study of the interpenetration of monastic and Nahua religion and ethics is Louise Burkhart, *The Slippery Earth: Nahua-Christian Moral Dialogue in Sixteenth-Century Mexico* (Tucson, 1989).

– Chapter 4 –

ICONIC DISCOURSE:
THE LANGUAGE OF IMAGES IN
SEVENTEENTH-CENTURY NEW FRANCE

☙❧

Margaret J. Leahey

IN THE OPENING MINUTES of the film *Black Robe*, we see a group of native people seated on the floor of a chapel in front of a ticking clock that has been placed before a tabernacle.[1] On the hour, the clock chimes and everyone murmurs with approval and wonder. One of the group turns to his companion and says, "'I told you. Captain Clock is alive. He speaks!'" His friend then turns to ask a priest, "What does he say?" The Jesuit answers, "It is time to go."

Anyone who has not read *The Jesuit Relations*, the reports from the seventeenth-century missions in Canada, may be forgiven for thinking that this scene is an invention of the screenwriter/novelist Brian Moore. It is not. The director has taken a bit of cinematic license (by placing the clock in front of the tabernacle, for example), but otherwise the scene appears very much as it does in the 1636 report of Jean de Brébeuf, S.J. (1593–1649): "The Hurons," he writes, think that the clock, which they call "captain of the day," is "some living thing, for they cannot imagine how it sounds of itself."[2] When it strikes, the Hurons say it is speaking. They "ask us about its food; they remain a whole hour, and sometimes several, in order to hear it speak."[3] Brébeuf adds that the Hurons have been told that when the clock strikes four, it is saying: "'Go out, go away that we may close the door.'"[4] He also notes that a few native people suspected the Jesuits of chicanery: "when [the clock] is going to strike, they look to see if we are all there and if some one has not hidden, in order to shake it."[5]

Reports of these sorts of encounters involving Jesuits, images, and native people occur with such great frequency in the *Relations* that we cannot afford to dismiss them. Even though the accounts may appear at first glance to offer only the Jesuits' interpretation of the events, a careful reading reveals a much more nuanced text. I will argue that the Canadian natives' responses to the Jesuits' images were highly complex, that their responses varied considerably and could involve the appropriation of the images for the Indians' own purposes.

An image, Hans Belding writes, "always participates in a dialogue with a recognizable form of reality."[6] A seventeenth-century French Jesuit's reality, however, was not necessarily congruent with a seventeenth-century Huron's. As a consequence, the dialogues that went on between the images and the viewers' respective "realities" were quite different, perhaps even mutually unintelligible. To understand how this was so, it is helpful to know what sorts of images the Jesuits presented to the Indians and how they were used.

Brébeuf's clock was but one of the many items in the Jesuit arsenal. The missionaries who took the Roman Catholic message to Canada followed the example of their Jesuit comrades in China, Japan, and Brazil, using precious cargo space to bring with them crosses, pictures, medals, emblems, statues, liturgical vestments, rosaries, bells and musical instruments, compasses, magnets, and other marvels.

These religious and secular objects were intended to persuade native people that the Europeans possessed superior knowledge, technology, and power, of course, but they were also to be used to introduce Indian people to what the Jesuits usually referred to as "our sacred mysteries." Beyond their propaganda and catechetical value, however, the objects served to help the missionaries learn the native languages in much the same way that twentieth-century language teachers use pictures and various objects: to elicit vocabulary, practice basic sentence structures, and make lessons more interesting.[7] More often than not, objects were expected to serve these three functions simultaneously.

Among the most important of all the items in their collection, the Jesuits thought, were pictures in the form of paintings and engravings. Persuaded that "fear is the forerunner of faith in these barbarous minds," Paul Le Jeune, S.J. (1591–1664), the head of the Jesuit mission in Canada, was especially eager to have images that depicted the Last Judgment.[8] The choice of this particular image is not surprising. Catholic Christendom in the seventeenth century, as Jean Delumeau writes, was characterized by a sense of the macabre.[9] The appeal of the macabre, he continues, "touched a large sector of the elite and left a deep imprint on the culture of the time."[10] At the heart of this "cultural melancholy," Delumeau says, is "the bitter certainty that humans are great sinners."[11] It is this deeply held conviction that drives the Jesuits' missionary efforts and explains their willingness to use every available means to save the Indians from perdition.

Le Jeune, moreover, thought that "heretics were very much in the wrong to condemn and to destroy representations, which have so good an effect."[12] Since "these sacred pictures are half the instruction that one is able to give the Savages," Le Jeune asked specifically for pictures to be painted for use in the missions that clearly depicted the sufferings of the damned: "three, four, or five demons tormenting one soul with different kinds of tortures—one applying to it the torch, another serpents, another pinching it with red-hot tongs, another holding it bound with chains."[13] Everything, he said, was to be very distinct, and rage and sadness should appear plainly in the face of the lost soul.[14]

Le Jeune's request did not go unheeded. We are told that on the baptismal day of one of the Jesuits' new converts, Tsiouendaentaha (renamed "Pierre"), the missionaries "exhibited an excellent representation of the judgment, where the damned are depicted—some with serpents and dragons tearing out their entrails, and the greater part with some kind of instrument of their punishment" (see Fig. 4.1).[15] Similar references appear throughout the reports and letters from the missions. In 1666, Claude Allouez, S.J. (1622–1689), described the decoration of a bark chapel he had established. He writes that he had "hung up in the Chapel various Pictures, as of Hell and of the universal Judgment, which furnish me themes for instruction well adapted to my Hearers."[16] Claude Dablon, S.J. (1619–1697), writes that Allouez had told him of showing the native people a "picture of the universal Judgment …[taking the] occasion to describe to them, in terms of their understanding, something of the happiness of the Saints and the torments of the damned."[17] "These poor people looked with wonder at this Picture," he continues, "having never seen anything like it, and [they] listened with an attention and silence full of respect—but with such eagerness that, not satisfied with the instructions given them through the day in public and in private … they assembled during the night, in crowds."[18] In a report

FIGURE 4.1 A redrawing by Margaret L. Bruns of an engraving of a "damned soul," by Pierre Landry. The original is in the Bibliothèque nationale, Paris. See Gagnon, *La conversion par l'image,* Plate 12.

for 1671–1672, yet another missionary, Louis André, S.J. (1631–1715), describes a picture he kept in his chapel representing the Last Judgment, "in the upper part of which the parents were glad to be shown the place that their baptized children would occupy; while below they saw, with horror, the torments suffered by the devil."[19] André adds that "their eagerness to come and to pray to God before these Pictures ... was such that many children used to come barefoot through the snow, over nearly a quarter of a league's distance."[20]

To enhance the power of the images, Jacques Bigot, S.J. (1651–1711), added music: "We have given here ... some Instructions on Hell by means of certain Mournful Songs, all that is best fitted ... to torment one damned."[21] Another Jesuit, Jean Pierron, S.J. (1631–1700), painted his own representations and even invented a card game, not only for catechetical purposes but also, he said, to learn more of the language while listening to native people talk about his pictures.[22] There is a remarkable description of Pierron's representation of the Last Judgment in a letter dated 1669 from Marie de l'Incarnation (1599–1672), an Ursuline nun at Quebec, to her son in France.[23] The painting, she writes, represents hell "full of demons so terrible (both in their faces and in the chastisements they are inflicting on the damned Savages) that it is impossible to look upon it without trembling. In it is depicted an old Iroquois woman, who is stopping up her ears so as not to hear a Jesuit [who] desires to instruct her."[24] The woman, she continues, is "surrounded by devils, who are hurling fire in her ears and tormenting her on other parts of her body."[25] Pierron, Mère Marie writes, had "represented the other vices by other suitable illustrations, accompanied by the devils that preside over these vices and torment those that have yielded to them during their lives."[26] The Ursuline notes that "All the Iroquois of this mission are so moved by them [Pierron's paintings] that they talk of nothing else in their councils.... These paintings are spoken of in the neighbouring nations, and the other missionaries wish to have their like."[27]

There was at least some attempt to accommodate the images to Huron tastes and preferences. Charles Garnier, S.J., for example, asked that the figures in representations sent from France not wear hats or have halos, that they have straight hair, and that men appear beardless and full face, not in profile.[28] Garnier was particularly interested in having a picture of a single damned soul, whose sufferings are clearly evident; too many people in the picture caused confusion.[29]

Apparently, paintings and engravings were sent to New France in fairly large quantities, since they not only hung in the Jesuits' chapels but also were distributed to Indian people. Some of these images were to be mounted in native dwellings as mnemonic devices to help the Indians remember what the Jesuits had told them (particularly, of course, the fate that awaited the sinner).[30] Others, however, were given to native men and women so that they could evangelize their own people.[31] For example, when the convert Tsiouendaentaha was given an image of Christ as Savior, Le Jeune tells us the Huron then "took the Picture and began to preach."[32] At the conclusion of his speech, Tsiouendaentaha is reported to have said, "'If we have to encounter any enemies on our return, let us raise this standard high and all cast our eyes upon it, and we shall be helped,'" and he asked the Jesuits to wrap the picture carefully, lest something happen to it.[33] Le Jeune tells of another Canadian native who, after he had been given a picture, told the story to others: "'Look,' said he, 'here is the picture of those who would not believe; see how they are bound in irons, how they are in flames, how mad with pain they are.'"[34]

Women, as well as men, were given catechetical responsibilities.[35] There is an account of a young woman, seventeen years old, who "so well remembered what [the missionary had said] about each picture of the Old and of the New Testament that she explains each one singly, without trouble and without confusion, as well as I could do—and even more intelligibly, in their manner."[36] The Jesuit adds that "I allowed her to take away each picture after I had explained it in public, to refresh her memory in private. But she frequently repeated to me, on the spot, all that I had said about each picture."[37] The young woman, he continues, "not only ... [explained] them at home to her husband, to her father, to her mother, and to all the girls who went there—as she continues to do, speaking of nothing but the pictures of the catechism—but she also explained the Biblical illustrations to the old and the young men whom her father assembled in his dwelling."[38]

The Jesuits described the images in such detail that art historian François-Marc Gagnon has been able to identify some of the works they probably used.[39] These representations, especially of the Last Judgment and the Crucifixion, were seen by hundreds of Indian people. Some were viewed in the mission chapels where there was some control over what was said about them, but others were carried far beyond the missionaries' hearing.

Le Jeune believed that these pictures "speak for themselves."[40] *What* they said, however, is more problematic. What sort of "iconic discourse" went on?[41] The Jesuits clearly expected native people viewing Last Judgment images to have no difficulty connecting what they saw with their own experience: for example, with torture at the hands of their enemies. Bigot writes that "The most natural picture that I place before their eyes, to make them fear the flames of hell, is [one] representing fire in which their enemy, the Iroquois, is burning them....I add that these torments are nothing in comparison with those of hell."[42]

Do we know—or can we know—what sort of interior dialogue went on in the mind of a Huron woman when she looked at, let us say, a picture of the Last Judgment? We can be fairly sure that the viewer "mentally places what [s]he sees in a ... context of memory."[43] What constituted a Huron "context of memory," however, is more elusive. Although it is true, as Ruth B. Phillips has argued, that there is not a sufficient body of documented Huron objects to "analyse a Huron visual system,"[44] we can be fairly sure that it did not have a great deal in common with that of a French Jesuit.

Moreover, the explanations that the Jesuits gave of the paintings may well have been utterly unintelligible to the indigenous viewer.

The Jesuits' linguistic achievements have been looked upon in a much more favorable light since the publication of the late Victor Hanzeli's *Missionary Linguistics in New France: A Study of Seventeenth- and Eighteenth-Century Descriptions of American Indian Languages* in 1969.[45] James Axtell, in *The Invasion Within: The Context of Cultures in Colonial North America*, for example, describes the Jesuits as "armed with a *native tongue.*"[46] Comparing the English and French Jesuits' experiences, Axtell, one of the most influential American historians of this period, writes that "the English [Jesuits] never became fluent in the native language or lived in native villages long enough to be adopted, given Indian names, or accepted as men of sense. Their French brothers did, and reaped a rich harvest of souls as a result."[47]

Hanzeli, however, does not argue that the Jesuits had achieved a high level of mastery but, rather, something much more modest: the missionaries had discovered a good deal more about the thorny syntax and morphology of the Indian languages than previous historians of linguistics had thought.[48] While the Jesuits' dedication, perseverance, and ingenuity are remarkable, it is very unlikely that the early missionaries were able to speak fluent Huron, Montagnais, Micmac, or any of the other languages of New France after only a few months or even a few years in the country.[49] The structures of the languages are utterly unlike any with which the Jesuits were familiar, and although Brébeuf did discover what he called the "clef du secret" of the Indian languages (their polysynthetic or incorporating feature), a significant breakthrough, that discovery was just the beginning. The missionaries themselves constantly alluded to their continuing difficulties.

The Jesuits make frequent mention of sharing their "most sacred mysteries" with Indian people, but it is difficult to imagine that these mysteries were understood in the way the Jesuits intended, if only because the missionaries were forced to invent words. Paul Le Jeune, for example, writes that he "coin[ed] words approximating to their language, which I made them understand."[50] It is very difficult to imagine, however, that "understanding" could have been substantial. As the missionaries discovered more about how the languages worked, they were able to put the invented words into something like the correct grammatical form; but these inventions must have sounded very curious indeed to native speakers, even to those who had been baptized and lived in Christian communities.

It is not surprising, therefore, that once European diseases began to ravage native populations and traditional medicine seemed powerless, there was a very perceptible negative shift in many Indians' attitudes toward the missionaries' pictures, rituals, and gadgetry. All of the Jesuits' innovations, including writing, became suspect.[51]

Desperate for an explanation as they watched their children, spouses, friends, and neighbors sicken and die, native people faulted the statues, the clocks, the windsock, the consecrated bread in the tabernacle, holy water, and even the Jesuits' posture at prayer. Le Mercier reports that after the Jesuits placed two pictures (one of Christ, one of Mary) on the altar in a Huron village, angry people from other villages insisted that the images were the source of illness and death. "In a few days," he writes, "the country was completely imbued with this opinion, that we were, without any doubt, the authors of this so universal contagion."[52] In fact, the intense anxiety about the nature of the images gave rise to one of the *Relations'* few reports of how native people interpreted what they saw in the Last Judgment images. Le Mercier says that "some persuaded themselves that this multitude of men [the damned], desperate and heaped one upon the other, were all those we had caused to die during the Winter; that these flames represented the heats of this pestilential fever, and these dragons and serpents, the venomous beasts that we had made use of in order to poison them."[53] Some of the images and other wonders had to be put away. Le Mercier writes in the 1638 report that "our clock was no longer visible, for they believed it to be the Demon of death, and our illuminated pictures represented to them nothing more than what was happening to their people."[54]

Even in these grim circumstances, some native people had more complicated psychological responses to the images. Le Mercier, for example, writes this account of a woman who visited the Jesuits' cabins:

> She was wonderfully surprised at the entrance of our cabin; she remained there for some time, without daring to advance and cross the threshold. It was amusing to see her in the struggle, for, on the one hand, she felt herself powerfully attracted by the novelty of this object; and, on the other, her fear, lest in approaching nearer our pictures, she would be immediately attacked by the disease, made her draw back.[55]

Le Mercier continues: "After a hard struggle, curiosity got the better of it. 'There is no help for it ... I must venture, I must see, even though it costs me my life.'"[56]

For some viewers, the "Indianization" of the European images may well have been accelerated by the fact that the Jesuits encouraged Christian converts to mix traditional native practices with the new rituals.[57] For example, neophytes continued to bring gifts to the images in the chapel; but instead of tobacco, they offered wampum beads. One Jesuit writes that his Huron congregation had "adopted a pious practice of making a little present every Sunday to the Virgin, each one giving a porcelain bead for each rosary recited during the previous week."[58] Some Jesuits actually allowed the continued use of tobacco offerings. There is even an account of a woman throwing tobacco on a crucifix. The missionary writer hastens to explain that "her intention [was] the same as that of those who kiss it devoutly,"[59] but it is more likely that the woman was following the native custom of using tobacco to propitiate forces in the spirit world.[60] The use of tobacco is especially significant because tobacco is closely linked to a powerful element in the spirituality of Northeastern Indian people: the dream. Tobacco and dreams "provided avenues to spiritual power," inducing a "state of mind that opened one to supernatural forces."[61] Brébeuf, for his part, gives a fairly benign account of the significance of tobacco. The Hurons, he says, believed that tobacco smoke gave them "intelligence and enable[d] them to see clearly through the most intricate matters."[62]

Dreams, however, were much more dangerous. The Jesuits repeatedly inveighed against the native people's attachment to dreams, which the missionaries thought had diabolical origins.[63] To Brébeuf, it seemed that the dream was "the oracle that all these poor Peoples consult and listen to … the usual Physician in their sicknesses, the Esculapius and Galen of the whole Country—the most absolute master they have."[64] The dream, he adds, "does everything and is in truth the principal God of the Hurons," an observation that he assures the reader is not an exaggeration, but rather a statement of fact based on "the experience of five years, during which I have been studying the manners and usages of our Savages."[65] The dreams are related to "a feast, or to a song, or to a dance, or to a game—or, lastly, to a certain kind of mania that they in fact call *Ononharoia*," which he translates as "turning the world upside down."[66]

It is not surprising, then, that at a time when the Indian people were surrounded by illness and death, the intersection of dreams, tobacco, and images (traditional and European) became more powerful and complex. The Hurons, for example, had a long tradition of rituals associated with curing sickness. Le Mercier writes that when the village of Ossossané was particularly hard hit by disease, a shaman, Tonneraouanont (whom he describes as a "little hunchback, extremely misshapen"), "began to sing, and the others sang after him.... After much singing, he asked for some tobacco which he threw upon these red-hot stones while addressing the devil."[67] On another occasion, Le Mercier writes, the Hurons "donned their masks and danced, to drive away the disease."[68] There is also an account of a Huron ritual dance performed for a sick man in which all of the dancers were "disguised as hunchbacks, with wooden masks, which were altogether ridiculous."[69] Le Mercier adds that "at the end of the dance, at the command of the sorcerer *Tsondacoune* all these masks were hung at the end of poles and placed over every cabin ... to frighten the malady."[70]

Brébeuf, writing about a ceremony he had observed, tells his readers: "you would have seen some with a sack on the head, pierced only for the eyes; others were stuffed with straw around the middle, to imitate a pregnant woman."[71] Some of those participating in the ceremony were "naked as the hand, with bodies whitened, and faces as black as Devils, and feathers or horns on the heads; others were smeared with red, black, and white ... each adorned himself as extravagantly as he could, to dance this Ballet, and contribute something to the health of the sick man."[72]

It should be noted that there are some curious silences in the Jesuit accounts of healing rituals. The Recollet lay brother Gabriel Sagard has left more graphic accounts of Huron healing ceremony behavior. In one case, he describes a ceremony during which a young man urinated into the mouth of a sick woman, "in order to carry out without any omission a dream she had had"; this is a feature of the dance that he says he "cannot excuse or pass over silent."[73] Sagard also observed another ceremony that involved young men and women having sexual relations in the presence of a sick woman, "either at her request, according to an imagination or dream she may have had, or by order of the Oki [powerful spirits] for her health and recovery."[74] Sagard notes that "they pass the whole night thus, while the two chiefs at the two ends of the house sing and rattle their tortoise-shells from evening till the following morning, when the ceremony is concluded."[75] The ritual, he adds, is "such a damnable and wicked ceremony."[76] If Brébeuf or Le Mercier or any of the other Jesuits witnessed such behavior in connection with the Huron ceremonies, they did not record it in their reports from the missions. They surely knew, however, that the rituals could involve sexual activity, which probably helps to explain the missionaries' antipathy toward the curing societies and their ceremonies.

Masks were a key element in the healing ceremonies, as we have seen. According to scholars who have studied Iroquoian masks, a significant change took place in the appearance of the masks: sometime after the middle of the seventeenth century, smooth-faced masks were replaced by distorted ones.[77] This is also a time when a large number of Hurons were adopted by other Iroquoian people, many of whom practiced the ritualized behavior associated with the curing ceremonies, but without the masks.[78] George Hamell has argued that as smallpox and other diseases took their toll among Iroquoian people, and their traditional medicine failed, they increasingly perceived supernatural beings as grotesque.[79] The changing perception is an aspect of the "broader pattern of psychological dislocations following European contact," Hamell says, and the "trauma is mirrored in the art of the carvers in the shift in style from naturalistic to grotesque forms."[80]

Since the grotesque masks appear at precisely the time when the Jesuits were most active among the Huron, it seems more likely that the inspiration for the change was related to the Hurons' experience of seeing the faces of the damned depicted in the Jesuits' macabre paintings and engravings of the Last Judgment. These images were widely distributed among native people in the mid-seventeenth century; and while the Jesuits believed that their listeners had understood their explanations of what the images represented, there is little evidence that this was the case; the dialogue between the images and a "recognizable form of [Huron] reality" would necessarily produce a very different understanding. It is much more likely that the twisted, distorted, gaping-mouthed faces of the damned of the Last Judgment appeared in a Huron's dream or a tobacco-induced vision, and that he or she then carved (or had carved) a grotesque wooden mask (see Fig. 4.2).[81] We know that the Iroquois False Faces of the nineteenth century were a response to disease (smallpox, cholera, and influenza).[82] It is certainly reasonable to conclude that in the mid-seventeenth century, contorted images were deliberately incorporated into Iroquoian curing society rituals in a desperate effort to counter the supposed effects of the Jesuits' images and/or to appropriate the power of European medicine into their own ceremonies.

FIGURE 4.2 The Six Nations Iroquois Confederacy has issued a policy statement on False Face masks that restricts their reproduction. In compliance with this policy, and out of respect for Iroquoian traditions, the artist, Margaret Bruns, has produced a drawing that represents only the basic lines of an eighteenth-century mask. See Fenton, *The False Faces of the Iroquois* (Norman, 1987), 42. Plate 2-9.

Notes

1. *Black Robe*, produced by Robert Lantos, Stephane Reichel, and Sue Milliken, directed by Bruce Beresford. Vidmark, Inc., 1992. Videocassette.
2. Reuben Gold Thwaites, ed. *The Jesuit Relations and Allied Documents*, 73 vols. (Cleveland, 1896–1901), 8:111. The English is the Thwaites translation unless the words appear in brackets.
3. Ibid.
4. Ibid., 113.
5. Ibid., 111.
6. Hans Belding, *The End of the History of Art?* trans. Christopher S. Wood (Chicago, 1987), 26.
7. For a more detailed description of how the Jesuits went about learning the indigenous languages, see my article "'Comment peut un muet prescher l'évangile?' Jesuit Missionaries and the Native Languages of New France," *French Historical Studies* 19, no.1 (Spring 1995): 105–32.
8. Thwaites, *Jesuit Relations*, 11:89.
9. *Sin and Fear: The Emergence of a Western Guilt Culture 13th-18th Centuries*, trans. Eric Nicholson (New York, 1990; 1983), 356.
10. Ibid., 189.
11. Ibid.; Delumeau notes (p. 59) that a "total of 20 Jesuit titles on death appeared between 1540 and 1620, as opposed to 139 titles between 1621 and 1700, and 101 from 1701 to 1800."
12. Thwaites, *Jesuit Relations*, 11:89. Le Jeune himself was a former "heretic." Brought up a Huguenot, he converted to Roman Catholicism at the age of sixteen and joined the Jesuit order six years later.
13. Ibid. This is an era, Delumeau writes, of "slicings, flayings, burnings, [and] tortures with red-hot pincers;" *Sin and Fear*, 242–43.
14. Thwaites, *Jesuit Relations*, 11:89. Michel de Nobletz, S.J., whose work the Canadian Jesuits knew (see, e.g., Thwaites, *Jesuit Relations*, 62:173), had commissioned a number of large paintings on lambskin to be used in catechizing Breton peasants. A number of the 2' x 3' paintings, including a *carte du Jugement*, survive and may be seen at the bishop's palace in Quimper, Brittany. The Breton *Last Judgment*, executed in 1636 by a marine cartographer named Allain Lestobec, depicts, among other things, a fairly benign dragon and a blazing cauldron representing hell. This particular *carte* is not fearsome enough to have been a model for the pictures Le Jeune requested.
15. Thwaites, *Jesuit Relations*, 14:103.
16. Ibid., 50:299.
17. Ibid., 55:201.
18. Ibid., 55:201–203.
19. Ibid., 56:135.
20. Ibid.
21. Ibid., 63:66–67. Bigot wrote his songs for the Algonquian Ottawa, but such songs may well have been written for Iroquoian people, too. It is interesting to note that in Iroquoian society, "those possessed of great supernatural power were also known as divine chanters…the Iroquoian root for 'power' is the same as that for 'song;'" Dean R. Snow, *The Iroquois* (Oxford, 1994–96), 101.
22. "I learn much of the language through the medium of these Pictures." Thwaites, *Jesuit Relations*, 52:118–19. See also Leahey, "'Comment peut un muet prescher l'évangile?'" 123.

23. Marie Guyart was born in Tours. Married at seventeen, a mother at eighteen, and a widow at nineteen, she entered the Ursuline order in 1633. Inspired by a dream of Canada, she went to Quebec in 1639 (a response that native people would have understood), establishing the Ursuline order in New France. She maintained a lengthy correspondence with her son, Claude, and her letters are full of wonderfully insightful commentary on New France. See Marie-Emmanuel Chabot, O.S.U., "Marie Guyart," in *Dictionary of Canadian Biography* (Toronto, 1981), 1:351–59. See also Anya Mali's recent study, *Mystic in the New World: Marie de l'Incarnation (1599–1672)* (Leiden, 1996).
24. *Word from New France: The Selected Letters of Marie de l'Incarnation*, trans. and ed. Joyce Marshall (Toronto, 1967), 352.
25. Ibid.
26. Ibid.
27. Ibid.
28. François-Marc Gagnon, *La Conversion par l'image: un aspect de la mission des Jésuites auprès des Indiens au Canada au XVIIe siècle* (Montreal, 1975), 45.
29. Ibid. It is true, as Gagnon says, that the "confusion" occurred in a catechetical context, but multiple representations also complicated the images' language-learning function. Jean Cousin's *Le Jugement dernier*, with bodies of those being judged heaped upon one another, is a good example of an image that is "too confused" to be useful in catechesis (or language learning, either); see Gagnon, *La Conversion par l'image*, plate 2.
30. Thwaites, *Jesuit Relations*, 65:80–81. Gagnon says that in the *Relations* the word *image* can be used to mean painting, statue, or engraving, and it is not always clear from the context which is intended; however, the representation is very similar, he says, from one medium to another; *La Conversion par l'image*, 124.
31. The Jesuits made extensive use of native catechists (*dogiques*), who "offer public prayers, and hold divine service, as strictly as if they were in their Church; they instruct and baptize, with much satisfaction and edification, in times of danger;" Thwaites, *Jesuit Relations*, 27:67.
32. Ibid., 12:253.
33. Ibid. In passages such as these, it is always difficult to know whether the event really occurred or has been invented by the writer to edify devout French readers.
34. Ibid., 11:89.
35. The Jesuits' attitudes toward women are not easily categorized. Karen Anderson's *Chain Her By One Foot: The Subjugation of Women in Seventeenth-Century New France* (London, 1991) does not represent the complexities and ambiguities of individual Jesuits' behavior toward women. In Canada, the members of the religious order founded by Ignatius of Loyola (1491–1556) often exhibit their founder's notorious misogyny. However, we also see the same "wealth, diversity, and subtlety" in their relationships with women that Jean Lacouture suggests was characteristic of Loyola. See *Jesuits: A Multibiography*, trans. Jeremy Leggett (Washington, 1995; Paris, 1991 and 1992), 137.
36. Thwaites, *Jesuit Relations*, 64:229.
37. Ibid.
38. Ibid.
39. François-Marc Gagnon, *La Conversion par l'image*, Plates 1–5, 9–15, 17–18. Works commissioned for the missions or executed by the Jesuits in the field do not appear to have survived.
40. Thwaites, *Jesuit Relations*, 5:259.

41. Michel de Certeau uses the term "iconic discourse" in an essay on the Jesuit proto-anthropologist Joseph François Lafitau's two-volume *Customs of the American Indians Compared with the Customs of Primitive Times* (1724). See "Writing vs. Time: History and Anthropology in the Works of Lafitau," trans. James Hovde, *Yale French Studies* 59 (1980): 37–64. Lafitau's work contains forty-two carefully chosen plates, and these plates, De Certeau writes (p. 40), "form an iconic discourse which traverses, from one section to another, the mass of the written discourse."

42. Thwaites, *Jesuit Relations*, 62:135.

43. Moshe Barasch, "Visual Syncretism: A Case Study," in *The Translatability of Cultures: Figurations of the Space Between*, ed. Sanford Budick and Wolfgang Iser (Stanford, 1996), 53.

44. "What is 'Huron Art'? Native American Art and the New Art History," *The Canadian Journal of Native Studies* 9, no. 2 (1989): 165.

45. Victor Hanzeli, *Missionary Linguistics in New France: A Study of Seventeenth- and Eighteenth-Century Descriptions of American Indian Languages* (The Hague, 1969). In 1984 Hanzeli published an article entitled "De la Connaissance des langues indiennes de la Nouvelle France aux dix-septième siècles;" it was a reprise of his book, in a special issue of *Amerindia: Revue d'ethnolinguistique américaine*, 209–25.

46. James Axtell, *The Invasion Within: The Context of Cultures in Colonial North America* (New York, 1985), 90; my emphasis.

47. "White Legend: The Jesuit Missions in Maryland," in Axtell, *After Columbus: Essays in the Ethnohistory of Colonial North America* (New York, 1988), 85.

48. Most scholars, Hanzeli writes, "in making their often tangential and undocumented comments upon the linguistic labors of the early missionaries, simply repeated the critical commonplaces which have customarily been directed against all pre-nineteenth-century linguistics efforts." *Missionary Linguistics in New France*, 16.

49. There were some situations in which the Jesuits' knowledge of vocabulary and basic syntax was probably adequate or even fairly proficient, but it is not possible to attain anything like native fluency in so short a time. My own interest in the Jesuits' study of the native languages began in 1978 when I encountered both the *Relations* and Hanzeli's book shortly after completing two years of teaching English as second language. When I read the Jesuits' accounts of their language experiences, I was struck by the sophistication of the missionaries' approach to language acquisition. The Jesuits used virtually every strategy (excluding technological ones, of course) familiar to present-day language teachers and their students: native informants, immersion, language partners, games, pictures, and songs, as well as phrase books, grammars, and dictionaries.

50. Thwaites, *Jesuit Relations*, 5:187.

51. A Huron once told the Jesuits that "Since you have described our country, our rivers, our lands, and our woods, we are all dying, which did not happen until you came here." Ibid., 9:207.

52. Ibid., 15:19.

53. Ibid., 14:103.

54. Ibid., 15:35.

55. Ibid., 14:97.

56. Ibid. Some Jesuits persisted in viewing native men and women as childlike and amusingly naïve.

57. Jesuit missionaries in other parts of the world, particularly in China (the Chinese Rites controversy) and South Asia (the Malabar Rites controversy), were accused by rival missionaries of permitting their converts to continue "pagan" practices (ancestor worship and the caste system, respectively).
58. Thwaites, *Jesuit Relations*, 41:165.
59. Ibid., 55:223.
60. This use of tobacco is discussed in Daniel Richter's *The Ordeal of the Longhouse: The Peoples of the Iroquois League in the Era of European Colonization* (Chapel Hill, 1992), 28.
61. Ibid.
62. Thwaites, *Jesuit Relations*, 10:219.
63. Ibid., 42:147. One Jesuit wrote that dreams "constitute the God and the great Master of those peoples;" Ibid., 53:281; see also 57:275. As Richter has observed, "probably no European before Freud could have begun to understand the psychological functions involved with these phenomena [dreams], and the Jesuits were at a loss to deal with them." *The Ordeal of the Longhouse*, 110.
64. Thwaites, *Jesuit Relations*, 10:169.
65. Ibid., 171.
66. Ibid., 175. Ononharoia, the Hurons' main winter festival, Bruce Trigger says, "belongs to the general category of soul-curing rituals;" during the three-day celebration, "people who felt ill dreamed of objects, then went about the village propounding riddles and seeking to find someone who could guess what these objects were and give them to them;" *The Children of Aataentsic*, 83.
67. Thwaites, *Jesuit Relations*, 13:131, 203.
68. Ibid., 175.
69. Ibid., 263.
70. Ibid.
71. Ibid., 10:203. William Fenton says that when he read Brébeuf's account to his Seneca mentors, "they immediately equated the name *Tsondacuané* with their own term for the individual who sponsors a medicine feast: *godɛsyoni*, 'she sponsors the ritual'; *sadɛsyoni*, 'you sponsor.'" The Huron form, he adds, may be the third person singular masculine. See *The False Faces of the Iroquois* (Norman, 1987), 74.
72. Thwaites, *Jesuit Relations*, 10:203. Some years ago, Marius Barbeau argued that the Huron-Iroquois masking was borrowed from the French carnival, but subsequent research has demonstrated that in fact there are few references to carnival in Quebec in the seventeenth century. See Fenton, *The False Faces of the Iroquois*, 499. Fenton here is relying on a paper by M. W. Walsh, "The Condemnation of Carnival in the Jesuit Relations," *Michigan Academician: Papers of the Michigan Academy of Science, Arts, and Letters*, 25, no.1 (1982): 13–26.
73. *Sagard's Long Journey to the Country of the Hurons*, originally published as Champlain Society Publication XXV, ed. George M. Wrong, trans. H.H. Langton (New York, 1968; Toronto, 1930), 118.
74. Ibid., 120.
75. Ibid.
76. Ibid.
77. Fenton, *The False Faces of the Iroquois*, 71. Snow notes that although there are masks on Iroquoian ceramic pipes dating back at least to the fifteenth century, the pipes "do not depict medicine masks with noses and mouths askew." Snow, *The Iroquois*, 105.

78. Fenton, *The False Faces of the Iroquois*, 72–73. Fenton and others have hypothesized that masks "may have been brought to the Iroquois by Huron captives late in the seventeenth century;" although the non-Huron Iroquoians had curing ceremonies similar to those of the Hurons, contemporary observers do not mention masks before 1650. Ibid., 75.
79. Ibid., 71.
80. Ibid., 72.
81. Amelia M. Trevelyan notes that "bursts of artistic and ritual activity developed in response to cultural crises." See "Continuity of Form and Function in the Art of the Eastern Woodlands," *The Canadian Journal of Native Studies*, 9, no. 2 (1989): 196.
82. Fenton, *The False Faces of the Iroquois*, 78.

– *Chapter 5* –

Mapping after the Letter: Graphology and Indigenous Cartography in New Spain

ⵛⵛ

Dana Leibsohn

IN THE WANING DECADES of the sixteenth century, the mapping of local territory continually brought indigenous and Spanish subjects face to face in New Spain. Among the remnants of these interactions are a corpus of hand-painted cartographs and thousands of pages of alphabetic text that document many of these cross-cultural negotiations. Indeed, by 1570 *merced*, or land grant, maps often displayed both images and alphabetic writings—some produced by native painters, others by Spanish officials. Typically Amerindian mapmakers rendered the territory of New Spain by way of pictorial and glyphic signs to which Spanish bureaucrats added explication and authentication in alphabetic script. This practice betrays, at least on the surface, a forthright colonial arrangement. As indigenous lands increasingly were managed by legal practices instituted and controlled by Europeans, the language and labor of representation felt the yoke of colonial rule and its cultural hierarchies. A map of Coatlinchan and its environs painted in 1579 offers an example (Fig. 5.1). One of hundreds of merced maps fashioned in New Spain, this document responds to a petition filed by a Spanish settler seeking rights to a parcel of land near an indigenous town. As part of the formal inquiry, an Amerindian painter fashioned an image of the site and its environs. Officials then viewed the scene and attested to its validity by penning their own words in black ink

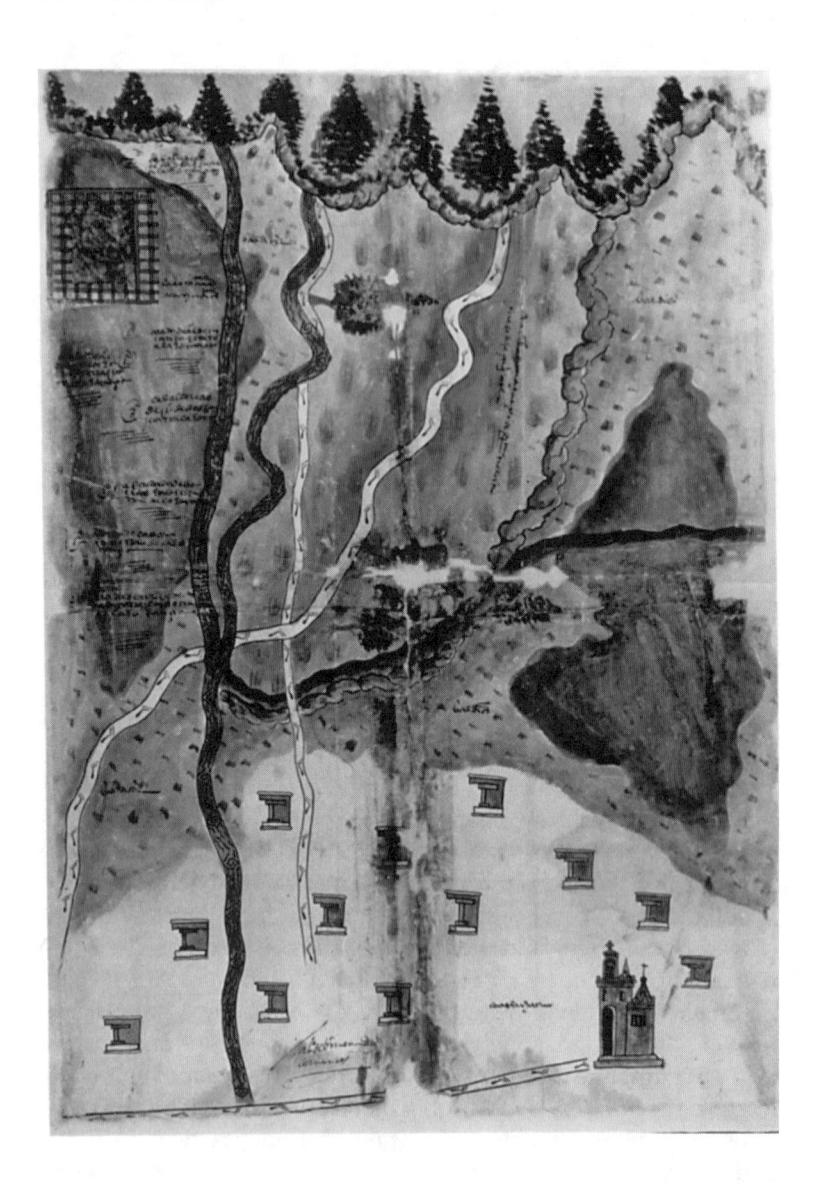

FIGURE 5.1 Map of Coatlinchan (Texcoco, Mexico), painted in 1579 for a merced of two caballerías de tierra. A church and scatter of pre-Hispanic-style houses toward the bottom of the painting identify the town of Coatlinchan. The surrounding region includes a forest, rocky outcroppings, a branching river, and, along the upper left edge of the map, land already under cultivation. Size of original: 60 x 42 cm (AGN #1678, Tierras, vol. 2688, exp. 35, fc. 373; reproduced with permission from the Archivo General de la Nación, Mexico City).

across the map. The result: a binding document of image and text forged by both indigenous and Spanish hands.[1]

While modern eyes might find this visual description of Coatlinchan stinting in mimetic detail and marked by a certain lack of visual abundance, in sixteenth-century New Spain the cartograph served its purposes well. On one hand, the map allowed its readers to scrutinize a specific slice of topography; yet it also registered, in durable form, traces of verbal exchange about, and movements across, this region. This compositing of functions was fundamental to the map's efficacy. Through picture and alphabet, merced maps documented the lay of particular lands as well as the vestiges of bureaucratic rites and negotiations that lent territory an officially acceptable form. Consequently these cartographs never served only as visual evocations of New Spanish landscapes. Merced maps took on meaning as material records of cross-cultural transactions—transactions carried out through travel, speech, writing, and painting. The merced process always embedded maps in a larger reservoir of writing and legal documentation that both engendered and hampered their potency. In this the cartographs share much with property documents crafted throughout the early-modern and modern worlds. Yet if we are serious about cross-cultural transit, as well as the meaning assigned to languages in the Americas, the idiosyncrasies of merced maps warrant sustained attention. For today these cartographs represent the most common surviving record from early colonial Latin America consistently capturing—albeit in a mediated way—the engagement of Amerindians and Spaniards in both visual and textual form. It is, then, the visuality and language of this engagement that anchors this essay.

In the following pages I use merced maps of the late-sixteenth and early-seventeenth centuries as a case study in colonial representation and argue two points. First, I claim that the visual aspects of alphabetic writing and pictorial imagery were no less significant—and at times, were more significant—than the iconographic or overtly denotative meanings of images and their texts. Put simply, although distinct in their signifying strategies and legal applications, pictures and writing at times suffered similar fates due to their physical properties. The materiality of ink and paper, the corporeal logic of document inscription and painting, and colonial rites of reading and verifying legal records all shaped the ways in which image and text took on meaning in New Spain. Second, I argue against an interpretive tradition that privileges the logic and clarity of historical documentation. Thus my conviction: unless we attend to signifying acts that appear inadvertent—or quasi-intentional—

we reduce archival documents unjustly. As material forms that elicit colonial landscapes, both literally and metaphorically, scripted word and painted picture worked effectively and auspiciously on merced maps. But not on every occasion. Therefore it is to both the efficacy and decrepitude of drawing and writing that I turn. My aim is to identify where "noise" operates at the interface of two systems. If this interference appears coincidental (and hence is easily dismissed as a mistake or lapse of expertise), it nevertheless turns out to be crucial to, and characteristic of, colonial practice.

Others have addressed the postconquest relations between pictorial images and alphabetic texts, both eloquently and in detail. In fact transformations of pre-Hispanic and indigenous expression wrought by the introduction of alphabetic writing have formed a prominent trope in recent analyses of the early colonial period in Mexico.[2] My objective here, however, differs from that of my predecessors. Although changes in the status of image-making after the Spanish conquest are important, I believe the topic offers little insight into how, or why, a document like the map of Coatlinchan presented a convincing image of local territory to sixteenth-century viewers, let alone to those of us who see it today. So the focus of this essay is neither the ascendancy of alphabetic script nor the tenacity of pre-Hispanic modes of expression. Rather my concern is the visual economy of graphic marks as it percolates through territorial constructions and colonial politics. Because land (as a valued commodity) and its management (as a lucre-driven system of claims) were the stakes in this game, the written and painted signs on merced maps carry considerable weight. Moreover, in the sixteenth century maps operated—and they operate today—complexly, as simulacra of a lived world. Consequently, the pictures and words of merced maps are well anchored in the operations and consequences of colonial life. Yet the rapprochement between cartographic image and alphabet has implications that extend beyond the edges of any single mapped page. Ultimately, then, this essay seeks to explore how the material and visual forms of written language circulate across cultural boundaries to both sustain and impede our construals of the past.

The Lineaments of Cartographic Claims

In New Spain between 1550 and 1630, maps were implicated in a labyrinth of social processes. By far the greatest numbers were created to aid in the administration of colonial lands and to serve those who dwelt upon them. Officials often commissioned maps that, in conjunction with oral and written testimony, buttressed entreaties for grants of land for ranching and wheat cultivation. Maps also figured in local conflicts over boundaries, in moves to resettle indigenous communities known as *congregaciones*, and in responses to royal investigations such as those of the Relaciones Geográficas. Still quantities of maps never crossed the threshold of Spanish attention; produced by indigenous painters for use within their own spheres of influence, these cartographs fulfilled local, familial, and intracommunal needs. Many of these paintings take the form of cartographic histories, a mode of representation that intertwined sites in the landscape, such as boundary markers, with auspicious tableaux from the past. Also surviving from the sixteenth century are cadastral maps and paintings that charted, in a census-like manner, the distribution of people and communities in particular regions. The historical situation, then, shows Spanish and Amerindian mapmakers lending order to the territory and affairs of daily life by applying color and ink to paper.[3] Indeed, the social heterogeneity of map patrons, along with the sheer number of surviving maps, underscores how in early colonial New Spain indigenous people and Spaniards alike relied upon—in fact grew attached to—the rhetorical clout of land charts.

Of all the maps surviving from this historical milieu, merced maps are by far the most prevalent.[4] Within a generation after the Spanish conquest, Antonio de Mendoza, the first viceroy of New Spain, began offering mercedes for cattle or sheep ranches as well as for the raising of crops. The amount of land given in merced depended upon a number of factors: the location of the grant, the nature of the terrain, the primary intended use of the land (i.e., grazing or cultivation), the proximity and density of indigenous settlements, and the political and economic status of the petitioner. As with many colonial practices, mercedes did not affect indigenous people or their access to natural resources to the same degree in all regions of New Spain. Some areas were far more frequently parceled than others, and opposition to grants varied with the occasion. Moreover, those who profited from land grants include men and women of Mesoamerican as well as those of European descent, although the number of petitions awarded to Spanish men outstripped those awarded to either Spanish women or indigenous people (or communities).[5]

Between 1550 and 1600 the merced process became a well-rehearsed bureaucratic rite. A typical example comes from a 1588 request by one Francisco Vásquez Coronado, who filed a petition with the *Audiencia* requesting rights to a parcel of land near the indigenous town of Atlatlauca, today in the state of Mexico. The Audiencia offered a stock response: soon after receiving the request it passed it to local officials with instructions to conduct an investigation. This inquiry required a visit to the proposed site to record its location, size, and current condition. Public announcements of the pending grant were read aloud in nearby indigenous communities, and testimony on the parcel's history was gathered from ten witnesses. Officials registered their findings in written, documentary form; as if to seal the affair, they commissioned a map depicting the site under petition, the nearest towns, and regional landmarks (Fig. 5.2). This cartographic artifact was filed at the bottom of the dossier before the papers were sent back to the Audiencia for final approval, which was conferred not long thereafter.[6]

In the sixteenth century, merced maps and papers rarely saw publication, nor did they leave New Spain to pass before royal or other European eyes. These records and cartographs were parochial in circulation, delineating land and its possessors for the inhabitants of New Spain. Unfortunately, the social practice of fashioning merced maps is not yet well understood. Written records associated with mercedes indicate that Spaniards as well as indigenous people were employed as mapmakers. The few names that are now known are all male, and scribal traditions in New Spain (both as introduced from Europe and as practiced in pre-Hispanic times) suggest that most indigenous map painters were, in fact, men. Yet the gender exclusivity of mapmaking is not sure, and the relations between mapmakers and their patrons are not clear. For instance, evidence has not yet come to light to clarify whether map painters were paid for their work. Also unknown is the extent to which they were obliged, or coerced, to paint in particular ways. Furthermore, while it seems reasonable to presume that Spanish map painters worked primarily for Spanish patrons and indigenous people worked for each other, mapping arrangements did not necessarily break cleanly along such lines. While Spanish mapmakers seem to have favored a European clientele, indigenous people painted cartographs for both Amerindian and Spanish patrons.[7]

What seems most certain, and crucial, to our knowledge of colonial mapping is that neither officials nor mapmakers wielded ultimate control over the ways in which territory took shape in the cartographic record. This can be sensed from the map of Atlatlauca made in conjunction with the merced for Vásquez Coronado (Fig. 5.2). Here, an indigenous painter familiar with graphic conventions

Mapping after the Letter | 125

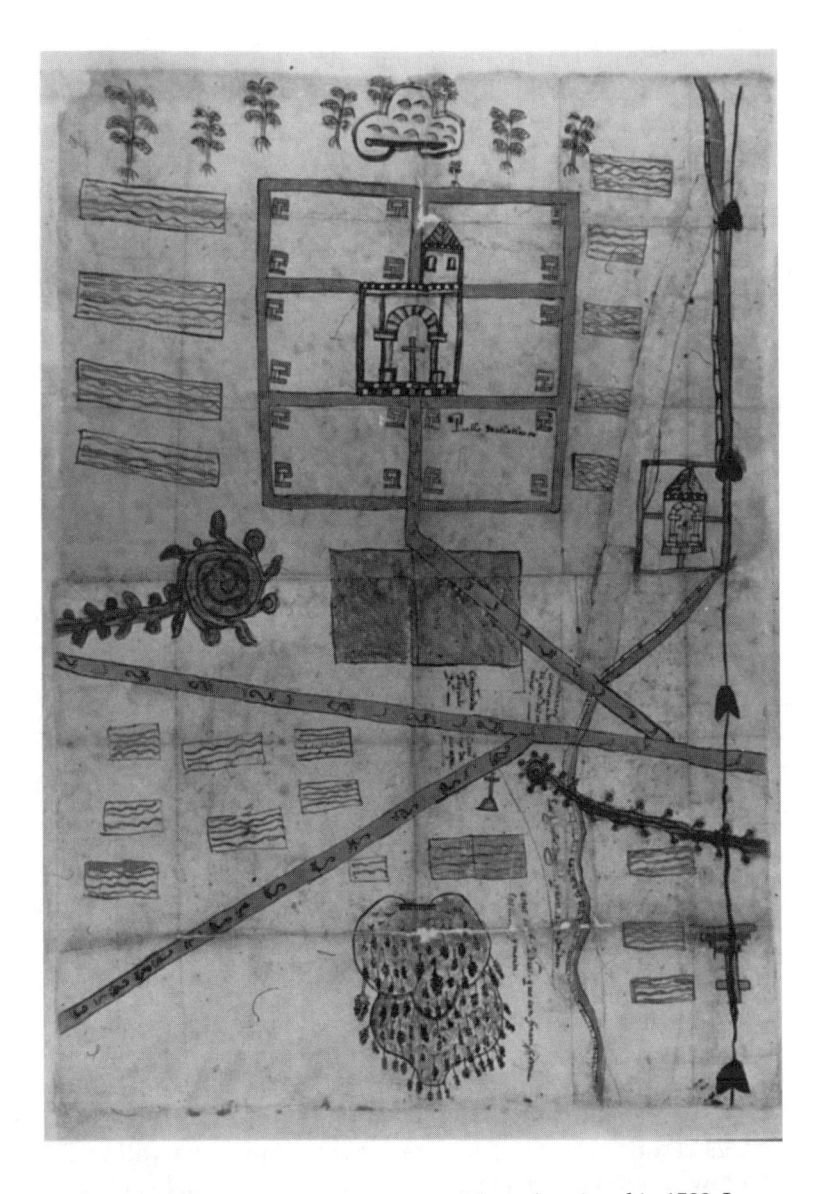

FIGURE 5.2 Map of Atlatlauca (Tenango, Mexico), painted in 1588. In addition to the town, the mapmaker has clearly defined the roads that traverse this region. At the top and bottom of the map, two mountain-like forms frame the scene. These elements, along with the houses of Atlatlauca, the swirling waters, and the footprints on the roads derive from pre-Hispanic graphic conventions. Size of original: 43 x 59 cm (AGN #1572, Tierras, vol. 2679, exp. 5, f. 9; reproduced with permission from the Archivo General de la Nación, Mexico City).

of both European and pre-Hispanic origin has set the townscape within the frame of a gold-brown rectangle. A church dominates the painted community, and small, pre-conquest-style houses frame the Christian structure. This arrangement parallels that of many merced maps, where communities are signed with church buildings that stand either alone or amid houses and grid plans. The territory surrounding the main community bears the stamp of intense cultivation, with twenty-one rectangles defining a network of local fields. Regions under cultivation were of no small concern, for mercedes could not be made—at least not in good faith—if they infringed upon lands already in use or under title to others. Prominent features of this map also include forked roads (often traversed by human footprints) and references to topography in the form of swirling blue skeins, which represent water, and mountains or hill glyphs that often define a fringe of rising peaks. The map was incomplete, however, without alphabetic lettering. Penned not by the map painter but by a Spanish official, written words identify the town by name. On this and other cartographs, writing also indicates the terminus of roads, locates the desired tract of land, and often identifies the colonial authorities who accepted and vouched for the mapped image. This painting of Atlatlauca also exhibits a correction: a piece of European paper, shaped like a long canal, affixed to the upper left side of the map. On this attachment the mapmaker has re-painted a new series of details, collaging them into the map's pictorial vocabulary. On other maps, corrections can be seen as areas abraded and painted over, or even as blatant crossings-through of an original image. Not every cartograph shows signs of emendation, but the frequency with which documents were doctored or patched suggests that the desire for accuracy was not incidental in colonial mapping.

At first glance the vocabulary of merced maps evokes, and presents, a very particular view: fixed firmly in the New Spanish landscape are communities, routes of passage, cultivated lands, waters, and mountains (Figs. 5.1–5.6). Upon closer scrutiny, these scenes can be seen to concentrate human dwelling within the shadow, if not centripetal pull, of a Christian church. In addition, agricultural productivity and paths of movement loom large. Where one travels matters greatly, as does the disposition of specific parcels of territory. Thus the merced maps fashion New Spain as a land structured by human occupation and the flux of short-lived possession and dispossession—or at least the possibility thereof. At one level, this is predictable, for the merced *acordados* (official directives) often specify that maps should include major towns close to the requested site, along with nearby ranches and fields. And many maps respond to written instructions outlining the features that mattered most to the gaze of colonial officials.[8] Furthermore, the places people lived, cultivated, and journeyed through, formed the warp and woof of daily existence. As such, these seem the obvious elements of cartographic reality.

Yet the ways in which maps organize territory should not be taken as self-evident or merely pragmatic. I know of no written guidelines specifying that map painters should craft their images in color (or not), or that indigenous mapmakers should include elements derived from pre-Hispanic painting. Rather, painters invented compelling images with whatever graphic elements and conventions they could summon.[9] In addition, although each merced map was charged with depicting an actual site or region in New Spain, the maps also responded to tangential desires, thwarted possessions, birds-not-in-the-hand. We might reasonably expect that a legal apparatus such as that of the merced would restrict free-floating aspirations in mapmaking; it is nonetheless evident that the representations of the map-world were dogged by appetites for fruits of the land, if not land itself. Fashioned upon demand, with each scene custom-made for a specific territorial inquest, these maps do not depict the lands of New Spain in general but, rather, particular sites and settlements that envelop sought-after parcels. In these documents, then, the surplus desire for an object swamps and suffuses the entire cartographic terrain, structuring the relations between paper and earthly ground.

Merced maps also share a utopian impulse. On the maps of Coatlinchan and Atlatlauca (Figs. 5.1 and 5.2), for instance, both painters rendered green trees, blue running waters, and forested mountains. Absent are hints of less verdant seasons, muddied or dry waterways, hillsides partially denuded. From this edenic landscape, we sense not only the traits of imaginary depiction (i.e., waters are typically blue or blue-green), but also the visual rhetoric of the mapmaker for hire.[10] Certainly these paintings were all the more convincing because they appeared to fuse daily experiences with the lands under petition. At the same time, through visual mechanisms of persuasion and idealization, merced images entreat viewers to believe not only in their pictorial veracity but also in the desirability of the bucolic scene set before them

This is not to suggest that maps were in the cynical business of "falsifying" or "misrepresenting" landscapes known, in fact, to be more humble. But neither did these images reveal to their viewers what actually could be seen from a particular vantage or geographical position. Indeed, the constraints and conventions of human vision concern merced maps only marginally. In this, the paintings share much with cartographic projects from other places and times. For maps rarely proffer scenes that correspond directly to either the perceptive or conceptual limits of human sight.

The principles of mapping—the abstractions or graphic codes that link merced maps to cartography in general—offer an avenue for further exploration. Yet to fairly examine the topic would require another essay. In the sections that follow, therefore, I focus on the visuality of alphabetic script as it bound text to image and land. Through this analysis, I aim to explore some of the complexities of language as it circulated, in material form, through New Spain.

The Grounds of Counter-Signature

Throughout the sixteenth century, many resources and much power flowed from Amerindians to Spanish colonists. Yet to find in merced cartographs only encroachment or loss is to fundamentally predispose the material evidence around a foregone conclusion—a finality that escaped the historical players themselves. If the prospects, especially for indigenous actors, were grim, they nevertheless were sufficiently complex to allow for play. And on merced maps we find the traces of diverse and often contradictory effects of picture, script, and paper.[11]

Of all the elements on these maps, perhaps the most intrusive for modern readers are the alphabetic passages and annotations penned across the front and sometimes the back of each cartograph. So distinct are the written passages that, in their absence, merced maps appear to founder as convincing and recognizable renderings of territory—at least when viewed by bureaucratic, legalistic eyes that seek specificity and repleteness from property charts. To assess merced maps apart from, or independently of, their scripted texts is to ignore one of the genre's principal features. Moreover, although cartographs required alphabetic inscription, standard writing formats such as those used for documenting the land grant procedure itself rarely sufficed. Special arrangements and multiple orientations for written words figure prominently in the mapping process. The orientation and dispensation of writing on merced maps thus responded to no fixed traditions of alphabetic transcription, nor to any pre-established templates. Rather the particularities of each pictorial and diagrammatic field structured the possibilities for the deployment of alphabetic text.[12]

In recent years the status of image-making after the introduction of alphabetic writing in the decades following the Spanish conquest has become a topic of serious discussion. Evidence suggests that pre-Hispanic scribal and documentary conventions contributed significantly to the rapidity with which indigenous communities appropriated alphabetic script. In high-status circles of pre-Hispanic society, specialists trained to create and interpret pictorial records played integral roles. Furthermore, prior to 1521, Mesoamericans had developed sophisticated techniques for producing permanent, portable records by applying colored inks to paper, cloth, and animal skin. Although the forms of European documents differed from those known before the conquest, materials and patterns of use were often similar. Indeed, in Maya, Mixtec, and Nahuatl, postconquest vocabularies for paper and other tools of the trade (as well as writing and reading) paralleled pre-Hispanic terminologies. Even so, as colonial religious, legal, and bureaucratic channels came to depend, increasingly, upon written texts, picture making and alphabetic writing pursued different trajectories. By the turn of the seventeenth century, indigenous records relied heavily upon alphabetic script but used images more sparingly than before.[13]

In the case of mercedes, however, the historical and notarial writings set down in indigenous languages in the sixteenth and early seventeenth centuries by Nahua, Mixtec, and Maya writers constitute a separate arena of record making. For seldom is the penmanship on merced maps that of an indigenous hand. Time and again we see texts drafted on cartographs in Spanish by colonial officials—presumably for the inspection of other officials or even members of the Audiencia back in Mexico City. The alphabetic script on merced maps may have taken on meaning against the backdrop of indigenous notarial practices for some sixteenth-century viewers, but the comments lettered across merced maps are, by and large, exemplary of Spanish, not Amerindian, writing.

An excellent gauge of the work performed by merced map texts can be traced on the cartograph in Figure 5.3, a document from 1630 that depicts the indigenous town of Coatepeque and its environs. On the front of the map, a pre-Hispanic-style place glyph stands at the center. Atop the over-sized hill teeters a lavender snake, and descending along one slope of the mound spill alphabetic letters. This writing tells its readers that the hill represents an actual mountain, named Coatepeque, or Snake Hill. The principal

FIGURE 5.3 Map of Coatepeque (Zacualpan, Mexico), painted in 1630. The land requested in this merced—which is identified alphabetically—stands just below the large hill glyph and thus occupies the very center of the map. While the forms in this painting have been loosely drawn, the colors are striking. The mapmaker has used green, blue, tan, rose, and orange. Size of original: 43 x 30 cm (AGN #1448, Tierras, vol. 2431, exp. 1, f. 47; reproduced with permission from the Archivo General de la Nación, Mexico City)

town, also called Coatepeque, appears on the map as a small church set just above the place glyph. The writing orients itself along multiple axes: in some instances it runs horizontally, in others it moves diagonally or vertically, depending upon the lay of the virtual topography. For the most part, the texts on the front of the map gloss pictorial elements; they comment upon each figural sign—road, river, town, and house. The alphabetic marks also cut into many of the map's unpainted spaces, commandeering them as documentary asides. Just below the hill glyph, for example, the sought-after parcel of land is identified via inscription.[14]

The encroachment of alphabetic signs reveals that imagery alone was not wholly sufficient—at least not for maps seeking the stamp of official recognition. This should not be surprising, for both pre-Hispanic and European custom demanded that pictorial images and other legal exhibits be proffered along with verbal or textual elucidation. Yet merced maps record no verbatim translation of some actual utterance. Neither the direct testimony of witnesses nor the words of administrative officials were set onto merced maps.[15] It is true that the topics addressed in writing, and the vocabulary of these texts, cleave to a litany of stock observations. This opens the possibility that alphabetic inscriptions distill actual statements into condensed formulaic phrases; however, there is no way to reliably reconstitute specific oral exchanges from the words set down on maps. The written comments therefore resemble disjointed descriptions of place, linked through the journey of map-readers' eyes as they pass from station to station, scanning each cartographic passage in its turn.

If we consider the genesis of the map in Figure 5.3, we can appreciate it as a laminate made up of discrete layers, each with its own internal rationale. European paper provides both symbolic and material ground, upon which rest the colored marks of an indigenous mapmaker. Then, as counter-signature over the native, pictorial hand, there appears alphabetic inscription, set down by an official to ascribe place and occasion. The Spanish hand seeks to clarify that this is not any community, but Coatepeque; not any canal, but the one leading to the property of don Francisco Alonso de Sosa. Once defined with pen and ink, the picture is transfigured into a less ambiguous portrayal of particulars. Seen in this light, writing fulfills a largely restrictive, or better, deictic, function.

It is almost required these days to interpret the superimposition of image by word as a Spanish attempt to wrest control from indigenous record keepers. Admittedly, a large number of merced maps were painted by indigenous people and subsequently inscribed by colonial officials. It is as if, in writing upon Amerindian images, authorities sought the final (and defining) imprimatur. In fact, many Spanish labels do aim to curb the ambiguity of pictorial imagery. In so doing, these inscriptions work to turn the paintings on maps into uniformly legible—and unequivocal—signs (at least for those conversant with written Spanish). While it is tempting to ascribe to this scenario an imperial will-to-dominate, I want to hold the interpretive door ajar, at least long enough to note that in the last quarter of the sixteenth century, the time when most merced maps were crafted, alphabetic writing could hardly be called a Spanish medium of control. Although introduced soon after the conquest along with Christianity and other colonial institutions, alphabetic lettering accrued a wide spectrum of meanings across the sixteenth century. After 1560, not only did indigenous notaries write often, and well, in their own languages, but we would be incorrect to assume that texts written in Spanish (or any other tongue) necessarily fulfilled the ambitions of their writers in a straightforward way. The history of writing offers a multitude of cases in which readers thwart, undermine, and transform the expectations of writers. And in colonial Latin America this is especially true. Both indigenous interpretations of Spanish alphabetic script and Spanish understandings of Amerindian writing confirm that a chasm could—and often did—open between an intended denotation and its reception. This does not mean that the objectives of Spanish writers can be easily dismissed. My point is that the presence of alphabetic words, even those set down by colonial officials, did not, a priori, undermine or limit the power of pictorial images on maps.[16]

This is the situation I imagine: script on merced maps is colored by the administrative roles of the officials who wrote, and the connotations that adhered to the Spanish milieu, of these texts. Yet the significance of writing did not unfurl against a blank ground. If map texts arise from an officious will to rein in images, the authority of scripted words nonetheless remains ill-defined. This is because each mode of expression—picture and word—transforms and undercuts the other. Moreover, since the manufacture of a cartograph is but one moment in its career, not the determining instant, we must also assess maps well after their birth, when both letter and image were already at play. New meanings do, in fact, emerge when attention turns to the "finished product," to that residue of designs that adhered to cartographs as they left local communities bound for Mexico City. To disentangle the politics and language of writing on maps, then, the question must shift.

What becomes crucial is not how writing controls or restricts maps but, rather, how alphabetic script intersects with and redirects the visual destiny of the cartograph.

Returning to the map in Figure 5.3, we can begin to assay just how the visual and physical disposition of script prompted cartographic meaning. Surveying the upper edges of the page, one notices that alphabetic words written on the reverse of the map bleed through and stain the obverse. This text notes the date of the legal inquiry and names the officials who participated in and oversaw the grant. The text also registers the signatures of the individuals who participated in the legal mechanics of the transaction.[17] In addition to other kinds of cartographic labor, the inclusion of date, descriptions, and signatures identifies a specific group of administrators who witnessed, verified, and authenticated the document. The inscription thus provides the trace of an official reading (or set of readings). The names and signatures of the functionaries also render the map proper and legitimate; in bringing the painting into the official registry, they level the idiosyncrasies of this particular page, transforming it into one more successful merced. The writing on this map matters not only because it records actual names or certain dates, but because it links this evocation of Coatepeque into a chain of administrative declarations on land, entitlement, and record keeping.

Beyond this, in occupying the back, and staining the face of the painting, alphabetic script interrupts the pictorial, spatial illusion that is key to this type of map, and by extension, proper to the painted scene of Coatepeque. Whether this was intentional or not, we cannot know. What is certain is that the bleeding inscription locks into place, and disrupts, other elements of the map: the written stain anchors the floating pre-conquest-style toponym, its creator, and the community of interlocutors into a lattice of colonial, legal order as it cuts them loose in a haze of dispersed ink. While the text may not explicitly set out to contaminate the face of the painted image, it effectively undermines patches of the pictorial ground by literally and metaphorically seeping into the foundation upon which an indigenous community and topographic features of New Spain rest. This process, however, is not symmetrical; writing does not absorb the landscape.

Continuing in this semiotic vein, I would note that to "properly" read the inscription on the map's reverse one must flip the map over. Hence, the text emerges on the front of the document as a kind mirror writing. And so it is transgression by the backside or nether region of alphabetic texts that mars the pictorial face of this map. Modern readers tend to demote the material presence of seeping words—by pretending not to see them, by overlooking their physical traits, and by bracketing them off as a dimension separate from the map's pictorial imagery. Once we acknowledge their presence, however, we must also recognize that their infiltration confounds our reading of the cartographic plane. No less importantly, the painted colors of the map's visage, and the words penned across the front of the map, also hemorrhage through the paper, complicating the task of deciphering the written text on the document's reverse. What we see, and what colonial officials probably detected but could not rescind, was the porosity of materials—ink, colored paint, paper—subverting and adulterating an ideal condition of both text and image, of indigenous painter and Spanish writer. Perceived as the visual and material presence that it is, this writing hardly explicates the painting. Rather letter and image suffer the same fate: each is infused and carried off in a new direction by the other.

This seepage of ink and paint through European paper is hardly unique to the cartographs of this mapmaker.[18] Across the surface of numerous other maps, word and picture saturate each other. A map painted in 1597 for a land request near to Jocotitlán, for instance, shows another way that written texts and images mutually infect one another (Fig. 5.4).[19] By and large the alphabetic letters gloss the pictorial elements and buttress the chart's veracity. Toward the left side of the map, however, extending across the tan house is a textual passage that takes its referent from elsewhere. The words assert that the painted edifice does not exist, at least not contemporaneously with the other scenery illustrated on the page. Moreover, below the house, the text drafted on the map informs its readers that the building represents the site requested in merced: this is the place where one don Baltasar Ximenez hopes to lay claim to two *caballerías de tierra*.[20] This phrase introduces prolepsis that the painted image, alone, cannot signify. Reading image and script together, we understand the house as a prediction. It foreshadows a successful outcome for this merced. This indicates that the maps made for land grants could give current arrangements visual form, but they could also describe expectations and anticipated transformations of territory.

Beyond this, we need to recognize that specific mapping conventions are at work in this document: people of this region did not build houses as tall as mountains, nor did Jocotitlán actually appear as a single green hill with a net across its surface and white ruffle at its lower extremity. Even so, the painted imagery insists

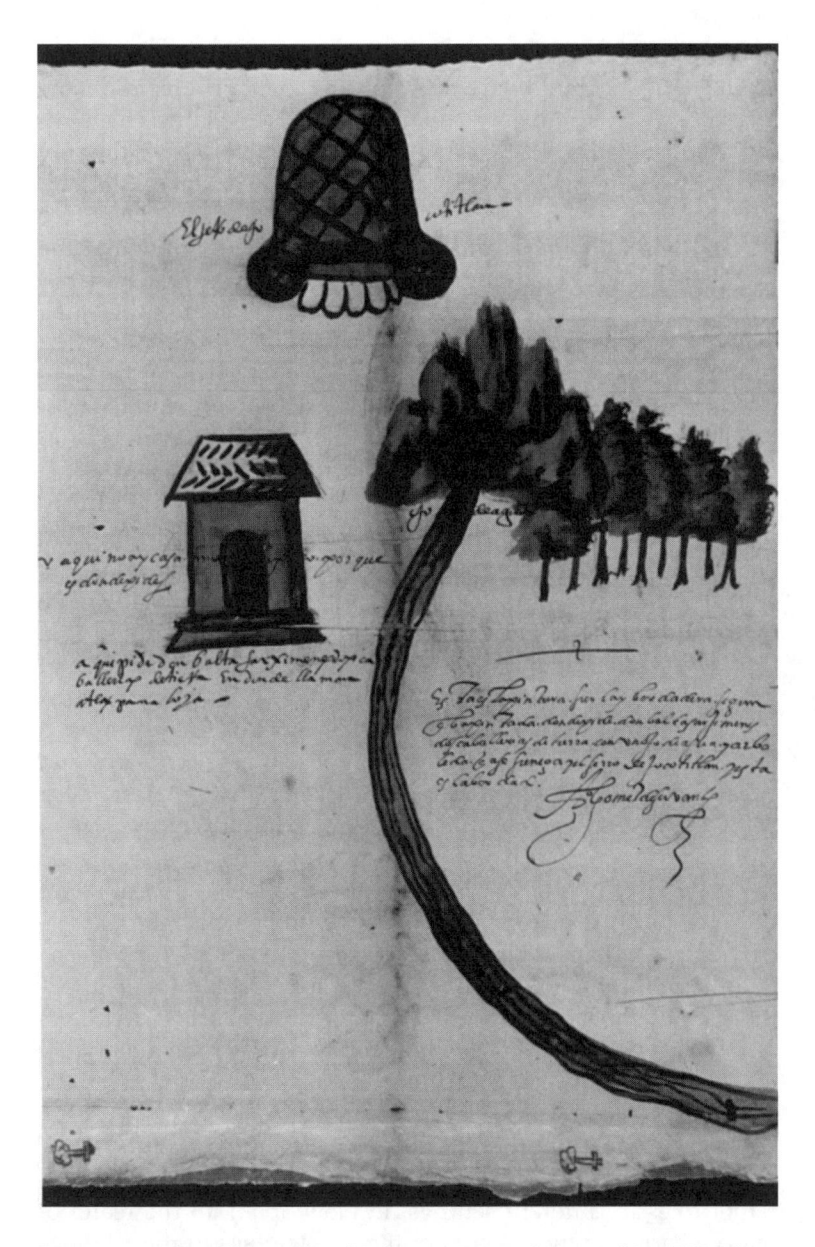

FIGURE 5.4 Map of Jocotitlán (Ystlauaca, Mexico), created in 1597. The unpainted background, absence of groundline, and combination of glyphic elements with more mimetic landscape imagery are all typical of the merced genre. Size of original: 41 x 31 cm (AGN #2083, Tierras, vol. 2764, exp. 21, fc. 289; reproduced with permission from the Archivo General de la Nación, Mexico City).

that, should one traverse this territory, commanding this scene would be a large building, a forest, and a mountain stream. Yet the inscription across the house qualifies this visual claim. This writing, which negates what is otherwise shown pictorially, is the only text on the map that crosses through, and, to an extent crosses out, painted signs. The script cuts through the house as if the edifice has only an ephemeral presence. From this we intuit that the power of alphabetic writing on maps is sometimes an exercise pitted against the actuality of visual signals. And still, in spite of the stated intent of the writing, this phantom house hardly "goes away." Alphabetic lettering does not effectively cancel the mapmaker's vision—it merely signals a temporal rift in the cartographic illusion.

This play between pictorial and scriptorial signs transforms the surface of the painting into a ground—not of existential contention—but of mutual, although partial, transparency. Sheldon Nodelman's work offers insight into this process, suggesting that as the elements bleed through one another they approach a state of simultaneous presence. Writing and painting suffuse and condition each other, at once begetting and subverting the integrity of graphic representation.[21] This may seem a small point. For the inks of written texts and the colored paints of images have seeped through paper and stained their supports in myriad places and times. Ubiquity, however, does not necessarily signal banality. Scholars have long recognized that the script, form, and size of alphabetic lettering lend texts extra-lexical significance; so, too, do the material properties of inks and their supports. To fail to see this is to construe historical documents—and particularly the role of written language set upon their surfaces—as sites where speech and thought can mysteriously take physical form but remain uninflected by the worldly conditions and corporal acts of writing. I would argue against this position and allege that the materiality and embodied acts that constitute writing are fundamental to the meanings staged by alphabeticized language.

This is not to propose some universal significance for the ink of all written words. The material and visual features of text play different roles in different settings. In New Spain, in the realm of merced cartography, the crux of the problem lies in the relations between alphabetic writing (of a Spanish hand) and pictorial imagery (of an indigenous painter). When we speak only of the hard boundaries between alphabetic and pictorial representation, we miss both the seepage of one into the other and a crucial feature of these graphic forms. At issue, then, is what it means for maps and their readers to tolerate the porosity of graphic conventions. In accepting the maps of Coatepeque and Jocotitlán, officials acknowledged that these documents did in fact pass muster. These maps thus disclose how writing and painting can transgress each other's boundaries and still forge persuasive meaning. That the words and images are themselves material objects invoked to renegotiate the existence (and visibility) of other objects renders the map even more complex. For these documents imply that the play between what is written and what is pictured is not necessarily incidental to either lived experience or the representation of imaginary spaces.

Cartographic Itineraries

The manifestation of language on maps, in the form of scripted words, suggests that the denotative sense of any particular phrase was only part of the story. Of equal consequence were the material and visual effects of alphabetic texts—both intended and otherwise. Yet written language made no appearances, and did no work, apart from readers and writers. Thus the writing on cartographs—as traces of embodied movement through landscape and across the real surface of paper—charts relationships among people, land, paper, and pen. Specifically, I want to propose that the words individuals inscribed with their hands, and then surveyed with their eyes, operate as a kind of circuit through the landscape. Written language, then, as it documents and diagrams human movements through space and across paper, summons both the land of New Spain and reasonable pathways through it.

The document in Figure 5.5 provides an apt example of this. In many ways, this work hardly seems to be a map at all. Created for a merced in 1591, this cartograph uses the expressive range of unmarked paper and handwritten text to depict a region near Huejotzingo, in the modern state of Puebla.[22] In the realm of pictorial representation, a conventionalized waterway, the Rio Apapastla, skirts the left border, distinguishing the northern edge of this region as the only place where land does not stretch unbounded across an undifferentiated plane. Otherwise, the map exercises extraordinary pictorial restraint: no hint of nearby mountains surfaces; and apart from the river, no clues about the types of land that frame the requested parcel appear. Even so, alphabetic writing alone would not suffice. The writer felt compelled to arrange his texts in a diagrammatic fashion, differentiating the writing of the

FIGURE 5.5 Map for a merced near Rio Apapastla (Huejotzingo, Puebla). Painted in 1591, this map's heavy dependence upon alphabetic writing in Spanish suggests little connection with indigenous graphic traditions, yet the river running along the left edge of the page strongly resembles pre-Hispanic depictions of running water. Size of original: 40 x 32 cm (AGN #1765, Tierras, vol. 2708, exp. 13, f. 10; reproduced with permission from the Archivo General de la Nación, Mexico City).

map, with its multiple orientations and dispersal across the paper, from the more formal writing of the rest of the merced.[23] Cardinal directions are indicated along the map's sides, and to the east, south, and west lands belonging to others surround the petitioned property. Centered on the page is a flourish of writing that locates the parcel requested by one Sancho Ortiz de Zúñiga, and gives primacy of place to the signature of Esteban de López, the official who both wrote and authorized the document.

If we follow the hand of Esteban de López as he marked this paper, we find that his script runs vertically, not horizontally, along the right and left edges of the page. To manage this shift of orientation, the writer turned either the paper or his body. In order to move himself, and perhaps beckon his reader to a particular bearing, he repositioned himself in space; both literally and symbolically, he negotiated the unfolding representation. The writing not only describes a site in New Spain; it traces an encounter with and invocation of a physical place via a diagrammatic surrogate. Admittedly, the marks on this page convey only a few clues about this landscape. For instance, there is no hint of the boundary markers or topography that define this region, nothing to suggest that near the requested land stands one of the tallest mountains in the area. Yet the work speaks volumes, as it were, about the possibilities for evoking place through a spare but visually compelling use of paper and ink. Even more importantly, at least for the argument here, the marks of the scribal pen turn writing into a trek—for map reader no less than mapmaker—across both page and place.

In contrast to this nearly alphabetic map, the richness of the paint, color, and mimetic design in a cartograph of Yzquyluca are nearly overwhelming (Fig. 5.6). The basic composition is forthright: an indigenous town occupies the bottom of the painting; above, looms a tree-covered hill, a road (with footprints), fields, grassy terrain, and outlying settlements. The full sun at the upper edge of the image marks the east, the half-sun below signifies the occidental rim of this world. At center stage, on the vertical axis of the painting and within a walled enclosure, stands the property requested in legal proceedings—vacant but for the writing that identifies it as ground awaiting tenancy. Through this composition, the map engages in clever visual rhetoric. The only open patch of map is the land requested in merced; that this parcel appears framed and centered, pinioned on the map's vertical axis, is no accident. The painting quietly, but firmly, insists that here, at the heart of this region, lies a void—indeed, just one empty space—the sought-after parcel of land. The subtext is not lost in nuance: the merced would conflict

140 | Dana Leibsohn

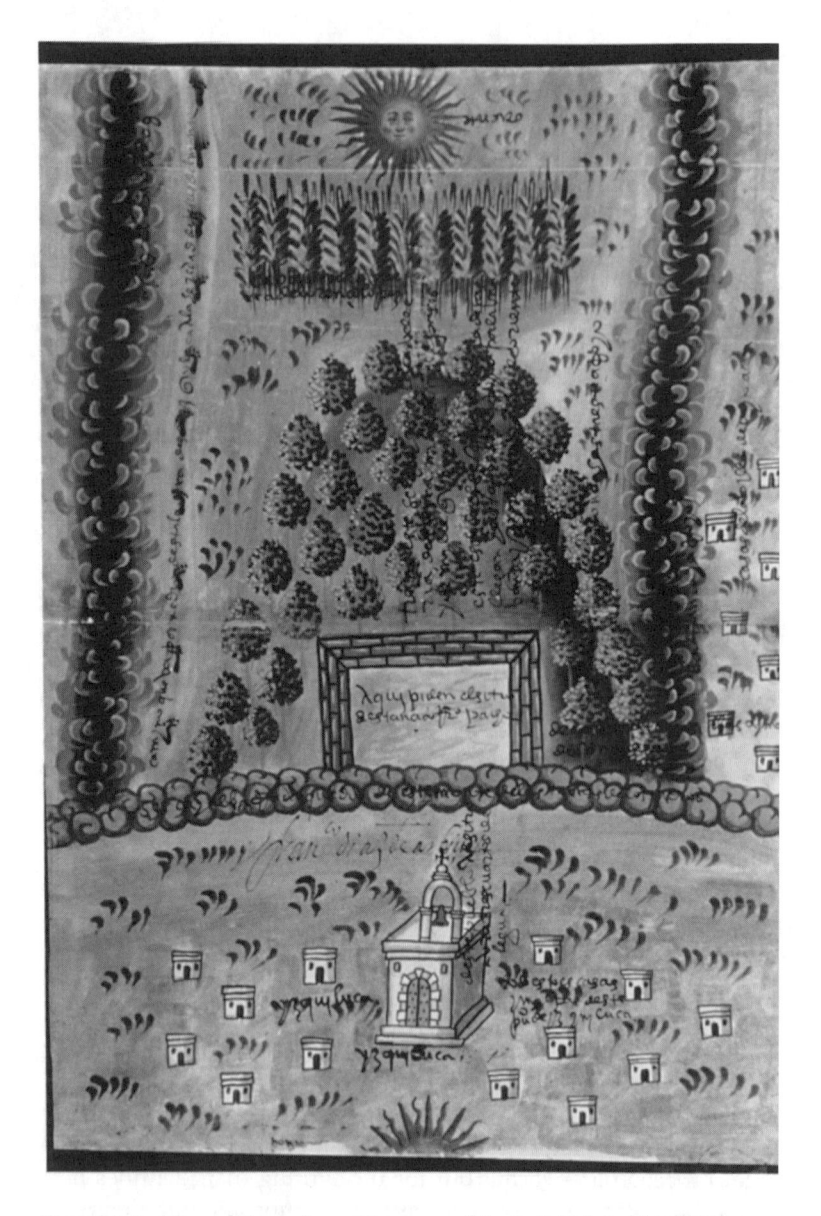

FIGURE 5.6 Map of Yzquyluca (Tenayuca, Mexico). Painted in 1594 for a request for grazing land, this is one of the most elaborately painted of all indigenous merced maps. The colors are vibrant, the scenery is lush, and the church is well-detailed. Like many merced paintings, east appears at the top and is signed with an image of the sun. Size of original: 43 x 31 cm (AGN #2230, Tierras, vol. 2812, exp. 16, fc. 455; reproduced with permission from the Archivo General de la Nación, Mexico City).

with the prior claims of no one and therefore should be awarded. In contrast to the pictorial scene, the writing of this map takes a less polemical role. It labels what can be seen, and it identifies the place under petition. Essentially, the words incorporate this map of 1594 into the fabric of colonial documentation and ownership.[24]

This painted record encourages us to raise one more issue in this discussion of cartographic language: map reading. Although we know very little about how maps were read in New Spain, the matter is significant. This painting, for instance, measures about a foot by a foot and a half, large enough to be attached to a wall or held up for display. Readers could certainly keep their distance from the map and nevertheless discern the spikes and curves of the script. From the mere presence of alphabetic writing—indeed, without decoding a single word of Spanish—they could grasp that the map had been seen and authorized by officials. Viewing from a distance would also make it easier to take in the whole of the painting, to better imagine the lay of this land. Deciphering the script, however, demands focus and proximity. Moreover, readers must turn the map or their bodies to follow the different orientations of the writing: horizontal in some places, vertical or inverted in others. Thus to grasp these words, readers must re-trace the interaction between scribal and painterly hands; they must track at least two journeys through this territory. In this context, to read is to travel—across both physical and conceptual boundaries. And yet we must acknowledge that many of the words on this map are difficult to discern; they are swallowed up, particularly along the rocky ravine, across the hill, and along the bushy barrier at the right. The writer's ink subsides into the paint of the imagery; it is as if the ground has, quite literally, absorbed the words. Certainly this could not have been the writer's primary intent: the alphabetic texts of colonial officials were, as far as we know, never crafted purposely so as to sink into the pictorial imagery of maps. Yet neither is the absorption of word by picture simply a naïve mistake. Rather we are viewing writing and painting as they operate at the margins of explicit intent. In this map of Yzquyluca the effect is not unique, just strong. Here, as alphabetic script enters and defines the territorial scene, paint and paper consume the writing and render it a piece of the landscape itself. Working with other indigenous materials of the sixteenth century, Gary Tomlinson speaks of inscriptive territory.[25] This phrase is fitting. For this document from Yzquyluca inscribes landscape as it territorializes written script. It is as if land, image, and word cultivate one another.

Conscripted Terrain

Ultimately merced maps and their writings escort us into difficult country. In New Spain, the ground was never level. Indigenous people and Spaniards hardly qualified as equals, and in some respects alphabetic writing does subdue the unruly energy of pictorial images. Even so, I would claim that in maps, such as those of Yzquyluca (Fig. 5.6) or Coatlinchan (Fig. 5.1) it is the pictorial imagery, not the writing, that seduces the eye, if not the mind. This is not to say that in the end indigenous images "triumph" in some contest between graphic and scriptorial signage. Rather my point is that the translation of experience into painted image and alphabetic word was precarious. In part, this is because the turbulent effects of graphic "systems" are themselves disruptive. Beyond this, there is the behavior of material things—be they words, pictures, documents or deeds—that mediates experience in uneven ways, ways that permit (if not invite) trespass by other terms. In short, in the sixteenth and seventeenth centuries, merced maps were neither writing nor image but rather sites where distinct forms of representation collided with, and permeated, one another.

Moreover, these cartographs were deeply embedded in practices that shaped daily experience. They therefore registered far more than the details of territorial exchange, or the trace of their makers' hands. By supporting individuals, especially people of Spanish descent, in their quest to possess land, mercedes helped transfigure the very ways in which New Spain was claimed, managed, and imagined. J. Brian Harley, a leading scholar of cartography, has seen in mapping "a teleological discourse, reifying power, reinforcing the status quo, and freezing social interaction within charted lines."[26] And perhaps, for some documents, this is an acceptable assessment. Certainly maps tend to affiliate upwards, looking to those possessing or seeking social and economic privilege. In New Spain this was unquestionably the case: merced maps were wielded by officials in contests over land that often favored Spanish settlers or indigenous people of means. These documents are not exempt, then, from the channels of power that organize the production and consumption of most cartographically assisted enterprise.

Yet there is another moral to this tale. As records of specific topographies, communities, and liens, merced maps purport to matter-of-factly describe New Spanish territory. Nevertheless, it is impossible, at least today, to read through these maps, to somehow look past their surface marks and shadows to retrieve a colonial landscape. This is not simply because the cartographs are reserved, if not absolutely silent, about so many things. Nor is the abstraction or spareness of images and texts to blame. Rather, as pictorial and alphabetic objects, merced maps belong to the world of visual representations, not only the world of lived experience. And so, the rapprochement between mapped space and that of daily life, no less than the concord between people and their graphic instruments, is one of uneasy balance.

But what of the writing on merced cartographs? What does it reveal of colonial experiences and exigencies? To answer this requires one more look at written language itself. Traditionally we have presumed that written words, with their ability to transcend specific contexts and convey meaning to any literate reader, help to secure and stabilize images. Yet the merced maps show how the intervention of pictorial imagery can profoundly structure the meanings that words create. Alphabetic writing, these maps teach us, was never an independent agent, and it rarely reigned unchecked. Indeed, if the social practice we call writing ever did its work, it was no more often because of, than in spite of, writerly intention. A few precious hints indicate that people of the sixteenth century did, indeed, recognize this fact. Whether this arrangement also troubled them remains unclear. More certain is that modern expectations for clarity and transparency in writing (if not also visual imagery) are quite different from those of New Spain. We sense this most pointedly, I believe, in the seeping ink and paint of so many merced documents.

If we take the bleeding pigment and stained paper of cartographs in a straightforward way—at face value, as it were—we begin to grasp something of what it meant to see and read in New Spain. To modern eyes, the mirror-reversed images and words that leak through the backs and fronts of each cartographic page make for untidy documents that complicate reading and decipherment. Yet the tolerance of such conditions by early colonial viewers implies that legibility, and perhaps even sight, rarely escaped turmoil in the visual register. This raises the possibility that people in the sixteenth century might have found pleasure in the physical effects of their record keeping materials and in the bodily acts of their manufacture. For other modes of managing the inscription of alphabetic and pictorial signs could have been devised, had impermeable supports and less fluid inks been crucial. This suggests that practices for making documents in New Spain indulged, not simply endured, the conditions set by the materials themselves. Taking this one step further, we might inquire about other locales and traditions that have also permitted documentary seepage. My analysis has tracked only the lettering on New Spanish cartographs, but similar queries about visuality, legibility, and the physicality of alphabetic writing could be pursued for other words—both penned and printed—that hemorrhage through their supports.

It would be shortsighted, however, to interpret the seeping of ink through paper as only a physical process. There is also an allegorical interpretation to be made. As the pictures and letters on merced maps bleed into their supports, they participate in, and point to, a realm of signifying process that shapes how language, gesture, and paint create meaning. Indeed, the infusion and inflection of one form of representation by another is a salient feature of many signifying acts, not only those of "artistic" expression. A fitting example, given this volume's concern with language and cross-cultural engagement, can be found in the art of translation, wherein the words and writings of one language must transcend their boundaries and—through no proviso of their own—create meaning in other tongues, for new interpreters.[27] As visual and material substances, the images and letters on merced maps fall victim to their own rules and historical contingencies, yet the porosity of these cartographs is evocative of the world of representations in which both leakage and firm boundaries compete to forge meaning. As modern historians, we have not been eager to acknowledge these properties in documents. Perhaps for good reason. For once we take the visual and physical labor of pen and ink seriously, our accounts of historical language must become, also, accounts of representation. In closing, then, I suggest that the alphabetic writing and pictorial imagery of merced maps are, indeed, material things. But their referents have proven ephemeral. If these marks on maps tells us anything at all of colonial language and history (and I believe that they do), perhaps it is this: alphabetic language cannot deny its own physicality; writing may thus be transcribable and readable, but it remains, nonetheless, always vulnerable.

Notes

This essay has benefited from comments and suggestions offered by panelists at two conferences: "Communicating with the Indians: Aspects of the Language Encounter with Indigenous Peoples of the Americas, 1492–1800" (Brown University, Providence, 1996) and "Entre la Pared y la Espalda: Visual and Alphabetic Literacy in the Formation of Colonial Culture" (American Anthropological Association, Washington, DC, 1997). I also thank D. Bridgman, B. Mundy, J. Rappaport, M. Schreffler, participants in the Colonial Latin American Representations Workshop at the University of Chicago (May, 1998), and the editors of this volume for reading and challenging this work.

1. The records of this merced, a request for two *caballerías de tierra*, are housed in the Archivo General de la Nación (AGN), in Mexico City, Tierras, vol. 2688, expediente 35. The painting, #1678 in the AGN Mapoteca, is one of a pair of images created by the same painter. The counterpart image (AGN Mapoteca #1679, Tierras 2688, exp. 36), which depicts a similar region for a different merced, was painted on indigenous rather than European paper. Generally merced maps appear on European paper; thus a single mapmaker's use of both European and indigenous papers raises interesting issues about the meaning of both maps and their material supports. The production of maps in series is not common, although there were a number of instances in the sixteenth century. For further discussion, see Dana Leibsohn, *Contingent Cartographies: Indigenous Paintings, Maps, and the Colonial Fabric of Mexico* (in preparation). For a description of the merced process, as well as a translation and transcription of one *acordado*, see Barbara Mundy, *The Mapping of New Spain: Indigenous Cartography and the Maps of the Relaciones Geográficas* (Chicago, 1996), 181–88, 233–34. Useful discussions also appear in Charles Gibson, *Aztecs under Spanish Rule: A History of the Indians of the Valley of Mexico, 1519–1810* (Stanford, 1964), 275–77; and James Lockhart, *The Nahuas after the Conquest: A Social and Cultural History of the Indians of Central Mexico, Sixteenth through Eighteenth Centuries* (Stanford, 1992), 163–70. The process otherwise can be pieced together from reading merced cases; the examples I cite come from the AGN, ramos Tierras and Mercedes.
2. Important recent discussions of the introduction of alphabetic writing and the implications of this process, especially vis-à-vis indigenous traditions of pictorial representation, appear in: Serge Gruzinski, *The Conquest of Mexico: The Incorporation of Indian Societies into the Western World, 16th–18th Centuries* (Cambridge, 1993), 6–69; Lockhart, *The Nahuas after the Conquest*, 326–73; Walter Mignolo, "Literacy and Colonization: The New World Experience," in *1492–1992: Re/Discovering Colonial Writing*, ed. René Jara and Nicholas Spadaccini (Minneapolis, 1989), 51–96; and Mignolo, "Signs and Their Transmission," in *Writing without Words: Alternative Literacies in Mesoamerica and the Andes*, ed. Elizabeth Hill Boone and Walter D. Mignolo (Durham, 1994), 220–70. Tzevetzan Todorov's study, *The Conquest of America* (New York, 1984), although widely read, has met with considerable criticism from many Latin Americanists. The essays in *Writing without Words*, however, consider a number of issues relevant to text and image debates; other comments of note appear in Enrique Florescano, *Memory, Myth, and Time in Mexico: From the Aztecs to Independence* (Austin, 1994), and Gary Tomlinson, "Unlearning the Aztec Cantares (preliminaries to a postcolonial history)," in *Subject and Object*

in Renaissance Culture, ed. Margaret de Grazia, Maureen Quilligan, and Peter Stallybrass (Cambridge, 1996), 260–86. Finally, a number of scholars of pre-Hispanic culture have also examined word and image interactions (see, e.g., Janet C. Berlo, ed., *Text and Image in Pre-Columbian Art: Interrelationships of Verbal and Visual Arts* [Oxford, 1983], and Elizabeth P. Benson, ed., *Mesoamerican Writing Systems* [Washington, DC, 1973]). Writing on sixteenth-century indigenous maps, in particular, has not yet received great attention, although both Serge Gruzinski, "Colonial Indian Maps in Sixteenth-Century Mexico," *Res* 13 (1987): 46–61, and Mundy, *The Mapping of New Spain*, 135–79, make prescient observations.
3. The literature on sixteenth-century maps has grown considerably in the last twenty-five years. To date scholars have worked most intensively on cartographic projects commissioned by Spaniards or collected by Europeans in the eighteenth and nineteenth centuries. Thus the maps (or *pinturas*) of the Relaciones Geográficas (which were created in response to a questionnaire issued by Philip II in the 1570s) and cartographic histories have received most of the attention—even though these maps traveled in quite restricted, if high-status, circles, and were crafted far less frequently than maps for congregaciones and mercedes. Key sources on the Relaciones Geográficas are Donald Robertson, "The Pinturas (Maps) of the Relaciones Geográficas," in *Handbook of Middle American Indians*, ed. Robert Wauchope and Howard F. Cline (Austin, 1975): 12:243–78, and Mundy, *Mapping of New Spain*. On cartographic histories, see Donald Robertson, *Mexican Manuscript Painting of the Early Colonial Period* (New Haven, 1959); Elizabeth Hill Boone, "Migration Histories as Ritual Performance," in *To Change Place: Aztec Ceremonial Landscapes*, ed. David Carrasco (Niwot, 1991), 121–51, and *Stories in Red and Black: Pictorial Histories of the Aztecs and Mixtecs* (Austin, forthcoming); also, Dana Leibsohn, "Primers for Memory: Cartographic Histories and Nahua Identity," in Boone and Mignolo, *Writing without Words*, 161–87. For cadastrals, see Barbara Williams, "Mexican Pictorial Cadastral Registers," in *Explorations in Ethnohistory: Indians of Central Mexico in the Sixteenth Century*, ed. H.R. Harvey and Hanns Prem (Albuquerque, 1991), 103–25. Maps from legal arenas, and general cartographic issues in sixteenth-century New Spain have also been discussed by Gruzinski, "Colonial Indian Maps"; Arthur G. Miller, "Transformations of Time and Space: Oaxaca, Mexico, circa 1500–1700," in *Images of Memory: On Remembering and Representation*, ed. Susan Küchler and Walter Melion (Washington, DC, 1991), 141–75; Walter D. Mignolo, *The Darker Side of the Renaissance: Literacy, Territoriality, and Colonization* (Ann Arbor, 1995); and Keiko Yoneda, *Los mapas de Cuauhtinchan y la historia cartográfica prehispánica* (Mexico City, 1981).
4. Although the exact number of maps created between 1550 and 1630 is not known, at least 560 cartographic images—some by Spanish hands, some by indigenous hands—are catalogued in the Tierras section of the Archivo General de la Nación, in Mexico City. Several of these were commissioned for congregaciones and other cases involving territory, yet the majority are merced maps.
5. This imbalance, although telling, does not speak to the complexities of colonial land management more generally. Indigenous people—and particularly community leaders—wielded maps as deftly as any in the pursuit of favorable judgments. Still, a survey of sixteenth-century mercedes reveals the most common petitioners and witnesses to be Spaniards, followed by individuals of Mesoamerican descent, with people of African ancestry surfacing in records only occasionally. Moreover, although cases of fraud and coercion

leading to indigenous land forfeiture have been documented, James Lockhart, through an analysis of Nahuatl documents, finds parallels between colonial mercedes and pre-Hispanic practices. Consequently, the degree to which mercedes may have imposed new expectations and land-use requirements upon indigenous communities requires further research. Beyond this, land practices—especially among indigenous people—were not fully subsumed by the merced process: land sales as well as inheritances were integral to the territorial practices of New Spain. Finally, Lockhart and others have noted that indigenous population losses all but ensured that available land was never a significant problem early in the colonial period. Thus, while the merced process was hardly benign, it produced effects and conditions different—in intensity, if not also in kind—across New Spain. Of central importance, then, were not mercedes, per se, but localized struggles and negotiations for control of resources and positions of power. The stakes held most dear in these conflicts: access to plots of land, local tribute revenues, and the symbolic and economic privileges that sundered nobles from commoners. See Gibson, *The Aztecs under Spanish Rule*, 263–70, 274–79; Robert Haskett, *Indigenous Rulers: An Ethnohistory of Town Government in Colonial Cuernavaca* (Tucson, 1991); Lockhart, *The Nahuas after the Conquest*, 163–64, 166–76; and Mundy, *Mapping of New Spain*, 183–87.

6. The records of this merced, a request for two caballerías de tierra, are housed in the AGN in Mexico City, Tierras, vol. 2679, expediente 5. This painting of Atlatlauca, #1572 AGN Mapoteca, has been executed with colored pigments on European-style paper.

7. For discussion of one indigenous mapmaker and the implications of his support for a Spanish merced petition, see Dana Leibsohn, "Mapping Metaphors: Figuring the Ground of Sixteenth-Century New Spain," *Journal of Early Modern and Medieval Studies* 26 (1996): 499–523. Also see Mundy, *The Mapping of New Spain*, 181–211, for discussion of several individual merced map painters and their work,.

8. Merced acordados often direct officials to create an image that shows the town and lands near the requested parcel and that identifies the people who already lay claim to these territories (see, e.g., Mundy, *Mapping of New Spain*, 233–34). In some cases instructions also ask for distances and major roads to be indicated, although in true bureaucratic fashion, most acordados rely upon highly standardized language and are quite terse. It therefore would be a mistake to presume that merced maps followed precise dictates or strict prescriptions in their portrayal of the land.

9. Mapmakers may have received oral instructions from local officials, although I have yet to find records that would confirm this. Moreover, painted images for mercedes depended not only on the mapmaker's skill and knowledge of sixteenth-century graphic conventions but also on the painter's understanding (or imagining) of what would be acceptable to viewers. This is not to say that colonial officials—Spanish or otherwise—determined, in any absolute terms, the design or style of merced maps. Rather, the process seems to have been somewhat fluid, with mapmakers working to both accommodate general guidelines and anticipate the kinds of imagery that viewers would find satisfactory.

10. Working with twentieth-century highway maps, Denis Wood and John Fels make a similar set of observations in their analysis of the semiosis of cartographs. See, "Designs on Signs/Myth and Meaning in Maps," *Cartographica*

23, no. 3 (1986): 54–103. Also, Gruzinski has noted that for pre-Hispanic painters, color formed a basic component of expression, capable of evoking a wide range of metaphoric and sacred meanings ("Colonial Indian Maps," 51–52). The extent to which color on maps of the sixteenth century invoked, or referred to, pre-Hispanic meanings remains unclear. Because indigenous cartographs rely upon colored pigments far more often and more extensively than do Spanish maps of the same period, we are probably correct to associate strong investments in pigment with native craftsmanship (at least in this context). Beyond this, the presence of color does not reflexively signify the persistence of pre-Hispanic traditions. Chromatism may point to indigenous craftsmanship, but indigenous practices of the late sixteenth century (even those of preconquest origin) were not necessarily also pre-Columbian. Moreover, Gruzinski argues that colored pigment drains from merced paintings over time (idem., 51–52). Yet I find maps painted by indigenous people in the 1580s as well as the early 1600s with extraordinary colors, while some cartographs by native painters dating from the 1570s rely solely upon black ink. Hence I suggest the colors on indigenous merced maps are best read as features that betray something of the rhetorical and material conditions of mapmaking. If coloration hints at remnants of preconquest tradition, it also indicates the allure of pictorial landscape conventions introduced from Europe. What becomes interesting in this light: how, in the hands of indigenous mapmakers, and in the eyes of colonial map readers, colored paints become open enough to accommodate a host of diverse meanings.

11. Several discussions of maps and other two-dimensional representations guide my analysis of visual and material objects here. Prominent among these are: Paul Carter, *The Road to Botany Bay: An Exploration of Landscape and History* (New York, 1988); Tom Conley, *The Self-Made Map: Cartographic Writing in Early Modern France* (Minneapolis, 1996); Hubert Damisch, "La Grille Comme Volonté et Comme Representation," in *Cartes et Figures de la Terre* (Paris, 1980), 30–40; Louis Marin, *Utopics: The Semiological Play of Textual Spaces*, trans. Robert A. Vollarth (Atlantic Highlands, NJ, 1990); Frank Lestringant, *Mapping the Renaissance World: The Geographical Imagination in the Age of Discovery*, trans. D. Fausett (Berkeley, 1994); and Thongchai Winichakul, *Siam Mapped: A History of the Geo-Body of a Nation* (Honolulu, 1994). Scholarly work on text and image relations has also influenced my thinking; one particularly useful analysis has been that of Avital Ronell, *The Telephone Book: Technology, Schizophrenia, Electric Speech* (Lincoln, NE, 1989).

12. Because painting and writing were closely linked in indigenous communities in the sixteenth century, relationships between the two acts are difficult to sort out (see discussion below). Even so, the role of alphabetic writing on indigenous maps has generally been understudied. Scholars have not exactly disregarded written texts, but most have emphasized the study of pictorial elements and conventions on indigenous cartographs (see, e.g., Joyce W. Bailey, "Map of Texupa (Oaxaca, 1579): a Study of Form and Meaning," *Art Bulletin* 54 [1972]: 452–79; Boone, *Stories in Red and Black*; Gruzinski, "Colonial Indian Maps"; Leibsohn, "Colony and Cartography"; Mundy, *Mapping of New Spain*; and Robertson, *Mexican Manuscript Painting*). There are many reasons for this. Cartographic histories and other genres of indigenous mapping often eschew alphabetic texts; no less importantly there exists a long history of anthropological, ethnohistorical, and art historical desire to reclaim from colonial contexts indigenous, if not also pre-Hispanic traditions, which were more

often pictorial than alphabetic. Yet analysis of the merced maps, in particular, shows that written words were as integral as pictorial images to the meanings assigned these documents in the sixteenth century (and since). Moreover, the behavior of alphabetic texts on maps, especially in visual and material terms, often reiterates or overlaps with that of pictorial signs. Alphabetic inscriptions therefore cannot be overlooked if we are to understand either the cartographic process or the visual qualities of these artifacts.

13. In New Spain, the presence of alphabetic writing was hardly ideologically innocent. Early on, alphabetism did register as a foreign mode of expression that displaced and undermined pre-Hispanic graphic traditions. By the 1570s, however, alphabetic script, used by indigenous people to write in their own languages, was tightly enmeshed in local and regional administrative processes. Nevertheless, important distinctions separated writing in Spanish from writing in Nahuatl, Mixtec, and other indigenous languages. Not only did these languages typically have different readers, but the occasions appropriate for writing in each language also differed. Thus possessing the skill or desire to write alphabetically—or even to read alphabetic letters—had multiple meanings in New Spain. On the transition from pre-Hispanic modes of record keeping to alphabetic writing in indigenous languages, see, e.g., Frances Kartunnen, "Nahuatl Literacy," in *The Inca and Aztec States*, ed. George Collier, Renato Rosaldo, and John Wirth (New York, 1982), 395–417; Lockhart, *Nahuas after the Conquest*, 327–73; Matthew Restall, *The Maya World: Yucatec Culture and Society, 1550–1850* (Stanford, 1997); Matthew Restall and Kevin Terraciano, "Indigenous Writing and Literacy in Colonial Mexico," *UCLA Historical Journal* (Special Issue, 1992): 8–28; and Kevin Terraciano, *Nudzahui History: Mixtec Writing and Culture in Colonial Oaxaca* (Ann Arbor, 1994). For analyses of alphabetism that accent ideological designs, see Mignolo, "Literacy and Colonization"; Gruzinski, *The Conquest of Mexico*, 6–69; and J.J. Klor de Alva, "Language, Politics, and Translation: Colonial Discourse and Classical Nahuatl in New Spain," in *The Art of Translation: Voices from the Field*, ed. R. Warren (Boston, 1989), 143–62. On the persistence, and meaning, of visual imagery in indigenous documents of the sixteenth century, see Elizabeth Hill Boone, "Pictorial Documents and Visual Thinking in Postconquest Mexico," in *Native Traditions in the Postconquest World*, ed. Elizabeth Hill Boone and Tom Cummins, 149–200 (Washington, DC, 1998).

14. The painting, #1448 in the AGN Mapoteca, is associated with written records held in Tierras, vol. 2431, exp. 1. Included in the same expediente is a nearly identical map, painted by the same person, also on European paper (AGN Mapoteca, #1449). Both documents were inscribed by a single scribal hand distinct from that of the painter.

15. Even within the written records of mercedes, scribes typically relied upon standardized language to describe and register proper protocol. Although lengthy responses occasionally appear, more typically the words of individuals are summarized. In the case of interpreters' statements, we usually find some combination of relatively rote response and individual word choice. In general, however, the written accounts of mercedes, like much colonial legal documentation, tend toward redundancy and bureaucratic language.

16. In taking this approach, I disagree somewhat with Mundy, who emphasizes the power of alphabetic script to control the meaning of indigenous cartographs and render these works increasingly inaccessible to indigenous readers (*Mapping of New Spain*, 164–79). In some instances, she is certainly correct: such

roles may have been played by writing. Yet I believe the evidence suggests that the denotative function of written texts did not dominate their behavior in sixteenth-century contexts (as Mundy's analysis of the Relaciones Geográficas maps seems to imply). Moreover, my reading of merced documents indicates that images alone did not properly constitute a merced map. In the absence of writing, at least for Spanish officials, there was no map. Gruzinski speaks of a collaborative arrangement in which indigenous painters anticipated writing and thus created images that would accommodate later inscription ("Colonial Indian Maps," 53). Certain images do reveal such a practice, but I also have found documents in which writing by a Spanish official preceded the creation of imagery by an indigenous painter. This suggests a historical situation in which text and image determined and shaped each other. Finally, instances of shifts and reinterpretations of the spoken and written language of "colonizers" have received much press in the last several years. Prime examples are discussed by Homi Bhabha, "Signs Taken for Wonders: Questions of Ambivalence and Authority under a Tree Outside Delhi," in *Locations of Culture*, 102–22 (London, 1994); and Vicente Rafael, *Contracting Colonialism: Translation and Christian Conversion in Tagalog Society under Early Spanish Rule* (Ithaca, 1988). For a telling example from colonial Latin America, see Joanne Rappaport, "Object and Alphabet: Andean Indians and Documents in the Colonial Period," in Boone and Mignolo, *Writing without Words*, 271–92.

17. In this instance, the primary transaction concerns Francisco Alonso de Sosa's request for land to build and operate a tannery in Coatepeque. The individuals named are: Francisco Gomez de Sotomayor, teniente del alcalde mayor; Juan Escobar, yndio ynterprete (sic); Luis Esteban, interprete del audiencia (sic); and Luis Valentín Carrillo, escribano público. Only the latter three actually sign the document.

18. Bleeding of this sort occurs with considerable frequency on merced maps and many alphabetic documents of the sixteenth and seventeenth centuries as well as countless written records from early-modern and modern times. On the implications of this, see the discussion below.

19. The painting, #2083 in the AGN Mapoteca, was executed on European paper. Written records of this merced, which appear in Tierras, vol. 2764, exp. 21, concern a request for two caballerías de tierra.

20. The words written across the house read, "aqui no hay casa sino que se puso por que es donde pide" [there is no house here, nevertheless it was placed [here] because it is where he requests it]. And below the building, the passage runs, "aqui pide don baltasar ximenez dos caballerias de tierra en donde llaman atexpanaloja (sic)" [here, in the place called Atexpanaloja, don Baltasar Ximenez requests two caballerias de tierra].

21. Sheldon Nodelman, *Marden, Novros, Rothko* (Houston, 1978), 48–49, 52–53.

22. The map, #1765 in the AGN Mapoteca, was painted on European paper. The accompanying documents, which request a grant of two caballerías de tierra for Sancho Ortiz de Zúñiga, can be found in Tierras, vol. 2708, exp. 13. This map seems to be one of several related paintings, all presented to and signed by Esteban de López in Huejotzingo in 1591 and 1592, but not necessarily painted by the same hand. See maps #1763, #1764, #1767, #1768 (*Catálogo de Ilustraciones*, vol. 4, Mexico City, 1979).

23. In the instructions, investigation, testimony, and approval of this and other mercedes, texts parallel those of many sixteenth-century legal and notarial writings. Words are set down in script, in lines that read left to right, with

successive lines descending along the page from top to bottom (as the pages of this printed essay, for instance, are expected to be read). Paragraphs can be found, although they are not employed consistently; and, apart from the blank spaces separating sections of the investigation or crossed-out segments, writing proceeds uninterrupted from page to page. In contrast, the alphabetic words penned on maps enjoy far more liberty, even when they register words or phrases identical to those on accompanying merced maps. To wit, cartographic writing changes orientations, sizes, and positions in ways that are denied other parts of the merced record. Thus, one often has to turn a map or shift positions to decipher its writing. For other, recent analyses of the visuality of written words in documents and manuscripts, see e.g., Tom Cummins and Joanne Rappaport, "The Reconfiguration of Civic and Sacred Space: Architecture, Image, and Writing in the Colonial Northern Andes,"(Washington, DC, 1997); Gretchen Geser, "A Visual Analysis of the Codex Telleriano-Remensis," (Northampton, MA, 1997); Brinkley Messick, *The Calligraphic State* (Berkeley, 1993), 231–50; and Rappaport, "Object and Alphabet."

24. The painting, AGN Mapoteca #2230, was painted on European paper. Written records, describing the request for "un sitio de estancia para cabras" [a site for an estancia for goats], appear in Tierras, vol. 2812, exp. 16.
25. Gary Tomlinson, "Unlearning the Aztec Cantares," 267. Although Tomlinson enlists this phrase to reference the realm of the written in Nahuatl and Spanish in the *Cantares mexicanos*, the phrase works well here to evoke the ways in which alphabetic writing calls into being far more than "just words."
26. J. Brian Harley, "Maps, Knowledge, and Power," in *The Iconography of Landscape*. ed. Denis Cosgrove and Stephen Daniels (Cambridge, 1988), 301–3.
27. For a provocative, and serious, discussion of this point, see Rey Chow, "Film as Ethnography; or Translation between Cultures in the Postcolonial World," in *Primitive Passions: Visuality, Sexuality, Ethnography, and Contemporary Chinese Cinema*, 174–202 (New York, 1995).

Part III

The Literate and the Nonliterate

– Chapter 6 –

CONTINUITY VS. ACCULTURATION: AZTEC AND INCA CASES OF ALPHABETIC LITERACY

José Antonio Mazzotti

IT IS WELL KNOWN that when the Spaniards arrived in both Mexico and Peru, the Amerindian cultures of these regions had already developed their own systems of recording information. In the case of the Aztecs, the extensive use of pictorial representations kept alive the memory of the ancestors and the myths of origin and also contained a great deal of information about the daily affairs of the state. In the case of the Incas, the prevailing form of representation was the *khipu*, a system of cords and knots that was used mainly for statistical purposes but also in the highly specialized art of recording political and military history.

Both the pictorial representations (compiled in códices after the Spanish invasion) and the khipu were systems not directly related to language. They helped one to recall a verbal account of the referred facts, but they did not represent a phonetic materialization of spoken language. In most cases, their signs and designs could be deciphered only by a specialist, someone capable of "reading" the representations and interpreting them for political authorities upon demand.

It is not my purpose here to enter into details about the complexity of the códices and khipu. There already exists a large bibliography on the subject, most recently Joyce Marcus's *Mesoamerican Writing Systems*, Robert and Marcia Ascher's *Code of the Quipu*, and the compilation by Walter Mignolo and Elizabeth Hill Boone entitled *Writing without Words*.[1] These works argue that in highly developed Amerindian cultures there were forms of literacy and inscription that differed from the alphabetic literacy considered by Europeans to be the only form of true writing.

In this chapter I intend to present a panoramic view of the most prominent cases in which colonial subjects appropriated alphabetic literacy for their own ends. In some of these cases, indigenous and mestizo writers managed to preserve elements of their Amerindian discursive traditions, not only in content but also in terms of original structures and modes of narration. In addition to adapting alphabetical writing to their native discursive backgrounds, these writers attempted to negotiate some economic and symbolic privileges before the Spanish authorities. As members of elite groups within the native cultures, these writers enjoyed privileged access to the technology of alphabetical writing, thus ensuring themselves cultural legitimacy within the colonial order. Part of the concern of current literary scholars in studying these indigenous and mestizo cases of alphabetic writing derives from the need to describe with textual and linguistic approaches in particular the complexity of the political struggle and the social processes by which these native leaders preserved and transformed their own cultural identity. This kind of approach complements a purely historical one, generally focused on explicit contents.

I will concentrate here on cases from the Andean world, referring only briefly to three very important cases from the Aztec context. Most of these cases will already be familiar to the specialized reader. However, I would like to put these cases within the context of the ongoing struggle in native culture between, on the one hand, acceptance of acculturation and on the other, the maintenance of continuity with their non-European past. I use the concept of acculturation here to mean assimilation and not simply "cultural contact," as Robert Redfield and others would have it.[2] By the term "continuity," I refer to both renewal and resistance but also to the inevitable adaptation to a new cultural and political order.[3] Sometimes, this process of adaptation leads to a phenomenon that recent Latin American cultural critics identify as "transculturation," even though this theoretical framework was originally applied to post-Enlightenment processes of cultural contact and exchange.[4]

To begin with the Aztecs, it is important to remember that after the first years of the siege and capture of the city of Mexico/Tenochtitlan in 1521 Spanish friars trained some of the *tlacuilos*, or scribes (painters, more exactly), of the old Aztec régime in the use of alphabetic literacy. In the late 1520s these scribes produced the first written versions of the conquest in Nahuatl, without neglecting the continuity of their ancient pictorial mode of representation. However, these manuscripts were practically unknown until the 1550s and 1560s when priests like Bernardino de Sahagún and Diego Durán began to compile ethnographic information on ancient Aztec beliefs.[5] Although subsequently edited and translated by Spanish and mestizo priests, these first indigenous alphabetic accounts of the conquest somehow survived to contest the imposition of the triumphalist and heroic versions of the same historical events narrated by such Spanish historians as López de Gómara and Cervantes de Salazar. At the same time, in his translations of original Nahuatl versions of ancient myths and royal genealogies, Sahagún consciously or unconsciously preserved some of the original formulaic structures and heroic depictions in the narration of the origins of gods like Huitzilopochtl and Tezcatlipoca.[6] Ángel María Garibay, one of the most important scholars of Sahagún's ethnographic endeavor, has recognized that the sixteenth-century Spanish version preserved the form of an indigenous epic poem.[7]

However, it was only over the course of succeeding generations that native authors writing in Spanish began to express their own perspectives. Two representative cases are those of Fernando Alvarado Tezozomoc and Fernando de Alva Ixtlilxochitl. The first is the author of *Crónica Mexicana* (ca. 1598), an account of Aztec history from pre-Hispanic times until the end of the sixteenth century. Tezozomoc, who declared himself a grandson of the late Moctezuma through his maternal line, was also a son of the cacique Diego de Alvarado Huanitzin, an Aztec noble who held the title of governor of the town of Ehecatepec until 1539, when he became governor of the city of Mexico/Tenochtitlan.[8] According to Mario Mariscal, *Crónica Mexicana* was originally written in Nahuatl (in an apparently lost manuscript) and later translated into Spanish by Tezozomoc himself or by an anonymous translator. Mariscal also presents a third possibility: that Tezozomoc dictated his historical version of the Aztec past in Nahuatl and that this version was simultaneously translated and written down by someone who did not have a strong command of Spanish.[9] *Crónica Mexicana* contains numerous repetitions of words referring to objects that probably had homonymous denominations in the Nahuatl version. There are also multiple syntactical structures that do not correspond to the style of late-sixteenth-century Spanish chronicles and that reflect underlying Nahuatl structures.[10] The use of the formulaic repetition of words and the presence of long descriptive and enumerative passages regarding the clothes and gifts of important personages are also possible remnants of an oral memorized version.[11] For many reasons, Tezozomoc's work constitutes an important stage in the long conquest of alphabetical literacy by members of the dominated society, reflecting as it does Aztec styles of narration and cultural resonance that ultimately modified the dominating Spanish modes of historical writing.

The second author is the mestizo historian Fernando de Alva Ixtlilxochitl, born in 1578 and a descendant of the lords of Texcoco, one of the city-states that formed part of the Aztec Triple Alliance of the Mexican central valley. While Alva Ixtlilxochitl did incorporate into his work the system of warrior values deployed by Spanish historians to explain and praise the actions of the conquerors, he also infused the actions of his indigenous ancestors with heroism, thereby restoring their dignity and honor. His mother's great-grandfather had been Ixtlilxoxhitl, the last king of the Texcoco ruling house according to mestizo Alva Ixtlilxochitl in his *Compendio Histórico del Reino de Texcoco*. It was his ancestor who, forming an alliance with Cortés, led thousands of troops against Moctezuma and helped determine the victory of the Christian faith and the Spanish forces.[12] Among many others, one example of the heroism of Ixtlilxochitl, ancestor of the mestizo historian, is the passage in which the king of Texcoco saves Cortés's life by cutting off the arms of several Aztec warriors (472). Thus Alva Ixtlilxochitl rectifies Spanish versions that declared Cortés was saved by his own soldiers. However, as Rolena Adorno has stated, "to acknowledge this complicity is not to deny the legitimacy of the position of the colonial subject, but rather to outline its features."[13] In this sense, Alva Ixtlilxochitl represents not so much the "vision of the vanquished" but the voice of indigenous elites who placed themselves on an equal plane with the Spaniards in terms of courage, moral values, and heroism.

In another of his works, the *Sumaria Relación de la Historia General de esta Nueva España*, Alva Ixtlilxochitl focuses on indigenous history before the arrival of the Spaniards. He establishes his authority in this complex matter by claiming that his sources are the authentic ones, that is, "las pinturas y caracteres con que están escritas y memorizadas sus historias ... y los cantos con que las observaban" ("the paintings and marks with which they write and memorize their stories ... and the song with which they observe them").[14] He disputed what Spanish historians had written, arguing that the *amoxtli* (the Nahuatl name for the book of folded parchments) and oral tradition contained much more accurate information. In this sense, the mestizo historian identifies himself as a colonial subject who claims his own legitimacy and privileges in a universalizing empire. At the same time, he intends to preserve indigenous history by utilizing the same mode of expression that Spanish historians used for colonizing purposes.

Turning now to Peru, the old *khipukamayuq*, or professionals in the use of the khipu, had managed to transmit their knowledge of the Incan past into alphabetic literacy almost from the first years of the conquest. However, the first document that records this knowledge was not directly written by the khipukamayuq themselves but dictated to translators and then written down by Spaniards. Nine years after the occupation of Cuzco by Spanish troops in 1533, Governor Vaca de Castro ordered an investigation into Incan history to be carried out by Spaniards with the help of Indian informers who were known to be the record keepers of historical memory. He sent for the khipukamayuq of the town of Paqariq Tampu, a place celebrated in Incan origin myths.[15]

The document that resulted from the interviews is known as the *Relación del Origen y Descendencia de los Incas*. Of the four khipukamayuq who participated in the interviews, we know the identity of only two: Collapiña and Supno. These informants indicated that before the cuzqueño régime of the Incas there had been a state of general chaos, and that—anticipating what all the later chronicles would state—it was Mankhu Qhapaq, the first Inca, who conquered and "civilized" the neighboring communities and founded the empire. The khipukamayuq also narrated the deeds and victories of succeeding Incas, until the arrival of the Spaniards in 1532.

Like many other documents of the period, the *Relación del Origen y Descendencia de los Incas* of 1542 was presented in the format of a particular Spanish legal document: the "relación de servicios," or account of services rendered by a vassal to a high authority or directly to His Majesty, the King of Spain, in order to obtain honors and compensations. That it was presented in this way is due to the personal interest of Pawllu Inka, one of the sons of the last Inca who ruled before the arrival of the Spaniards. Pawllu Inka, who had cooperated with the Europeans, sought to manipulate some of the information rendered by the four khipukamayuq in order to gain favor for his own lineage. In fact, the only copy we have of the written testimony of the four khipukamayuq is dated 1608, precisely at the moment when the grandson of Pawllu Inka was in the process of petitioning the Spanish crown in Madrid for some privileges.[16]

Despite the process of translation, some traces of the original Quechua oral version of the khipukamayuq can be noted within the

Spanish prose into which it was transformed. If we remember that in Andean Incan tradition information contained in each khipu was organized in sequences of actions and characters, it is most likely that the "reading" of the knots and cords by khipukamayuq was performed by using formulas and repetitive structures in Quechua traditional oral style. In the manuscript of the *Relación*, each one of the biographies of the Incas begins and ends in a similar form, repeating the same patterns. Furthermore, several syntactic structures of the written Spanish version mirror the order of Quechua syntax, such as placing the verb after the modifiers in the predicate.

Such commonality with the original Quechua version of the khipukamayuq can be understood because the Spanish written text is basically a transcript of the literal translation undertaken by two Castilians and a mestizo interpreter. They translated the original Quechua version orally into Spanish, which other Spanish scribes then recorded. The result reflects some of the patterns and formulas that the khipukamayuq had used in their own original oral version.

Another element of continuity concerns the direction of the genealogy within both the narration of the khipukamayuq and the written Spanish text. While some Incas are credited with the expansion and consolidation of the cuzqueño state, others (identifiable as the ancestors of the contemporary rivals of Pawllu Inka) receive little recognition. In this sense, even the content of the *Relación* preserves the selective manipulation of the past so characteristic of the "historical poems"[17] attributed to the Incan court and in which the khipukamayuq of each royal family of Cuzco were well trained. This was an ancient tradition of narration whose existence is attested by several of the early chroniclers.[18] The "epic" form and historical recital of the past was an institutionalized and formal practice among the Incas, and it was controlled by the state in order to strengthen the power of the sovereign.[19] Both the khipukamayuq, professional bookkeepers and historians who recorded the information that would be used in the poems, and the *harawiq*, or composers, also in charge of public representations, were supported by the royal families as a specialized staff that contributed to the glorification of their ancestors. An understanding of the forms and uses of this ancient discursive practice is essential to our reading of the particularities of the *Relación*. Although generally following the format of the Spanish genre of the account of services, this early colonial document still presents traces of a specific kind of Quechua orality that literary critics and historians have overlooked.

A few decades later, in 1569, twenty-two descendants of the royal family of Tupaq Inka Yupanqi (the tenth ruler) presented two documents, or "memorias," to the Spanish authorities of Cuzco in order to claim lands and tributary benefits. The first "Memoria" is a list and description of the descendants and of ten witnesses from Incan times who can testify to the identity of the plaintiffs. The second document is called "Memoria de las provincias" and contains a long enumeration of the regions, towns, and military sites that Tupaq Inka Yupanqi conquered, presumably between 1463 and 1493. Both documents were studied by John H. Rowe in 1985, after he found them in the Departmental Archive of Cuzco.[20]

What really matters here is that the order of the provinces and towns of the second "Memoria" is organized in a way that can only be explained through the logic of the khipu system of recording. Although there are several other documents of the period in which descendants of different indigenous noble families petition to recover or preserve their privileges under the colonial régime, this "Memoria," in particular, represents a complex intermingling of Spanish legalistic discourse and Incan historical forms of recording. As Rowe observes, some of the places named in the narration of Tupaq Inka Yupanqi's conquests appear before others that are geographically closer to Cuzco, the point of departure for the ruler's military campaigns.[21] This apparent inconsistency reveals the existence of a subtext that models and structures the Spanish written narration according to the characteristics of the khipu cords. In a khipu, there is always a transversal horizontal cord from which several vertical cords hang. These vertical cords may also hold several other small cords that extend from them. It seems that in our case the khipu-source was organized in vertical cords signifying the conquered provinces, and the subsidiary cords would have represented fortresses and local chiefs who accepted or were crushed by the power of Tupaq Inka Yupanqi. The knots in each cord would remind the khipukamayuq of the number and order of the fortresses and conquered *kurakakuna*, or local chiefs. As Rowe explains, each khipu can be read vertically or horizontally. In the first case, the narration of the conquests by provinces would include their fortresses and local chiefs. In the horizontal "reading," the fortresses and chiefs from different provinces would appear juxtaposed in the same category regardless of chronology, thus raising possible confusion in a Westernized lineal reading.

Moreover, the "Memoria" also reveals that some campaigns are narrated in a circular order, first naming the northern *suyu*, or province, and then the eastern one, the southern one, and the western one. This particular spatial order is related to a ritual procedure of Incan military expansion, likened to the form of a spiral that expands itself from a central point of departure.[22] The "Memoria" itself presents the campaigns of Tupaq Inka Yupanqi throughout the entire Andean territory, following a similar order at the macro-regional scale: first the provinces conquered in Chinchaysuyu (north), and then in Antisuyu (east), Qullasuyu (south), and Kuntisuyu (west). Regarding style and formulas, Rowe notes that the narrative connections between conquered places consists of stereotypical phrases such as "y luego conquistaron" ("and after they conquered") that repeat the probable oral account made by an indigenous khipukamayuq in charge of keeping the memory of the family's ancestor.[23]

One year later, in 1570, another important document emerged from one of the last surviving Incas who resisted the Spanish colonization in the exiled government of Vilcabamba. Titu Kusi Yupanqi dictated his version of the conquest in order to negotiate privileges under a potential peace with the Spanish régime. This Inca in exile narrated that the Spaniards had committed all kind of abuses against his father, Mankhu Inka, and that his father was justified in carrying out a rebellion against those same Spanish conquerors. The document, called *Relación de la Conquista del Perú*, or merely *Instrucción del Inca*, originated in Titu Kusi's oral narration, which was translated by an Augustinian friar, Marcos García, and then written down by a mestizo scribe, Martín Pando.

Some studies have noted that the translation of Titu Kusi's account manages to keep the form and finality of the oral genre within Incan tradition of the historical poem or "ritual homage" to a dead Inca, ordered by his successor in order to glorify the deeds of his father.[24] However, in Titu Kusi's case, due to the severe conditions of exile under which he had to dictate his account, the function of this "historical poem" was also informed by the Spanish genre of the account of services, since the text was directed to ex-governor Lope García de Castro, who was to mediate with the Spanish king to obtain some privileges for the rebel Inca if he surrendered.

Putting aside the political and strategic intentions of *Instrucción del Inca*, scholars like Luis Millones have also noted the presence of Quechua orality in the style of the document.[25] *Instrucción* presents a heterogeneous structure, since most of the narration consists of long speeches by the principal characters in the drama of the conquest. Thus, Pizarro, Ataw Wallpa, Mankhu Inka, "Vila Oma," or supreme Incan priest, and others intervene with their own words, reproduced by the main narrator, Titu Kusi. According to Millones, this format is consistent with the narrative strategy of Quechua language, in which it is impossible to paraphrase a quote, because prepositions and conjunctions are absent. For example, to say that Mankhu Inka stated that he disapproved of the Spaniards' behavior, in Quechua you would need to quote Mankhu Inka's words directly. This is common in Amerindian languages in which the distance between the narrated facts and the main narrator has to be openly indicated by directly quoting the exact words of the participants in the events described. Generally, a verbal form closes the quotation. The narrator then appears as a simple intermediary between the narrated facts and dialogues and the public who hears or reads the narration. In addition to this characteristic, the theatrical or representational nature of the so-called "historical poem" of the Incan court also explains why many of the voices within the text are presented as if they were part of a dramatic script.[26]

At least 70 percent of the text of *Instrucción* consists of long speeches in the voices of the historical characters of the conquest of Peru. Through their words, as presented by Titu Kusi, the reader is presented with a history that deeply criticizes the behavior of the conquistadores and accepts the Spanish presence in the Andes only for the purpose of evangelization. Although some features of the text reveal the intervention of the translator and the scribe in the deployment of the Christian defense, it also is possible to affirm that important components of this document depend upon an indigenous point of view. This is clear not only in the sharp condemnation of the greed and lust of the conquerors but also in some of the categories of space and time the document utilizes. One example: While narrating the Great Rebellion of 1536 led by his father, Mankhu Inka, Titu Kusi describes the Incan armies as moving in a counterclockwise direction when descending upon Cuzco. Such troop movement is in contrast to the traditional clockwise spiral movement that Incan armies followed setting out from Cuzco on campaign. However, during the Great Rebellion, each of the four provinces in which the Incan empire was divided deployed thousands of soldiers whom Titu Kusi's narration describes as marching in a direction opposite from that of an expansion campaign, since Cuzco was the end point of the Rebellion rather than the point of departure. In its description of the rebellion led by Titu Kusi's father, then, the narrative reveals an adaptation of an Incan ritual and military strategy.

Another important case of the use of alphabetical literacy in the Andes is Inca Garcilaso de la Vega's *Comentarios Reales*, first published in two parts in 1609 and 1617.[27] Garcilaso was a mestizo of high standing in the existing social hierarchy of Peru. However, his work was written in Spain after 1590, more than thirty years after he left Peru. He managed to manipulate some of the most prestigious literary and philosophical topoi of Renaissance culture in order to paradoxically propose both a pro-Incan and a pro-encomendero vision of Peru. Garcilaso represents the emergence of a new social group, that of the noble mestizos of Cuzco, who glorified the deeds of their ancestors on both sides, the Spanish conquerors and the wisdom and greatness of the Incan régime. Since Garcilaso makes use of a vast array of European references in his *Comentarios Reales,* his work traditionally has been read as a typical case of the assimilation of the dominant culture by colonial subjects, who do little more than repeat and mimic the style and gestures of their Spanish masters.[28]

A principal shortcoming of such an interpretation of Garcilaso is that it pays no attention to the subtleties of the first editions of his work. The most important editions produced during our century—those of Ángel Rosenblat in 1943–44, Carmelo Sáenz de Santa María in 1960, and Carlos Araníbar in 1991—have served as the exclusive source for many contemporary studies of *Comentarios Reales.* All of these editions, however, severely modify Garcilaso's original punctuation, assuming the potential reader of the text to be a learned Westerner. As a result, Garcilaso's prose is transformed into a clear example of how well a *mestizo* subject of the Spanish king was able to master the Castilian written language.

Despite apparent mistakes and misprints, the rhetorical mechanisms embedded in the first editions of *Comentarios Reales* achieve a high degree of authority, both by evoking some of the most prestigious European literary and religious topoi as well as some key symbols of Incan imagery and by incorporating elements of an Incan mode of narration. With this understanding of his history as a double-voiced discourse, we can deduce the strategy of a writer who is dealing with a European audience and censorship but who is, at the same time, transforming original Andean themes and styles in order to accommodate them within a projective future, just as Alvarado Tezozomoc and Alva Ixtlilxochitl had done in the Mexican case.

For example, when reading the original text aloud, the continuous use of formulaic structures to open the chapters that narrate Incan expansions, and the similarity of certain foundational passages to the versal duality (the syntactical/semantic couplets) of Quechua poetry, become perceptible. Such a reading would respect the original punctuation of *Comentarios Reales,* a punctuation that modern editions have severely modified in order to better meet the requirements of a visual reading.[29]

Similarly, certain images used in the work to describe the Andean spiritual ages reflect not only European but also ancient Andean imagery. These images generally have been identified only with prestigious literary and rhetorical topoi such as the *præparatio evangelica* and the Augustinian scheme of the human ascension to the "City of God." But in the metaphors used in the work to talk about Andean spiritual history, there is also a syncretic but contradictory conformation of Incan and European images. For example, Garcilaso used the allegory of the climatic and temporal phenomena of Obscure Darkness, the Morning Star, and the Sun of Justice to refer to the ages of barbarism, the Incas, and the Christian faith.[30] If we compare the images of Garcilaso's allegory with the Inca pantheon as described by chroniclers who wrote about Inca religion, we find that Garcilaso's images would not have been at all unfamiliar to the surviving Inca aristocracy of the early seventeenth century.[31] The "Morning Star," or Venus, was generally characterized as a servant of the Moon, and it presided over the dawn and the Spring as a symbol of fertility. The "Sun" represented a dual entity, divided into the solstices of Summer and Winter. In the case of the Summer, the Apu Inti, or major sun, was the symbol of the power of a higher celestial god, Wiraqucha. It announced the climax of the rainy season and harvest during the months of December to May. The other sun, P'unchaw, was the weak sun of Winter, when the celestial body is furthest from the point of observation, Cuzco, in the southern hemisphere. This sun announced a time of preparation and renovation of the cosmic cycle and was worshipped during the Inti Raymi celebration of June.[32]

The two Inca suns imply a complexity that any linear reading of the Christian "Sun of Justice" does not capture. For if we consider the Incan references, which one is the "Sun of Justice" implied by Garcilaso's text: the major sun of December, or the weak sun of June? If we follow a narrative succession based on the temporality of the day, the arrival of the Spaniards would represent the sun immediately following the dawn and thus could be compared to a sun that has not yet arrived at its potential maturity and power. In this sense, the text would be implying a "fourth age" surpassing the colonial order, which would be represented by a major sun that is not present within the trifold description of the Andean spiritual ages.[33]

This example illustrates the possibility of a quite different interpretation of Garcilaso's work, an interpretation that de-centers and even contradicts a purely Europeanized reading of the text. By attending to the Andean resonance of style and semantic fields within the work, we can begin to discern some of the features of an author who is more complex than the traditionally accepted commonplace of the fully neoplatonic, "acculturated," and "harmonious" mestizo.

I could not finish this brief account of indigenous and *mestizo* appropriations of alphabetical literacy without referring to the *Nueva Coronica* written by the Andean cacique Guamán Poma de Ayala. Although peripheral to the Cuzco center (Guamán Poma wrote from Huamanga and declared himself a descendant of local noble ancestors, yet related to the Incan court), his work is a clear example of adaptation of the European historical recording system.[34] The last registered date in his manuscript is 1615, and the text constitutes a long narration about the pre-Incan and Incan past as well as a description of a chaotic and infamous colonial order. It is a clear denunciation of the exploitation and injustices suffered by the indigenous population under the Spanish régime. It was intended to reach King Phillip III in Spain, although we do not know if it was examined by any leading Spanish authority. The work was not published during the colonial period, and was found only in 1908, in the Royal Library of Copenhagen, where the manuscript still remains.

Guamán Poma's prose is frequently informed by his Quechua-speaking background. In fact, he introduces several passages directly written in Quechua, and in his use of the Spanish language he shows several syntactical and morphological forms that belong to the Quechua structure. For example, he frequently accompanies feminine nouns in Spanish with masculine adjectives, thus breaking the Spanish grammatical principle of gender agreement between noun and adjective. Quechua, like English, is a language that does not distinguish gender or number in adjectives. Therefore, Guamán Poma standardizes all adjectives in Spanish with one single masculine form. It is easy to mix such categories when Spanish is a second language at a very early stage of learning. For many years, traditional historians like Raúl Porras Barrenechea scorned Guamán Poma's prose for being so "imperfect" and "illegible." Porras did not recognize that, despite its multiple grammatical "mistakes," Guamán Poma's prose is the genuine expression of an Andean Spanish language that has become one of the most characteristic features of Peruvian popular culture in postcolonial times. *Nueva Coronica* is also well known because Guamán Poma adds to his narrative version of the pre-Hispanic past and the colonial present some four hundred illustrations related to the topics and situations in the written account. European iconographic models appear in many of these illustrations, but there are also a significant number of icons and a specific use of the structuring of space that belong to native Andean practices of visual representation.

Commentary by Rolena Adorno and others has shed light on the multiple sources, both Andean and European, that Guamán Poma used in his long account of Andean history.[35] *Nueva Coronica* provides a clear example of how colonial writers utilizing discursive strategies borrowed from the Spanish in order to serve indigenous interests. It is a challenging work in many senses and represents an example of what León-Portilla would call the "counter conquest" of the Americas. It is important to note, however, that its use of Andean themes and cosmogonic categories is intertwined with its defense of evangelization and its partial similarity to the Spanish genre of the *letras arbitristas*. *Nueva Coronica* is also, then, a good example of regional indigenous elites managing to accommodate themselves within the colonial apparatus.

As is obvious from this brief look at some indigenous and *mestizo* writers, the appropriation of alphabetic literacy assumes different forms depending upon the specific purpose of a text and its degree of closeness to an oral indigenous source. In the Andean area, other peripheral works, such as the *Huarochirí Manuscript* (ca. 1608), compiled by the *mestizo* extirpator of idolatries Francisco de Ávila in the area of Yauyos, and the *Relación de Antigüedades del Pirú* (ca. 1615), by the indigenous *kuraka* Joan de Santacruz Pachacuti Yamqui Salcamaygua, of the Collao region, would fit perfectly in the list of native uses of alphabetical literacy. In all cases these strategies of resistance or coexistence are visible enough to compare with the native appropriation of other European means of domination, such as the horse or gun powder. Despite these native endeavors, however, the Spanish construction of a "city of letters" or "ciudad letrada," as Uruguayan critic Ángel Rama called it, implied new limitations for the indigenous population, which then had to depend on Spanish scribes and lawyers to make claims before the Peninsular power.[36]

In many cases, assimilation into the European privileged form of communicating and recording information was complete, as is evidenced by thousands of legal documents filling the shelves of archives in Spain and Latin America.[37] However, in other cases— and I have described only a portion of them here—indigenous and *mestizo* cultures managed to survive and transmit some features of their heritage, transforming the European forms and functions of alphabetical writing into a complex discourse that is an original feature of early Latin American culture. It is thanks in part to those early writers that many features of contemporary Latin American literature (such as the *indigenista* movement) can be better understood within their own specific contexts and social and political function. It is also thanks to them that we can now better appreciate the real nature and sophistication of Amerindian cultures and the means by which they were able to maintain continuity with their past during colonial and postcolonial times.

Notes

1. See Joyce Marcus, *Mesoamerican Writing Systems: Propaganda, Myth and History in Four Ancient Civilizations* (Princeton, 1992); Marcia Ascher and Robert Ascher, *Code of the Quipu: A Study of Media, Mathematics and Culture* (Ann Arbor, 1981); and Elizabeth Hill Boone and Walter Mignolo, eds., *Writing without Words: Alternative Literacies in Mesoamerica and the Andes* (Durham, 1994). Also, for an interpretation of the khipu as a mnemonic device used to record historical information, see Carlos Radicati di Primeglio, *La "Seriación" como Posible Clave para Descifrar los Quipus Extranumerales* (Lima, 1964).
2. For an early definition of "acculturation," see Robert Redfield, R. Linton and M. J. Herskovits, "Memorandum on the study of acculturation," *American Anthropologist* 38 (1936): 149–52. The term was later used by anthropologist Gonzalo Aguirre Beltrán in its original meaning to refer to the Mexican context. He objected to the use of "transculturation," arguing that "acculturation" (from the Latin *ad-cultura*) already implied cultural exchange and not only assimilation. See *El Proceso de Aculturación* (Mexico City, 1957), introd.
3. For Andean cases of cultural continuity like Titu Kusi Yupanqui, Joan de Santa Cruz Pachacuti, and Guamán Poma de Ayala, see Raquel Chang-Rodríguez, *La Apropiación del Signo* (Tucson, 1989) and Rolena Adorno's compilation *From Oral to Written Expression* (Syracuse, 1982).
4. The term "transculturation" was coined by the Cuban anthropologist Fernando Ortiz in his classic essay *Contrapunteo Cubano del Tabaco y el Azúcar* (Havana, 1940). In the realm of literary criticism, Ángel Rama used it to describe the work of neo-indigenist and neo-regionalist Latin American novelists such as José María Arguedas and Juan Rulfo (see Ángel Rama, *Transculturación Narrativa en América Latina* [Mexico City, 1982]). More recently, "transculturation" has been used as a theoretical framework to describe pictorial, ritual, and literary phenomena dating back to the sixteenth century (e.g., Silvia Spitta's *Between Two Waters: Narratives of Transculturation in Latin America* [Houston, 1995]). However, I prefer not to use the term in this work because of its implicit relationship with the concept of "mestizaje," which implies a harmonic syncretism of Amerindian and European cultures not always easy to find in the colonial authors I am examining. The applicability of Rama's concept of "transculturation" in the field of colonial studies is discussed by Gustavo Verdesio,

"Revisando un modelo: Ángel Rama y los estudios coloniales," in *Ángel Rama y los Estudios Latinoamericanos*, ed. Mabel Moraña (Pittsburgh, 1997), 235–48.
5. The subject has been extensively developed in Walter Mignolo's *The Darker Side of Renaissance* (Ann Arbor, 1996), ch. 2. The most accomplished compilation, but also interpretation, of the original dialogues of 1524 between the Aztec wise men and the first twelve Franciscan priests who arrived in Mexico was made by Bernardino de Sahagún in his *Coloquios y Doctrina Cristiana*, written ca. 1565 but published for the first time in 1924. A recent edition and translation of the Aztec originals was made by Miguel León-Portilla (Mexico City, 1986). Diego Durán extracts some important information from manuscripts in Nahuatl in his *Historia de las Indias de Nueva España y Islas de Tierra Firme*, 3 vols. (Mexico City, 1867), which also was written in the second half of the sixteenth century.
6. See book 3, chaps. 1 and 2 of Sahagún's most comprehensive narration of Aztec history, the *Historia General de las Cosas de Nueva España*, ed. and notes by Ángel María Garibay (Mexico City, 1956), vol. 1.
7. Ibid., 265.
8. The title of *tlatohuani*, or "chief of warriors," that Moctezuma and his predecessors bore was maintained after the conquest by the surviving Aztec nobles. They were recognized as such by the Spanish authorities, although with the obvious deprivation of political power. Mario Mariscal states that there were twenty-one known tlatohuani until Cuautemoc (the defeated successor of Moctezuma in 1521) and that eleven more held the same titles and privileges until 1609, the year in which Tezozomoc finished a manuscript written in Nahuatl to complement his Spanish-language *Crónica Mexicana*. The Nahuatl manuscript was attributed to another indigenous writer, Domingo de San Antón Muñón Chimalpaín, until 1943, when Mariscal discovered the true author. According to the Nahuatl manuscript, Diego de Alvarado Huanitzin, Tezozomoc's father, was governor of the city of Mexico/Tenochtitlan between 1539 and 1541. Mariscal takes most of the information about Tezozomoc's life and lineage from the 1609 Nahuatl manuscript, given the sparse biographical information contained in the *Crónica Mexicana*. See Mariscal's "Prólogo" to his edition of *Crónica Mexicana*, by Fernando Alvarado Tezozomoc (Mexico City, 1943), especially XXII–XXVIII.
9. See Mariscal, "Prólogo," XLI–XLII.
10. See Mariscal, "Prólogo," XLII–XLIII.
11. See, e.g., chapter XXXVI, devoted to the detailed description and enumeration of the first Moctezuma's jewels and clothes. Eric Havelock (*The Muse Learns to Write: Reflections on Orality and Literacy from Antiquity to the Present* [New Haven, 1986]) and Walter Ong (*Orality and Literacy: The Technologizing of The Word* [New York, 1982]) have argued that the extensive use of chains of elements that are remembered during an oral narration (according to their place in a sonorous sequence) is typical of nonliterate societies. This is credible if we believe Tezozomoc's own declaration that he took his information only as it was directly told by kings and nobles ("muy de boca, tal como dijéronla los amados reyes y los amados nobles," ["by word of mouth, exactly as our beloved kings and noblemen told us"]). See Mariscal, "Prólogo," XXV. For a criticism of Havelock's and Ong's arguments, see Jack Goody, *Interfaces between the Oral and the Written* (Cambridge, 1987), ch. 2.
12. See Fernando de Alva Ixtlilxochitl, *Obras Históricas*, ed. Edmundo O'Gorman (Mexico City, 1975), 1: 415–522.

13. Rolena Adorno, "Arms, Letters and the Native Historian in Early Colonial Mexico," in *1492–1992: Re/discovering Colonial Writing*, ed. René Jara and Nicolás Spadaccini (Minneapolis, 1989), 216.
14. Fernando de Alva Ixtlilxochitl, *Obras Históricas*, vol. 1, 327.
15. Paqariq Tampu literally means "lodge of dawn." Many foundational myths identify this place as the point of departure of the four brothers Ayar and their sisters-wives in order to find a place in which to found the capital of the empire. After several adventures, only one of the brothers, Ayar Mankhu, also known as Mankhu Qhapaq, survived to initiate the organization of the Inca state in the valley of Cuzco. The importance of Paqariq Tampu as a place of antiquity and veneration was probably the main reason that governor Vaca de Castro chose to seek informants from that place.
16. The most recent edition of the *Relación* was made by Juan José Vega (Lima, 1974). For a short analysis of the contents and a discussion of the veracity of the *Relación*, see Franklin Pease G. Y., *Las Crónicas y los Andes* (Lima, 1995), 23.
17. Jan Vansina, *Oral Tradition: A Study in Historical Methodology*, trans. H. M. Wright (Chicago, [1961] 1965), 155.
18. For example, Juan Díez de Betanzos, *Suma y Narración de los Incas* [1548–1556], ed. María del Carmen Martín Rubio (Madrid, 1987), 86, is very explicit about the origin of these poems, attributing them to the initiative of Inca Pachakutiq, the great reformer of the Inca state. Possibly because of the formalized structure of the poems, Betanzos compares them with the Spanish "romance" poetic form and calls them "cantares." For recent approaches to Betanzos's text and its relationship to an oral indigenous "epic" source, see Martin Lienhard, *La Voz y su Huella: Literatura y Conflicto Étnico-social en América Latina, 1492–1988* (Havana, 1990), chap. 6; and José Antonio Mazzotti, "Betanzos: de la 'épica' incaica a la escritura coral: aportes para una tipología del sujeto colonial en la historiografía andina," *Revista de Crítica Literaria Latinoamericana* 40 (1994): 239–258. References to these poems are also very detailed in Pedro de Cieza de León, *El Señorío de los Incas* [ca. 1552] (Madrid, 1985), chaps. 11–12; and they appear in Bartolomé de las Casas, *Apologética Historia Sumaria* [1552] (Madrid, 1958), 2: 391, 422; Antonio de la Calancha, *Chronica Moralizada del Orden de San Agustín en el Perú con Sucesos Exemplares Vistos en esta Monarchia* (Barcelona, 1638), 90–92; and Inca Garcilaso's *Comentarios Reales* (part 1, book 6, ch. 5), among others.
19. The term "epic" here refers basically to the oral transmission of those poems (*epos* = voice). Robert Bynum ("The generic nature of oral epic poetry," in *Folk Genres*, ed. Dan Ben-Amos [Austin, 1976], 35–58, at 47), and Paul Zumthor (*Oral Poetry: An Introduction*, trans. Kathryn Murphy-Judy, foreword by Walter J. Ong [Minneapolis, 1990], 81) have convincingly argued for the multiple forms of epic discourse throughout several cultures. However, it is important to insist on the differences between the Incan mode of historical narration and the classical epic genre. The immediate political purposes of the former and its ritual and representational/theatrical appeareance in the Incan court are elements to be considered in a specific characterization of the Incan "epic" genre. Regarding those differences, see also Francisco Lisi, "Oralidad y escritura en la crónica de Pedro Cieza de León," *Hispamérica* 56–57 (1990): 175–85.
20. See John H. Rowe, "Probanza de los Incas nietos de conquistadores," *Histórica* IX, 2 (Lima, 1985): 193–245. Although Rowe recognizes that the original mention of the documents was made by the Peruvian historian Horacio Villanueva, the first detailed approach to these important manuscripts is the one

in Rowe's article. The documents are catalogued under the section "Intendencias, causas ordinarias, Legajo 23, 1790." They are actually copies made in 1656 and then included in a file from 1790. They were sewn together with a document of that year, unrelated to the claims of the Incan descendants of 1569.
21. See Rowe, "Probanza," 197.
22. Franklin Pease G. Y. has explained this tactic in *Los Incas* (Lima, 1972), 24–25: "puede apreciarse que los incas inician sus conquistas por el Norte, saliendo siempre del Cuzco y regresando a él, continuándolas después en el sentido de las agujas del reloj. Aún considerando que hay variantes en los textos de las distintas crónicas, esa información permite explicar una representación ritual de las mismas conquistas. Parece, además, que estas conquistas, así presentadas dentro de un contexto ritual, formaran una espiral que se amplía." ("the incas began their conquests going North, departing from Cuzco and then returning to it; later, they continued in a clockwise direction. Even considering that the chronicles present different versions of Incan conquests, it is possible to discern in them a ritual representation of those conquests. It also seems that the conquests by the Incas followed an expanding spiral pattern").
23. Rowe, "Probanza," 198.
24. See, e.g., Martín Lienhard, *La Voz*, 235–41.
25. Luis Millones, "Introducción," in *Ynstruçion del Inca Don Diego de Castro Titu Cussi Yupangui* (Lima: Ediciones El Virrey, 1985). See also Wolfgang Wölck, *Pequeño Breviario Quechua* (Lima, 1988), 53–55, for a detailed explanation of the morpho-syntactical structure of Quechua and its use of direct speech and suffixes of verbal validation.
26. In Quechua, a narrator has to directly quote the words of a character in his narration in order to keep verisimilitude and syntactical correctness. The grammatical structure of the language does not allow a different way of incorporating a third person's speech. For example, if we want to relate that Tupaq Inka Yupanqi was worshiping the sun at a determined moment, we would have to say *Tupaq Inka Yupanqi nirqa Intita kunan muchashani, nispa*. A literal translation is: "Tupaq Inka Yupanqi said: 'I am now worshiping the Sun,' saying." This is understandable due to the use of multiple suffixes and infixes instead of prepositions and conjunctions more typical of Indo-European languages.
27. The original titles are *Primera Parte de los Commentarios Reales, que tratan del origen de los Yncas, Reyes que fueron del Peru, de su idolatria, leyes, y govierno en paz y en guerra: de sus vidas y conquistas, y de todo lo que fue aquel Imperio y su Republica, antes que los Españoles passaran a el* (Lisbon, 1609), and *Historia General del Perú: Segunda Parte de los Commentarios Reales* (Córdoba, 1617).
28. For an argument against the acculturated view of Garcilaso's works, see José Antonio Mazzotti, *Coros Mestizos del Inca Garcilaso: Resonancias Andinas* (Lima, 1996).
29. For a more detailed explanation and examples of this argument, see Mazzotti, *Coros*, 118–166. For a further explanation of Quechua pre-Hispanic poetry and its use of syntactical/semantic couplets, see Jean-Phillipe Husson, "La poesía quechua prehispánica: sus reglas, sus categorías, sus temas a través de los poemas transcritos por Waman Puma de Ayala," *Revista de Crítica Literaria Latinoamericana* 37 (1993): 63–86; and Husson, *La poésie Quechua dans la Chronique de Felipe Guamán Poma* (Paris, 1985).
30. *Comentarios Reales*, part 1, book 1, ch. 15.

31. See Cristóbal de Molina, called "El Cuzqueño," *Ritos y Fábulas de los Incas* [written ca. 1573] (Buenos Aires, 1959); Blas Valera, called "el Jesuita Anónimo," *Relación de las Costumbres Antiguas de los Naturales del Pirú* [written ca. 1595], in *Tres Relaciones de Antigüedades Peruanas* (Asunción, 1950) 133–203; and Bernabé Cobo, *Historia del Nuevo Mundo*, ed. Marco Jiménez de la Espada, 4 vols. (Sevilla, [1653] 1890–93).
32. See R. Tom Zuidema, "La imagen del sol y la *huaca* de Susurpuquio en el sistema astronómico de los incas en el Cuzco," *Journal de la Societé des Americanistes* 63 (1976): 199–230; and Arthur Demarest, *Viracocha: the Nature and Antiquity of The Andean High God* (Cambridge: Peabody Museum of Archaeology and Ethnology, Harvard University, 1981), 13–15.
33. For a further explanation of these arguments, see Mazzotti, *Coros*, 175–202.
34. Guamán Poma's authorship cannot be fully challenged until there is clear proof of the authenticity and veracity of a seventeenth-century manuscript recently found by Professor Laura Laurencich in Naples, Italy. In that document, the Italian Jesuit Anello Oliva affirms that the real author of *Nueva Coronica* is the mestizo Jesuit Blas Valera and that Guamán Poma was used as a screen to prevent political and religious prosecution from the Church against both Oliva and Valera.
35. See Rolena Adorno, *Guaman Poma: Writing and Resistance in Colonial Peru* (Austin, 1986) and *Cronista y Príncipe* (Lima, 1989).
36. Rama argues that the social institution of literacy worked as a means of domination in which a group of specialists in law and literature began the construction of a prestigious form of representation that would later become the only accepted form of national high culture. See Ángel Rama, *La Ciudad Letrada* (Hanover, 1984), chaps. 1–3.
37. Bruce Mannheim, *The Language of the Inka since the European Invasion* (Austin, 1991), ch. 6, points out the existence of manuscripts in Quechua as early as 1540, according to the *Bibliographie des Langues Aymará et Kichua* by Paul Rivet and Georges de Créqui-Monfort (Paris, 1951–56). Most of these documents are mere legalistic claims, confessions, and questionnaires that reflect the general process of acculturation after the arrival of the Spaniards.

– Chapter 7 –

Native Languages as Spoken and Written: Views from Southern New England

୧୫୬

Kathleen J. Bragdon

Introduction

RECENT ANTHROPOLOGICAL STUDIES have paid much attention to the language(s) of domination and to the process by which the indigenous "other" is "invented" through description and categorization,[1] although the applicability of the identified processes and patterns to the earliest periods of colonization in the New World and elsewhere has received less attention. Examination of early colonial language studies in what is now southern New England demonstrates the significant role that language and linguistic studies played in the establishment of colonial rule. In addition, seventeenth-century representations of native languages have implications for modern understanding of native language distribution and use in southern New England. The presence of a corpus of writings by native speakers themselves, however, challenged seventeenth-century attempts at domination through categorization, and challenges modern understandings of the effects of the encoding of native languages.

The Linguistic "Map" of Native Southern New England

Colonial description, writings by native speakers, and modern linguistic analyses indicate that the languages spoken by the indigenous people of southern New England in the seventeenth century were of the Eastern Subgroup of the Algonquian language family and shared a number of innovations that marked them as a distinctive regional grouping within this larger group.[2] The languages included Loup A and B, spoken by people occupying the region centering around the middle and upper Connecticut River, who later came to be known as the Nipmuck and the Pocumtuck; Narragansett and Niantic, spoken on what is now the western shore of Narragansett Bay; Massachusetts, the language of the coastal regions of Massachusetts as far south and east as Cape Cod and the Blackstone River, including the islands of Nantucket and Martha's Vineyard; Mohegan-Pequot-Montauk, including those languages of coastal eastern Connecticut and eastern Long Island; and Quiripi-Unquachog, including those spoken in coastal western Connecticut and central Long Island.

At the time of first encounters with European explorers and later English settlers, the native people of coastal southern New England were horticulturalists with a heavy dependence on marine resources and game, and lived in socially stratified communities linked to one another through networks of kinship and trade.[3] However, these linkages did not preclude significant dialectal and language variation within the region, or a strong likelihood of multilingualism, at least among the elite.[4]

Southern New England Languages and the Creation of a Shared Communicative Practice

Southern New England was the site of several European exploratory ventures, and by the late sixteenth century it became a target of English colonization, although prolonged interaction between native people and English colonists did not begin until the establishment of Plymouth in 1620. Within two decades, however, English population surpassed that of the natives of the region, due both to the effects of two tragic epidemics in 1617–1619 and 1633 and to the arrival of a large number of English immigrants during the "Great Migration" of the 1630s.[5]

Native fortunes underwent dramatic alterations following the Pequot war of 1637, when many native communities found themselves increasingly bound by colonial rule. While colonial expansion has been examined from numerous perspectives, its impact on native language use has received little attention. The ensuing "contest" of cultures in southern New England was increasingly played out in more intimate contexts, in all of which language played a crucial, if unrecognized, function. Chief among these was the struggle for the minds and souls of the native people, carried out by missionaries who with dramatic effect, practiced the politics of language. It was those missionaries, for example, who were most responsible for describing native languages and who soon provided the metaphorical models that helped determine the treatment of those who spoke them. Symbols employed in the rhetoric and writing of missionaries passed into the domain of colonial policy, when, in Bernard Cohn's words, the command of language became the language of command.[6]

It goes without saying that in colonial encounters the establishment of channels of communication is vital. However, as Johannes Fabian argues, such a precondition goes "beyond the (trivial) fact of verbal exchanges," because in the long run such exchanges depend on a shared communicative practice, which provides the "common ground on which unilateral claims [can] be imposed."[7] The seventeenth-century English colonizers of what is now southern New England sought to implement such a shared communicative practice in their dealings with the native people of the region, with, as Ives Goddard has shown,[8] mixed success in the earliest period of contact. However, these efforts shaped contemporary events and interactions as well as modern understanding of language distribution and use there.

Early Descriptions of Southern New England Languages

The earliest detailed descriptions of native people in southern New England employed language in their categorization. Several recurrent themes emerged in William Wood's "Small Nomenclator" appended to his 1634 *New England's Prospect*. It was a list of words in a northern dialect of Massachusett, designed to complement his "experimental" description of the native people of Naumkeag, now Salem, Massachusetts. Wood provided his readers a sample of language not only as a curiosity, but as a set of labels for significant landscape features, rulers, and everyday objects, as well as a local manifestation of some larger (European) language family. Similarly, Thomas Thorowgood, whose influential *Iewes in America* was published in 1650, and Roger Williams's extraordinary *Key into the Language of America* (1643), drawn from languages spoken near what is now Providence, Rhode Island, supported the theory that

American Indians were descended from the Lost Tribes of Israel and thus detected similarities between their languages and those of the ancients. Williams, for example, wrote "others, (and my selfe) have conceived some of their words to hold affinitie with the Hebrew."[9] Others, like Thomas Morton, a settler near what is now Quincy, Massachusetts, remarked that "the Natives of this Country, doe use very many wordes both of Greeke and Latine, to the same signification that the Latins and Greekes have done."[10] The theory of shared humanity implied by these humanistic models of language origin was espoused by many seventeenth-century English writers. Native languages were soon identified as the medium for the "instruction" of colonized people.[11] Thomas Lechford wrote of President Henry Dunster of Harvard in 1642 that, "He will make it good, that the way to instruct the Indians, must be in their owne language, not English; and that their language may be perfected."[12]

In spite of the interest of Dunster and others, few missionary efforts were undertaken in New England before 1650. However, the Society for the Propagation of the Gospel in New England, established in 1649, and known after 1660 as the New England Company, dedicated itself to the conversion of the Indians of New England and funded the majority of Protestant missionary activities in the colonies.[13] Significantly, its funds were administered in New England not by missionaries but by the Commissioners of the United Colonies, a body established in 1643 to provide mutual aid in the event of Indian attack.[14] This marriage of military and missionary efforts, although only one among many such in the history of colonial relations worldwide, was to affect the distribution and survival of indigenous languages in southern New England and our understanding of those languages today.

The New England company funded two significant and long-standing missions, including one on Martha's Vineyard under the sponsorship of Thomas Mayhew and Thomas Mayhew Jr., and the other by John Eliot of Roxbury.[15] Both missionary efforts resulted in a substantial number of translations of English religious texts into, and descriptions of, Massachusett.[16] Other missionary efforts among the natives of coastal Connecticut led to additional, if less meticulous, translations into Quiripi-Unquachog.[17]

John Eliot's description of Massachusett, particularly in his *Indian Grammar Begun*, first printed in 1666, was a remarkably sophisticated study for its time (Fig. 7.1). His analysis, based on work with skilled native bilinguals, approaches modern standards of language description. He proceeded with the assumption that

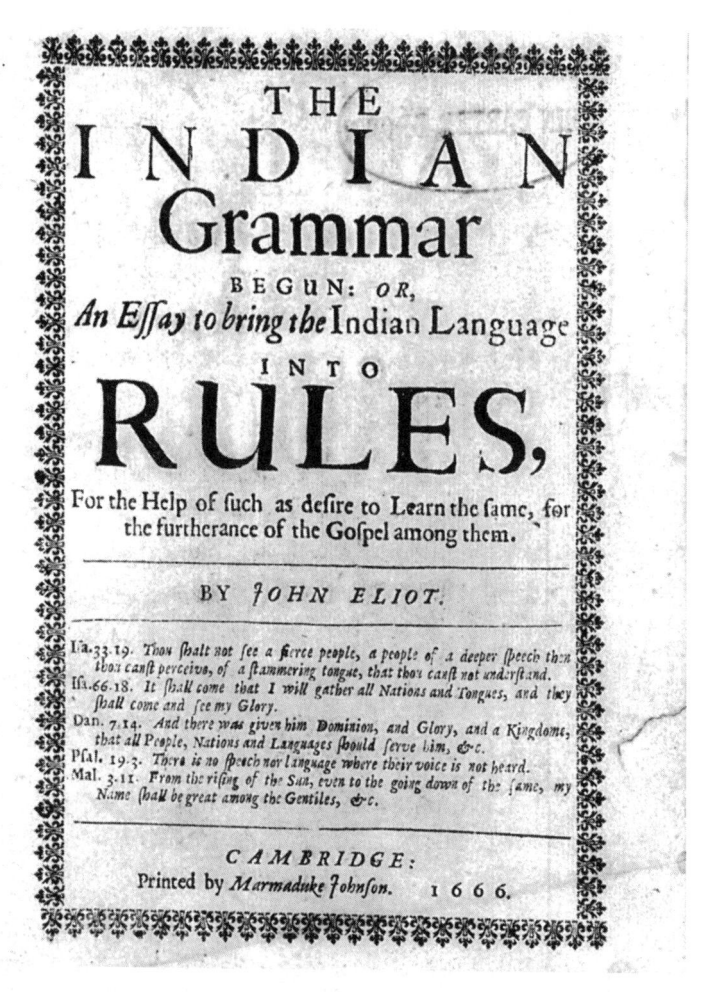

FIGURE 7.1 John Eliot. *The Indian Grammar Begun* (Cambridge, 1666). (Courtesy of the John Carter Brown Library at Brown University)

Massachusett, the language of "these Sons of our Morning," was in fact capable of being described according to a limited number of rules, as were the classical languages that formed the basis of his own education. Eliot promised his benefactor and then governor of the New England Company, Robert Boyle, "to set upon some essay & beginning of reducing this language unto rule; which, in the most common & usefull poynts, I doe see, is reducible."[18] His work, like that of Williams, and like Experience Mayhew's eighteenth-century treatments of Massachusett and related languages,[19] was generally based on the realities of native communicative interaction and on a deep knowledge of the language and people gained through years of familiarity with them.

Algonquian languages contain a number of features that made them unfamiliar to scholars of classical languages, features that Eliot identified and described with remarkable clarity, given the paucity of linguistic terminology available to him. Among these were the animate/inanimate gender distinction; the obviative mode marking the relative contributions of two third persons to action within a sentence or utterance; and the "irregular" dependent nouns such as *nuttah* (my heart), formed by "affixing the Noun with the pronoun."[20]

Although far superior to the earliest "word lists" and speculative language histories characteristic of the earliest decades of colonization, his work was not free of categorical treatment of native languages. Eliot, in part for lack of alternatives, employed grammatical categories familiar to classical scholars in his description of Massachusett, sometimes when those categories were not appropriate. However, his linguistic work was acknowledged at the time to be authoritative, so his other generalizations about southern New England languages and their speakers came to have significance in colonial policy making as well.

Language Studies and the Establishment of Colonial Rule

Historians of colonization in southern New England have noted that the ideas and ideologies of colonialism were formulated and perpetuated in the discourse of missionization. The metaphors of space, metonymic equations of languages and cultures, and evaluations of native cognitive abilities implicit or overt in missionary linguistic commentary, entered the discourse of political action as well. Because of their knowledge of native languages, missionaries became key figures in colonial governments' increasing infiltration into native political and legal affairs. Thomas James, first minister of the East Hampton, Long Island, Congregational church, stated in 1667, for example, that as a result of his proficiency in the local language, "I am employed from one end of the Island to th'other about setling matters between English & Indians." Daniel Gookin, Eliot's longtime assistant and a fluent speaker of Massachusett and Nipmuck, became the overseer of the native magistrates "in respect of Civill Government."[21]

Furthermore, missionaries working with native languages in southern New England understood them according to a spatial model, in Fabian's words, as "regions to be explored, as bounded systems to be monographically described, as the possessions of territorially defined groups (so that linguistic, ethnic and geographic labels could become interchangeable)."[22] Missionaries and colonial apologists counted it an achievement to have "another tongue brought in," and translations themselves were thought to be visible proof of missionary effort, if not success. Roger Williams's *Key* was in part a linguistic Baedeker designed to serve all English residents of the region, as "a little Key [which] may open a Box, where lies a bunch of Keyes."[23]

The study of language in the seventeenth century recognized few distinctions between linguistic and philosophical approaches and unlike the dominant schools of modern linguistics, did not isolate language as a separate object for study. Lacking our concept of culture, seventeenth-century observers sometimes used linguistic labels to refer to ethos, behavior, and what we might call ethnicity.[24] Failing to discover categories of expression for the "lofty" emotions attributed to the classical languages, Eliot proposed to introduce these forms to Massachusett. The *Logick Primer*, an original work in the Massachusett language, was authored and published by Eliot in 1672 to familiarize native students, and especially native teachers, with the explicit principles of logic; to provide, as he wrote, "subtilty to the simple." With this volume, accompanied with interlinear translations in English, Eliot hoped to provide his native converts an "Iron Key ... to open the rich treasury of the holy scriptures." Not content to leave the matter there, he also set up "a lecture in logic and theology at Natick."[25]

Interference with Massachusett and other southern New England languages by English missionaries and others went beyond their "objectification" in linguistic and ethnographic descriptions. "Translators" such as Eliot also coopted Massachusett terms for concepts of vastly different meaning. Among the most visible were the words for dieties. *Manit* (god, spirit) from Massachusett, which meant roughly "spiritual or supernatural force" and was used by the peoples of southern New England to refer not only to powerful beings such as *Cautanntowwit*, the benign if distant overseer of the afterlife, but to any quality or ability that struck observers as marvelous, unexpected, or extraordinary, became the standard term for "God."[26] Likewise, *Chepi*, the name of the powerful *manitou* whom powwows sought in curing rituals, became the standard term for "devil."[27] As Jean and John Comaroff have pointed out in another context, while such usage does not imply an overnight revision of worldview for the missionized "native," it signals a new awareness of relativity of meaning and the marking of non-English terms or concepts as "pagan."[28] At the same time, various native-language terms came to be associated with the structure of Christian mission communities, contributing to a kind of Anglicization of their use. Everyday terms such as *notompeantog* (leaders) came to mean "ministers."[29] Such subtle shifts of meaning were reinforced by other infiltrations, particularly the use of English loanwords in native languages, many of which were adopted to refer to the unfamiliar crops, animals, goods, and measurement practices introduced by English settlers.[30]

Literacy and Its Impact on Massachusett Speakers

The creation of a controlled communicative practice in southern New England did not end with descriptions of native languages or symbolic domination through commandeering native linguistic signs. As part of the missionization process, supported by the colonial government, Eliot and others also sought to introduce the natives to literacy by teaching natives to read and write in their own indigenous languages.[31] In 1650 he wrote to Edward Winslow, now serving in England as an advocate of the missionary effort in New England, "for their own language we have no book; my desire therefore is to teach them all to write, and read written hand, and thereby with pains taking, they may have some of the Scriptures in their own language."[32] Eliot's plan to encourage vernacular literacy among the Massachusett-speaking people was consistent with his religious and education philosophy; Eliot believed true conversion required intense personal study of scripture, preferably in its original languages. At the same time, however, his increasing familiarity with native culture convinced him that conversion would be more likely to take place if achieved within the context of native family and community and through the medium of the native language.[33] Although his ultimate goal was to introduce his converts to literacy in English, he clearly saw the merits of a gradual transition.[34] Even his orthography, based on the Roman alphabet but adapted to the Massachusett sound system, was an accommodation to these ends. This orthography was adopted by other missionaries working on the Cape and islands, and became the basis for widespread vernacular literacy among the Massachusett people. Native teachers soon spread the system to the numerous Indian communities in the colony, such that by the late seventeenth century nearly 30 percent of the Massachusett-speaking people could read, and many could write as well. Adults and children, male and female alike, learned in local schools while in service to white families or taught themselves.[35]

For the further instruction of literate native converts, Eliot produced several works in Massachusett reflecting his classical training. Although some historians have dismissed Eliot's translations and original works as "the least useful," of the productions of the Harvard College Press, seventeenth-century sources suggest otherwise.[36] The *Indian Primer* was widely used in native schools and was reprinted in 1687. Eliot wrote to Robert Boyle the previous year that "though the last impression [printing] be not quite spent, yet quickly they will."[37] Eliot's catechisms, primers, and the anonymously authored *The Indiane Primer*, which was probably based on Eliot's *Indian Primer*, were still sought on Martha's Vineyard in the 1740s. Natives instructed according to Eliot's methods and using Eliot's materials taught hundreds of others in turn.

Jack Goody has argued that the introduction of writing can lead to the "domestication" of colonized peoples. Writing, according to Goody, not only permits but encourages codification and regulation,[38] and literate Massachusett-speakers frequently participated in the regulation of those native communities most directly under Puritan control. It is probably no accident that many of the publications available for new converts in Massachusett were lists of laws and rules of conduct such as the tract entitled *Hatchets to Hew Down the Tree of Sin* issued in 1705 (Fig. 7.2). Native rulers heard disputes and handled local judicial matters, which were then reported on by Massachusett scribes; native clerics kept vital statistics and native clerks maintained land records. There is also some evidence that the availability of Eliot's "standardized" Massachusett in published translations, served to "level" dialectic diversity in that language.[39] Both in describing the languages themselves and in introducing vernacular literacy, missionaries contributed to the definition of a communicative practice in which the English controlled the form and substance of exchange not only between Indian and non-Indian but among the Indians themselves.

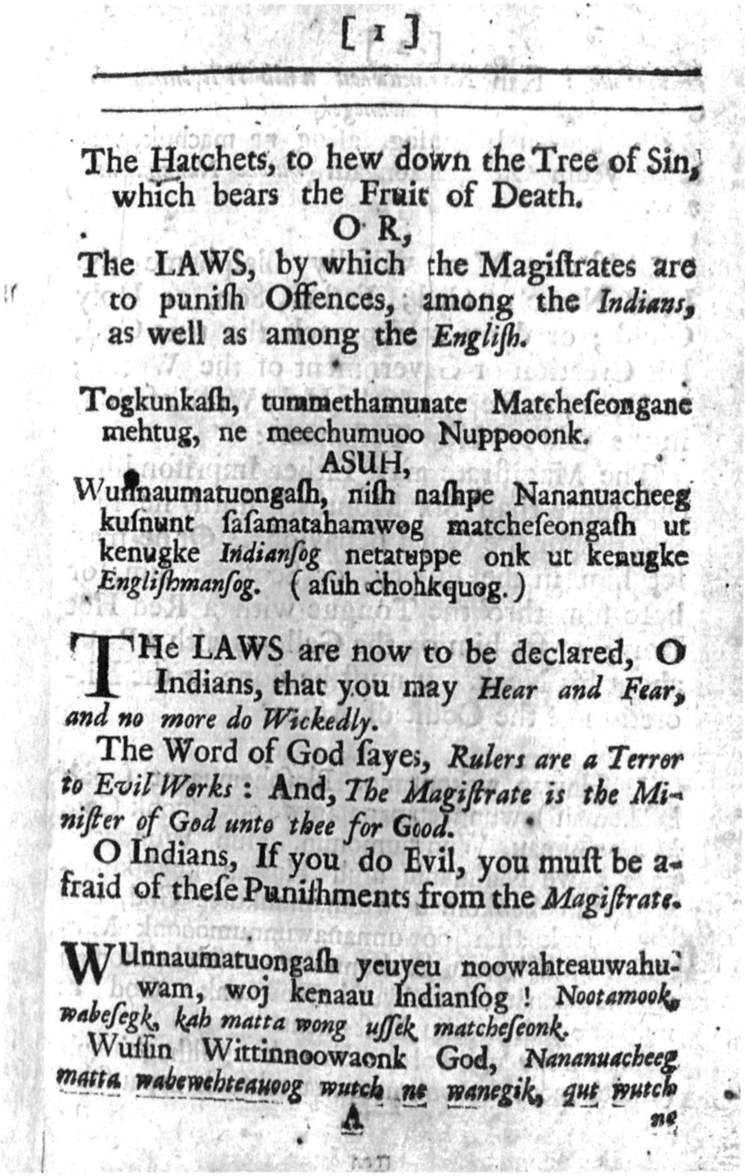

[1]

The Hatchets, to hew down the Tree of Sin, which bears the Fruit of Death.
OR,
The LAWS, by which the Magiftrates are to punifh Offences, among the *Indians,* as well as among the *Englifh.*

Togkunkafh, tummethamunate Matchefeongane mehtug, ne meechumuoo Nuppooonk.
ASUH,
Wunnaumatuongafh, nifh nafhpe Nananuacheeg kufnunt fafamatahamwog matchefeongafh ut kenugke *Indianfog* netateppe onk ut kenugke *Englifhmanfog.* (afuh chohkquog.)

THe LAWS are now to be declared, O Indians, that you may *Hear and Fear, and no more do Wickedly.*

The Word of God fayes, *Rulers are a Terror to Evil Works* : And, *The Magiftrate is the Minifter of God unto thee for Good.*

O Indians, If you do Evil, you muft be afraid of thefe Punifhments from the *Magiftrate.*

WUnnaumatuongafh yeuyeu noowahteauwahuwam, woj kenaau Indianfog ! *Nootamook, wabefegk, kah matta wong uffek matchefeonk.*

Wufun Wittinnoowaonk God, *Nananuacheeg matta wabewehteauoog wutch ne wanegik, qut wutch*
A *ne*

FIGURE 7.2 [Cotton Mather], *The Hatchets, to hew down the Tree of Sin* (Boston, 1705). (Courtesy of the New York Public Library)

Questioning the Texts

At the same time, however, vernacular literacy in Massachusett had effects not intended by its sponsors. The texts created by native speakers document the preservation of numerous aspects of native discourse style, a style as rhetorically elegant in its own way as any classical text.[40] In so doing, it helped preserve an indigenous social structure based on hierarchy and advocacy well into the eighteenth century. This is so because of the continued importance of "high style" language use among leaders. These writings also preserve another rhetorical convention of petition and underscore the reciprocal relations between advocate, petitioner, and superior authority typical of traditional social and supernatural relations (Fig. 7.3). The texts reflect dialectic diversity even in Massachusett inconsistent with English descriptions of widespread linguistic homogeneity. It is noteworthy, for example, that although many Englishmen comment on the similarities of native languages in the earliest periods of colonization, by the late seventeenth century linguistic diversity is a source of concern. Finally, the existence of these texts documents the lack of significant change in the Massachusett language as a result of its "contact" with English and the persistence of native language use to the end of the eighteenth century.

The controversy over the impact and role of literacy on languages of previously nonliterate people centers on the ways in which literacy is or is not employed by its initiates for uniquely local purposes.[41] The history of literacy in Massachusett suggests that the uses to which it was put were complementary to the continuing emphasis on orality in that language. Literacy was integral to the new native Christianity; it was used for recordkeeping and for communications with the non-Indian authorities. Far from contributing to the decline in native language use, literacy reinforced its survival in some contexts. Literacy also served in Massachusett culture as a *boundary-maintaining* device, demarcating domains where English and Indian interests intersected.

Literacy was not always, or necessarily, the individuating, isolating experience postulated by Goody and others. Among Massachusett speakers, literacy was often a manifestation of group encounters. Single readers read passages or "lined" phrases for a group to follow. Books had multiple owners, or users, who seem to have communicated with one another with annotations left on margins or endpapers (Fig. 7.4).

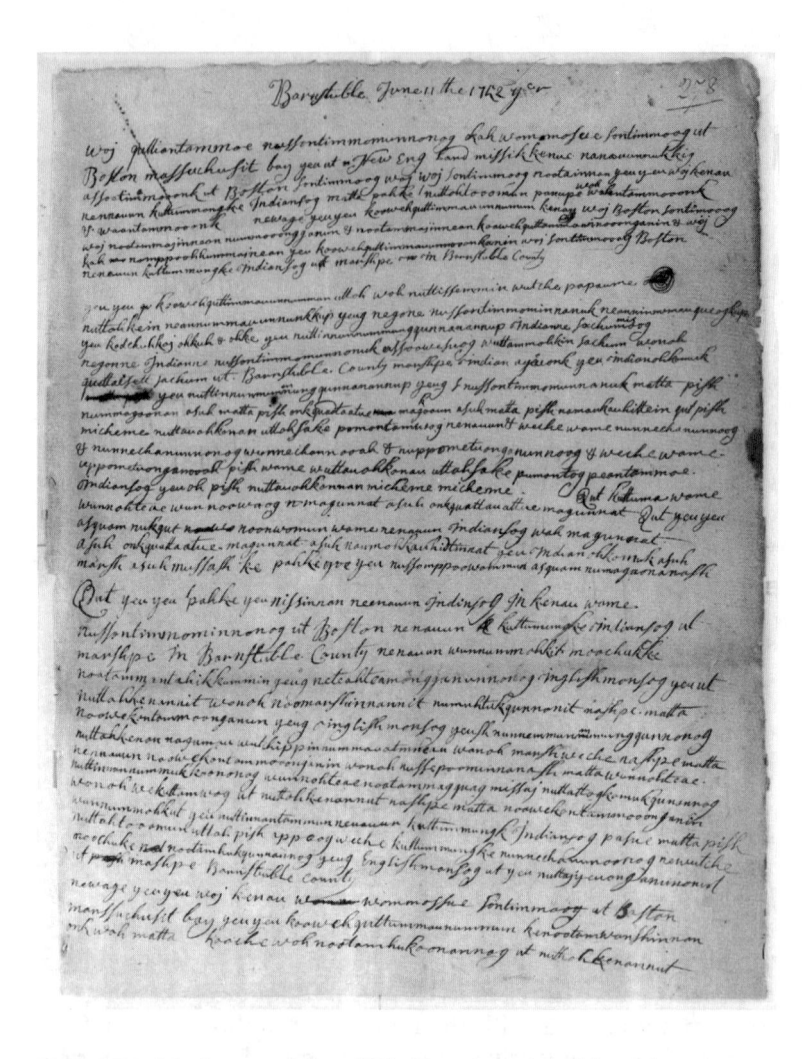

FIGURE 7.3 Mashpee petition, 1752. (Courtesy of the Massachusetts Archives)

Conclusions: The Politics of Language Description and Literacy

Classical theories premised on the autonomy of language often do not take into account the political implications of language use or the ways in which colonial powers have created and perpetuated a specific linguistic practice that determines not only the context and mode of communication but also the medium of expression. Nearly

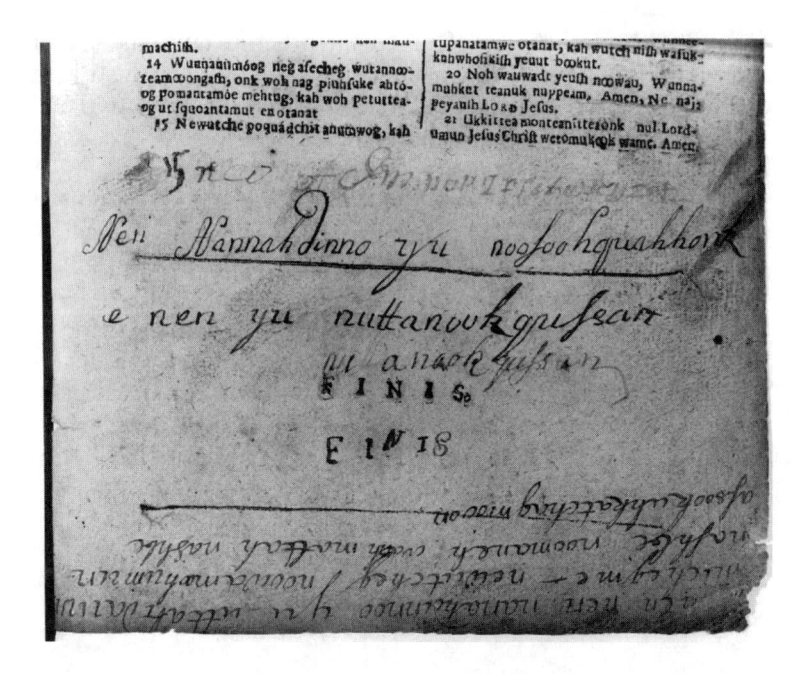

FIGURE 7.4 Eliot Indian Bible printed in Cambridge, Massachusetts, in 1685, with annotations on the endpaper. (Courtesy of the Congregational Library of Boston, Massachusetts)

two centuries before the study of "exotic" languages in India, Africa, and other outposts of the British empire facilitated the "domestication" of their speakers, similar methods were framed within an ideology of common humanity. In seventeenth- and early eighteenth-century southern New England, this ideology and the idea that one language was easily substituted for another was used to promote the gradual substitution of English for the region's various native languages.

The political uses of language description in the seventeenth and eighteenth centuries, I would argue, have also had an impact on the way in which modern historians and anthropologists have understood native cultural identity in southern New England. Far from "neutral" sources of information about language and its uses in the past, these linguistic analyses have shaped interpretations of political boundaries, political leadership, and social relations among native peoples of the region. The likelihood of multilingualism or multidialectism among native elite, for example, casts doubt on any sociopolitical model based on a premise of linguistic and cultural isomorphism. The elegant structure and phrasing of natives' writings amply demonstrate the "lofty" and sophisticated quality of their rhetoric. In addition, the survival of native discourse practices within the confines of the new colonial order and the adoption of literacy suggests that the native languages of southern New England were long resistant to the imposition of colonial authority, and the surviving writings by native speakers are eloquent testimony to the persistence of a native voice.

Seventeenth-century linguistic descriptions of southern New England languages thus tell us about theories of humanity, and of language current at the time, even as they provide us with valuable data about languages that are no longer spoken. However, native writings and comparative studies of "linguistic colonialism" indicate that the linguistic landscape of southern New England was a contested one.

Notes

1. E.g., Pierre Bourdieu, "The Economics of Linguistic Exchanges," *Social Science Information* 16, no. 6 (1977): 645–68; Michael Foucault, *Power/Knowledge* (New York, 1980); Bernard Cohn, "Representing Authority in Colonial India," in *An Anthropologist among the Historians and other Essays* (New Delhi, 1987), 632–82; Bernard Cohn, "The Command of Language and the Language of Command," in *Subaltern Studies: Writings on South Asian History and Society*, Vol. 4, ed. R. Guha (New Delhi, 1985); Patrick Harries, "The Roots of Ethnicity: Discourse and the Politics of Language Construction in South-East Africa," *African Affairs* 87, no. 346 (1988): 25–52; Edward Said, *Culture and Imperialism* (New York, 1993).
2. Ives Goddard, "Eastern Algonquian Languages," in *The Handbook of North American Indians*, vol. 15, *Northeast*, ed. Bruce Trigger (Washington, DC, 1978), 71–72; Bert Salwen, "The Indians of Southern New England: Early Period," in *The Handbook of North American Indians*, vol. 15, *Northeast*, ed. Bruce Trigger (Washington,DC, 1978), 161.
3. For a recent description of the native cultures of southern New England, see Kathleen Bragdon, *Native People of Southern New England 1500–1650* (Norman, OK, 1996).
4. Kathleen Bragdon, "Language and Cultural Identity in Native Southern New England," paper delivered at the Second Mashantucket-Pequot History Conference, 20 April 1993, Mystic, CT.
5. David Quinn, *North America from Earliest Discovery to First Settlements: The Norse Voyages to 1612* (New York, 1975), 390–91.
6. Bernard Cohn, "The Command of Language and the Language of Command."
7. Johannes Fabian, *Language and Colonial Power: The Appropriation of Swahili in the Former Belgian Congo 1880–1938* (Cambridge, England, 1986), 3.

8. Ives Goddard, this volume.
9. Roger Williams, *Key into the Language of America* (Providence, 1936[1643]), A4.
10. Thomas Morton, "New English Caanan or New Caanan, containing an Abstract of New England,"(1632) in *Tracts and Other Papers, Relating Principally to the Origin, Settlement, and Progress of the Colonies of North America*, vol. 2, ed. Peter Force (New York, 1947).
11. Thomas Lechford, *Plain dealing; or, Newes from New-England* (London, 1642), 53.
12. The missionization effort in southern New England has captured the interest of several generations of scholars, reflecting various schools of thought. Works representative of these varying perspectives include Alden Vaughan, *New England Frontier: Puritans and Indians 1620–1675* (Boston, 1965); Neal Salisbury, "Red Puritans: The Praying Indians of Massachusetts Bay and John Eliot," *William and Mary Quarterly*, 3s, no. 31 (1974): 27–54; William Simmons, "Conversion from Indian to Puritan," *New England Quarterly*, 52, no. 2 (1979) 197–218; James Axtell, *The Invasion Within: The Contest of Cultures in Colonial North America* (New York, 1985); and Harold Van Lonkhuyzen, "A Reappraisal of the Praying Indians: Acculturation, Conversion, and Identity at Natick, Massachusetts, 1646–1730," *New England Quarterly*, 62 (1989): 396–428.
13. William Kellaway, *The New England Company, 1649–1776* (New York, 1962), 1, 16, 46.
14. The society even went so far as to import arms and ammunition for sale in the colonies as part of its effort to raise funds for missionary work (ibid., 62, 69).
15. The most comprehensive contemporary discussions of the missionary effort in southern New England appear in Henry Whitfield, "A Farther Discovery of the Present State of the Indians in New England," *Collections of the Massachusetts Historical Society* 3, no. 4 (1834): 107–47; Daniel Gookin, *An Historical Account of the Doings and Sufferings of the Christian Indians in New England in the Years 1675, 1676, 1677* (New York, 1972); John Eliot and Thomas Mayhew, "Tears of Repentance: or, A further Narrative of the Progress of the Gospel Amongst the Indians in New-England," (London, 1653), reprinted in *Collections of the Massachusetts Historical Society*. 3s no. 4 (1834): 197–287; John Wilson, "The Day-Breaking, If Not the Sun Rising of the Gospel with the Indians in New England," *Collections of the Massachusetts Historical Society*, 3s no. 4 (1834): 1–23; Edward Winslow, "The Glorious Progress of the Gospel amongst the Indians in New England," *Collections of the Massachusetts Historical Society*, 3s no. 4 (1834): 69–99. For a scathing critique of these reports, see Francis Jennings, *The Invasion of America: Indians, Colonialism and the Cant of Conquest* (New York, 1975). The Eliot mission is also described in Ola Elizabeth Winslow, *John Eliot, Apostle to the Indians* (Boston, 1968), and the Mayhew mission is summarized in Lloyd C. Hare, *Thomas Mayhew, Patriarch to the Indians 1593–1682* (New York, 1931).
16. James Constantine Pilling, *Bibliography of Algonquian Languages*, Bureau of American Ethnology bulletin 13 (Washington,DC, 1891), 103–4, 127–84, 347– 51.
17. Abraham Peirson, *Some Helps for the Indians…* (London, 1658).
18. John Eliot, letter to Robert Boyle, 30 September 1670, *Collections of the Massachusetts Historical Society* 1, no 3 (1810): 177–88.
19. Experience Mayhew, who said of himself "I learnt the language by rote, as I did my mother tongue," was the great-grandson of Thomas Mayhew, a prominent early missionary on Martha's Vineyard, and a widely recognized scholar of the Massachusett language. In addition to several translations of native texts, Mayhew published a translation of the psalms, the *Massachusett Psalter* (Boston, 1709), and a short letter on the language which appeared in 1722,

"Letter of Experience Mayhew, 1722, on the Indian Language," *New England Historical and Genealogical Register* XXXIX (1885): 10–17.
20. Eliot, *Indian Grammar Begun*. For a more thorough discussion of the influences on Eliot's grammatical studies, see Kenneth Miner, "John Eliot and the Beginnings of American Linguistics," *Historiographica Linguistica* I, no. 2 (1974): 169–83; and Stephen Guice, "The Linguistic Work of John Eliot" (Ph.D. Thesis, Michigan State University, 1990).
21. Kellaway, *The New England Company*, 104.
22. Michael Foucault *The Order of Things: An Archaeology of the Human Sciences* (New York, 1973). For a discussion of similar strategies in eighteenth-century African missions, see Fabian, *Language and Colonial Power*, and John L. Comaroff and Jean Comaroff, "The Colonization of Consciousness," in Comaroff and Comaroff, eds., *Ethnography and the Historical Imagination* (London, 1992): 250–58.
23. Williams, *Key*, A2. For a discussion of Williams's *Key* as an example of emblematic writing, see John J. Teunissen and Evelyn J. Hinz (eds), *A Key Into the Language of America by Roger Williams. Edited with a Critical Introduction* (Amherst, 1973).
24. Stephen K. Land, *The Philosophy of Language in Britain: Major Theories from Hobbes to Thomas Reid* (New York, 1986).
25. John Eliot, *Logick Primer* (1672).
26. E.g., Williams, *Key*, 126.
27. See Eliot, *The Holy Bible: Containing the Old Testament and the New* (Cambridge, MA, 1663, 1685).
28. Comaroff and Comaroff, "The Colonization of Consciousness."
29. James Hammond Trumbull, *Natick Dictionary*, Bureau of American Ethnology, bulletin # 25,(Washington, DC, 1903); Josiah Cotton, "Vocabulary of the Massachusetts (or Natick) Indian language," *Collections of the Massachusetts Historical Society* 3, no. 2(1820): 147–257.
30. Kathleen Bragdon, "'Another Tongue Brought In': An Ethnohistorical Study of Native Writings in Massachusett" (Ph.D. Thesis, Brown University, 1981).
31. Ives Goddard and Kathleen J. Bragdon, *Native Writings in Massachusett*, 2 vols. (Philadelphia, 1988).
32. Henry Whitfield, *A Farther Discovery* (London, 1834 [1651]): 144.
33. E.g., Eliot, "Strength out of Weakness," (London, 1834[1651]): 168.
34. Bragdon, "Another Tongue Brought In," 51.
35. Eliot, *Indian Grammar Begun*, 4–5.
36. Samuel Eliot Morison, *Harvard College in the Seventeenth Century* (Cambridge, MA, 1936), 345.
37. Ibid., 252–53.
38. Jack Goody, *The Domestication of the Savage Mind* (Cambridge, England, 1977).
39. Goddard and Bragdon, *Native Writings*, 482ff.
40. Ives Goddard, "Two Mashpee Petitions, from 1752 (in Massachusett) and 1753 (in English)," in *American Indian Linguistics and Ethnography in Honor of Laurence C. Thompson*, Anthony Mattina and Timothy Montler, eds. Occasional Papers in Linguistics 10 (1993): 397–416.
41. For a sample of the large literature on the impact of literacy, see Nico Besnier, "Literacy and the Notion of the Person on a Nukulaelae Atoll," *American Anthropologist* (1991): 570–87; and Wallace Chafe and Deborah Tannen, "The Relation between Written and Spoken Language," *Annual Reviews in Anthropology* 16 (1987): 383–407.

– Chapter 8 –

THE MI'KMAQ HIEROGLYPHIC PRAYER BOOK: WRITING AND CHRISTIANITY IN MARITIME CANADA, 1675–1921

ତ୨୦

Bruce Greenfield

ONE OF MANY INTERESTING ASPECTS of the Mi'kmaq hieroglyphs, whose documented history begins in the late seventeenth century, is the evidence that they were founded in indigenous practice. Although French missionaries seem to have developed the script used to represent Catholic prayers and teachings, and although we are dependent on their reports for most of what is known of its earliest uses, the missionaries' accounts point to local graphic practices as giving them the idea in the first place and as providing the basis for a remarkably swift and extensive diffusion of the new, or elaborated, script among Mi'kmaq groups in eastern Canada. Another important fact is that the hieroglyphic script has played a role in Mi'kmaq culture since the end of the seventeenth century, even during periods, spanning several generations, when there were no Catholic missionaries, and during periods of Protestant evangelization, when missionaries promoted literacy in alphabetic Mi'kmaq. So when David Schmidt and Murdena Marshall, editors and translators of the *Mi'kmaq Hieroglyphic Prayers* (1995), describe a recent Good Friday service at Eskasoni, Cape Breton, Nova Scotia, in which the *komqwejwi'kasikl*, or hieroglyphs, figure prominently, we glimpse a recent manifestation of a three-hundred-year tradition:

> An elderly man praying from his tattered hieroglyphic missal ...; the young nujialasutmat [prayer leader] reciting the Passion from a version recently published in the script; hieroglyphic characters ... painted on church walls, embroidered on the priest's vestments, and stitched into the altar cloth.... In Mi'kmaq homes, silk-screened hieroglyphic prayers hang from kitchen walls, and drawings of hieroglyphic figures decorate classrooms in the reserve grade school.[1]

Renewed educational efforts of the Catholic Church in this century, along with those of governments, both of which insisted on English or alphabetic Mi'kmaq as the medium of instruction, have hastened the decline of the hieroglyphs. Schmidt and Marshall note, however, that "a series of hieroglyphic workshops sponsored by the Mi'kmaq Association of Cultural Studies were held in the late 1980's ... led by Wilfred Prosper, an elder whose knowledge of the script is unparalleled."[2]

This essay focuses mainly on the period of the script's early development, from 1675 to about 1760, and is based primarily on the writings of two missionaries of this period, Chrestien LeClercq, a Recollect, and Pierre Maillard, a Spiritan, both of whom describe, and claim credit for, the introduction of the hieroglyphs; secondarily, two later missionaries, Silas Rand, a Baptist (1810–1889), and Father Pacifique (Henri Buisson de Valigny) (1863–1943), a Capuchin, offer insights into the history and role of the hieroglyphic prayer book during the nineteenth and early twentieth centuries. Though there are few extant hieroglyphic writings other than the prayer book that was developed by Pierre Maillard in the eighteenth century, three centuries of cultural practice tied to these religious texts constitutes an ongoing, real (if hard to document), expressiveness, an intriguing example of how a written text can play an important function in a culture without necessarily producing other written texts. Having made this claim, however, I confess that this essay circles round this expressiveness, without claiming knowledge of its specific nature. Because I know English and French but not Mi'kmaq, I have more to say about the mentalities of the missionaries than about their Mi'kmaq partners.

I use the word "partners" advisedly. The indigenous roots and the endurance of these hieroglyphic texts over centuries suggests a complex interplay of influences across the frontiers of language, culture, and imagination. Missionaries learned Mi'kmaq language and adapted pictographic writing in order that they might teach their own faith and values; some Mi'kmaq people, in turn, adapted their graphic practices in order that they might apprehend certain aspects of French Catholic Christianity, and then went on to live with these in various ways. Though this essay has more specific things to say about the missionaries than about the Mi'kmaq people who were in contact with them, the 250-year existence of the hieroglyphic prayer book points to a history that ultimately must be understood as centered in Mi'kmaq life.

The long history of the prayer book, along with what we can recover of the early period of this exchange, with its evident complexities and nuances, challenges a common model of the linguistic interactions of early-modern Europeans and peoples of the Americas, a model according to which more or less monolithic European alphabetic literacies confront native oralities across a chasm of wonder. The European reporters of these encounters posit a native response that elevates European writing to the level of "magic" and renders European literates as all-knowing. Conforming to this model are missionary and travel reports in which the European writer notes the great power ascribed to him by native contacts because he can make "that which is white" (paper) speak,[3] and in which the European ascribes a lack of "history" to a people who have no written records.[4] Modern theories of "literacy and orality," as well, have tended to posit contrasting modes of thought, social organization, and understanding of language, with the contrast determined by the alphabetic literacy of Europeans and the complementary lack of such literacy among non-Europeans.[5] Peter Wogan has questioned the accuracy of this stark contrast between writing and nonwriting both as depicted in contact narratives and as formulated by modern scholars; he calls for more attention to "the socio-cultural factors that mediate and determine the uses of literacy in any given culture" and for "more detailed studies of native attitudes toward writing."[6] A response to such a call might include the story of the Mi'kmaq hieroglyphs, a history of sophisticated communication across linguistic and cultural frontiers in which more than one kind of writing and several different understandings of how writing functions in a society are at play. At times in this story, moreover, there seemingly are greater differences between European Catholics and Protestants over the role of writing than there are between Catholic missionaries and the Mi'kmaq.

First, let us describe the script and provide a bibliographic synopsis. David Schmidt and Murdena Marshall, the editors and translators of *Mi'kmaq Hieroglyphic Prayers*, explain that:

> [Mi'kmaq] hieroglyphic texts are composed of individual symbols (called *glyphs*) written horizontally from left to right. Each glyph represents a word in the Mi'kmaq language. Glyphs, in turn, are comprised of one or more discrete *graphemes* that signify the morphemes

(meaningful subunits like stems, prefixes, and suffixes) of that word. By combining glyphs and their constituent graphemes in various ways, we believe that hieroglyphic-literate Mi'kmaq were able to write and read information they had not previously memorized. The *komqwejwi'kasikl* [hieroglyphs] ... comprise one of the most formidable scripts in history with an inventory of approximately 2,700 graphemes.[7]

Until the mid-nineteenth century, these hieroglyphic texts circulated in manuscript only, copied and recopied and passed on from generation to generation within families and bands. (No prayer manuscript in hieroglyphs from the eras of LeClercq or Maillard is known to survive.) (See Fig. 8.1.) In the mid-nineteenth century, a Catholic missionary, Christian Kauder, arranged for the many and variant manuscripts to be copied, collated, and finally printed in Vienna, an exercise that required cutting about 2,700 individual typefaces.[8] (See Fig. 8.2.) In 1921, Father Pacifique arranged a second edition based on Kauder's. This book is the principle archive of texts in Mi'kmaq hieroglyphs. The English title of the 1921 edition is *Manual of Prayers, Instructions, Psalms, and Hymns in the Micmac Ideograms*. This title would seem to reflect the original purpose, and the predominant use over the centuries, of the Mi'kmaq hieroglyphic script.

The first missionary to use the hieroglyphs, Chrestien LeClercq, intended them to foster the learning of Catholic prayers and instructions, and the hieroglyphic books remained devoted to sacred matters for generations after. Having learned the local language himself, LeClercq, like earlier and later missionaries, translated prayers, catechisms, hymns, and liturgies into Mi'kmaq. LeClercq and his fellow Catholic missionaries wanted these learned exactly, word for word, and repeated from memory. As presented by LeClercq and Maillard, the process of evangelization was centered on what Maillard in the 1730s, '40s, and '50s would call "acts of prayer," exact and heartfelt repetitions of the texts. Neither of these missionaries was naive about the differing degrees of understanding that accompanied these repetitions. Maillard, for example, quotes one Mi'kmaq man telling him that "everything you have given us to learn is truly Mi'kmaq in terms of its words and their arrangement, but we do not catch the sense of what you want to say."[9] Maillard's memoir of his missionary years includes numerous dialogic interrogations of the meaning and implications of his teachings in which neither side is depicted as simplemindedly promoting or accepting rote learning. The French approach seems to have been to establish these visual representations in order to promote the "act" of repeating them aloud and to foster

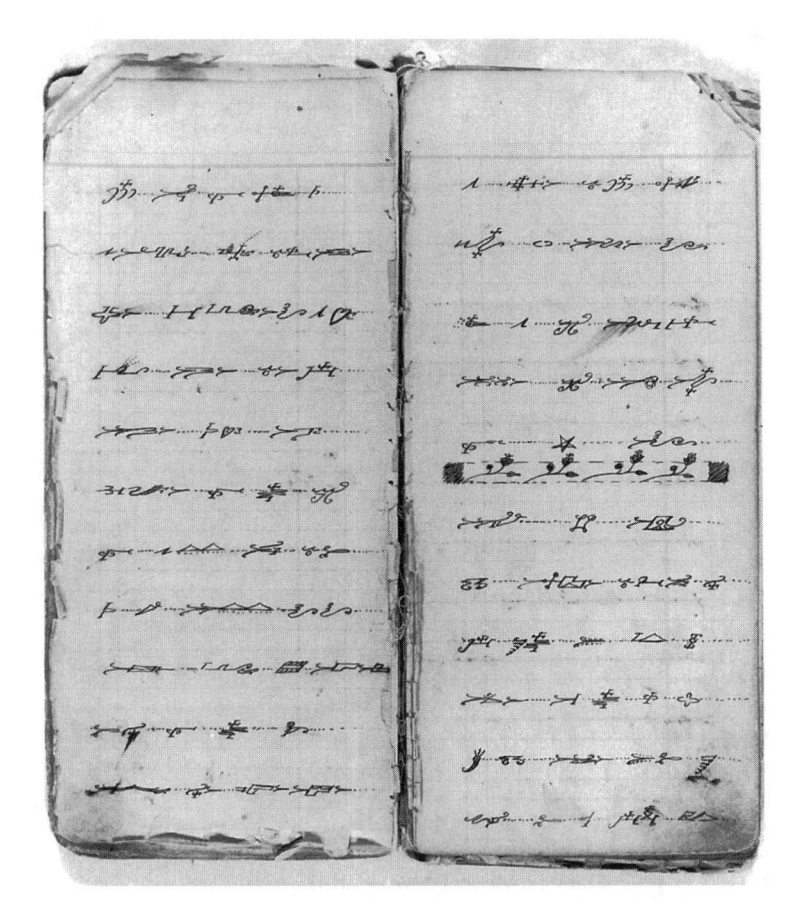

FIGURE 8.1 Pages from a manuscript prayer book in Mi'kmaq hieroglyphics, ca. 1900. There are no known surviving manuscripts from the period of the French missionaries, and very few from the nineteenth century. (Courtesy of the Nova Scotia Museum)

further understanding in relation to them as time passed. As Atlantic Canada increasingly became a battleground for the French and English, French missionaries encouraged the Mi'kmaq to identify themselves through these acts of prayer, to distinguish themselves, *"les Priants,"* the "praying," who were trained to the performance of correct "acts of prayer," from the "non-praying," which included Protestant Englishmen. During the wars of the 1740s, for example, a prisoner of the Mi'kmaq is tortured and killed by them when he is unable to correctly make the sign of the

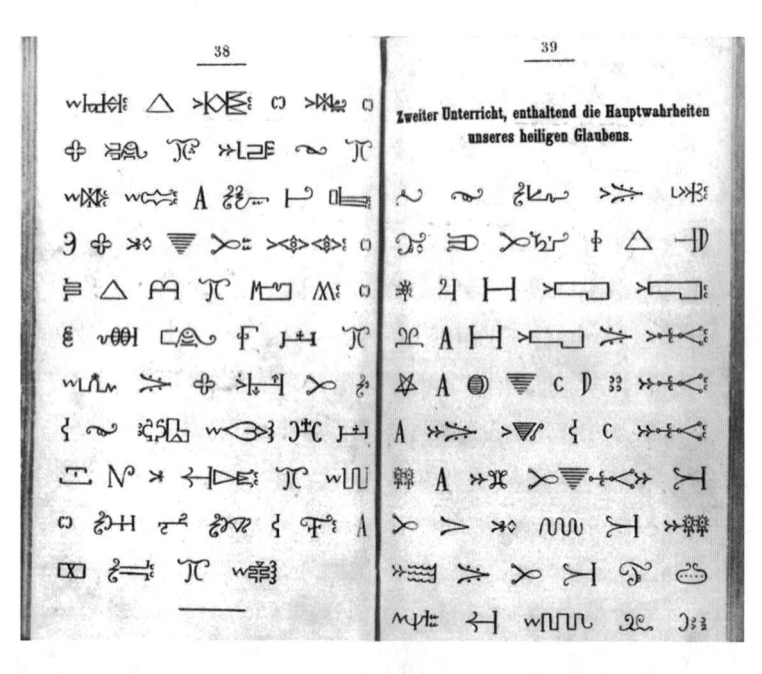

FIGURE 8.2 "Zweiter Unterricht, enthaltend die Hauptwahrheiten unseres heiligen Glaubens." Two pages from Christian Kauder's *Buch das gut, enthaltend den Katechismus, Betrachtung, Gesang* [The Good Book, containing the Catechisms, Meditations, Hymns] (Vienna: Imperial Printing Office, 1866). This is the first printed version of the hieroglyphic prayer book. Christian Kauder, a Catholic missionary, collected and collated surviving manuscripts in use in the mid-nineteenth century. (Courtesy of the Nova Scotia Museum)

cross: "Il n'est donc pas Priant, il est anglois" [He is thus not praying, he is English].[10] Neither missionary refers to his Mi'kmaq contacts as "converts," or as "Christians." They emphasize, rather, the performance of hymns and prayers, responses to catechizing, attendance at mass—*actions* in the form of witnessing and performing sacred words and gestures, which make a person "*Priant.*"

LeClercq and other missionaries who promoted this kind of word-perfect voicing of prayers complained about the "bad memories" of their subjects. But the same missionaries acknowledged, even marveled at, prodigious feats of memory in other contexts, and this apparent contradiction directs us to the precise nature and significance of the verbal tasks conceived by the missionaries. LeClercq and Maillard (the latter knew the Mi'kmaq language well) recognized high intelligence in individuals and sophistication in the language and culture. For the initial Mi'kmaq contacts, Christian narrative and doctrine certainly would have been unfamiliar, probably conceptually bizarre, and therefore difficult to remember; but additionally, the missionaries' demand that exact sequences of words be remembered and repeated exactly may also have been strange. Father Biard's *Relation* of 1616 encapsulates the problem from a missionary's point of view:

> They have a very good memory for material things, such as having seen you before, of the peculiarities of a place where they may have been, of what took place in their presence twenty or thirty years before, etc.; but to learn anything by heart—there's the rock; there is no way of getting a consecutive arrangement of words into their pates.[11]

Imparting this "consecutive arrangement of words" was fundamental to the French missionary project, and it would seem that some of the difficulties they encountered sprang in part from this requirement. Codified, exact sequences of words—creeds, the Decalogue, prayers—are, of course, characteristic of literate religions, whose "dogma and services are rigid (that is, dogmatic, ritualistic, orthodox)."[12] Mi'kmaq people of the seventeenth century, on the other hand, did not found memory and knowledge on alphabetic documents purporting to represent the sounds of exact sequences of words.

The chapter in which LeClercq recounts his formation of a system of "characters" begins with a complaint that resembles Biard's, but LeClercq's leads to an insight as to how he can realize his desire to convey "consecutive arrangements of words" to his Mi'kmaq catechumens. The Mi'kmaq, he says, "do not know how to read nor how to write. They have, nevertheless, enough understanding and memory to learn how to do both, if only they were willing to give the necessary application." But their minds are "fickle and unstable," he says, and "they are willing to apply [them] only in so far as it please them."[13] LeClercq's task is to motivate what he sees as innate intelligence and good memory to the task of memorizing the "prayers":

> The facility I have found in a method for teaching the prayers to our Gaspesians by means of certain characters which I have formed, fully persuades me that the majority would soon become educated; for, in fact, I should find no more difficulty in teaching them to read than to pray to God by means of my papers, in which each arbitrary letter signifies a particular word and sometimes even two together. They have so much readiness in understanding this kind of writing that they

learn in a single day what they would never have been able to grasp in an entire week without the aid of these leaflets.[14]

Note the distinction that LeClercq makes here between what his people have learned and what they might learn: he has taught them, by means of his characters, to "pray to God," and on the basis of their facility in this task, he is confident that they could learn to "read." LeClercq treats alphabetic reading and the deciphering of his characters as related, but distinct, skills. The achievement of one predicts success in the other, but in his mind they are not the same. It seems, then, that as used by LeClercq, the hieroglyphic script played a mediating role between, on the one hand, a culture with alphabetic literacy and the linguistic habits of a "religion of the book" and, on the other hand, a culture with an economy of language that combined oral systems of knowledge creation and transmission with visual representations of ideas. The hieroglyphs in combination with memorization of the "consecutive arrangement of words" (and all the missionaries stress memorization as their goal, to which the written characters are an aid) preserve the sense of language essential to a seventeenth-century Catholicism founded on canonical texts, but in the Mi'kmaq context they are regarded primarily as a script for oral enactment. In its fixing of "consecutive arrangements of words" the missionaries' hieroglyphic script preserves, or adapts, the concept and values of an alphabetic text, a visualized matrix that purports to enable the exact repetition of sequences of words. But for these French missionaries it is the repetition aloud that matters. Relevant here, perhaps, is Walter Ong's observation that, even in alphabetic, literate religions, "the spoken word functions integrally in ceremonial and devotional life," that we have the sense that the gods *speak* to humankind, and that we invoke their power through our own voicing of words.[15] It seems that such spoken "acts of prayer" made ceremonial sense to the Mi'kmaq as well, even when the acts were scripted by alien missionaries.

The relation of the priest to his Mi'kmaq congregation in late-seventeenth-century Nova Scotia may have resembled, in some respects, the analogous relationship in contemporaneous rural France, where literacy rates were low, where reading and especially writing were specialized skills (and access to books was restricted); where the authority to read and interpret sacred scripture was highly centralized and restricted; where official religious practice was constituted in visual icons (such as architectural carvings, paintings, symbolic vestments and objects), rote repetition, and priestly instruction and interpretation.[16] LeClercq describes the notebooks (*cahiers*) that he created for his people, and that they reproduced for themselves, as their "hours," as in a "book of hours" or basic collection of canonical prayers. He describes Mi'kmaq during the Mass as holding their cahiers "between their hands as we do our hours."[17] In her article on the education of fifteenth-century English writer Marjorie Kemp, Melissa Furrow describes the common practice among parishioners who knew little or no Latin of following "familiar Latin texts [in their book of hours], perhaps as the priest read the same words aloud."[18]

Pierre Maillard, the second and most important Catholic missionary, began his missionary labors among the Mi'kmaq in 1735, and he remained active even after the British regime took over, until his death in 1762. He was an accomplished linguist who appears to have mastered the Mi'kmaq language, producing a grammar, another version of the hieroglyphic script, and an alphabetic system of writing the language. Maillard's account of his introduction (or reintroduction) of the hieroglyphs reiterates LeClercq's, in that when he recounts the use of the hieroglyphs—he uses this word as well as LeClercq's "characters"—he makes clear that their purpose is to aid the accurate memorization of prayers, hymns, and religious instructions:

> In order to make them more promptly and easily ... learn the prayers, hymns, and instructions that we wished them to know, we distributed to them notebooks in which we had traced in hieroglyphs, which we invented ourselves, all the words that make up the prayers, hymns, and instructions. With the help of these characters, they learn in very little time everything they wish; and once they have got into their heads the shape and meaning of each character, they name with an astonishing ease all that is likewise written in their notebooks.... We congratulate ourselves strongly for having found this means of making them learn by heart the prayers ...; for it is this that so diminishes the pains that otherwise we would have to take in order to engrave these things in their memories.[19]

The distinction between kinds of literacy that I am suggesting was operative for LeClercq was also part of the conceptual framework within which Maillard worked some seventy-five years later. Maillard consciously chose to use the hieroglyphs over the obvious alternative of introducing the Roman alphabet (which he had already adapted to Mi'kmaq for his own use). His defense of this decision reveals a lot about Maillard's vision of the cultural and political landscape of *Acadie* in the era of his mission and about his sense of how technologies of language interact with politics and culture. That access to the written and printed word was a contested, and defining, division within early-modern European culture is a truism; for example, English colonies in North America were printing their own books in the seventeenth century, while New France had no printing press until the late eighteenth century. One can perhaps see in the French missionaries' use of hieroglyphic script an attempt to stake out a position on the contested ground between authoritarian and liberal approaches to the dissemination of knowledge, with the added consideration that, by the first half of the eighteenth century, control of information in the colonies was crucially associated with the European powers' struggle for hegemony.

Generally, Maillard's views are conservative and hierarchical. When writing to a correspondent in France, he openly states his desire to remain in control of the flow of information between French missionaries and the Mi'kmaq. He says that if the Mi'kmaq "should be in a state to use, as we do, our alphabet, be it to read or to write, they inevitably would abuse this knowledge through this spirit of curiosity ... which hurriedly drives them to know bad things rather than good."[20] He goes on to say that "they would surely emancipate themselves ... if they could make use of our alphabet ...; they would not hesitate strongly to persuade themselves that they knew much more than those who are intended to instruct them."[21] In the context of the wars between the French and British in what is now Maritime Canada, moreover, Maillard thought that alphabetic literacy could make the Mi'kmaq a strategic threat: "[T]hey would be capable of causing great harm amongst the people, as much with respect to religion and behavior as with respect to politics and government."[22] I am certain, he concludes, "[t]hat to ... substitute the alphabet for the characters which the Indians use to read and write, this would work very badly, for them as for us."[23] There are already some among them, he explains, who speak French well and who would soon be reading.

Maillard goes on to claim that writing and the sacred are equated by *"le sauvage"*; in particular, a Mi'kmaq person will not believe that you are actually "reading" the book you are holding if what you say does not have to do with religion:

> If what you read in his presence does not strike his ear with words like God (*Nixkam*), Jesus Christ (*jèchouk'lit*), the savior (*ouèchtaoulk*), the Redeemer of humankind (*mechta ouschedaoui ouet*), the excellent Virgin Mary (*ouèlinaxkouet Mali*), prayer (*Elajoudmakan*), etc., or at least

something that relates to praying, he will believe that you are joking and that all you make the book say it does not really say. From where does this savage's way of thinking come? It is that he believes firmly that those things mentioned above are all that merits being consigned to writing, and to printing as well."[24]

This view of the nature of writing Maillard does nothing to alter. He is content that, for the Mi'kmaq, books should pertain to nothing other than faith. "Patriarch" is the word used for the missionary in his role in the Mi'kmaq communities; it is a self-reference, and it is attributed to the lips of Mi'kmaq speakers: "You are a Patriarch ... what do you not know how to do? You know what has been, what is, what will be; a thousand kinds of writing teach you: you are so unlike us!"[25] This *Patriarche* is the conduit from these "thousand kinds of writing" to the Mi'kmaq, and the hieroglyphs are the sanctioned records of his teaching. In his account, Maillard sketches an evangelized Mi'kmaq society informed, and also isolated, by the hieroglyphic texts. During calm moments on long canoe voyages, he says, he will have his Mi'kmaq companions recite "some pieces from their prayer notebooks that I know they do not have well by heart. Often it happens that they ask me to explain what we have sung, particularly some psalm that, although very well rendered in Mi'kmaq, is not intelligible to them."[26] Maillard equates the role of the hieroglyphic cahiers with that of the catechism for French believers: "it is from these explicated symbols that they draw all kinds of excellent responses when one questions them on whatever point of religion, for they all know their notebooks by heart."[27] Maillard's idyllic world of faith is embattled, however, threatened by forces (English) whom Maillard personifies as the "Seducer," tempting the *"vrais Priants"*[28] with goods and promises of various kinds, as well as ridiculing their prayers and characterizing the missionaries as "men who deceive them, who trick them, who lure them, and who are sent to them expressly to prevent them from enjoying freedom of thought as other men do."[29] As we saw above, Maillard associates this "freedom of thought" with access to alphabetic writing, which, he says, would dangerously gratify the "spirit of curiosity" that is part of Mi'kmaq character.[30]

Considered in relation to the motives and mentality of the Catholic missionaries, then, the Mi'kmaq hieroglyphs are an understandable choice as an evangelization tool. As texts, they convey, with the verbal precision that was an essential part of an alphabetic religion, the key elements of doctrine and practice. As a writing system unique to the Mi'kmaq language, however, they also satisfied the desire, common among Catholic elites, to limit lay access to the Bible as well as to other writings, sacred and secular. And from the point of view of a colonial power, they were an exclusive system of communication not likely to be used by any other power and that offered the Mi'kmaq only limited access to French society.

These considerations, however, do not explain why the hieroglyphs worked for the Mi'kmaq, why hieroglyphic literacy became widespread among the Mi'kmaq, and why the prayer book endured for generations, even during long periods when no missionaries were present and there was very little contact with priests of any kind. Part of an explanation may be derived from strong indirect evidence that the hieroglyphic writing developed by the missionaries grew out of, and was grafted onto, graphic practices that predated the missionaries' activities; there is evidence that, at least at the level of the type of sign system used, there were strong continuities from the pre-missionary period to the postmissionary period. In summary, the evidence is as follows: (1) pictographic and signing practices are well documented throughout the Americas, and in Mi'kmaq territories there are petroglyphs known to predate the earliest missionaries; one of these has been identified with one of the missionary glyphs; (2) numerous missionary reports describe people spontaneously keeping notes for themselves as missionaries talk; (3) the rapid diffusion of the script suggests a pre-existing base in the culture; LeClercq describes what seems like spontaneous cooperation in the copying and teaching of the script; (4) the survival of the hieroglyphs suggests that hieroglyphic practice was culturally so deep-rooted that it did not need constant tending by missionaries.

Nineteenth-century American ethnographer Garrick Mallery's comprehensive study, *Picture-Writing of the American Indians* (1888–1889), includes scores of examples of conventionalized pictographs that were understood among the speakers of numerous different Native American languages; and Mallery regarded the extensive array of sophisticated picture-writing systems in North America both as the "intellectual remains of the ancient inhabitants" and as serving "living Indians for purposes as important to them as those of alphabetic writing."[31] Mallery's theory placed picture-writing on an evolutionary continuum of increasing abstraction and of ever-greater ideational sophistication and suppleness, with the alphabet as the telos of this development. Within this developmental framework picture-writing was understood as one stage in a series through which human cultures evolved, a stage that alphabetic societies were seen as having surpassed. Implicitly, however, the scope and detail of Mallery's data, as well as remarks such as those just quoted, testify to the importance of written signs in indigenous cultures north of Mexico; a synchronic view of these cultures includes their visual representations of ideas serving many different functions. Historically, the alphabet has been a powerful component of European expansion, but the situation in the Americas was never a case of writing societies confronting nonwriting societies. Rather, it was one of various kinds of writing and degrees of literacy interacting in complex, historically specific ways.[32]

Schmidt and Marshall do not equate any of the missionaries' glyphs with any native glyphs known to exist prior to LeClercq, but Ruth Holmes Whitehead of the Nova Scotia Museum has argued that the missionaries' glyph for the sun is the same sign as a petroglyph in Bedford, Nova Scotia, that definitely predates LeClercq.[33] Many characters are clearly European in origin; but, regardless of how few particular local characters missionaries may have adapted to their purposes, the missionaries are clear that indigenous picture-writing practices existed and were part of their strategy of teaching the new hieroglyphs.

LeClercq presents himself as the initiator of the script ("certains caracteres que j'ay formez"), but he says that he got the idea from local practices and describes the adoption and proliferation of the script as a phenomenon beyond his imagining and control.[34] During the second year of his mission, he says, he was at a loss as to how he was going to teach the "Gaspesiens" to pray to God:

> I noticed that some children were making marks with charcoal upon birch-bark, and were counting these with the finger [sic] very accurately at each word of prayers which they pronounced. This made me believe that by giving them some formulary, which would aid their memory by definite characters, I should advance much more quickly than by teaching them through the method of making them repeat a number of times that which I said to them. I was charmed to find that I was not mistaken, and that these characters which I had formed upon paper produced all the effect that I could wish.[35]

He goes on to describe the "ardor" and "spirit of emulation" with which the Mi'kmaq took up these writings, an ardor that made it difficult for him to keep up with demand.[36] He describes how the Mi'kmaq taught the characters to each other, little children even teaching their grandparents, and how they read and repeated them together in their homes.[37] In fact, when LeClercq returned after a long absence from the Gaspé, intending to present his writings to those gathered there to be instructed, he found that "they could already decipher the characters with as much ease as if they had always lived among us. This was because some whom I had formerly instructed had returned to their homes and had taught the others, thus performing, in regard to them, the office of missionary."[38]

William F. Ganong, the editor and translator of LeClercq for the Champlain Society edition of his *New Relation of Gaspesia*, connects LeClercq's description of existing writing practices and of the facility with which some Mi'kmaq absorbed the characters with analogous situations recounted in *Jesuit Relations* prior to LeClercq's missionary work. Of the five instances Ganong cites from the 1640s and 1650s, the one that most resembles what LeClercq recounts is that of Father Druillettes in the *Relation* of 1651–1652, referring to the Abnakis:

> Some would write their lessons after a fashion of their own, using a bit of charcoal for a pen, and a piece of bark instead of paper. Their characters were new, and so peculiar that one could not recognize or understand the writing of another,—that is, they used certain signs corresponding to their ideas; as it were a local reminder, for recalling points and articles and maxims which they had retained. They carried away these papers with them, to study their lessons in the quiet of the night.[39]

Maillard, too, describes the facility with which the people he taught reproduced the texts among themselves:

> This manner of reading and learning by means of these characters suits them, and the characters are a serious concern of theirs. They themselves collect the written sheets that have been distributed to them, and at their leisure they transcribe the characters from them, very faithfully and in the same order in which they found them inscribed, into other notebooks which should serve them in church to pray, sing, and to follow the Patriarch in his interrogations ... [T]hey themselves, the men and the women, make their books of hymns, prayers and instructions.[40]

Maillard describes occasions—such as when they are becalmed on a voyage—when his people will ask him to explain things that they have learned by heart but which raise questions for them. Perhaps eager to impress his reader with the fruits of his twenty years of missionary work, Maillard claims that on such occasions they forget nothing of what he explains:

They listen, then, with the greatest attention, because they want all the good things they hear to remain well inscribed in memory. If what they hear escapes them, they make the Patriarch repeat it; they even go so far as to beg him immediately to trace for them in characters what they see they cannot retain as faithfully as they would wish.... They occupy themselves with their notebooks during the long evenings of winter.[41]

The dynamism and interactivity conveyed in these accounts of the hieroglyphs' inception—note-taking and participation in the dissemination of Christian texts—is strong counterevidence to the notion that societies without alphabetic writing are always profoundly impressed by it, that they "will attribute some form of extraordinary 'magical' properties to writing."[42] The Mi'kmaq would seem to have been technologically well prepared to understand the use of writing and receive the words of a foreign faith by means of texts. The one instance of magical veneration of texts described by LeClercq is instigated by LeClercq himself: he carefully retrieves the charred fragments of one of his notebooks, which a Mi'kmaq woman has burned in a moment of anger and rebellion, and subjects them to a pantomime of grieving and reverential gestures (146–149).[43]

One can see how the hieroglyphs served the purposes of French missionaries, initiating and regulating Christian forms of religious speech and action among the Mi'kmaq. It does not follow necessarily, however—indeed, it is not likely—that the script functioned strictly along the lines intended by the missionaries. The writing system seems to have remained bonded to the Christian message that the missionaries conceived it to bear; but it may also be the case that the texts served Mi'kmaq people in ways that their missionary "Patriarchs" did not envision. The surprisingly easy inception and the vigorous and long life of the hieroglyphs suggest that Mi'kmaq religious practice associated with the hieroglyphic notebooks resonated in various and complex ways within the existing, and changing, culture that the missionaries intruded upon and then left behind. Perhaps because the hieroglyphic texts were insulated from the universe of alphabetic commentary and authority, the religious ideas they conveyed may have been more available for adaptation to Mi'kmaq cultural norms and traditions. According to Carlo Krieger, Christian Kauder's letters (1857–1862) describing Kauder's work among the Mi'kmaq in the 1850s and 1860's demonstrate how Mi'kmaq headmen's roles as lay priests reinforced their traditional authority: the Mi'kmaq "had lay priests with full authority long before the Catholic church ever thought of tolerating or introducing this position."[44] Kauder describes the various ceremonial actions of such a headman, noting that "all prayer[s] and hymns are in the hieroglyphic book, as they should be sung and said during the ritual."[45]

A contemporary of Kauder, Silas T. Rand, the first important Protestant missionary to the Mi'kmaq, also witnessed occasions when the headmen led services. In "early June" of 1851, for example, Rand visited "Indian [Chapel] Island" in Cape Breton, where he was allowed to attend the Sabbath service: "One old man led on the rest, and after the singing was over, he gave them an exhortation. As he spoke slowly, and in measured style, I could understand the most of it. He said many good things, seated, by the way, like the Rabbins of old, and some which were not so good."[46] Rand's diaries and his letters to the Micmac Missionary Society contain numerous references to the hieroglyphic Prayer Book, although it is impossible to tell whether to manuscripts or, after 1866, to Kauder's volume. As a Baptist, Rand regarded individual reading of the Bible as fundamental to Christian faith, and his mission centered on the translation, printing, and dissemination of the Bible in alphabetic Mi'kmaq. His references to the hieroglyphics suggest that he understood his translations of the Gospels as offering the complete story, to which the Catholic missionaries' prayer book gave only partial access:

> I shall not soon forget an afternoon spent last winter in the place where he [a Mi'kmaq man with whom he has been discussing religion] and another large family resided. How attentively did they all listen to our Saviour's farewell address to his disciples, and his closing prayer, in John xvii. 'Oh why did they not give us all that in our book?' asked the other man, of whom I have been speaking.[47]

Rand could be sharply critical of the hieroglyphs, which, he once said, had "no value except to show how ponderously foolish learned and clever men [the Catholic missionaries] can be when they desire to darken counsel by words without knowledge."[48] For Rand, truth lay in holy scripture, and each believer needed to be able to seek it there; the hieroglyphs, for Rand, denied access to the "knowledge" in scripture that lay behind the "words" in the hieroglyphic prayer book. At other times, however, he seems more inclined to afford the hieroglyphic prayer book some value: "Sabbath afternoons I always spend at the camps. We read the scriptures together and discuss their sacred contents; we also read and compare their hyeroglyphic [sic] prayer book, and I can assure you we find some good things there too."[49] In this instance, the hieroglyphs enable a conversation about Christian belief. Rand's evangelizing often consisted of his reading aloud from his Mi'kmaq translations of the Bible; and even when the hieroglyphic texts were not on site, he knew he was dealing with people whose lives had been, and continued to be, significantly influenced by the texts' existence. Rand did not require formal conversion, or the renunciation of Catholicism, as an index of his success as a missionary (and in any case, according to this own estimate, he effected very few, if any, such conversions in the course of forty years of work). In an important sense, however, Rand's career was a long polemical response to Maillard's position on which writing system was the appropriate form of mediation between Euro-Christian and Mi'kmaq culture. Rand rejected the Catholic missionaries' retention of priestly authority and their limiting of access to the Bible, but he recognized that he was engaging people who had internalized Catholic teaching. In language that is less temperate than Rand's own, but in terms that reflect his ideas, the editors of the *Third Annual Report of the Micmac Missionary Society* write that an "obstacle" to Rand's success was

> the fact that the minds of the Micmac Indians were not, like those of aboriginal tribes in some countries, comparative blanks in religious matters, prepared, in a manner, for the reception of whatever truths might be communicated to them; but had already been filled with a multiplicity of erroneous fancies and dogmas, by the Missionaries of the Church of Rome.... Sunk in degradation—without school—without books (*except a prayer book, written, not printed, and often incorrect and hurtful in its teachings*) sitting in the region and shadow of death— access to them with the truth as it is in Jesus seemed in a great measure barred out.[50]

Here theological and liturgical assumptions are bound up with their respective systems of written communication. What Michel de Certeau says of French Calvinist Jean de Léry could be said as well of Rand: "He prefers the letter to a church body; the text to the voice of a presence; origins related by writing to the elocutionary experience of a fugitive communication."[51] And in spite of Rand's forty years of work, the hieroglyphic prayer book seems to have remained far more important in Mi'kmaq society during his lifetime than the alphabetic Mi'kmaq translations of the Bible he introduced.

An important Catholic missionary of the twentieth century, Father Pacifique, writing in an era when English was becoming the language Mi'kmaq children learned in school, expressed somewhat contradictory opinions with respect to the usefulness of the hieroglyphs. In one instance, he looked ahead to a time when the hieroglyphs would fall completely out of use: "[T]hey are now almost abandoned, and it is hardly regrettable. Very useful to express general ideas, the hieroglyphics are rather useless and even harmful when it is a matter of being precise about nuances. Alphabetic writing is much more advantageous, and it is now the only kind in use among the Mi'kmaq."[52] However, a decade later, in the preface to the new edition of Kauder's hieroglyphic prayer book he brought to press, Pacifique seems to have revised this estimate of the hieroglyphics' importance in Mi'kmaq culture. Most copies of the Kauder edition, he says, have been lost:

> Those that escaped have been worn out for a long time. The Mi'kmaq do their best to reattach the leaves, to make them last longer, or they even want to bind them, several times over, to the great discouragement of the binders. They preserve the debris as relics. How many times they have asked me to reprint this work for them![53]

He seems here to explain his own role in reprinting the Kauder prayer book by alluding to the demand for it among the Mi'kmaq. In spite of his earlier opinion that the hieroglyphs are less useful than the alphabet, he seems to recognize and accede to something autonomous in Mi'kmaq culture of which the hieroglyphic prayer book is an index, and which has won his respect and cooperation. Indeed, explaining the history of their book, he recounts that

> the Mi'kmaq, almost completely deprived of the services of priests during long years, have conserved their faith with a perseverance and a unanimity that is almost prodigious. They have copied and recopied without giving up the notebooks of their apostle [Maillard]. And, in spite of inevitable gaps, in such a case where there is no person in authority, the book they call their Bible has sustained them in the knowledge and practice of their religion. For 128 years they have conveyed one to another these sacred hieroglyphs.[54]

The Mi'kmaq among whom Pacifique lived and worked were corresponding with each other and publishing a monthly newspaper in alphabetic Mi'kmaq.[55] Yet in these comments, and in helping reprint the Kauder prayer book, Pacifique seems to recognize the important role of this unique book in Mi'kmaq culture and history. Whatever its future, and regardless of the various motives and understandings of Euro-Christian missionaries in connection with this book, it would seem that the Mi'kmaq had long ago made it their own.

One approach to further study of the hieroglyphic prayer book is to regard it as an artifact—a material and symbolic entity with an attendant social practice— instigated by the missionaries but retained and recontextualized within Mi'kmaq culture. However it is determined that the hieroglyphs function as a "writing system," if one regards the prayer book as one artifact, one can explore how this bonded unit—the material sign in the birch bark or printed book and the prayer spoken aloud—circulated in Mi'kmaq culture. Such an approach to the hieroglyphic prayer book would be different from regarding the characters themselves as a neutral technology, a writing system that, once acquired, could have been adapted to any use. In fact, Wogan notes, studies of the "ethnography of literacy" have "stressed the importance of social-cultural factors that mediate and determine the uses of literacy in any given culture."[56] Writing systems are not "neutral" technologies; they develop in relation to verbal and cultural practices; they are always rhetorical, in the sense of serving certain ends in a society. To today write the history of the hieroglyphic "Great Book" would be to begin to explore it as a site of expressiveness and creativity even though it has not resulted in other known hieroglyphic texts. Such an account of the prayer book might be analogous to the performance history of a liturgy or a play, in which one tries to recover the sites, actors, costumes, settings, occasions, and audiences of a succession of enactments. The texts of Shakespeare's plays were established and printed in the seventeenth century, but considering the performance of his plays by succeeding generations reconnects text to historically specific realizations. That succeeding generations in many different locations can locate themselves in relation to exactly the same words is an effect of the technologies of writing and printing; but the history of such realizations is more the history of those who have produced and acted the play than it is the history of the original writer, or of "the text itself" (if the text, in isolation, has any meaningful existence at all). Still, Mi'kmaq people have preserved, copied, and passed on their hieroglyphic texts, and so a knowledge of the history of particular texts, of who has held them and when and where, of where they have been read and in what circumstances and by whom, can be the beginning of a history of their fuller life as realized "acts."

Notes

My thanks to Edward Gray for the many insights and sources I gleaned from his Ph.D. dissertation, particularly chapter two, "Language and Conversion." I also would like to thank Ruth Holmes Whitehead, staff ethnologist and assistant curator in history at the Nova Scotia Museum, for her generous sharing of materials, for her insightful comments and advice, and for the inspiring example of her own work.

1. David L. Schmidt and Murdena Marshall, eds. and translators, *Mi'kmaq Hieroglyphic Prayers: Readings in North America's First Indigenous Script* (Halifax, 1995), 2. Schmidt is a linguistic anthropologist and an assistant professor of culture and heritage; Murdena Marshall is a grandmother and designated Prayer Leader of *the Santewi Mawio'mi* (Grand Council) of the Mi'kmaq First Nation, and an associate professor of Mi'kmaq Studies; both are at the University College of Cape Breton.
2. Ibid., 15.
3. Louis Hennepin, *Déscription de la Louisiane, Nouvellement Découverte au Sud-Ouest de la Nouvelle France*, 2 vols. (Paris, 1683), 1:249.
4. In the late seventeenth century, Hennepin, writing about the native peoples of New France, connects lack of writing with their supposed uncertainty as to their own origins, and he sees this uncertainty as a reason that native peoples ought to recognize European civilization as superior. It was hardly surprising, he said, that European historians were unable to determine the origins of the Americans, "since the inhabitants [of North America], who ought to be the best informed, know nothing about it themselves." But, he continues, "if in Europe we were, like them, deprived of writing, if we had not the use of this ingenious art, which makes the dead live again and the past return, and which conserves for us an eternal memory of all things, we would be no less ignorant than they" (*Déscription de la Louisiane*, 2: 8). Translations of Hennepin are my own.
5. For an overview of the theory and for an analysis of "literacy in contact situations," see Peter Wogan, "Perceptions of European Literacy in Early Contact Situations," *Ethnohistory* 41, no.3 (Summer 1994): 407–29.
6. Wogan, "Perceptions of European Literacy," 408.
7. Schmidt and Marshall, *Mi'kmaq Hieroglyphic Prayers*, 4.
8. Christian Kauder, *Buch das gut* (Vienna, 1866) was rare from the outset, because the ship carrying most of the volumes back to Nova Scotia was lost.
9. Pierre Antoine-Simon Maillard, "Lettre de M. l'Abbé Maillard sur les missions de l'Acadie et particulairment sur les missions Micmaques," in *Les Soirées Canadiennes* (Québec, 1863) 3: 409–10.
10. Ibid., 319.
11. Quoted by William F. Ganong, trans. and ed., in Chrestien LeClercq, *New Relation of Gaspesia: With the Customs and Religion of the Gaspesien Indians* (Toronto, 1910), 23.
12. Jack Goody, *The Logic of Writing and the Organization of Society* (Cambridge, England, 1986), 9.
13. Ganong, trans., *New Relation*, 125. "Ils ne scavent ni lire, ni écrire: ils ont cependant assez de jugement & de memoire, s'ils vouloient avoir autant d'application qu'il en faut pour apprendre l'un & l'autre; mais outre l'inconstance & l'instabilité de leurs esprits, qu'ils ne veulent gener qu'autant qu'il leur plait " (*Nouvelle Relation*, 127).

14. Ganong, trans., *New Relation*, 126. "La facilité & la metode que j'ay trouvé d'enseigner les Prieres à nos Gaspesiens, avec certain caracteres que j'ay formez, me persuadent efficacement que la pluspart se rendroient bien tôt sçavans: car enfin, je ne trouverois pas plus de difficulté à leur montrer à lire, qu'à prier Dieu par mes papiers, dans lesquels chaque lettre arbitraire signifie un mot particulier, quelques-fois même deux ensemble. Ils ont tant de facilité pour concevoir cette sorte d'écriture, qu'ils apprennent dans une seule journée, ce qu'ils n'eussent jamais pû retenir en une semaine entiere sans le secours de ces billets ..." (*Nouvelle Relation*, 129–30).
15. Walter Ong, *Orality and Literacy: The Technologizing of the Word* (London, 1982), 74.
16. Henri-Jean Martin, *Print, Power and People in Seventeenth-Century France*, trans. David Gerhard (Metuchen, NJ, 1993), 2–4.
17. Ganong, trans., *New Relation*, 132, 130.
18. Melissa Furrow, "Unscholarly Latinity and Margery Kemp," in *"Doubt Wisely": Papers on English Language and Literature for E. G. Stanley*, ed. M. J. Toswell and E. M. Tyler (London, 1996), 246.
19. All translations of Maillard are my own. See Schmidt and Marshall, *Mi'kmaq Hieroglyphic Prayers*, 10, for a discussion of the apparently conflicting claims of LeClercq and Maillard to have "invented" the hieroglyphs. "Pour leur faire apprendre plus promptement et avec beaucoup plus de facilité qu'ils ne faisoient cy-devant les prières, les chants et les instructions que nous souhaitons qu'ils sachent, nous leur distribuons des cahiers sur lesquels nous leur avons tracé en hiéroglyphs, que nous avons inventez nous-mêmes, tous les mots dont se trouvent composez ces prières, ces chants et ces instructions. A l'aide de ces differens caractères, ils apprennent en très-peu de temps tout ce qu'ils veulent apprendre; et quand ils ont une fois mis dans la tête la figure et la valeur de chaque caractère, ils nomment avec une facilité etonnante tout ce qui se trouve écrit de même dans leurs cahiers.... Nous nous félicitons fort d'avoir trouvé ce moyen de leur faire apprendre si facilement par coeur les prières ...; car c'est ce qui diminue beaucoups des peines qu'autrement nous aurions à graver toutes ces choses dans leurs mémoires" (Maillard, "Lettre," 355–57).
20. "S'ils étoient une fois en état de se servir comme nous de notre alphabet[,] soit pour lire, soit pour écrire, ils abuseroient infailliblement de cette science par cet esprit de curiosité, que nous leur connaissons, qui les domine pour chercher avec empressement à sçavoir plutôt les choses mauvaises que les bonnes" (ibid., 358).
21. "Mais s'ils s'émanciperoient bien ... s'ils pouvoient faire usage de notre alphabet, soit pour lire, soit pour écrire; ils ne tarderoient pas à se fortement persuader qu'ils en sçavent beaucoup plus que ceux qui sont faits pour les instruire" (ibid., 360).
22. "Seroient-ils capables de causer de grands maux parmi la nation, tant par rapport à la religion et aux bonnes moeurs, qu'au gouvernment politique" (ibid., 361).
23. "De vouloir substituer notre alphabet aux caractères dont nos sauvages se servent pour lire et pour écrire, ce seroit fort mal travailler et pour eux, et pour nous" (ibid., 362).
24. "Si ce que vous en lisez en sa présence ne luy frappe pas l'oreille des noms de Dieu (*Nixkam*), de Jésus-Christ (*jèchouk'lit*), de sauveur (*ouèchtaloulk*), de Rédempteur du genre humain (*mechta ouschedaoui ouet*), de Marie Vierge par excellence (*ouèlinaxkouet Mali*), de Prière (*Elajoudmakan*) &c, au moins de

quelque chose qui ait relation à la Prière, il croira vrayment que vous badinez et que vous faites dire au livre tout ce qu'il ne dit pas. D'ou vient cette façon de penser du sauvage? c'est qu'il croit fermement que ce que je viens de rapporter ci-dessus, est ce qui mérit seul d'être consigné par écrit, et imprimé de même" (ibid., 362–63; transcriptions of Mi'kmaq words are Maillard's).

25. "'Tu es Patriarche ... que ne sçais-tu pas faire! Tu connois ce qui à été, ce qui est, ce qui sera; mille sortes d'écrits te l'apprennent: que tu nous es dissemblables!'" (ibid., 313).

26. "Quelques ... morceaux de nos cahiers de prières que je sçay qu'ils ne possèdent pas bien par coeur. Souvent il leur arrive de me demander l'explication de ce que nous aurons chanté, surtout de quelque psaume qui quoique fort bien rendu en mikmaque, ne leur est pas intelligible" (ibid., 409).

27. "C'est de ce symbole expliqué qu'ils tirent toutes sortes de bonnes et excellentes réponses, quand on les interroge sur quelque point que ce soit de la religion, car ils sçavent tous leurs cahiers par coeur ..." (ibid., 410).

28. Ibid., 339.

29. "De gens qui les dupent, qui les trompent, qui les leurrent, et qui ne leur ont été envoyez qu'exprès pour les empêcher de jouir de la liberté de penser ... comme tous les autres hommes" (ibid., 342).

30. Ibid., 359.

31. Garrick Mallery, *Picture-Writing of the American Indians*, 2 vols. (1893; New York, 1972), 1:28.

32. See Wogan, "Perceptions of European Literacy," 413–14; and Michael Harbsmeier, "Writing and the Other: Traveller's Literacy, or Towards an Archeology of Orality," in *Literacy and Society*, ed. Laren Schousboe and Mogens Trolle Larsen (Copenhagen, 1989), 220–21.

33. Ruth Holmes Whitehead, "A New Micmac Petroglyph Site," *The Occasional* 13, no.1 (1992): 7–12.

34. LeClercq, *Nouvelle Relation*, 129.

35. Ganong, trans., *New Relation*, 131. "Je m'apperçûs que quelques enfans faisoient des marques avec du charbon sur de l'écorce de bouleau, & les comptoient avec leur doigt fort éxactement, à chaque mot de Prieres qu'ils prononçoient: cela me fit croire qu'en leur donnant quelque formulaire qui soulageàt leur memore par certain caracteres, je pourrois beaucoup avancer, que de les enseigner en les faisant repeter plusiers fois ce que je leurs disois. Je fus ravis de connoître que je ne m'étois pas trompé, & que ces caracteres que j'avois formez sur du papier, produisoient tout l'effet que je souhaitois" (*Nouvelle Relation*, 141–42).

36. Ibid., 142.

37. Ibid., 131.

38. Ibid., 130. "Ils en déchifroient déja les caracteres, avec autant de facilité que s'ils étoient toujours demeurés parmi nous; d'autant que ceux que j'avois auparavant instruits étant retournez chex eux, avoient enseigne ceux ci, & avoient fait à leur égard l'office de Missionnaire." (*Nouvelle Relation*, 139).

39. Ibid., 22–23.

40. "Cette façon de lire et d'apprendre par le moyen de ces caractères, leur plait, quoiqu'elle les occupe fort sérieusement. Ils rassemblent eux-mêmes les feuilles écrites qu'on leur à distribuées, et à leur loisir ils en transcrivent les caractères très fidèlement et dans le même order qu'ils les trouvent tracez sur d'autres cahiers qui doivent leur servir à l'Eglise pour prier, pour chanter, et pour suivre le Patriarch dans ses interrogations.... [I]ls font eux-mêmes, les

femmes commes les hommes, leurs livres de chants, de prières et d'instructions" (Maillard, "Lettre," 357–58).
41. "Ils écoutent alors avec une attention des plus grandes, parcequ'ils veulent tout de bon que ce qu'ils entendent leur reste bien gravé dans la mémoire. Si ce qu'ils ont écouté de même, leur échappe, ils se le font répéter par le patriarche; ils vont même jusqu'à le prier instamment de leur tracer en caractères ce qu'ils voyent ne pouvoir aussi fidèlement retenir qu'ils le souhaiteroient.... Entre'eux ils s'en [i.e., with their notebooks] entretiennent dans les longue soirées de l'hyver" (ibid., 409–10).
42. Wogan, "Perceptions of European Literacy," 408.
43. Ganong, trans., *New Relation*, 146–49.
44. Carlo Krieger, "Ethnogenesis or Cultural Interference? Catholic Missionaries and the Micmac," *Actes du vintième congrès des algonquinistes*, ed. William Cowan (Ottawa, 1989), 197.
45. Quoted, ibid., 197.
46. Silas T. Rand, in *First Annual Report of the Micmac Missionary Society* (Halifax, 1851), 9–10.
47. *Tenth Annual Report of the Micmac Missionary Society* (Halifax, 1859), 11.
48. Quoted in Schmidt and Marshall, *Mi'kmaq Hieroglyphic Prayers*, 14.
49. *Thirteenth Annual Report of the Micmac Missionary Society* (Halifax, 1863), 5.
50. *Third Annual Report of the Micmac Missionary Society* (Halifax, 1852), 7 (my emphasis).
51. Michel de Certeau, *The Writing of History* (1975), trans. Tom Conley (New York, 1988), 217.
52. Père Pacifique (Henri Buisson de Valigny), *Une tribu privilégiée* (Québec, 1910), 6–7. "Ils sont presque laissés de coté maintenant, et c'est à peine regrettable. Très commodes pour exprimer les idées générales, les hiéroglyphes sont plutot inutiles et meme nuisibles, quand il s'agit d'en préciser les nuances. L'écriture alphabétique est bien plus avantageuse, et c'est maintenant la seule en usage parmi les Micmacs." (Translations of Pacifique are my own.)
53. *Micmac Manual: Manual of Prayers, Psalms, and Hymns in Micmac Ideograms: New Edition of Father Kauder's Book published in 1866* (Restigouche, Québec, 1921; 3d ed., Ste-Anne-des-Monts, 1995), 1. "Ceux qui ont échappé sont depuis longtemps plus qu'usés. Les Micmacs en rattachent les feuilles de leur mieux, pour les faire durer encore, ou bien ils veulent les faire relier, à plusieurs reprises, au grand découragement des relieurs. Ils en conservent les débris comme de reliques. Combien de fois ne m'ont-ils pas demandé de leur faire réimprimer cet ouvrage!"
54. Ibid. "Les Micmacs, presque complètement privés de service religieux pendant de longues années ont conservé leur foi avec une persévérance et un unanimité qui tient du prodige. Ils ont copié et recopié sans relache les cahiers de leur apotre [Maillard]. Et, malgré des lacunes inévitables, là ou manque le controle de l'autorité vivante, le livre qu'ils appellent *leur Bible* les a maintenus dans la connaissance et la practique de la religion. Pendant 128 ans ils se sont transmis les uns aux autres ces hiéroglyphes sacrés."
55. Pacifique, *Une tribu*, 6–7.
56. Wogan, "Perceptions of European Literacy," 408.

Part IV

Intermediaries

– *Chapter 9* –

INTERPRETERS SNATCHED FROM THE SHORE: THE SUCCESSFUL AND THE OTHERS

ତ୨୦

Frances Karttunen

I do not know the language, and the people of these lands do not understand me nor I them, nor does anyone on board. And these Indians whom I took along I often misunderstood, taking one thing for the opposite, and I don't trust them much, for many times they have tried to flee.

> Christopher Columbus (as quoted in S. E. Morison, *Journals and Other Documents of the Life and Voyages of Christopher Columbus*)

BEGINNING IN THE FIFTEENTH CENTURY the great oceans ceased to be barriers and became highways carrying explorers around the globe to touch on the shores of land masses small and great. In a short time, populations hitherto ignorant of each other were linked by an active maritime network. Coastal peoples and those inland behind them shared no common language with the explorers. The separation from one's own context and immersion in another that is necessary for language acquisition under such circumstances were accomplished in large part through kidnapping. Some Europeans, too, learned indigenous languages through voluntary or involuntary isolation among the indigenes. This paper deals with interpreters operating in that interval before a bilingual/bicultural generation grew up to serve as cultural brokers. For individuals pressed into service, the requirements of survival were flexibility, youth, sharp intellect, and sheer good luck.

Kidnapped Individuals

Monday, 12 November, 1492 ... Yesterday came aboard the ship a dugout with six young men, and five came on board; these I ordered to be detained and I am bringing them. And afterwards I sent to a house ... and they brought seven head of women, small and large, and three boys. I did this because the [Indian] men would behave better in Spain with women of their country than without them; for already many times I happened to take men of Guinea that they might learn the language in Portugal, and after they had returned and it was expected to make some use of them in their own country ... but in reaching home it never proved to be so ... But these, having their women, will find it good business to do what they are told, and these women would teach our people their language.[1]

On the return leg of his first voyage, Columbus succeeded in bringing back to Spain a small group of indigenes for exhibition at court and potentially to serve as interpreters on subsequent voyages. On his next voyage he brought back a larger number for the slave market in Seville, and then the floodgates were open to one-way forced transport from the Caribbean.[2] Despite debate in Europe about the moral and religious acceptability of enslavement of newly contacted people, the practice spread. In 1501 Gaspar Corte-Real shipped to Lisbon a group of men and women, about fifty altogether, taken from the shores of Newfoundland or thereabouts. A quarter century later, his fellow countryman Estevão Gomes shipped out at least as many Algonquians. Jacques Cartier carried off two Iroquoians he caught as they fished off the Gaspé peninsula in the summer of 1534. Two years later he kidnapped ten more and took them to France, where they all died, but he succeeded in getting support for exploration of their land in 1541 and 1542.

From their base in Cuba, Spanish ships had begun nudging their way along the mainland early in the sixteenth century. Following a clash with Mayas on a Yucatecan beach in 1517, the Spaniards carried off two men, whom they baptized Julián and Melchor, with the specific purpose of making them into interpreters. Soon came Hernán Cortés to those same shores, and the Mayas did their best to buy him off with goods and servants. One of twenty women the Mayas included in the bribe was already a victim of kidnapping and resale among the Mayas. Baptized doña Marina, this bilingual, and eventually trilingual, woman served Cortés as the key to communication throughout what soon became New Spain.[3]

After the fall of Montezuma and the Aztec capital to Cortés in 1521, Spaniards fanned out through South America in search of more kingdoms to conquer. Several Andeans were carried off to learn Spanish. Two, baptized Felipe and Martín, returned with the Pizarros to participate in the conquest of Peru. In one of the drawings illustrating Guaman Poma de Ayala's *Nueva Coronica*, a man in Spanish clothing interprets between Spaniards and the ruler Atahualpa. Written on his sleeve are the words "Felipe indio lengua" (Felipe, Indian interpreter).[4]

Meanwhile about sixty indigenes were taken from the coast of what is today South Carolina to Hispaniola/Santo Domingo to labor on the *encomienda* of don Lucas Vásquez de Ayllón. One of them, who was baptized Francisco and known as "de Chicora" (apparently from Shakori, an indigenous group of the general area), traveled with Vásquez de Allyón to Spain. For three years in Spain, Francisco served don Lucas as personal servant and provided accounts of the great resources and desirability of his land, assisting his master in getting permission and support for a colonizing expedition there with Francisco himself as interpreter.[5]

In the mid-sixteenth century an indigenous nobleman of what became Virginia fell into the hands of Spaniards exploring up the coast in the direction of Chesapeake Bay. They took him to Mexico, it seems, and then to Spain. He received the name Luis de Velasco after the Viceroy, who sponsored him in baptism. In Spain don Luis, like Francisco de Chicora before him, fervently testified to the richness of his homeland and of his great desire to bring Christianity there. After several false starts over an entire decade, don Luis finally was attached to a group of Jesuits setting out from Havana to carry the faith to his people. Their mission site lay just a short way from where the English would establish Jamestown less than forty years later, in 1607.[6]

An early and frequent visitor to Jamestown was a prepubescent girl called Matoaka and also known as Pocahontas. She became attached to the English at the age of eleven or twelve and served as an important emissary between them and her people.[7] In 1613 Pocahontas was taken into custody by the English. Within the year she had been instructed in the Christian faith, baptized as Rebecca, and married to the Englishman John Rolfe. With the passage of another year, she was the mother of a son. After his weaning, the young family, in the company of ten or a dozen of her people, made a trip to London, where they were presented at court. It is not clear where kidnapping had ended and domesticity had begun.[8]

In March of 1621, three months after the English settlers on the *Mayflower* had debarked at Plymouth, a man walked out of the woods and greeted them in their language. He introduced himself as Samoset and asked for some beer (it appears he had to settle for rum). His ability with English was the result of long association with European fishermen and traders along the Maine coast. He had, in fact, just come down to Massachusetts Bay with an English captain in whose company had been another English-speaking indigene, Tisquantum ("Squanto"). A few days later, Samoset brought Squanto to meet them. Squanto was one of twenty people from the immediate area who had been carried off in 1614 by an English captain, Thomas Hunt, to be sold in Spain as slaves. Somehow, Squanto had escaped and made his way to London, where he had lived with a merchant named John Slany. Upon return to his home after an absence of four years, he found all his people dead of an epidemic that preceded the arrival of the *Mayflower*, leaving vacant the area taken over by the English. Squanto, now a man alone, attached himself to the Plymouth Plantation and made himself useful in practical matters and especially in negotiating with members of other indigenous groups in the area.[9]

It had taken Cortés only a short time to press inland from the shore of the Gulf of Mexico to the heart of Central Mexico. It took much longer for explorers from the eastern United States to reach the continental divide, cross it, and complete the overland trek to the Pacific Northwest coast. Sacajawea—the Shoshone woman who accompanied them in 1805–6 and provided help with negotiation, passage through the mountains, and the everyday business of getting enough to eat—had also been placed on the path of interpretation through kidnapping and subsequent exchange. Lewis and Clark acquired her services when they signed on a French fur trader, Toussaint Charbonneau, who had bought or won her and another young girl from their Hidatsa captors.[10]

Castaways and Exchanges

Columbus remarked upon the practice of carrying men off the Guinea coast in West Africa to learn the Portuguese language. The Portuguese also put ashore on that same coast men with no prospects of returning home. Of these exiles, known as *lançados*, it was expected that those who survived would father children, and that these children, being able to communicate with both their fathers and their mothers, could also facilitate future trade.

In 1511 two Spaniards found themselves similarly isolated among the Mayas of Yucatan. Not deliberately cast away, but the sole long-term survivors of shipwreck, both were enslaved by the Mayas. Gonzalo de Guerrero adopted Maya ways, made himself useful to his master, was rewarded with responsibilities, married, and became a family man in a way familiar to readers of James Axtell and John Demos.[11] His companion, Jerónimo de Aguilar, had taken holy orders and did not assimilate, although both men, through their immersion, became speakers of Maya. When Cortés, who had great need of their talents as interpreters, arrived to rescue them, Aguilar hastened to the beach, anxious to know the day and date to be sure he had been observing the Christian calendar without error. Guerrero declined rescue and lived out the rest of his life with his adopted people.[12]

Having lost all the people he had taken to France in 1536, Cartier left two French boys behind at the conclusion of his 1541/42 voyage to learn the local language for trade purposes. As New France developed, Europeans continued to trade places with indigenes for periods of time; intermarriage of Frenchmen and local women was sanctioned; and efforts were made to secure Catholic missionaries.

Missionaries

The Peruvian Garcilaso de la Vega, "El Inca," had this to say about reciprocal language learning:

> There are some who think it would be wise to oblige all the Indians to learn the Spanish language, so as to spare the priests the vain labor of learning the Indian language. Anyone who hears this argument will realize it arises more from weakness of spirit than from dullness of understanding ... If the Spaniards, who are sharpwitted and versed in learning, cannot, as they say, learn the general language of Cuzco [Quechua], how can they make the Indians, who are untutored and uninstructed in letters, learn Spanish?[13]

The missionary friars were in fact committed to carrying out evangelization in the languages of the people to whom they carried the Christian faith. In the sixteenth century Franciscans, Dominicans, and Augustinians all compiled dictionaries and grammars of indigenous languages, and the Jesuits carried on the commitment, supported by solid funding and rigorous training.[14] The Franciscan Bernadino de Sahagún immersed himself in the company of Nahuatl speakers (crediting his Nahua associates by name, and, in fact, never taking a Spanish-speaking colleague) to produce an immense corpus of religious and ethnographic material in the language. In Yucatan, Diego de Landa, also a Franciscan, received permission to go alone and unprotected among very hostile Mayas to learn to dispute with them in their own language. Landa was less generous than Sahagún in naming his prime sources of information about Maya language and culture, but we know that among them were the mature Nachi Cocom and the young Gaspar Antonio Chi.[15] Guaman Poma de Ayala, the Andean who illustrated the efforts of Felipe to interpret between Atahualpa and the Spaniards at Cajamarca, sharply satirized Catholic priests preaching in Quechua, not only for their failings but also for virtuoso grandiosity,[16] demonstrating that the proposal of his contemporary Garcilaso, that Spaniards learn Quechua, was partially implemented.[17]

Although the Jesuits' missionizing of the mid-Atlantic coast was unsuccessful, their efforts in New France prospered despite sporadic destruction of mission posts. Circulation of their reports, the *Jesuit Relations*, proved influential in the founding of Montreal in 1642. The "savages" who so threatened the New England towns in the seventeenth and eighteenth century were in considerable part Catholics and conversant with French.

The English looked upon the numbers of Catholic conversions and deemed it scandalous that they themselves were so uncompetitive. Rather than the corporate approach to evangelization taken by Franciscans, Dominicans, Augustinians, and Jesuits, it fell to the consciences of individuals among the English settlers to go among the native peoples and acquire their languages. Those who did so in New England included John Eliot, Roger Williams, the father-and-son team of Thomas Mayhew and Thomas Mayhew Jr., and Peter Foulger. Without the institutional support and specific training that evangelists in Catholic missionary orders received, each had to approach learning the local language on his own. Eliot secured the assistance of Cockenoe, a Montauk boy taken during the Pequot war and made into a house servant. Through this immersion experience, Cockenoe had acquired fluent English and became "the first I made use of to teach me words and to be my interpreter," according to Eliot.[18]

In the case of Roger Williams's gathering the information from which he compiled his *Key into the Language of America*, he does not explicitly state how he found his way into the language; but in his introduction he speaks of being called to the deathbed of a Pequot named Wequash, whom he describes as an "old friend" with whom he had had "many discourses." At the conclusion of their reported final conversation, Wequash shifts into English, demonstrating his own imperfect but serviceable bilingualism.[19]

The first convert and longtime associate of the Mayhews and Foulger on Martha's Vineyard was Hiacoomes. His son, Joel Hiacoomes, was sent to study at Harvard's Indian School, but whether the father had acquired some English ahead of the Mayhews is as yet unclear to me. The Mayhews' enterprise took place on islands with large indigenous populations and, initially, no English settlements. As settlers moved to Nantucket beginning in 1659, Foulger served as interpreter there.

Whether as members of an order or individually, missionaries seeking to acquire the languages of those they would evangelize have often chosen the role of voluntary castaways. To some extent the same principle of language acquisition by brute force applies to them as to the indigenes carried off against their wills. However, in addition to metagrammatical background in Latin, Greek, and Hebrew and the driving force of religious motivation, Christian missionaries typically have also had the assistance of indigenes who had already become somewhat bilingual under coercive circumstances.

Ritual Kin

Both Axtell and Demos describe in detail the practice of taking European captives and making some of them into ritual kin. It was a scandal and a heartbreak to relatives and communities left behind that, after a period of time with their captors, some of these people refused rescue or, having been wrested away from their new families, did everything in their power to escape and return to their kidnappers. Fearing the prospect of being forcibly returned to their original homes, these deeply assimilated people typically did not serve as interpreters. But sometimes assimilation failed to take, and an individual did return and assist in future parleys. In Demos's story of the unredeemed captive, we see both courses: silence and refusal on the part of Eunice Williams, who steadfastly refused redemption; and active interpretation on the part of Joseph Kellogg, who returned from his captors and then made a life's work of carrying messages back and forth between worlds.

Success?

By what criteria can one measure success among coerced language-learners? Survival? Escape? Assimilation or staunch refusal to assimilate? Ability to translate? Ability, beyond translation, to make sense of each side to the other?

Mortality

The survival rates for snatched indigenes was abysmal. A half-dozen or so of Columbus's first captives managed to make the trip all the way to Barcelona for presentation at court and baptism. On his second voyage from Spain, Columbus took with him several of those who had been baptized in Barcelona along with a couple more who had remained behind in Palos and not made the journey all the way to the eastern coast of Spain. Of the group returning home from their sojourn in Spain, apparently only four survived. Three of these disappear from the records upon arrival. The last, baptized Diego Colón, is mentioned repeatedly as an active interpreter.[20] One indigene who had received baptism with royal sponsorship and putatively had learned fluent Spanish was left behind in the service of the prince don Juan. In his second year of residence in Spain he died.[21] Of the 550 Columbus shipped to Spain in 1495 to labor as slaves, most died in transit or not long after arrival. Of the two Mayas taken from Yucatan, Julián died in captivity. The legend that doña Marina traveled to Spain and was presented in court is baseless. Less than a decade after she fell into the hands of the Spaniards, she died, apparently of postpartum infection following the birth of her second child. Pocahontas lived to accompany her English husband to London and satisfy the curiosity of the English court, but she died before the ship returning her party to Virginia even cleared the Thames, and she lies buried in a place aptly named Gravesend. Squanto lived only a year and a half after meeting the Plymouth pilgrims. On an autumn reconnoitering voyage along the ocean shore of Cape Cod, he suddenly fell sick and died. It is not clear whether Sacajawea succumbed to "putrid fever" not long after the conclusion of the Lewis and Clark expedition or whether she survived.

Flight

Provided that one managed to stay alive, successful escape meant being cooperative while biding one's time. When one of the survivors of Columbus's return voyage from Spain was put ashore in Hispaniola to carry a message of good will from the rulers of Spain, two others waited for cover of night to jump overboard and swim for shore. None were ever heard from again. Melchor, the Maya brought back to Yucatan, served the Spaniards under Cortés until an interpreting session went sour and precipitated a battle with wounds and fatalities on both sides. Bernal Díaz del Castillo wrote, "When Melchorejo was looked for he could not be found as he had run off with the people of Tabasco, and it appears that the day before he had left the Spanish clothes that had been given him hung up in a palm grove, and had fled by night in a canoe. Cortés was much annoyed at his flight, fearing he would tell things to his fellow countrymen to our disadvantage."[22]

Over a period of five years in Santo Domingo and Spain, Francisco de Chicora gained the trust of his master, don Lucas Vásquez de Ayllón, who (according to the chronicler Oviedo) described him as a person of good judgment, an apt language learner, a sincere Christian, and a devoted servant. It must have been as painful for don Lucas as it had been for Cortés when his prime interpreter fled at the first opportunity. Within days of the arrival of the 1526 fleet on his familiar coast, Francisco was gone.[23]

Even more devastating were the actions of don Luis de Velasco. Returned to his people, he was treated as one risen from the dead, according to a letter dispatched by the Jesuit Luis de Quirós. The company immediately set to building a mission compound, much aided and encouraged by don Luis, who nonetheless did not stay with them but went off with his kin. Soon the Jesuits began complaining of his un-Christian behavior and pointing out their great need of his interpreting services. Apparently don Luis's patience gave out, for in response to importuning letters and visits he returned to the mission with a party of his people and killed everyone save one boy, Alonso de Olmos. It took two years for the Spanish to rescue Alonso, who in the meantime had ceased to speak Spanish and had formed a deep bond of friendship with an indigenous boy of his own age. Inseparable, they swam out to the Spanish ship together.[24]

If Sacajawea did not die at Fort Manuel on the Missouri River in 1812, then she probably was the woman who eventually rejoined the Shoshones, served as an interpreter for years, died in advanced old age, and is buried on the Wind River Reservation in Wyoming. Shoshone tradition recounts a very long period of separation, travel, and temporary connections with other peoples before her return.[25]

Competence

For competence in interpreting, it is instructive to compare how Garcilaso de la Vega describes the efforts of Felipe at the encounter between the Spaniards and Atahualpa with how Sahagún's Nahua assistants describe doña Marina's performance before Montezuma. Concerning the speech of fray Vicente de Valverde informing Atahualpa of the tenets of the Christian faith and the authority of the Spanish sovereign, Garcilaso writes:

> All agree that it was short and harsh, with no touch of softness or any other concession, and that the interpretation was much worse.... It is to be remarked that Felipe ... was a native of the island of Puna, a man of very plebian origin, young—for he was scarcely twenty-two—and as little versed in the general language of the Incas [Quechua] as in Spanish. He had in fact learned the language of the Incas, not in Cuzco, but in Túmbez, from Indians who speak ... as foreigners: we have already explained that to all Indians but the natives of Cuzco this is a foreign language. He had also learnt Spanish without a teacher, but merely by hearing the Spaniards speak.... Though baptized, he had received no instruction in the Christian religion.... As to his translation, he did it badly and often reversed the sense, but this was not done out of malice, but because he did not understand what he was interpreting ... Instead of God three in one, he said God three and one make four, adding the numbers.... This is shown by the tradition of the *quipus*, or annual records in knots.... He could not express it in any other way; for there are no words or phrases in the Peruvian language for many of the concepts of the Christian religion, such as Trinity, three in one, person, Holy Spirit, faith, grace, church, sacraments, and other similar words.... As regards the second part of the speech, he rendered this less ill than the first, for it dealt with concrete matters of war and arms.[26]

Immediately after this, Atahualpa is reported to have spoken scornfully of what he had just heard, requested a Bible or breviary, turned the pages, and flung it on the ground. Not surprisingly, Spaniards and Andeans fell to fighting.

Unlike unfortunate Felipe, doña Marina was not in the position of translating badly understood Spanish into another poorly acquired language. The redeemed captive Jerónimo de Aguilar translated the Spanish of Cortés and his chaplain into Maya for her, and she then translated the Maya into Nahuatl, a language native to both her and Montezuma. Nonetheless, the strangeness of the Christian message remained, a strangeness she had had only a short time to try to understand. Moreover, the rhetoric of the Nahua nobility known as *tecpillahtolli* 'lordly speech,' was far too convoluted and indirect for even a native speaker, if not trained in it, to comprehend. Montezuma's speech to Cortés as reconstructed in Book 12 of the *Florentine Codex*, produced by Sahagún's Nahua associates under his direction, is a classic example of tecpillahtolli. The drama of the encounter as it is related there is that doña Marina understands Montezuma's language in all its significance and chooses to convey Cortés's speech in bluntly direct terms, denying Montezuma reciprocal honorific speech. If the encounter was as Sahagún's associates portray it, doña Marina used language to wound the Aztec lord as deftly as with an obsidian blade.[27] The next thing Montezuma knew, he was being stared at, touched, and jostled along by the Spaniards, while his associates offered no effective resistance. The process of demystification whereby Montezuma lost the awe and protection of his subordinates had been largely accomplished on the spot, with words.

Summary and Conclusion

The lives examined here abundantly demonstrate those qualities necessary for survival mentioned at the beginning of this paper.

For captives, flexibility was an absolute necessity. No matter who the kidnapper, nonfunctioning captives were summarily dispatched. Those who would survive were those not immobilized by the trauma of kidnapping. If one remained committed to escape in the long run, in the short run it was necessary to cooperate, to make oneself useful and valuable to one's captors. A forced choice of allegiances is implicit in any sort of long-term captivity; the pressure is to become like one's captors in behavior, appearance, and beliefs. These survival strategies are the very ones for which doña Marina has been vilified since Mexico's independence from Spain and the ones that led Eunice Williams to break her father's rigid Puritan heart.

Youth, too, is significant, not only for stamina and the likelihood of going forward rather than looking back but because capacity for direct language-learning, unmediated by explicit instruction, atrophies in most people as they move into adulthood. Yet for competent bilingual interpreters (as contrasted with kin replacements, in whom maintenance of the first language was generally discouraged), taking very young children defeated the purpose, because they soon ceased speaking their first language and moved on to that of their captors. Additive bilingualism was best achieved with adolescents. Individuals who acquired fluency in their captors' language during adolescence could potentially teach their own language and answer questions about it, as Sahagún's and Eliot's informants did. Demos makes the point that among the captives carried off from Deerfield (and more generally in the struggle between New England and New France), infants, the old, and the weak were killed at the beginning. The men were held for ransom. Strong, mobile children were kept, assisted, and encouraged. Vigorous young women also stood a good chance of survival as mothers of captive children and as potential wives. Eunice Williams, kidnapped at age seven, became a family member among her captors, converted to Catholicism, married and raised her children among her adopted people, and steadfastly refused to return to her anguished father and siblings. So did Joanna Kellogg, taken in the same 1704 raid on the town of Deerfield. Her brother Joseph Kellogg, age twelve at the time of the raid, returned, admitting that he had wavered to the point of participating in Catholic observances. He then invested years in interpreting and mediating. The young women did not.

As we have seen with Columbus, women were valued by European kidnappers as instruments for keeping male captives in line and as potential language teachers. I doubt Europeans ever intended to use women as interpreters. The famous women interpreters such as doña Marina and Sacajawea emerged from circumstances beyond European control and soon proved too valuable to dispense with.

Sharp intellect was absolutely necessary. Not everyone was equally gifted or equally prepared. For all interpreters, whether their immersion in another language and culture was involuntary or voluntary, it was necessary to observe and gain an understanding of how the new language, and its speakers, worked; what would please the strangers and set them at ease; what would make them angry and distrustful. Consider the comparison between the two *lenguas* Felipe and doña Marina. Bernal Díaz says doña Marina was of noble birth, and it certainly appears that she had received the special training of the Nahua nobility, since she was able to understand and speak persuasively to the Tlaxcalan, Cholulan, and Aztec rulers. She also was remarkably capable of attending to the communalities of dialectal varieties of Nahuatl and Maya and untroubled by superficial local differences. She impressed the Spaniards she served as completely trustworthy, and in their negotiations with the Spaniards Nahuatl-speakers preferred her over other potential interpreters.[28] From the sustained success of her negotiations, it seems clear that she was able to grasp novel Spanish ideas and recast them in terms understandable to the people to whom Cortés addressed himself.

And finally, good luck. No matter how bright, how willing to learn, how young and healthy a person might be, contact with pathogens to which one had no prior exposure was often lethal. Among messengers between worlds, long life has been exceptional.

Perhaps the most successful interpreter was the Maya Gaspar Antonio Chi.[29] Not literally snatched from a shore, he had been handed over to the Franciscans as an adolescent for baptism and education. The corpus of his surviving writing demonstrates that he became a powerfully competent multilingual. He claimed to have written a grammar of Maya for the Franciscans. He also composed sermons for them in Maya and transcribed depositions, made translations, and produced civil documents. He had a professional career while retaining his Maya identity. A husband, father, great grandfather, he outlived everyone, Spaniard and Indian alike. He even outlived the sixteenth century. Yet over those many years he saw terrible things and was implicated in many of them. It is hard to imagine that he could have looked upon his long life and service with satisfaction, and this, I suspect, was generally true for the coerced interpreters who lived long enough to reflect on their experiences.[30]

Notes

After presentation of this paper at the John Carter Brown Library in October 1996, I learned that William Sturtevant published a paper in 1993 dealing with many of the same individuals from the perspective of indigenous people seeing the homelands of their captors ("The First American Discoverers of Europe," *European Review of Native American Studies* 7: no. 2 (1993): 23–29).

1. Christopher Columbus, quoted in S. E. Morison, *Journals and Other Documents of the Life and Voyages of Christopher Columbus* (New York, 1963), 93.
2. Michele de Cuneo, 28 October 1495, in Morison, *Journals*, 226.
3. F. Karttunen, *Between Worlds: Interpreters, Guides, and Survivors* (New Brunswick, 1994), 5, 86–87.
4. Karttunen, *Between Worlds*, 120–121. Illustration reproduced in Rolena Adorno, *Guaman Poma: Writing and Resistance in Colonial Peru* (Austin, 1986), 96.
5. Gonzalo Fernández de Oviedo y Valdés, *Historia general y natural de las Indias*, I, IV, *Biblioteca de autores españoles*, vols. 117 and 120 (Madrid, 1959), 120: 323–325; Paul Hoffman, *A New Andalucia and a Way to the Orient: The American Southeast during the Sixteenth Century* (Baton Rouge, 1990), 48.
6. C.M. Lewis and A.J. Loomie, *The Spanish Jesuit Mission in Virginia, 1570–1572* (Chapel Hill, 1953), 15–18.
7. The extreme youth of Pocahontas may seem incompatible with this service, but doña Marina, interpreter for Cortés, was very young, as was Sacajawea

during her service to the Lewis and Clark expedition and also the African girl Krotoa/Eva, who performed similar service for the Dutch during a tense and hostile period at the Cape of Good Hope. Earlier, in 1613, the crew of an English ship had snatched two Khoikhoi men from the Cape and taken them off to England. One died aboard ship, and the other suffered through a London winter before being returned to provide interpreting services, which he did for a dozen years before disappearing. Thereafter, the Dutch transported their potential interpreters from the Cape to Java and back for their language immersion experience. Eva, however, learned Dutch and Portuguese as a child servant in the household of the commander of the post. Karttunen, *Between Worlds*, 248–52.

8. Helen C. Rountree, *Pocahontas's People: The Powhatan Indians of Virginia through Four Centuries* (Norman, OK, 1990), 38–39, 43–44, 53, 58–65.
9. Edward Arber, *The Story of the Pilgrim Fathers, 1606–1623. A.D. as told by Themselves, their Friends, and their Enemies* (New York, 1969), 451–61; William Bradford, *Of Plymouth Plantation, 1620–1647* (New York, 1963), 81.
10. Karttunen, *Between Worlds*, 24–25.
11. See the chapter on "The White Indians" in James Axtell, *After Columbus: Essays in the Ethnohistory of Colonial North America* (New York and Oxford, 1988); and John Demos, *The Unredeemed Captive: A Family Story from Early America* (New York, 1995).
12. Karttunen, *Between Worlds*, 5, 85, 88.
13. Garcilaso de la Vega, *Royal Commentaries of the Incas and General History of Peru ...* (Austin, 1994), part 1: 407–408. Garcilaso here advocates promoting the Cuzco dialect of Quechua as an areal lingua franca in Peru just as Nahuatl served that purpose in New Spain.
14. F. Karttunen, "The Roots of Sixteenth-Century Mesoamerican Lexicography," in *Cultures, Ideologies, and the Dictionary: Studies in Honor of Ladislav Zgusta*, ed. Braj B. Kachru and Henry Kahane (Tübingen, 1995), 75–88.
15. Karttunen, *Between Worlds*, 107.
16. Karttunen, *Between Worlds*: 122, 126.
17. The best survey of the language situation in contact-period and colonial Peru is Bruce Mannheim, *The Language of the Inka since the European Invasion* (Austin, 1991).
18. Ola E. Winslow, *John Eliot, "Apostle to the Indians"* (Boston, 1968), 89–91. Margaret C. Szasz, *Indian Education in the American Colonies, 1607–1783* (Albuquerque, 1988), 111–12. After an excellent description of the practice of linguistic elicitation and analysis as practiced by Eliot and by linguistic fieldworkers to this day, Winslow unfortunately describes each question as directing "a searchlight into some dark corner of an Indian's mind" (p. 93). More than a century later, with the works of Williams and Eliot before them as models and with 'Opukaha'ia, a young refugee native speaker of the language, having been among them for several years, the Congregational missionaries to Hawai'i nonetheless seem to have reinvented the wheel in their efforts to compile a grammar of the Hawaiian language. A.J. Schütz, *The Voices of Eden: A History of Hawaiian Language Studies* (Honolulu, 1994).
19. R. Williams, *A Key into the Language of America* (Detroit, 1973), 88.
20. Cecil Jane, *The Four Voyages of Columbus: A History in Eight Documents, Including Five by Christopher Columbus, in the Original Spanish, with English Translations* (New York, 1988), 122, 124, 154, 160.
21. Oviedo, *Historia general*: 117: 31.

22. B. Díaz del Castillo, *The Discovery and Conquest of Mexico, 1517–1521* (New York, 1979), 52.
23. Hoffman, *A New Andalucia*, 67.
24. Lewis and Loomie, *The Spanish Jesuit Mission*, 44–46, 53–54, 89.
25. Karttunen, *Between Worlds*, 37–41.
26. Garcilaso de la Vega, *Royal Commentaries*, part 2, 681–82.
27. James Lockhart, *We People Here: Nahuatl Accounts of the Conquest of Mexico* (Berkeley, 1993), 116, 118.
28. An admiring Díaz del Castillo asserted that doña Marina was the daughter of Nahua rulers in the Tabasco region, that she was shrewd, and that before the crucial moment of first meeting with Montezuma she had demonstrated her persuasiveness in dealing with priests in the city of Cholula. Díaz del Castillo, *Discovery and Conquest*, 64, 174, 176. For testimonials to her trustworthiness, see Karttunen, *Between Worlds*, 22; and Karttunen, "Rethinking Malinche" in *Indian Women of Early Mexico*, ed. Susan Schroeder, Stephanie Wood, and Robert Haskett (Norman, OK, 1997), 229, 300, 307.
29. Karttunen, *Between Worlds*, 84–114.
30. Gaspar Antonio Chi's career is paralleled by that of Cockanoe, John Eliot's first Algonquian language associate. Szasz, *Indian Education*, 111–13. Cockanoe began his total immersion in English as an adolescent. After working with Eliot for ten years, he left Bible translation, returned to his own people, and supported himself as a civil interpreter.

– Chapter 10 –

Mohawk Schoolmasters and Catechists in Mid-Eighteenth-Century Iroquoia: An Experiment in Fostering Literacy and Religious Change

William B. Hart

AFTER FOUR DECADES (1704–42) of trying to spread the gospel to Mohawk Indians in the province of New York without native help, the Society for the Propagation of the Gospel in Foreign Parts (SPG), the English foreign mission society, realized that Mohawk schoolmasters and catechists had a significant role to play in helping the organization "promote the Glory of God" among the "Heathens and Infidels."[1] Cultural and language barriers that rendered communication difficult made obvious the need for native help. None of the first few SPG missionaries to the Mohawks achieved fluency in their catechumens' language, finding "much Confusion" in it. To their Anglo ears, the local language sounded like "sev[era]l words Tumbled up together." And yet, to translate prayers, sermons, hymns, and passages from the Bible into Mohawk, the society's ministers turned not to Mohawk speakers but to several English-Dutch- and Dutch-Mohawk-speaking interpreters of European descent.[2] Moreover, a lack of native exhorters to read prayers during long and frequent absences of the missionaries caused many of the SPG ministers to complain about chronic apostasy among their flock whenever they returned to Mohawk country, or following a hiatus of SPG activity in the region. Tiononderoge, the

Mohawk town nearest Fort Hunter, the site of the SPG's mission to the Mohawks about fifty miles west of Albany, was without an instructor of Protestant Christianity from 1746 to 1750. When the missionary, John Ogilvie, arrived in 1750 to assess the health of Protestantism there, he found the residents "universally degenerate ... intirely given up to Drunkenness ... hav[ing] lost all sense of religion."[3]

The various difficulties of communication, as well as alleged backsliding among new converts, soon made it clear to the SPG that it had to alter its strategy of harvesting Mohawk souls. In 1740, Henry Barclay, the SPG's minister at Albany and at Fort Hunter, made a bold proposal to the society: appoint from among the "several Indians well qualified" a "Schoolmaster to Instruct their Indian youth (upon whom the greatest hopes are to be built) to read their own Language." Without hesitation, the society "agreed that an Indian Schoolmaster with a Salary not Exceeding 15 [pounds] per annum be appointed by Mr. Barclay with the approbation of the Lieutenant Governor of New York and the Commissioners for Indian Affairs."[4]

Between 1742 and 1750, the SPG hired three Mohawk headmen—Daniel, Cornelius, and Paulus Sahonwadi—to be schoolmasters, and Old Abraham Caunauhstansey, an uncle to Paulus, to be catechist. The three schoolmasters were to teach Mohawk children and adults literacy in their own language, and Old Abraham was to read morning and evening prayers. In fact, at least two of the schoolmasters performed both duties. Barclay observed that Cornelius, who "Instructs severall young Men and Women, and is much beloved of his betheren," also "Reads Prayers to them in my Absence." Paulus did the same at Canajoharie. The two men promoted the philosophy of Protestant Christians that piety and literacy went hand in hand. William Andrews, the missionary to the Mohawks between 1712 and 1719, articulated this connection when he asserted that if the children "Learn[ed] their books," it would "be the principle [sic] means of laying a good and lasting foundation of religion among them [the Mohawks]." In theory, literate, pious Mohawks, especially the children in whom the missionaries hoped to implant a new religious worldview, would sell Christianity to succeeding generations throughout Mohawk country and the rest of Iroquoia.[5]

In truth, none of the SPG missionaries believed that they had laid a good foundation of Protestant Christianity among the Mohawks. When Andrews resigned from the Fort Hunter mission in 1719, he lamented that, although the Mohawks had had "a

Considerable time Plentifull of instruction line upon line and precept upon precept, the scripture constantly read and all the points of Religion fully explained to them together with the Practice of a holy life," his religious instruction "had made but little impression on their Minde." He complained: "Heathens they were, and heathens they will still be." To Andrews they were a "sordid mercenary, beggerly people," who "returned to their former ill lives, like the dog ... to his vomit."[6] John Stuart, the last SPG missionary to the Mohawks, upon his arrival in 1770 found an unspecified heinous custom "injurious to their temporal as well as spiritual welfare."[7]

Nevertheless, in 1761, with the Mohawk nation in spiritual and physical decline from alcoholism and disease, Little Abraham, a pious Christian headman, spoke for many Mohawks when he called for "a Minister [to] remain constantly amongst us" to pray for them and to administer the sacraments so that they may be "happy in this, and the next World."[8] Moreover, in 1758, Mohawk parents at Canajoharie so valued the instruction offered by Paulus Sahonwadi that they complained to John Ogilvie when the native schoolmaster spent too much time away with war parties and, thus, neglected their children's education.[9] Additionally, when Ogilvie left Fort Hunter in 1760 for a three-year assignment in Montreal, and with Paulus on furlough, several Mohawk converts repeatedly asked Sir William Johnson for prayer books, as well as "Indian Almanack[s]," sometimes "daily enquiring for them." Presumably they were concerned that no one was available to instruct them, which forced them to either turn to others in their community who were literate or to read the texts themselves.[10] Finally, Christian Mohawks at Canajoharie were so fed up with having to make the twenty-mile journey to Fort Hunter and the two-day trip to Albany to attend church services that they raised money among themselves to "Build a Church at Cannojohery," which must also have the all-important steeple bell. The Canajoharies viewed the presence of the physical structure of a church in their own community as critical to their becoming "Religious and lead[ing] better lives."[11]

By the mid-eighteenth century, a growing number of Mohawks considered Christianity as viable as Iroquois sacred traditions, a concept either unthinkable or unimportant to most Mohawks in the early decades of the eighteenth century. This rising interest in Christian knowledge and practice was in part the result of increasing familiarity with Protestantism, growing dissatisfaction with traditional sacred practices in a changing world, and material and cultural change.[12] However, two other interrelated factors, this essay argues, contributed significantly to religious change and practice among the Mohawks: the desire of many to become literate; and the power invested in the Scriptures that were translated into the local vernacular and communicated by respected local leaders. Despite the complaints of SPG missionaries about the difficulties and "savageness" of the Mohawk language, most supported the experiment of translating the gospel into the tongue of their native hearers. Those who endorsed this effort believed that their catechumens could best learn the gospel in their native tongue. After all, many Church of England clergymen believed that all human beings, regardless of language differences, were capable of receiving the word of God. All that was required were patience to listen to sermons, a good memory for retaining and internalizing the Lord's Prayer and one's catechism, and "a capacity to read" the Bible—"and scarcely that, for what is constantly used," wrote one clergyman, "will in a short time, be treasured up in the Memory." The Church needed only a small army of ministers of good *"breeding up"* who could learn and "understand the great variety of Languages of those [Indian] Countries in order to be able to *Converse* with the Natives, and Preach the Gospel to them."[13]

Supporting such a program required the publication of Christian texts in Mohawk. In essence, the early-eighteenth-century Church of England allied itself with the thinking of the Renaissance humanist Desiderius Erasmus (d. 1536), who called for the mysteries of Christ to be "published as openly as possible."[14] In publishing Christian texts in the local vernacular, the SPG continued the long tradition of translating the Scriptures into local languages. In such cases, when the local vernacular carries the word of God—the ultimate authority of the universe, according to teachers of Christianity—and individuals are then able to communicate directly with God through their own language, their language takes on a power hitherto not accorded it. As several students of orality and literacy have argued, missionaries who sponsored vernacular translations of Christian texts unwittingly conferred upon the local languages an indisputable authority. Putting the Mohawk language in print in the form of passages from the Scripture, the catechism, rudimentary dictionaries, psalms, prayers, and hornbooks elevated the language to the level of English, the language in which the SPG missionaries introduced the word of God. To use the Mohawk words *Niyoh* for God and *Raniha* for Father, for example, invited a unique indigenous reading of these two concepts, which Western Christians easily conflate cognitively. This phenomenon stamped the local languages with a seal of approval, although missionaries usually found other aspects of the indigenous culture deficient and in need of replacement.[15] In time, these texts excited "local ambition," to quote one scholar of Christian missionary history in West Africa, and made apparent myriad possibilities for an individual's identity, from becoming a literate person to recognizing that one could autonomously receive Christian knowledge and know God's truths.[16]

Local ambition and autonomy could not have arisen, I argue, had it not been for native schoolmasters and catechists who helped to "domesticate" Christianity. These headmen were viewed by both the SPG and by fellow Mohawks as men with God, and thus were individuals of special merit who could exercise power through prayer to God. Moreover, as headmen they already owned authority and status within Mohawk society. This status was further enhanced by their own literacy skills. When literacy is introduced into oral-based societies, argues one authority on the subject, elders, who traditionally are the keepers and teachers of knowledge, are bypassed. Books and other printed matter fix that knowledge that previously only elders could provide. This consequence of literacy—making elders redundant—did not occur in this way in Mohawk society, for throughout the eighteenth century only a small number of Mohawks were literate in either English or Mohawk. Oral and written texts coexisted. Nevertheless, the role and status of the schoolmasters and catechists changed as their influence and authority expanded beyond the confines of their local villages.[17]

To understand the impact of Mohawk schoolmasters on literacy and religious change, it is first important to understand both these individuals' new role in serving the Church and their traditional role as *sachems*, or headmen.

Headmen in Iroquois Society

One way to view these Mohawk teachers is as culture brokers. Modern scholars have sometimes referred to such persons as intermediaries and go-betweens. Culture brokers, who were often translators, interpreters, guides, diplomats, traders, civil servants, teachers, and catechists, offer unique perspectives on cultural change and continuity within Indian societies, acting as windows into the construction, maintenance, and evolution of personal identity. They were uniquely situated, living "between worlds," as one historian has noted, occupying the spaces at the margins of society.[18]

Not all brokers lived liminal lives, however. Some, like the SPG's native teachers, were deeply rooted in their native societies. But they were able to maneuver between two or more cultural worlds. The four Mohawk teachers, who probably ranged in age from their thirties to their early sixties (Old Abraham being the eldest), were sachems, or headmen, who were community leaders of significant social and political standing in their respective towns of Tiononderoge (Cornelius and Paulus, although Paulus taught principally in Canajoharie), and Canajoharie (Daniel and Old Abraham). A headman was essentially a chief, a political office for which several ranks existed in Iroquois society. These included Peace Chief, or League sachem, an inherited title at the confederated League level; *rotiyanehr*, or clan chief, also an inherited title; Pine Tree Chief, a title earned through personal charisma and accomplishment; war chief, also an earned title; and wise clan elder, a title earned through longevity. The historical record refers to the four teachers as "sachems," but because there are no explicit references to their being League sachems, we might assume that they were either clan chiefs, war chiefs, or, in the case of Old Abraham, a wise elder. A headman's sphere of influence was local, although he could sometimes pool support and resources from nearby communities and thereby expand his sphere of influence. The headmen in each village met collectively almost daily to discuss matters of the day, especially war and peace. They reached decisions by consensus, but always in consultation with clan matrons, who carried enormous influence in matrilocal and matrilineal Iroquois society.[19]

In order to hold the title of sachem, a headman had to possess several personal qualities that Iroquois people valued. They had to be even-tempered, selfless, and patient, and have copious amounts of good will. They also had to be skillful orators. Good speaking skills were essential, for sachems were routinely asked to officiate at condolence ceremonies for the dead. With soothing words, they calmed the raging hearts and wiped away the tears of the next of kin. An early historian of the Iroquois noted the importance of oratory among "the People of the *Five nations* [who] are much given to *Speech-making*," for "where no single Person has a Power to compel, the Arts of Persuasion alone must prevail." Community consensus guided the decision-making process, often influenced by powerful, persuasive speeches given by eloquent headmen.[20]

The combined qualities of authority, eloquence, and piety made the four headmen ideal candidates as SPG religious instructors to

Mohawk children and adults. Old Abraham, for example, fit well the model of the headman who used his authority, eloquence, and piety to spread the gospel. The old sachem worked as an itinerant catechist, traveling from village to village, expanding his sphere of influence beyond his own community. As a result of his being "always among them [the Mohawks], while in one Castle, and then in another," Old Abraham, according to Sir William Johnson, was "much liked by them all." He was so committed to spreading the gospel that, in John Ogilvie's opinion, he had "intirely neglected his hunting in order to instruct his Brethren in the principles of Religion." Moreover, while presiding at condolence ceremonies and at council meetings, Old Abraham often would chastise the attending colonial officials, which often included William Johnson, named Superintendent of Indian Affairs in 1756; the presiding governor of New York or his representative; and sundry Commissioners of Indian Affairs for neglecting the spiritual, educational, and material needs of the Mohawk people. The 1740s and 1750s were difficult times for the Mohawks. Disease, warfare, and alcoholism brought about a feeling of social self-destruction. Many Mohawks grew convinced that they needed a new moral code, and thus it was time to learn to read the Holy Bible.[21]

By the 1750s, most Mohawks could boast of being baptized. Nevertheless, most continued to observe traditional Iroquois sacred practices and concomitantly participate in some Christian rituals, most significantly baptism and communion. This "alternation," that is, the supplementation rather than substitution or blending of one religious form with another, defined the sacred practice of most baptized Mohawks. The native converts were most interested in being baptized, which they believed offered protection against present and future calamities, and in taking communion, which conferred upon the communicant a coveted status in the community. Still, many converts insisted upon supplicating various spirits with sacrificial offerings, participating in thanksgiving festivals, and conducting condolence ceremonies. One scholar of late-twentieth-century Chinese converts could have spoken for the majority of eighteenth-century Mohawks when he observed that "it is not necessary to become a believer in a 'world religion' to be a convert."[22]

Fostering Literacy and Religious Change

To Henry Barclay, Daniel and Cornelius were "some of the better sort of Indians" in the Mohawk nation. By that, Barclay meant that these men were sober and pious, identified as Christians, and had the capacity to be gentle in their teaching and loving in their reprimands. Moreover, the two men possessed literacy skills, which the Church of England valued highly. In November 1742, Henry Barclay informed the Society that part of a fifteen-pound advance he had received went to furnish "Cornelius a Sachem at the Lower [Tiononderoge] and ... Daniel att [sic] the Upper Town [Canajoharie] ... with paper [and] Ink." Cornelius apparently was very diligent about teaching his students reading and writing, for six months later Barclay found him taking "great pains, Being obliged to write manuscript to Instruct them by having no Books printed in the Indian Tongue proper for that Purpose."[23]

Paulus, too, was literate in Mohawk and English. In 1755, five years after the SPG hired him as the schoolmaster at Canajoharie at an annual salary of seven pounds, ten shillings, missionary John Ogilvie reported that several of the more than 40 children whom Paulus taught "every day ... begin to read, & some to write" in Mohawk. In the 1760s, Paulus switched to teaching literacy in English, as instructed by the SPG. Sir William Johnson, who, by reason of his status and his marriage to Molly Brant (sister of the celebrated warrior, Joseph Brant) of Canajoharie, was one of the Mohawks' benefactors, disagreed with this decision, for he was convinced that literacy in English would result in the Mohawks losing their culture and their identities as warriors, and thereby would become useless to the English as allies.[24]

Eighteenth-century Protestant Christian ideology maintained that literacy, piety, and politics were closely linked. Good Protestants were supposed to read the Bible regularly in order to remain steadfast in their belief and regular in their practice. Then as now, Protestantism privileged "the word," especially the printed word; the first sentence in the Gospel of John begins "In the beginning was the Word...." The words were God's, passed down to humanity, which had to discern the symbols, metaphors, and meanings of Christianity through prayers, the liturgy, psalms, and so on.[25] Those who supported translating the Scriptures into indigenous languages—in this case, the Mohawk tongue—believed in the essential universalism of God's truths. Even a native language such as Mohawk whose mysteries were difficult to penetrate could not obscure God's truths.[26]

Additionally, good Protestants made good allies. Seventeenth- and eighteenth-century European political theory held that nations that observed a common religion also forged political ties. In 1764, the Bishop of Peterborough articulated this theory when he remarked in an annual SPG sermon that the "seeds of [established] Religion ... will be the firmest bond, the most assured pledge of ... fidelity" between nations. John Ogilvie, the SPG missionary who succeeded Henry Barclay, represented the hopes of the Church and the Crown when he wrote in 1755 that "nothing will contribute more to make them [the Iroquois] firm friends, than uniting them to us by the sacred ties of Christianity." Indians also invoked this theory when it suited their political needs. In 1755, the Catholic Mohawks at Kahnawake near Montreal informed Sir William Johnson that they could not join him in battle against the French, their allies, to whom "by Religion and Treaties, they were so united, [that] they must obey their orders."[27]

The SPG reasoned that pious, enculturated Mohawk teachers who allied themselves with England could facilitate this task of laying a solid religious foundation among the Mohawks upon which political fidelity could be built. According to Anglo-American accounts, the four native teachers performed this task admirably. By the fall of 1742, Cornelius and Daniel were successfully plying their trade, the former at Tionondoroge, the latter at Canajoharie, at annual salaries of ten pounds, New York currency. Barclay described Cornelius as "very faithful and diligent and vastly successful" at his post. The following May, Barclay boasted that many of the Tionondoroge Mohawks "attend the School very Steadily, and make a great Proficiency under the Schoolmaster [Cornelius], who is very diligent, and takes great pains to Teach them." The missionary had not yet visited Canajoharie but had heard that Daniel was doing an equally diligent job of instructing Mohawk children and adults. By November 1743, the two Mohawk schools flourished under the Mohawk schoolmasters, who, according to Barclay, "carried on with great Diligence and no less Success."[28]

Likewise, Old Abraham Caunauhstansey, the brother of venerable headman King Hendrick, went about his job as catechist faithfully and diligently, according to Anglo-American eyewitnesses. Old Abraham had traveled to several of the Mohawk castles to read prayers and instruct children and adults "in the fundamentals of religion" for three years prior to Governor Clinton's recommendation in 1749 that the SPG formally hire the old headman. His catechumens were said to be "more desirous than ever of his praying to them." During his tenure at Stockbridge, Massachusetts, in the late 1740s and early 1750s, Jonathan Edwards met Old Abraham, whom he characterized as "a remarkable man; a man of great solidity, prudence, devotion, and strict conversation; [who] acts very much as a person endowed with simplicity, humanity, self-denial and zeal of a true Christian."[29]

The desire to learn to read and write motivated several Mohawk families to enroll their children in the Stockbridge, Massachusetts, mission. In 1751, Old Abraham, King Hendrick, and eleven other Mohawk headmen led a delegation of ninety-two Mohawks to Stockbridge to inform Edwards they wanted their children to "learn the English language and to read the Bible."[30] According to Edwards, many parents considered the ability to read and write "a great attainment." They held in high esteem anyone who could "read and understand the Bible," and thus were particularly "fond of their children learning the English tongue." Undoubtedly, the Mohawks especially valued the acquisition of literacy skills at this time because of the uncertain presence of SPG missionaries among them. More and more, they felt compelled to turn to literate members of their own community to teach them the principles of Christian doctrine and practice. Moreover, in a rapidly changing, uncertain world, it was increasingly important to develop bicultural skills.[31]

No Mohawk supported the move to Stockbridge more than Old Abraham, whom Edwards characterized as an informant to him on Iroquois matters. According to Edwards, Old Abraham exhorted his fellow Mohawks to go to the dissenting mission in order to receive religious instruction. His brethren lived in darkness at Canajoharie, he reportedly informed his catechumens, but at Stockbridge they would find light. He claimed that he knew little and therefore could teach them little. Because of his piety and because he now advised converts who had aligned themselves with the Church of England to now embrace the dissenting church, Old Abraham suffered "a sort of persecution" among some Mohawks, probably warriors who increasingly questioned the authority and pronouncements of sachems. From Old Abraham's ecumenical perspective, however, his community's desperate need of regular instruction in Christianity outweighed doctrinal differences among ministers.[32]

There is little doubt that many Mohawks wished to become literate in both English and Mohawk in order to read religious and secular texts in either language, which would enable them to better negotiate the two worlds they now inhabited. But it is difficult to determine exactly how the Mohawk teachers communicated Christianity to their catechumens and how the teachers themselves understood and practiced their new faith. They left no accounts of how and what they taught, nor of what Christianity meant to them or to their catechumens. Nor does the extant written record—letters, reports, and other documents left by European and American missionaries, diplomats, and other colonial officials—shed much light on the meaning of Christianity to Mohawk believers. Too often, their observations are superficial, and they tend to merely depict Mohawk conformity to Church of England practices and notions of piety. Sir William Johnson, for example, commenting on Old Abraham's prayer services before the Battle at Lake George in 1755, noted that "Good Old Abraham performed Divine Services every morning and evening."[33] This remark contains little with which to assess Old Abraham's reading of the prayers or the content of them. Yet if the Mohawk teachers were as responsible and as dedicated to their work as those who wrote about them believed, then we may assume that their activities were in line with SPG expectations and adhered to the guidelines followed by society missionaries.

In order to try to achieve maximum results when preaching to Indians and Africans, the missionaries consulted religious treatises and instruction manuals. One such book, used by Barclay and Ogilvie in Mohawk country, was a tract penned in 1740 by Thomas Wilson, the Bishop of London in the 1730s and '40s, entitled *An Essay Towards an Instruction for the Indians*. His extended essay is an imaginary dialogue, in the tradition of John Eliot's *Indian Dialogues*, between a missionary of great tolerance, wisdom, and patience, and an extremely articulate, yet skeptical, Indian catechumen. Wilson's missionary persuades the reluctant "heathen" to cast off his life lived in darkness and choose the lighted path of Christianity. Wilson's book became very popular among missionaries throughout the colonies, who regarded it as a kind of training manual. Henry Barclay, for example, asked for and received several copies of the book so that he might have it translated into Mohawk, presumably so that he, Cornelius, Daniel, and their Mohawk catechumens could use it. When Barclay quit the Mohawk mission in 1746 to accept the rectorship at Trinity Church in New York City, his successor, John Ogilvie, took possession of many of his books, the Wilson treatise no doubt among them, which Ogilvie and Paulus, too, would have consulted to instruct their Mohawk pupils.[34]

Through his fictional missionary, Wilson advised ministers to keep their religious lessons plain and simple when propagating the gospel to Indians and to black slaves. Unlike some of his contemporaries, Wilson did not question whether Indians were "capable of receiving ... Christian Knowledge." He believed that

Indians "can reason as well as Christians." Moreover, in this monotheistic world, "we [humans]," he argued, "are the Creatures of one and the same God," and therefore were capable of grasping God's truths, regardless of differences of birth, station, language, or culture.[35]

Perhaps the most fundamental truth that Christian Indians were required to grasp, according to Wilson, was the tenet that God was incomparable and omnipotent. Some Mohawk catechumens may have found this "truth" difficult to understand, for according to Iroquois religion, no single entity held such supreme power and authority. The Great Creator, or Great Spirit, existed but he was one of many gods and spirits that animated the world. All things, in fact, possessed spirits. Each individual had his or her own guardian spirit, or *orenda*, who guided him or her through life and thus was far more important than the Great Creator. To endow a single deity with total omnipotence ran counter to Iroquois religion, which was polytheistic, valued a world in balance, and regarded the world as animated by multiple forces.[36]

Perhaps Wilson recognized that Indians believed in multiple forces at play in the Iroquois world, for he cautioned missionaries about what he saw as a particularly troubling aspect of Indian thought and behavior: Indians, he claimed, had a strong and natural inclination toward evil. Neophytes, especially, had to be constantly vigilant, Wilson warned, for "evil Spirits [were] always ready to take Possession" of them.[37] Interestingly, Wilson noted an aspect of Iroquois religion with which Iroquois believers and converts to Christianity would have agreed: evil spirits existed and, depending upon one's universe of discourse, one either supplicated them or asked for God's intervention.

The actual means for getting Indians, first, to acknowledge God as the supreme authority of the universe, and, second, to cast off their "evil, superstitious ways," required teaching them the Church's catechism. The catechism contained the fundamental "truths" of Church of England Protestantism. Its lessons consisted of a series of questions posed orally by the catechist to the catechumen, who was compelled to respond with rote answers. The drill was designed to impel the student to renounce the devil and the wicked, sinful ways of the world and of the flesh; to believe sincerely in the "Articles of Faith"; and to become a devout person by worshipping God and following His holy commandments.

In reciting the first few lines of the "Articles of Faith," which establish God as incomparable and supranatural, and Jesus Christ as the Lord in human form—"I Believe in God the Father Almighty, maker of heaven and earth: And in Jesus Christ his only Son our Lord"—a Mohawk catechumen would have said: "Tewakightaghkouh Niyohtseragouh ne Raniha ne agwegouh tihhaeshatste, raonissouh ne Karonia, neoni Oghwhentsya Neonoi Jesus Christtseragouh raonha-a Rahawak Songwayaner."[38] In this passage, key Mohawk words—*Niyoh* for "God," *Raniha* for "Father," *Karonia* for "heaven"—carry images and meanings that are specific to Iroquois thought. There is, however, no comparable Iroquois word for "Jesus Christ." Converts either had to place their faith fully in Christ or make room for him in their pantheon of gods. Whether the new Christians exercised the first or second option—it is nearly impossible to tell who did what—those who claimed Christ as their savior surely felt empowered by this secret knowledge, which also set them apart from non-Christian Indians.

Old Abraham, Paulus, and the others also would have conveyed to their catechumens that their daily duty to God was to praise Him through prayer and psalms. Their pupils would have had to commit to memory a number of prayers, including the Te Deum laudamus—"Thee, God, we praise," a prayer of thanksgiving to God—recited at morning prayers on Sundays, Wednesdays, and Fridays, and on other holy days at which a prelate convened services. The first three lines of this prayer reinforced the first of God's ten commandments, that is, singular devotion to God alone:

We praise thee, O God: we acknowledge thee to be the Lord.
O Niyoh wakwaneandon; kwayenderist-ha Sayaner.
All the earth doth worship thee: the Father everlasting.
Oghwhentsiagwegouh, yesenideghtasisk: Ne Raniha tsiniyeheawe.
To thee all angels cry aloud: the heavens, and all the powers therein.
Karonghiyageghronontseragwegouh, neoni Kaeshatsteghtitserhogouh,
Karonghiyagehogouh yederon.[39]

Frequent, regular recitations of the Lord's Prayer, led by the native teachers at morning and evening prayers, at catechetical lessons, at communion, and at church services, also undergirded the convert's view of God as incomparable and sovereign, and reminded the proselyte of his or her responsibility to God:

Our Father which art in Heaven,
Songwaniha Karonghyage tighsideron;
Hallowed be thy Name;
Wafaghseanadogeaghtine.
Thy kingdom come;
Sayanertsera sewe,

Thy will de done in earth, as it is in Heaven.
Tagserre eghniawanea tsiniyought Karonghyagouh, oni Oghwentsiage.
Give us this day our daily bread:
Niyadewighniserage Takwanadaranondaghsik nonwa:
And forgive us our trespasses, as we forgive them that trespass against us.
Neoni Tondakwarighwiyoughstouh tsiniyughtoni Tsiakwadaderighwiy oughsteani.
And lead us not into temptation:
Neoni toghsa tackwaghsarineght Dewaddatdenageraghtonke
But deliver us from evil:
nesane sadyadakwaghs ne Kondighseroheanse;
For thine is the kingdom, and the power, and the glory,
ikea Sayanertsera ne na-ah, neoni ne Kaeshatste, neoni ne Onweseaghtak
for ever and ever. Amen.
ne tsiniyeheawe neoni tsiniyeheawe. Amen.[40]

Genesis was a critical place where missionaries began to reshape the Iroquois foundational view of the cosmos. The Christian creation myth significantly contradicts that of the Iroquois religion. Consider God's creation of the world:

1. In the beginning God created the heaven and the earth.
1. *A Daghsaweghtseragouh raonissouh Niyoh neKaronya ne Oghwhentsya.*
2. And the earth was without form, and void:
2. *Neoni Oghwhentsya Karagouh keghne, neoni oriwagouh:*
   and darkness was upon the face of the deep:
   neoni Tsi-Yoghnod Aghsadakonghtsera naah:
   and the Spirit of God moved upon the face of the waters.
   neoni ne Ronigoghriyoughstouh Niyoh t'hio-auwe Oghnekage
3. And God said, Let there be light:
3. *Neoni Niyoh waheanrouh Weankehak*
   and there was light.
   neoni weande ondon.[41]

The Iroquois creation myth begins quite differently. Sky Woman either fell or was pushed from the Sky World above. As she fell to earth, her fall was broken by the wings of birds, who set her gently down on the back of a turtle. Earth divers dived down into the seas and brought up earth, which they fashioned into land. Soon Sky Woman gave birth to a daughter, who, grown, was impregnated by a warrior-god when he laid several arrows across her body as she slept. In time, she gave birth to twin boys, Teharonghyawago, the Good Twin, and his evil sibling, Tawiskaron. The evil twin, favored by their grandmother, killed their mother. In retaliation, Teharonghyawago cut off his grandmother's head, which he tossed up into the sky, where it became the moon. The twins battled each other. Eventually, Teharonghyawago vanquished his evil brother, and banished him to the edges of the world, from where he tempted the souls of men. Teharonghyawago then went about making all the living things on the earth and teaching men and women how to live and how to keep thanksgiving festivals.[42]

The Iroquois creation myth is at odds with the Christian myth in a number of areas, including gender (a female progenitor of Iroquois life in Sky Woman versus the traditional Christian male God); a world of gods prefiguring humankind; and the preexistence of a primordial world rather than a void, from which God created the world. To accept the Christian foundational myth was to reconceive the essence of the world. This was difficult for many converts to do, and so many held on to both concepts of the world. John Norton, an early nineteenth-century Scot-Cherokee writer who identified ethnically as Mohawk, explained that many Christian Iroquois throughout southern Canada did not discredit the Iroquois creation myth that featured Sky Woman, her daughter, and her daughter's twin sons. Rather, they "endeavour[ed] to accommodate it [the myth] to the Scriptural account of our Blessed Lord." One day, Norton "asked one of these old men, who in his youth had had much conversation with the Roman Catholic Priests, if he remembered the name of the Mother of Teharonghyawago." His informant answered "not in our language, but in that of the Europeans, she is called Maria."[43]

Although the Scriptures in Mohawk carry the essential meanings of God's truths, the Mohawk language conveys images that are specific to Iroquois thought. This does not mean that Mohawk converts interpreted Christianity in ways antithetical to Protestant precepts; rather the Mohawk language facilitated an Iroquois worldview to inform the practice of Mohawk converts. As such, some Mohawk converts interpreted some Christian practices, such as the sacraments—baptism and communion—in distinctly Iroquois ways. Although the Church of England practiced infant baptism, its ministers baptized many adults and adolescents. The message that SPG missionaries tried to convey to their Mohawk catechumens was that baptism, like communion, sealed one's covenant with God by symbolizing that one had been received into the holy church of Christ. Baptism secured one's place in the kingdom of God by spiritually regenerating one's soul through the mystical act of washing away one's sins with holy water. Once adult and adolescent Mohawks demonstrated a grasp of Protestant tenets by reciting the Church catechism and by manifesting outward signs of pious living, they were permitted to enter into covenant with Christ and the Church through baptism. Concomitant with the blessing of baptism, the new convert took a Christian name, which further symbolized rebirth.

Many Mohawk converts, however, interpreted the act of baptism—*n'eadatnekoserhouh*—differently. For most, baptism constituted evidence enough of Christian identity and membership in the Church. Nothing further was required—no further instruction, no compensatory attendance at church, no outward sign of constant sobriety, and no putting away of old customs and practices. The mystical washing away of sin with sanctified water—*Snegadogeaghtist ne keagaye ne akanohharete ne Karighwanerea*—was all that was necessary to make one a Christian.[44] Moreover, baptism, according to some adults, acted as a powerful curative medicine, capable of wiping out all faults and illnesses. One Mohawk man, who had become ill and feared that he might die, grew "troubled that he had not yet been baptized and therefore earnestly desired" that the attending SPG missionary administer that sacrament to him. After balking at the request, the missionary relented, reassured by other members of the community that this "vary wicked Indian" was repentant. After being baptized, the sick man recovered, but quickly "forgot all his promises of amending his life ... and became as wicked as ever he was."[45] It was not necessary for this "convert" to accept Christ as his Savior or to believe in the principles of Christianity to be convinced of the power of baptism.

The Mohawk interpretation that baptism offered a form of protection against illness and other misfortune coincided with the concept of orenda, one's personal guardian spirit or power. Mohawk mothers continuously sought out ministers—French, Dutch, German, English, it did not matter—to have their children baptized with holy water in order to protect them from future harm. It is likely that the Mohawk schoolmasters and the SPG missionaries conveyed this idea by taking a cue from Bishop Wilson, who insisted that ministers explain to their Indian catechumens that God "will give his holy Angels charge concerning you, to guard you against the Power and Malice of evil Spirits.— And this All-powerful Spirit will guide and assist you in the Way you should go...."[46] Perhaps some Mohawks conceived of orenda when Old Abraham spoke of *Karonghiyagaghronouh* (angels) in heaven (*Karonghyage*).

Many Mohawks also viewed the other sacrament, communion, differently than SPG clergymen. According to the Church, communion represented the baptized worshipper's worthiness in joining a community of worshippers in covenant with God. However, many Mohawk converts viewed admittance to communion as an imprimatur affirming his or her social standing. To be refused communion reduced the individual "to a kind of Dispair," which often led the individual "to commit worse crimes than before, for they then are pointed at as bad Persons unfit for Society." More than one disgruntled "convert," annoyed at being barred from communion, usually for excessive drunkenness, threatened to harm an SPG missionary.[47]

The fact that Mohawk converts held complex views of the sacraments, informed partly by Iroquois cognition and partly by Christian interpretations of these rites, suggests that Christian texts translated into Mohawk and explained by baptized and pious Mohawk headmen played a significant role in religious change among many Mohawks. Texts written in the local vernacular and explained by local leaders enabled the Mohawks to realize that they could communicate with God on their terms. With texts and native teachers, they did not even need the services of a missionary. In 1764, the Mohawks at Canajoharie, the Upper Castle, politely refused the services of 75-year old Jacob Oel, a German minister to families on the German Flatts since the 1720s. For the past forty years, Oel had occasionally visited the Upper Castle to read prayers, catechize the youths, and baptize both white and Mohawk children and infants.[48] Now, however, Oel could not "excite any desire in his Indians in the upper castle for public worship, or the use of the sacraments." In reality, the Mohawks, who had been without the services of Paulus Sahonwadi for a few years, preferred to work with Philip Jonathan, a young Mohawk from Canajoharie who had received an English-style education. Already, he had two star pupils who were "pretty fur [sic] advanced in their Learning" and for whom Jonathan sought from Brother Waronghyage (Sir William Johnson) "two of our printed Books."[49]

Conclusion

In 1771, Sir William Johnson wrote to Arthur Lee and explained that "the customs and manners of the Indians are in several cases liable to changes, which have not been thoroughly considered by authors and therefore the description of them (as is usual) at any one particular period must be insufficient."[50] Through this astute observation, Johnson acknowledged that cultures—notably Indian cultures—are dynamic and in constant flux. The mid-eighteenth century marked one particular period of change for the Mohawk. At this time, the majority of Mohawks were baptized, but most continued to cling to Iroquois sacred ways, which they supplemented with Christian practices. This praxis was partly evolutionary, a by-product of enculturation, but also was sparked by Mohawk schoolmasters and catechists, who were hired by the Society for the Propagation of the Gospel in Foreign Parts to generate and sustain Mohawk interest in Protestantism.

The instruction that most of the native teachers provided their Mohawk catechumens included reading prayers and teaching literacy. According to some missionaries, most Mohawks now valued literacy highly. The community held in high esteem those individuals who could read the Holy Bible, read prayers, and teach literacy. By example and by practice, these men helped Mohawk converts and nonconverts alike to imagine new ways of being.

The SPG experiment of using Mohawk schoolmasters and catechists to teach literacy and spread the gospel was confined primarily to these four headmen—Cornelius, Daniel, Paulus, and Old Abraham. When three of the four teachers ceased working for the SPG—Old Abraham died in 1757, and Cornelius and Daniel abruptly quit their posts in 1746 following a dispute with Henry Barclay over unspent funds—the society did not replace them with native teachers but hired white Protestant schoolmasters in their stead. Through this strategy, the SPG no doubt intended to "reduce"—that is, lead back to the established church—Mohawks who had strayed to dissenting ministers. For the next several decades, Paulus remained one of the very few native schoolmasters on the SPG's books, continuing to teach Mohawk children in Canada after the American Revolution (see Fig. 10.1).[51]

From the perspective of the SPG, Old Abraham and the three schoolmasters performed their tasks well. Between 1746, following Henry Barclay's departure from Fort Hunter, and 1750, when John Ogilvie arrived at Fort Hunter to be the new SPG missionary, Old Abraham was virtually the only Christian schoolmaster in the entire Mohawk valley. Ogilvie found the Mohawks at Tiononderoge (the town nearest the fort) "intirely given up to Drunkenness." At Canajoharie, however, Old Abraham's primary post of operation, Ogilvie found that drunkenness had been "greatly prevented by a very pious Indian whose name is [Old] Abraham."[52]

Old Abraham surely played a role in keeping some Canajoharies pious and sober. But to credit him with single-handedly sustaining a new moral code in his community for four years is to oversimplify Indian-missionary relations. It is tempting to read

248 | William B. Hart

FIGURE 10.1 Engraving by James Peachey, in Daniel Claus, *A Primer for the Use of Mohawk Children* (London, 1786). A Mohawk classroom, Grand River, Ontario. The teacher may be either Paulus Sahonwadi, who was among the first schoolmasters to use this primer, or Thomas. The author, Daniel Claus, was the son-in-law of William Johnson. (Courtesy of the John Carter Brown Library at Brown University)

the drunkenness at Tiononderoge as apostasy, as Mohawks returning to their old ways during the four-year absence of SPG missionaries. Ogilvie would soon learn, however, that shortly after he left a Mohawk village, many residents would retrieve their hidden rum and resume drinking. In this way, Mohawks engaged in drunkenness as a form of public protest. At Tiononderoge, disgruntled Mohawks used drunkenness to protest SPG neglect. At Canajoharie, however, native etiquette required that the residents not embarrass Old Abraham, perhaps because he was the only native teacher on the SPG payroll at that time.[53]

The Revolutionary War scattered most Mohawks across southern Canada. At Montreal, Paulus Sahonwadi continued to teach children from Tiononderoge whose families had gathered near the city. He was assisted by another Fort Hunter Mohawk, Thomas, who had once served as John Stuart's clerk. Together, they taught the children the alphabet from scraps of paper until Daniel Claus, a son-in-law of the late Sir William Johnson, could provide them with primers and prayer books that he had translated into Mohawk. Many Indians and whites believed that Claus was the only person, "White or Indian," with the "competent knowledge of both languages" to accomplish this task. Aaron Hill, a.k.a. Kanonraron, a Mohawk living at Niagara, thanked Claus for sending copies of the primers and prayer books to him and the refugee community at Niagara, comprised significantly of Mohawks from Canajoharie. The texts would keep the spirit of Christianity alive there, where, Hill professed, the religion was "upheld among us." On Sundays, Thomas (formerly of Montreal?), "a pious Mohawk," read prayers in a log house "built for them to meet in for the purpose of Divine Worship." Despite worshipping in stone and clapboard churches in Iroquoia, the community evidently felt the need to quickly build a house of worship using a familiar design: that of a longhouse.[54]

Notes

I wish to express my gratitude to the editors of this book, and to James Merrell, Albert Raboteau, Marianne Mithun, and members of the 1998–99 Religon and Culture Workshop at Princeton University who read earlier drafts of this essay and offered invaluable commentary.

1. Charter of the Society, 16 June 1701, as cited in C.F. Pascoe, *Two Hundred Years of the S. P. G.: An Historical Account of the Propagation of the Gospel in Foreign Parts, 1701–1900* (London, 1901), 932; Minutes of SPG Meeting, 28 April 1710, Records of the Society for the Propagation of the Gospel in Foreign Parts, The Journals, 1701–1850, vols. 1–50 with Appendices A-D (microfilm) [hereafter SPG Journals] (London, 1964), vol. 1:479.
2. William Andrews to Secretary, 17 October 1714, Records of the Society for the Propagation of the Gospel in Foreign Parts, The Letter Books, Series A, 1702–37 (microfilm) [hereafter SPG Letters A] (London, 1964), vol. 10, no. 1 (folio 158). One missionary complained about using unchurched interpreters of European ancestry to communicate his sermons. His ideas, he claimed, were too often "Imperfectly Convey'd to them [the Mohawks] by the means of an Ignorant Interpreter, whose Immorall life Contributes to Lessen the Impression of the Dictates." See John Miln to Secretary, 5 November 1729, Records of the Society for the Propagation of the Gospel in Foreign Parts, The Letter Books, Series B, 1701–86 (microfilm) [hereafter SPG Letters B] (London, 1964), vol. 1, no. 53 (folio 205). A Mohawk-Dutch woman, Hilletie van Olinda, was employed by the provincial government at the end of the seventeenth century and the beginning of the eighteenth century as official interpreter for Indian affairs, both secular and religious. However, she worked primarily with Dutch ministers in the area. The French Jesuits in New France, the Church of England's main competitors in the contest for Iroquois allies and souls, sought the help of native exhorters to assist them in their work. The Jesuits routinely employed native *dogiques*, or Indian "prayer captains," to read prayers, to catechize children, to occasionally baptize other Indians, and, in general, to put a familiar face on Christianity and the process of religious conversion. See James Axtell, *The Invasion Within: The Contest of Cultures in Colonial North America* (New York, 1985), 125.
3. John Ogilvie to Rev. Sir, 27 July 1750, SPG Letters B, vol. 18, no. 102; John Wolfe Lydekker, *The Faithful Mohawks* (New York, 1938), 67. Three of the first five SPG missionaries assigned to the Mohawks were responsible first to congregations in Albany or Schenectady. Even the Dutch ministers assigned to the Mohawks had first serviced congregations in either Albany, Schenectady, Schohare, or the German Flatts. Most SPG ministers attended to the Mohawks at Fort Hunter only a few weeks out of the year. When there, they divided their attention among the Indians, English soldiers stationed at the garrison, local Euro-American settlers, and African slaves. For a brief history of Dutch pastors to the Mohawks, see Charles E. Corwin, "Efforts of the Dutch-American Colonial Pastors for the Conversion of the Indians," *Journal of the Presbyterian Historical Society* 12 (1924–27): 225–46. For SPG missionaries to the Mohawks, see Lydekker, *Faithful Mohawks*.
4. Henry Barclay to Secretary, 15 October 1740, SPG Letters B, vol. 7, part II:143; Minutes of SPG Meeting, 20 March 1740/41, SPG Journals, vol. 8:233.
5. Henry Barclay to Secretary, 4 November 1743, SPG Letters B, vol. 11, no. 155; Minutes of SPG Meeting, 17 February 1743/44, SPG Journals, vol. 9:234 (Cornelius); Memoir of John Stuart, n.d., *Documentary History of New York* [hereafter *DHNY*] (quarto), E.B. O'Callaghan, ed. (Albany, 1851), vol. 4:314 (Paulus); Andrews to Secretary, 15 October 1714, SPG Letters A, vol. 10:186. To "read prayers" is to lead the congregation in prayer. This meaning is akin to a common late-seventeenth-century definition of "to read," which is "to give instruction in."

6. William Andrews to Secretary, October 1717, SPG Letters A, vol. 12:318–24; *idem*, 18 October 1717, SPG Letters A, vol. 12:325–26; *idem*, 17 April 1718, SPG Letters A, vol. 13:321, 319; *idem*, 1 September 1717, SPG Letters A, vol. 12:331; *idem*, 2 July 1719, SPG Letters A, vol. 13:467.
7. John Stuart to Rev. Worthy Sir, 22 June 1771, SPG Letters B, vol. 2, no. 197 (folio 680–81); Minutes of SPG Meeting, 18 October 1771, SPG Journals, vol. 19:110–11.
8. James Sullivan, Alexander C. Flick, and Milton Hamilton, eds., *The Papers of Sir William Johnson*, 14 vols. (Albany, 1921–62), vol. 10:241–42.
9. Minutes of SPG Meeting, 15 June 1759, SPG Journals, vol. 14:186. In response to Paulus going AWOL, Ogilvie withheld three and a half pounds—half his salary. When Ogilvie rehired Paulus several years later, he paid him a salary of only five pounds per year rather than his customary seven.
10. Sir William Johnson to Daniel Claus, 10 March 1761, Sullivan, *Papers of Sir William Johnson*, vol. 3:355; Johnson to Ogilvie, 1 February 1766, Sullivan, *Papers of Sir William Johnson*, vol. 5:29; John Stuart to Richard Hind, 9 August 1774, Sullivan, *Papers of Sir William Johnson*, vol. 8:1195–96. Despite Johnson's efforts to publish such tracts, their lack of availability remained a problem beyond Johnson's death in 1774, after which time John Stuart, the SPG missionary, took over the translation project. For further evidence of Johnson, Ogilvie, Stuart, Daniel Claus (Johnson's son-in-law), and others trying to meet the repeated demands of Mohawk converts for texts printed in their language, see Sullivan, *Papers of Sir William Johnson*, vol. 3:384, 630; vol. 4:72; vol. 8:1039–40; vol. 10:264, 333, 935.
11. Journal of Indian Affairs, Meeting at Fort Johnson, 15 March 1761, Sullivan, *Papers of Sir William Johnson*, vol. 10:241; Council at Albany, 28 June–11 July 1754, *DHNY* (quarto), vol. 2:345; Minutes of SPG Meeting, 15 March 1765, SPG Journals, vol. 16:329; *idem*, 15 November 1765, SPG Journals, vol. 16:469.
12. By this time, the Mohawk people resided virtually "in the Heart of [white] Settlements," and lived much like their white neighbors, almost entirely isolated from the other five Iroquois nations. Sir William Johnson asserted that the Mohawks had "less Intercourse with the Indians & more with us [the English]," and consequently blended some of "their Ancient usages ... with Customs amongst ourselves." See Sullivan, *Papers of Sir William Johnson*, vol. 10:237; *DHNY* (quarto) vol. 2:336; and for evidence that a European lifestyle was adopted by most Mohawks by the time of the American Revolution, see Gansevoort to Sullivan, 8 October 1779, Gansevoort Military Papers, Gansevoort-Lansing Collection, New York Public Library, cited in Barbara Graymont, *The Iroquois in the American Revolution* (Syracuse, 1972), 219.
13. George Pigot, *A Vindication of the Practice of the Ancient Christian...* (Boston, 1731), 16, as cited in John Calam, *Parsons and Pedagogues: The S. P. G. Adventure in American Education* (New York, 1971), 78; Rev. Gilbert Burnet, Bishop of Sarum, *A Sermon Preach'd at St. Mary-le-Bow, February 18, 1703/04* (London, 1704), 17–18, collected in Society for the Propagation of the Gospel in Foreign Parts, *Sermons & Abstracts, 1701–10* (London, n.d.), n.p.; Rev. Richard Willis, Dean of Lincoln, *A Sermon Preached before the S. P. G. ... February 20, 1701/02* (London, 1702), 17–18, collected in S. P. G., *Sermons & Abstracts*, n.p.
14. Desiderius Erasmus, *Christian Humanism and the Reformation*, ed. John C. Olin (New York, 1965), 96–97, as cited in Lamin Sanneh, *Encountering the West: Christianity and the Global Cultural Process: The African Dimension* (Maryknoll, NY, 1993), 73.

15. The scholarship on orality, literacy, and the consequences of translating Christian texts into local languages is large. My thinking on this matter has been influenced by several scholars, especially Sanneh, *Encountering the West*; Jack Goody, *The Interface between the Written and the Oral* (Cambridge, 1987); Robin Lane Fox, "Literacy and Power in Early Christianity," in *Literacy and Power in the Ancient World*, eds. Alan K. Bowman and Greg Woolf (Cambridge, 1994), 126–48; and Edward G. Gray, *New World Babel: Languages & Nations in Early America* (Princeton, 1999). James Axtell argues in "The Power of Print in the Eastern Woodlands," *After Columbus: Essays in the Ethnohistory of Colonial North America* (New York, 1988), 86–99, that for Indians the power of print lay in the magic of a printed foreign language, such as English or French. I disagree with this position and contend that having one's own language in print is empowering, as Sanneh has so persuasively demonstrated.
16. Sanneh, *Encountering the West*, 17.
17. On power through prayer to God, see Fox, "Literacy and Power," 130. On literacy displacing the authority of elders, see Goody, *Between the Written and Oral*, 164. For an initial investigation into the degree of literacy in late-eighteenth-century Mohawk society, see William B. Hart, "For the Good of Our Souls: Mohawk Authority, Accommodation, and Resistance to Protestant Evangelism, 1700–1780" (Ph.D. Thesis, Brown University, 1998), ch. 5.
18. Frances Karttunen, *Between Worlds: Interpreters, Guides, and Survivors* (New Brunswick, NJ, 1994). Other recent studies on Indian brokers, intermediaries, and go-betweens include James Clifton, ed., *Being and Becoming Indian: Biographical Studies of North American Frontiers* (Chicago, 1989); and Margaret Connell Szasz, ed., *Between Indian and White Worlds: The Cultural Broker* (Norman, 1994). For a brief historiographical overview of the scholarship on brokers, see the "Introduction" in Szasz, *Between Indian and White Worlds*.
19. Memoir of John Stuart, n.d., *DHNY* (quarto) vol. 4:314. For a cogent summary of the various offices and duties of Iroquois "headmen," see Daniel K. Richter, *The Ordeal of the Longhouse: The Peoples of the Iroquois League in the Era of European Colonization* (Chapel Hill, 1992), 40, 42–46. See also Jose Antonio Brandao, *"Your fyre shall burn no more": Iroquois Policy toward New France and Its Native Allies to 1701* (Lincoln, 1997), 32–33, for the role played by war chiefs. For a detailed, but partially flawed, account of the intricate system of headmen and other leaders, see Lewis Henry Morgan, *League of the Iroquois* (1851; New York, 1962), 62–77, 84–90. Note that clans "owned" the titles of "Peace Chief" and *rotiyanehr* and that clan mothers granted the titles to worthy male successors.
20. Richter, *Ordeal of the Longhouse*, 45–47; Cadwallader Colden, *The History of the Five Nations of Canada, Which Are Dependent on the Province of New-York in America....* (London, 1747), 14, as cited in Richter, *Ordeal of the Longhouse*, 46 (quote).
21. Sullivan, *Papers of Sir William Johnson*, vol. 10:241–42; Ogilvie to Rev. Sir, 27 July 1750, SPG Letters B, vol. 18, no. 102; Lydekker, *Faithful Mohawks*, 67; Hugh Hastings, ed., *Ecclesiastical Records, State of New York*, 6 vols. (Albany, 1901), vol. 5:77–78; Council Meeting in Court house, Albany, 6 July 1754, ed. E.B. O'Callaghan, *Documents Relative to the Colonial History of the State of New York* [hereafter *DRCHNY*], 15 vols. (Albany, 1853–87), vol. 6:876–77; Minutes of SPG Meeting, 21 September 1750, SPG Journals, vol. 11:258–59.
22. See David Snow and Richard Machalek, "The Sociology of Conversion," *Annual Review of Sociology* 10 (1984): 169–74, for a summary and analysis of

the various categories that sociologists of religion have used to explain conversions. David K. Jordan, "The Glyphomancy Factor: Observations on Chinese Conversion," in *Conversion to Christianity: Historical and Anthropological Perspectives on a Great Transformation*, ed. Robert W. Hefner (Berkeley, 1993), 286 (quote on Chinese converts). For Mohawk converts practicing Iroquois religion and Protestantism concomitantly, see Hart, "For the Good of Our Souls," esp. chaps. 3 and 5.
23. Henry Barclay to Secretary, 12 March 1744/45, SPG Letters B, vol. 14:99; Frank J. Klingberg, *Anglican Humanitarianism in Colonial New York* (Philadelphia, 1940), 77; Barclay to Secretary, 17 November 1742, SPG Letters B, vol. 10, no. 112; idem, 31 May 1743, SPG Letters B, vol. 11, no. 153. For the personal qualities and qualifications required by the SPG of its ministers, see Pascoe, *Two Hundred Years of the S. P. G.*, 63– 64, 845, 837–38; Alfred W. Newcombe, "The Appointment and Instruction of S. P. G. Missionaries," *Church History*, ed. Matthew Spinka, et. al. (New York, 1936), vol. 5:342–44, 347–49; and Calam, *Parsons and Pedagogues*, 23–24, 31.
24. Minutes of SPG Meeting, 19 November 1756, SPG Journals, vol. 13:182; Lydekker, *Faithful Mohawk*, 83; William Webb Kemp, *The Support of Schools in Colonial New York by the Society for the Propagation of the Gospel in Foreign Parts* (New York, 1913), 220. In opposing the SPG's mandate to teach Mohawk children in English, Sir William Johnson went to great expense to have Protestant texts translated into Mohawk. Johnson died in 1774, never seeing the publication of his pet project, which was delayed by myriad translating and printing problems. See Johnson to Daniel Claus, 22 November 1761, Sullivan, *Papers of Sir William Johnson*, vol. 10:333; Johnson to Lords of Trade, 13 November 1763, *DRCHNY*, vol. 7:580; Hastings, *Ecclesiastical Records*, vol. 6:3902; Johnson to Henry Barclay, 24 November 1763, Sullivan, *Papers of Sir William Johnson*, vol. 10:935.
25. For an introduction to the discourse, or rhetoric, of religion, see Lawrence A. Palinkas, *Rhetoric and Religious Experience: The Discourse of Immigration Chinese Churches* (Fairfax, VA, 1989), intro., 1–18. For a study of the rhetoric of religion, see Kenneth Burke, *A Rhetoric of Religion: Studies in Logology* (Berkeley, 1970).
26. For a discussion of the Massachusett language and the Eliot Bible obscuring God's truths, see Gray, *New World Babel*, esp. chap. 3.
27. Richard Terrick, Bishop of Peterborough, *A Sermon before the SPG* .... February 1764 (London, 1764), 28, cited in Calam, *Parsons and Pedagogues*, 160; Minutes of SPG Meeting, 19 November 1756, SPG Journals, vol. 13:184 (Ogilvie); Johnson to Lords of Trade, 3 September 1755, *DRCHNY* vol. 6:994. The Kahnawake interpretation of fidelity premised upon religious ties is an example of what Richard White calls "middle ground" discourse, in which one party appeals to another party based on what the former believes to be the values of the latter. The Iroquois of the seventeenth century did not share the view that religion bound nations together, for in the 1640s and 1650s they devastated the Huron nation, which, as Iroquois people, shared similar religious beliefs. For most Iroquois people, kinship rather than religion was a stronger bonding agent. See White, *The Middle Ground: Indians, Empires, and Republics in the Great Lakes Region, 1650–1815* (Cambridge and New York, 1991), esp. intro. and chap. 2.
28. Henry Barclay to Secretary, 17 November 1742, SPG Letters B, vol. 10:112 (Cornelius and Daniel); Minutes of SPG Meeting, 21 October 1743, SPG Journals, vol. 9:199 (May 1743 visit); Barclay to Secretary, 31 May 1743, SPG Let-

ters B, vol. 11, no. 153; *idem*, 4 November 1743, SPG Letters B, vol. 11, no. 155; Minutes of SPG Meeting, 17 February 1743/44, SPG Journals, vol. 9:234 (November 1743 visit).

29. Minutes of SPG Meeting, 15 December 1749, SPG Journals, vol. 11:176; *idem*, 20 July 1750, SPG Journals, vol. 11:246–47; *idem*, 21 September, SPG Journals, vol. 11:259; *idem*, 18 January 1750/51, SPG Journals, vol. 11:299–300; Jonathan Edwards to Jaspar Mauduit, 10 March 1752, Andover Newton Theological Seminary [hereafter ANTS], folio 2. (I am indebted to Rachel Wheeler for recognizing the relevance of Edward's Stockbridge correspondence to this essay.) Old Abraham earned a salary of five pounds per year. Compare this to the salaries of English schoolmasters in the colonies, whose pay ranged from a low of 5 pounds per year to a high of 20 pounds between 1714 and 1763. See Calam, *Parsons and Pedagogues*, 103–104. No Mohawk women were hired to proselytize Christianity. This was despite the fact that the early education of Iroquois children was an activity conducted in the village, and therefore, was the responsibility of mothers, and despite the fact that Mohawk women, the most zealous proselytes, constituted the backbone of the Mohawk Protestant church.

30. Jonathan Edwards to Jaspar Mauduit, 10 March 1752, ANTS, folio 2; Edwards to Thomas Hubbard, 1751, ANTS, folio 2; Kellogg to Hendrick Petris, 20 June 1750, SPG Letters B, vol. 18, no. 104; Axtell, *Invasion Within*, 196–204. Some of the delegates were not at all interested in literacy and Christian instruction but had come along with the hope of receiving survival goods, in the manner of receiving goods at the missions in New France. They left in disgust when they learned that only those children and their families attached to the school would receive clothing.

31. Edwards to Joseph Paice, 1752, ANTS, 1752B, no. 6a–6b, no. 7. To have known how to read both Mohawk and English during King George's War (1744–48) would have been invaluable for the Mohawks. During that time, rumors circulated that the English intended to "cut off" the Iroquois. While a Dutch trader was probably the source of these rumors, several Mohawks blamed Barclay, their missionary. They specifically identified his books, which they believed were written by the devil, as the source of the trouble. Anti-Barclay feelings among the Mohawks were so virulent that Daniel and Cornelius resigned their posts. See Barclay to Secretary, 12 March 1744/45, SPG Letters B, vol. 13, no. 314; *idem*, 21 October 1745, SPG Letters B, vol. 13, no. 316; Minutes of SPG Meeting, 15 November 1745, SPG Journals, vol. 10:83; *idem*, 18 April 1746, SPG Journals, vol. 10:124; Barclay to Secretary, 9 December 1746, SPG Letters B, vol. 14:99.

32. Edwards to Thomas Hubbard, 1751, ANTS, folio 2. Edwards believed that Old Abraham was made catechist by the SPG in order to counter the Stockbridge mission and keep the Mohawks home. John Ogilvie opposed the removal of the Mohawks to Stockbridge for two reasons: (1) he feared that their removal would "divert the Trade from us [Albany] & leave our Frontiers naked & defenceless"; and (2) he believed that it was unwise to expose the Mohawks to "the unhappy Divisions subsisting among Protestants," for to do so "may so prejudice their minds as to render them a more easy Prey to the craft of Popish Missionaries." Ogilvie worried needlessly about Indian knowledge of the "unhappy divisions" among Christians. Iroquois Indians, who had long been evangelized by French Jesuits, were well aware of doctrinal differences. Ogilvie, quoting John Sergeant, the founder of the Stockbridge

mission, believed that the solution to keeping Indians "faithful" to the Church and Crown lay in changing "their present Habits of thinking and acting, and instill[ing] the Principles of Virtue and Piety, into their minds in such a Way as may make the most lasting Impressions, and withal introduc[ing] the English Language among them, instead of their present barbarous Dialect." See Ogilvie to Secretary, 7 August 1751, SPG Letters B, vol. 19, no. 72; Minutes of SPG Meeting, 20 March 1752, SPG Journals, vol. 12:114.
33. Minutes of SPG Meeting, 19 November 1756, SPG Journals, vol. 13:182–83; Lydekker, *Faithful Mohawks*, 83.
34. Thomas Wilson (Bishop of Sodor and Man), *An Essay Towards an Instruction for the Indians; Explaining the Most Essential Doctrines of Christianity* ... (London, 1740). Wilson compiled this essay after extensive conversations with General Oglethorp of Georgia, gleaning from those conversations some rudimentary understanding of Cherokee (an Iroquoian-speaking people) sacred beliefs (see Wilson, p. i). Minutes of SPG Meeting, 19 September 1740, SPG Journals, vol. 8:178; SPG to Henry Barclay, 14 June 1743, SPG Letters B, vol. 20, no. 196; Johnson to Daniel Claus, 10 March 1761, Sullivan, *Papers of Sir William Johnson*, vol. 3:355; Daniel Claus to William Johnson, 2 May 1761, Sullivan, *Papers of Sir William Johnson*, vol. 3:384; *idem*, 1 May 1761, Sullivan, *Papers of Sir William Johnson*, vol. 10:264.
35. Wilson, *Essay Towards an Instruction*, ii, iii, xvi, 12, 69. Jonathan Edwards may have read Wilson's book while he was the missionary at Stockbridge in the 1750s. An observer noted that when Edwards preached to the Indians, his style was that of "a very plain and practical preacher." Gideon Hawley, "Narrative of his Journey to Onohoghgwage, July 1753," Hastings, *Ecclesiastical Records*, vol. 5:3399.
36. Axtell, *Indian Peoples of Eastern America*, 174–79; Axtell, *Invasion Within*, 15–16; Richter, *Ordeal of the Longhouse*, 9–11; Donald P. St. John, "Iroquois Religion," ed. Mircea Eliade, *The Encyclopedia of Religion*, 16 vols. (New York, 1987), vol. 7:284. The Great Creator was Teharonghyawago, the "Good Twin," a grandson of the Sky Woman, who was the progenitor of the Iroquois people. As such, he did not prefigure the world, although believers in Iroquois religion credited him with making the world in a fashion similar to that outlined in Genesis: Teharonghyawago made the animals and humans, and he showed humans how to live and how to conduct thanksgiving ceremonies.
37. Wilson, *Essay Towards an Instruction*, 120.
38. Church of England, *The Book of Common Prayer and Administration of the Sacraments and Rites ... to which is added the Gospel according to St. Mark, translated into the Mohawk Language by Capt. Joseph Brant* (London, 1787), 86, Catechism.
39. Ibid., 14–15, Morning Prayers.
40. Ibid., 8–10, Morning Prayers.
41. Ibid., 138, Genesis.
42. This summary of the Iroquois creation myth is a composite drawn from a number of sources. Each has a different ethnic origin (e.g., Mohawk, Onondaga, Seneca) and each offers slightly different aspects of the myth. See John Norton, *The Journal of Major John Norton* (1816), ed. Carl F. Klinck and James J. Talman (Toronto, 1970), 88–97, for an Onondaga version; Hazel W. Hertzberg, *The Great Tree and the Longhouse: The Culture of the Iroquois* (New York, 1966), 12–19, for a Cayuga version; J.N.B. Hewitt, "Iroquoian Cosmology," pt. I, Bureau of American Ethnology, *Annual Report, 1899–1900* (Washington, D. C., 1903), 141–339, for Onondaga, Seneca, and Mohawk versions.

43. Norton, *Journal of Major John Norton*, 91. Here is evidence of Jesuit missionaries and their catechumens syncretizing, or blending Catholic teachings with Iroquois beliefs: they substituted Teharonghyawago and his mother for Jesus Christ and the Virgin Mary respectively.
44. Church of England, *Book of Common Prayer*, 461–62, Baptism; Andrews to Secretary, 26 September 1717, SPG Letters A, vol. 12:339.
45. Andrews to Secretary, 17 October 1718, SPG Letters A, vol. 13:334–35.
46. Wilson, *Essay Towards an Instruction*, 96; J.N.B. Hewitt, "Orenda and a Definition of Religion," *American Anthropologist*, n. s., 4 (1902): 33–46. I thank Ives Goddard for pointing out to me that *orenda* is a Huron term that nineteenth-century Tuscarora ethnologist Hewitt used as a synechdoche for all Iroquois references to "spirit," despite the fact that each nation used a slightly different term due to differences in dialectics. Mohawks and Cayugas, for example, used the terms *orrenna* or *karenna*; Oneidas *olenna* or *kalenna*; Onondagas and Senecas, *gaenna* or *oenna*. See Hewitt, "Orenda," 33–46.
47. See, for example, William Andrews to Secretary, 26 September 1717, SPG Letters A, vol. 12:338; *idem*, 1 September 1717, SPG Letters A, vol. 12:328–29; John Stuart to Rev. Sir, 20 July 1772, SPG Letters B, vol. 2, no. 99 (folio 686–87); Minutes of SPG Meeting, 20 November 1772, SPG Journals, vol. 19:313–14; Stuart to Rev. Sir, 9 August 1774, SPG Letters B, vol. 2, no. 201 (folio 690); Minutes of SPG Meeting, 17 March 1775, SPG Journals, vol. 20:329; Stuart to Rev. Sir, 17 October 1775, SPG Letters B, vol. 2, no. 202 (folio 694); *idem*, 27 October 1775, SPG Letters B, vol. 2, no. 203 (folio 700); Minutes of SPG Meeting, 25 January 1782, SPG Journals, vol. 22:369; Memoir of John Stuart, n.d., *DHNY* (quarto) vol. 4:314.
48. Minutes of SPG Meeting, 17 February 1747/48, SPG Journals, vol. 11:89; *idem*, 20 May 1748, SPG Journals, vol. 11:22–23; *idem*, 20 December 1754, SPG Journals, vol. 12:406 (living at German Flatts); *idem*, 21 January 1725/26, SPG Journals, vol. 5:76; *idem*, 19 March 1730, SPG Journals, vol. 5:290; *idem*, 17 November 1758, SPG Journals, vol. 14:106 (instructing Palatines); *idem*, 19 March 1762, SPG Journals, vol. 15:203 (age); *idem*, 19 February 1762, SPG Journals, vol. 15:191 (teacher).
49. Minutes of SPG Meeting, 19 February 1762, SPG Journals, vol. 15:191; *idem*, 19 October 1770, SPG Journals, vol. 18:437–38; Schoolmaster at Canajohary to Johnson, 22 March 1764, *DHNY* (quarto) vol. 4:216–17.
50. Johnson to Arthur Lee, 28 February 1771, *DHNY* (quarto) vol. 4:270.
51. For the basis of the dispute between Barclay, Cornelius, and Daniel, see Barclay to Secretary, 12 March 1744/45, SPG Letters B, vol. 13, no. 314; *idem*, 21 October 1745, SPG Letters B, vol. 13, no. 316; Minutes of SPG Meeting, 15 November 1745, SPG Journals, vol. 10:83; *idem*, 18 April 1746, SPG Journals, vol. 10:124; Barclay to Secretary, 9 December 1746, SPG Letters B, vol. 14:99. Jacob Oel, a German minister operating in the German Flatts, took over the duties at Canajoharie after Old Abraham's death. Beginning with John Ogilvie's tenure as missionary and continuing into the American Revolution, the SPG appointed a series of white schoolmasters to teach white and Iroquois children at the Fort Hunter post. See, for example, evidence of Cornelius Bennett, who fled Fort Hunter in 1764 during a smallpox epidemic, Minutes of SPG Meeting, 15 March 1765, SPG Journals, vol. 16:329; *idem*, 15 November 1765, SPG Journals, vol. 16:469. Little Abraham, a Tiononderoge headman, extolled the benefits of Christianity to other Mohawks throughout the 1750s, '60s, and '70s but was not paid by the SPG. For Oel, see Minutes of SPG Meeting, 17 February

1747/48, SPG Journals, vol. 11:89; *idem*, 20 May 1748, SPG Journals, vol. 11:22–23; *idem*, 20 December 1754, SPG Journals, vol. 12:406 (living at German Flatts); *idem*, 21 January 1725/26, SPG Journals, vol. 5:76; *idem*, 19 March 1730, SPG Journals, vol. 5:290; *idem*, 17 November 1758, SPG Journals, vol. 16:106 (instructing Palatines); *idem*, 19 February 1762, SPG Journals, vol. 15:191 (teacher). A few Algonquian schoolmasters, educated by the dissenting minister, Eleazar Wheelock, taught school at some of the Mohawk villages in the 1760s and 1770s but were not recognized by the SPG. See Margaret Connell Szasz, *Indian Education in the American Colonies, 1607–1783* (Albuquerque, 1988). Most historians of missionary-Indian relations understand the concept of "reducing Indians" to mean to lessen their savagery and haughtiness, to tame them, to bring them to "civility." See Axtell, *Invasion Within*, chaps. 4 and 7. However, "reduce" also meant at this time "to lead back to." Christian theory held that all of humankind were once Christians, but a few unfortunates—Indians and Jews, for example—got lost and fell away from the faith. See Hart, "For the Good of Our Souls," 97–100.

52. Ogilvie to Rev. Sir, 27 July 1750, SPG Letters B, vol. 18, no. 102; Lydekker, *Faithful Mohawks*, 67; Ogilvie to Secretary, 14 April 1751, SPG Letters B, vol. 19, no. 71.

53. Ogilvie to Secretary, 14 April 1751, SPG Letters B, vol. 19, no. 71. Politeness, dissemblance, and refrainment from publicly contradicting others constituted Iroquois etiquette at this time. See John Webster Grant, *Moon of Wintertime: Missionaries and the Indians of Canada in Encounter since 1534* (Toronto, 1984), 250, and Richter, *Ordeal of the Longhouse*, 45.

54. Minutes of SPG Meeting, 25 January 1782, SPG Journals, vol. 22:368–69; *idem*, 20 December 1782, SPG Journals, vol. 23:2, 6–8 (Aaron Hill's letter). For a narrative of life for the Mohawks in Ontario, Canada, following the American Revolution, see Isabel Thompson Kelsay, *Joseph Brant, 1743–1807: Man of Two Worlds* (Syracuse, 1984), chaps. 18–29.

– Chapter 11 –

THE MAKING OF LOGAN, THE MINGO ORATOR

Edward G. Gray

HISTORICAL WRITING about the native societies of colonial North America has changed dramatically in recent years. In addition to its emphasis on Native American experiences and perspectives, this new work has established the diversity and distinctiveness of the various indigenous societies of North America. To speak of "Indians," we now know, is to invoke about as much cultural specificity as is suggested by the term "Europeans." Much like Europe, indigenous North America was a place of enormous diversity in language, belief, manners, and morals. Aside from transforming what was once assumed to be a virgin wilderness into a world a lot like our own—diverse, complex, and riddled with conflict—this new sensitivity to the cultural diversity of native North America presents an opportunity to reevaluate some old generalizations about Indian societies.[1]

Few such generalizations have been as pervasive as the assertion that the native peoples of North America have a unique and natural capacity for eloquent public speech. Indeed, in the eighteenth century, particularly during the decades of the American Revolution, it is difficult to find a case in which Euro-American commentators did not praise Native-American orators, attributing to them sobriety, formal genius, and, most of all, a capacity to move listeners' emotions and inspire them to action.[2] A closer look at some of the assumptions behind this praise suggests that, as portrayed by Europeans, Indian orators were typical not so much of actual Native American speakers but of an idealized primitive speaker, a speaker whose capacities included the unique ability to transcend the literary intrusions of interpreters.

Nowhere is this image more evident than in Euro-American writings about the popular Revolutionary-era Indian orator Soyechtowa, or Logan as he was more widely known. Logan's reputation as an orator came from a speech he delivered in 1774, as he conceded his people's defeat at the hands of a band of Virginia militiamen. The speech, as it has been handed down to us, is short enough to quote in full:

> I appeal to any white man to say, if ever he entered Logan's cabin hungry, and he gave him not meat; if ever he came cold and naked, and he clothed him not. During the course of the last long and bloody war, Logan remained idle in his cabin, an advocate for peace. Such was my love for the whites that my countrymen pointed as they passed, and said, "Logan is the friend of white men." I had even thought to have lived with you, but for the injuries of one man. Col. Cresap, the last spring, in cold blood, and unprovoked, murdered all the relations of Logan, not sparing even my women and children. There runs not a drop of my blood in the veins of any living creature. This called on me for revenge. I have sought it: I have killed many: I have fully glutted my vengeance. For my country, I rejoice at the beams of peace. But do not harbour a thought that mine is the joy of fear. Logan never felt fear. He will not turn on his heel to save his life. Who is there to mourn for Logan?—Not one.[3]

Logan's words acquired nearly immediate and lasting celebrity. Less than a year after he was reported to have delivered the speech, Thomas Jefferson remembered that it "became the theme of every conversation in Williamsburg."[4] James Madison was so impressed that in January 1775—as he and fellow Virginians were "very busy ... in raising men and procuring the necessaries for defending ourselves and our friends in case of a sudden invasion"—he took the time to send a copy to his friend William Bradford, who praised Logan's words for raising "a crowd of ideas and at one stroke [setting] in a strong light the barbarity of [his enemies], the sufferings of Logan and his contempt of death." So taken was he with the oration that Bradford saw it into print. "I thought it a pity," he explained to Madison, "that so fine a specimen ... should languish in obscurity and therefore gave a copy of it to my brother who inserted it in his paper; from which it has been transcribed into the others and has given the highest satisfaction to all that can admire and relish the simple beauties of nature."[5] In late winter of 1775 the speech found its way into newspapers in New York, Pennsylvania, Virginia, and even France. And through the 1780s the oration appeared in numerous European and American philosophical tracts as an example of the artfulness of Indian oratory. The most familiar of these is Thomas Jefferson's only published book, *Notes on the State of Virginia*.[6]

Jefferson's interest in Logan's speech had less to do with the plight it described than with what he perceived to be its more representative qualities—qualities that in Jefferson's view disproved European theories that American nature had a deleterious effect on human culture. "I may challenge the whole orations of Demosthenes and Cicero," he wrote, "and of any more eminent orator, if Europe has furnished more eminent, to produce a single passage, superior to the speech of Logan."[7] The claim—made principally by the French natural historian Le Comte de Buffon and the disillusioned Jesuit, and critic of colonization, the Abbé Raynal—that the humidity and variability of the American climate would forever prevent Americans from achieving the creative greatness of Europeans, Jefferson was suggesting, defied evidence of the sort Logan's speech represented.[8] The undeniable emotional power of Logan's speech, Jefferson argued, was all the more remarkable given that it emanated from a figure whose people lacked writing. Indeed, Jefferson compared these Native Americans to Europeans north of the Alps before the Roman conquest. Although the latter benefited from what Buffon, Raynal, and other philosophers of the age assumed to be a climate more favorable than any other to human genius and creativity, they too lacked what must be regarded as the greatest human technological achievement: alphabetic writing. Furthermore, Jefferson asked, "how many good poets, how many able mathematicians, how many great inventors in arts or sciences, had Europe north of the Alps then produced?"[9] What made Logan's speech important was thus not so much that it represented the highest levels of technological or creative achievement but that it cast doubt on the correlation between a moderate climate and human cultural growth.

If American Indians were comparable to preconquest Northern Europeans in terms of technology, in other ways Jefferson believed them to be closer to the conquering Romans—particularly in their form of government. For it was almost universally accepted in Jefferson's day that the Native American talent for eloquent speech was indicative of the republican nature of Indian government. "The principles of [Indian] society forbidding all compulsion," Jefferson explained, "they are to be led to duty and to enterprise by personal influence and persuasion. Hence eloquence in council, bravery and address in war, become the foundations of all consequence."[10] Expressing a similar view, one of Jefferson's political opponents, the Connecticut Federalist Jedediah Morse, exclaimed, "what civilized nations enforce upon their subjects by compulsory measures, [Indians] effect by their eloquence."[11] And earlier in the century, another writer explained that "speech making is the certain effect of a republican government. These Indians have such high notions of liberty, that there is not one slave among them, nor can anyone claim the least preeminence, but what his age and wisdom give him among his fellow citizens. The only way to shew this wisdom is by shining in councils, and public assemblies."[12] Given the state of Indian society, in other words, it made sense to assume, as the Jesuit father Le Jeune had of the Algonquians, that "all the authority of their chief is in his tongue's end; for he is powerful in so far as he is eloquent."[13] These remarks reverberate with echoes of a classical republican ideal in which persuasion, not coercion, held nations together and induced them to action. As Cicero explained in his *De Inventione*, "how could it have been brought to pass that men should learn to keep faith and observe justice and become accustomed to obey others voluntarily ... unless men had been able by eloquence to persuade their fellows of the truth of what they had discovered?"[14] On the basis of such reasoning, Jefferson and others portrayed Logan as a vanquished chief or sachem whose gift for eloquent speech befitted his elevated station among his people. There is, however, good reason to believe that in Logan's case, anyway, the connection between eloquence and authority was, at best, an exaggeration; at worst, a downright fabrication. The evidence for this lies partly in what little is known about Logan's past.

He spent his childhood and early adult life in central Pennsylvania, at the town of Shamokin, a town inhabited by Iroquois migrants known as Mingos. His father, Shikellamy, had been an important figure in the town; but contrary to what earlier biographical accounts suggest, he was not a sachem, but rather a go-between, serving as an Iroquois liaison and diplomat in central and western Pennsylvania. Although Pennsylvania provincial authorities urged one of Shikellamy's sons to succeed him in this role, it seems clear that that son was not Logan, but his older brother, Tachnechdorus. Even if Logan was able to achieve some influence, events conspired to deny him much opportunity to exercise that influence. The French and Indian war devastated Shamokin, and Logan's efforts to remain neutral compromised his reputation among both White and Indian allies. With no village to return to and little real influence among the native peoples of western Pennsylvania, the end of the War left him with little to lead. After several years' residence in Mifflin County, Logan moved with his family to the Ohio Valley, west of Pittsburgh, and it was there that he became involved in the series of events that culminated in what would come to be known as Lord Dunmore's War.[15]

In the spring of 1774, while Logan was on a trading mission up the Ohio River, a band of squatters, allegedly led by the failed Maryland merchant and farmer Michael Cresap, attacked and murdered members of Logan's home camp. The attack left as many as nine Mingos dead, among them Logan's mother, brother, and sister. Logan responded with a series of retaliatory strikes against Whites in the region. This, in turn, allowed Virginia's governor, Lord Dunmore, to justify a military campaign to wrest parts of the Ohio country from Mingo and Shawnee occupants. While Dunmore's military campaign was ultimately indecisive, Shawnee leaders chose to accept a negotiated settlement rather than risk further bloodshed.[16]

At the start of these negotiations, Logan delivered a personal statement to be carried by messenger to Dunmore. The statement, as transmitted by Dunmore's agent, the militiaman, fur trader, and interpreter John Gibson, became Logan's famed oration. According to Gibson, Logan approached him at a preliminary meeting underway at a Shawnee camp and requested that together they take leave of the meeting so that Logan could make a personal statement to his enemy, Dunmore. As Gibson explained it, in "a copse of wood ... [we] sat down, when Logan, after shedding [an] abundance of tears, delivered to [me] the speech."[17]

Writing in his *Notes*, Jefferson offered an explanation for Logan's motives that has since become part of Logan lore, but that in fact presumed that Logan addressed Gibson from a position of authority. That position, in Jefferson's mind, was confirmed by the measures Logan took to preserve his honor. For Jefferson, "so distinguished a chief" chose not to address Dunmore and his agents because he could not make a compact with the people who murdered his family.[18] At the same time Logan was selfless enough to see that such an accord would save the lives of his own people. Jefferson's analysis suggests the possibility of an alternative scenario in which Logan would have directly addressed the diplomatic council, and would have been in a position to shape opinion and influence negotiations. In all probability, however, Logan was never an integral or influential member of the Shawnee delegation.

While no doubt he was known by provincial authorities and other Iroquois and Shawnee groups in the region, Logan's influence, even among his fellow Mingos, was minimal. Indeed, when Logan initially approached Gibson, he did so, according to Gibson, not as an actual participant in negotiations but as an uninvited outsider. Far from a proud sachem or an imposing member of the tribal council, Logan was probably a peripheral figure—the refugee second son of a father who had straddled two worlds and never acquired much influence in either.[19]

If biographical details cast doubt on Jefferson's depiction of Logan as a chief, what little is known about northeastern Indian speechways raises even more questions about the assumption that Indian leaders were by definition eloquent orators. Indeed, if in fact Logan was a gifted orator, this may have marked him not so much as an Indian leader but as a mere spokesman or tribal functionary with no real power. Although one of the ways for northeastern Indian leaders to distinguish themselves was with oratorical talent, leaders who were gifted speakers often did not reveal this talent to European agents or diplomats. Instead, they regularly relied on spokesmen—such as Logan may at some point have been—chosen for their abilities as public speakers and commonly mistaken for headmen or chiefs.[20] These spokesmen, the French Jesuit Father Joseph François Lafitau explained, had to possess "knowledge of councils, a complete knowledge of all their ancestor's ways, wit, experience and eloquence. Not considered at all in the qualifications is whether they are of a ranking maternal household; their personal merits and talents are the only things considered."[21] None of this, however, gave them singular authority. They functioned, instead, as the collective voice of a group of headmen, who often punctuated diplomatic oratory with ritual shouts that affirmed group unity. As one observer of an Iroquois council explained, "in their Treaties with the white people, or by white people to them, they make the Io ... han, or shout of Approbation, which is performed thus: The speaker, after a pause, in a slow Tone pronounces the U—huy; all the other Sachems in perfect Silence: so soon as he stops, they all with one voice, in exact Time, begin one general Io', raising and falling their Voices as the Arch of a Circle."[22] Such practices meant that White negotiators rarely negotiated with a single, authoritative voice but with spokesmen who spoke for the whole group, the Io ... han indicating the speaker's conformity with tribal opinion.

Another assumption implied by Jefferson's portrayal of Logan is that a Native American orator might speak apart from his community—as some sort of isolated, yet dignified speech-giver. In reality, northeastern Indian orators rarely acted alone. As they delivered their messages, Father Lafitau tells us, Indian spokesmen usually had near them "one or two persons to remind him what he is to say, to refresh his memory on what decisions have been reached and to watch that he says things in proper order."[23] This is not to say that orators had no influence over the course of council meetings. As the historian Daniel Richter has written, "the greatest of Iroquois orators were far more than mouthpieces. In an oral culture they were the repositories of ancient wisdom, the masters of diplomatic protocol, and the purveyors of the powerful words of condolence and peace. The few who possessed the skill and talent wielded enormous influence." They were in a position, that is, to manipulate dialogue through both their words and their gestures. But this in no way meant that they had anything like singular or unilateral authority.[24]

One final aspect of Jefferson's portrayal of Logan's motives deserves scrutiny, and that is the very notion that Native American leaders—by definition—used the spoken word as the primary means of expressing their authority. In fact, for local elders, silence more than speech was often a mark of social distinction. In the early seventeenth century, William Wood observed that among the Massachusett "[he] that speaks seldom and opportunely, being as good as his word, is the only man they love." "Garrulity," on the other hand, "is much condemned of them."[25] Writing of Huron and Algonquian headmen, Lafitau further noted that "as the chiefs consider one another, and as none wishes to appear to arrogate to himself any superiority which might arouse jealousy, they manage themselves more than others in the councils; and, although they may be its guiding spirit, political expediency obliges them to talk little and listen to others' opinions rather than express their own."[26]

Leaders' sense of propriety and restraint is also suggested in what some European observers regarded as an inordinately deliberate and rehearsed approach to negotiations, an approach dictated in part, no doubt, by the fact that spokesmen generally did not have the authority to make unilateral agreements. As recorded in one treaty between the Iroquois and the three colonies of Pennsylvania, Virginia, and Maryland, "after a short pause, the Governor ordered the Interpreter to tell the Indians, that as they had greatly exceeded their appointed Time for meeting the Commissioners, he recommended to them to use all the Expedition possible in giving their answer to what had been said." In response to this, the Iroquois spokesman "repeated to the Interpreter the substance of what the

Governor had spoke; in order to know if he had understood him right (a method generally made use of by the Indians) and ... proceeded to return the thanks of the Six Nations for the Governor's kind Advice, promising to follow it as far as lay in their Power; but ... they would take time till the afternoon ... and would then give their Answer."[27] Elsewhere, the colonial traveler and natural historian John Bartram recalled learning from an official interpreter to an Onandaga council that, "there is nothing [the Indians] condemn so much as precipitation in publick councils; indeed they esteem it at all times a mark of much levity in any one to return an immediate answer to a serious question however obvious, and they consequently spin out a treaty, where many points are to be moved, to a great length of time."[28] When relating to Whites, in particular, it appears that northeastern Indians resorted to silence as a means of controlling the pace and course of ambiguous social situations. For Indian leaders were well aware that the spoken word, unlike the written, was irretrievable. Beyond this, highly ritualized Indian speaking protocol may have functioned as a mechanism for social control. By limiting and formalizing the range of expression available to Indian orators, native societies secured the authority of their nonspeaking leaders.[29]

* * * *

GIVEN THE APPARENT DISPARITIES between Jefferson's portrayal of Native American oratory and the actual practice of public speaking in northeastern Indian societies, it is perhaps not surprising to find that the authenticity of Logan's speech—as Jefferson presented it—has been the source of controversy, at least since 1797, when one of Jefferson's political enemies—the Maryland Federalist Luther Martin—began publishing accusations that Jefferson fabricated the speech. In addition to being marred by political partisanship, it seems that Martin's judgments also were influenced by personal passion. Michael Cresap, the Maryland squatter who Jefferson portrays as the murderer of innocent women and children, happens to have been Martin's father-in-law. Jefferson, however, took the accusation seriously enough to append a collection of affidavits to the 1800 edition of the *Notes*.[30] While there is almost no evidence to suggest that Jefferson knowingly manipulated the form or content of Logan's speech, one question about its authenticity is relevant for the purposes of this essay: was the speech a work of translation? Jefferson clearly accepted it as such, and this position would have been consistent with his assumptions about eastern Indian communication practices—assumptions that were somewhat better grounded than those concerning the relationship between eloquence and authority.

Although Logan's contact with English speakers had been lifelong, and a number of accounts testify to his competence in the language, a preference for his native tongue would have been consistent with Iroquois custom.[31] Eastern native peoples generally refused to conduct diplomatic discussion in any language but their own, even though they often were bilingual. As Witham Marsh, a member of a Maryland delegation to a 1744 Iroquois council reported, "most of them understood English, though they will not speak it when they are in treaty."[32] Even in discussions between two distinct Native groups, Indians tended to rely on interpreters rather than capitulate to other nations by speaking a language not their own. Hence, the North Carolina trader John Lawson explained that "the most powerful of these [North Carolina Indians] scorns to treat or trade with any others (of fewer numbers and less power) in any other tongue but their own."[33]

For Jefferson, this aspect of Native-American life explained the staggering number of distinct Native American tongues—"probably twenty in America for one in Asia."[34] In an undated manuscript note in his own copy of the *Notes*, he wrote that "we know that the Indians consider it as dishonorable to use any language but their own. Hence in their councils with us, though some of them may have been in situations which from convenience or necessity have obliged them to learn our language well, yet they refuse to confer in it, and always insist on the intervention of an interpreter, tho he may understand neither language so well as themselves." The general consequence of this, in Jefferson's mind, was a self-imposed linguistic difference that encouraged social and political disintegration. When "a faction of a tribe from domestic feuds has broken off from its main body to which it is held by no law or compact," he added, "and has gone to another settlement, may it not be the point of honor with them not to use the language of those with whom they have quarreled, but to have one of their own[?]"[35] Jefferson was suggesting that the same absence of coercive government that made eloquence so meaningful in Indian societies left those societies to resolve internal disputes with the crude tactic of linguistic atomization.

While Jefferson's general sense that Indians preferred to speak their mother tongue may have been valid, his explanation for the phenomenon as a matter of impulse, passion, pride, and the absence of legal obligation is less convincing. Aside from the greater clarity of thought and understanding that comes from speaking one's native tongue, it is likely that Native peoples made this choice for concrete social reasons. Linguists studying polyglot societies have long observed the practice among bilingual people of using specific tongues or dialects in specific social situations. A familiar example of this is the practice of using some dominant language—English, for example—in public situations, while retaining a regional dialect or language—such as Spanish, in the United States—for more intimate, familial interactions. Doing so allows speakers to affirm traditional identities, patterns of thought, and social ties. Ethnolinguists have identified similar processes among multilingual indigenous peoples in South America. As one scholar has written of peoples living in the Northwest Amazon River basin, in oral exchanges, "each individual initially speaks in his own father-language ... in order to assert his tribal affiliation and identification."[36] We can conjecture that something similar to this occurred in early American diplomatic councils: bilingual Indians used their nation's tongue as a way of affirming group allegiance in the presence not only of Europeans but also of members of their own and other kin groups.

Given the likelihood that Logan would have delivered his speech in his own tongue, it is remarkable how rarely his admirers acknowledged the translator's probable influence on the shape of the oration.[37] This is not to say that they failed to acknowledge any impact whatsoever. In his remarks to Bradford about the speech, Madison asked him to "make allowances for the unskillfullness of the Interpreter," and Jefferson himself recognized that the quality of the various transcriptions of the speech might have varied somewhat.[38] But neither writer suggested that translation might explain the oration's distinctive qualities—including the obvious allusions in the first line to Matthew 25 or in the final line to Deuteronomy 32.[39] Nor did they acknowledge the probability that Gibson considerably condensed what he heard. As an experienced interpreter, he no doubt was practiced in formulating the words of others into close, but abbreviated versions of what was said. For the common practice at Anglo-Indian diplomatic councils was for the interpreter to speak at the end of an Indian oration, conveying the substance of a speech, while permitting the audience to interpret much of its content from gesture, tone, and demeanor.[40]

One might simply attribute this confidence in the authenticity of the speech to careless scholarship on the part of Logan's admirers. But given the logic of eighteenth-century language philosophy, this explanation seems unlikely. More probably, they assumed a certain intellectual affinity between Logan and his interpreter—an affinity that muted the effects of translation.[41]

To begin with, Bradford's point that Logan's oration raised "a crowd of ideas ... at one stroke,"[42] suggests that what was singular about the oration was that it was closer to poetry than to prose. Its strength lay in its powers of evocation, powers that transcended verbiage by appealing to a universal language of feelings. That Logan spoke in this way was perfectly consistent with prevailing eighteenth-century assumptions about the relationship between speech and social refinement. The foundation of those assumptions was the belief that the diversity of the world's languages was not the result of a primordial catastrophe, as Christians had assumed for millennia, but a reflection of the diversity of human experience itself. And in the case of the most refined peoples, the nature of that experience yielded languages rich in their vocabularies and systematic in their grammars. Conversely, the narrower the range of experience, the narrower a people's vocabulary and the less systematic their grammars. Hence, only those peoples forming wide and diverse social ties—those nations that incorporated groups with different habits and languages—could experience linguistic refinement, since it was only those nations that were forced to assimilate the words and concepts of others. In doing so, they introduced novel terms, representing experiences they themselves had not had; such terms were therefore abstract terms, lacking for most speakers any palpable relation to experience. In addition, only expanding, sociable nations standardized and codified inflections. As Adam Smith explained, "when two nations came to be mixed with one another, either by conquest or migration ... each nation, in order to make itself intelligible to those with whom it was under the necessity of conversing, would be obliged to learn the language of the other." Without grammatical and lexical innovation, this could result in a vocabulary expanded to the point of incomprehensibility, leaving people "extremely perplexed by the intricacy of its declensions and conjugations."[43] For nations experiencing social expansion, however, a natural process of accommodation and simplification eventually would yield a standard set of inflections applicable to the diverse experiences of diverse constituencies. Rather than an enormous array of nouns signifying different actions, such nations would formulate a limited number of verb infinitives and conjugations.

According to this doctrine, the evolution of language was not without its costs. As language grew more complex and refined, speech grew alienated from feeling. That is why, according to the

Scottish social theorist and historian Adam Ferguson, poetic genius diminished as nations aged. The poet of former times "delivers the emotions of the heart, in words suggested by the heart: for he knows no other [and] he appears to speak from inspiration, not from invention; and to be guided in the choice of his thoughts by a supernatural instinct, not by reflection." All of this was because "the language of early ages, is in one respect, simple and confined; in another, it is varied and free: it allows liberties, which, to the poet of after times, are denied."[44]

The connection between eloquence and verbal primitivism commonly was thought to be revealed not only in the emotional content of primitive speech but in the very character of Indian languages themselves. "I am convinced," wrote the Moravian missionary John Heckewelder, that Logan's speech was "delivered precisely as it is related to us, with this only difference, that it possessed a force and expression in the Indian language which it is impossible to transmit into our own."[45] And in prefatory remarks to a Creek oration, one eighteenth-century writer explained, "it is impossible to do it justice in our language, which is very different from the Indian Phraseology. The Indian orators have a certain loftiness of expression, boldness of figures, and pomp of imagery, which we want abilities to naturalize." The reason for this was that "tho' their language has but few roots, yet they render it copious and extremely fit for oratory, by varying, compounding, and decompounding their words, and by having constant recourse to metaphors, & c."[46]

Without the abstract terms and complex verbiage of refined societies, so the reasoning went, the uneducated or "uncivilized" experienced none of the alienation of words from the feelings they excited. When a "savage" spoke, he did so from the heart; his language was thus no mere representation of reality. It was not simply a collection of signs with no necessary relation to human experience but instead was a collection of symbols intrinsically related to sensations.[47] Applying this reasoning, one early-nineteenth-century Euro-American commentator explained that, "[Indians] utter what their subject inspires and never advert to approved models as their standard." In the end, "this is more pleasing and powerful than the smooth harmony of studied [tongues]."[48]

No eighteenth-century thinker made more of the loss that came with linguistic refinement than Jean-Jacques Rousseau. For him, the most primitive speech consisted not merely of words but of the exchange of passions through all those things that denote passion, all those things that are shaped not by convention—grammar, vocabulary, and syntax—but by natural human emotions: "accents, cries, lamentations." Such speech was, quite simply, poetry or even song—the media of sensation and feeling. As Rousseau explained, "it would have to correspond to its initial object, presenting to the senses as well as to the understanding the almost inevitable impression of the feeling that it seeks to communicate," all of which would allow it to "persuade without convincing, and ... represent without reasoning." Rousseau lamented the dissipation of such speech for the simple reason that a person's speech could never be true to his natural feelings when obstructed by the complex conventions and rehearsed patterns of modern languages. "To the degree that needs multiply, that affairs become complicated, that light is shed, language ... becomes more regular and less passionate. It substitutes ideas for feelings. It no longer speaks to the heart but to reason.... Language becomes more exact and clearer, but more prolix, duller and colder."[49]

This reasoning explains in part why Logan was so often spoken of in the company of another exemplar of passionate and moving speech: the third-century Scottish bard Ossian. In 1760 and 1763 the Scottish poet and critic James Macpherson published a collection of verse recounting the valor and virtue of ancient Scottish tribes that he claimed was composed by Ossian and handed down through the centuries by word of mouth.[50] Writing in 1806, the Scottish-trained physician and professor of botany at the University of Pennsylvania, Benjamin Smith Barton, declared that Logan's speech "would not have disparaged one of Ossian's heroes."[51] One year earlier, another Euro-American commentator defended the natural poetic brilliance of Ossian and Logan: "Who at this day, except the untutored sons of nature, can utter the language of Ossian and Homer? What man, trammeled with the forms of modern art, can speak like Logan? The language of nature alone can arrest attention, persuade, convince, and terrify; and such is the language of the Indians."[52] Jefferson's own remarks about Ossian—made in a letter to Charles Macpherson just two years before Logan delivered his speech—could just as well have characterized his response to Logan's words: "The tender, and the sublime emotions of the mind were never before so finely wrought up."[53] But perhaps no remark better conveys the perceived affinity of Logan and Ossian than Adam Ferguson's general point that "the artless song of the savage, the heroic legend of the bard, have sometimes a magnificent beauty, which no change of language can improve, and no refinements of the critic reform."[54] Both figures, because of the literalness of their words, upheld an idiom of transcendence, an idiom that communicated emotion despite the literary intrusions of translators and critics.

Similar thinking informed the rather perverse notion that the best interpreters had to be as culturally debased as Indian orators supposedly were. "Considering the interpreters who have undertaken to give the meaning of Indian speeches, it is not a little surprising that some of them should approach so near to perfection," the mayor of New York City, Dewitt Clinton, explained in the first decade of the nineteenth century. "The major part of the interpreters," he continued, "were illiterate persons, sent among [the Indians] to conciliate their favor, by making useful or ornamental implements; or they were prisoners who learnt the Indian language during captivity." Such persons, without the burdensome baggage of a liberal education and refined speech, could best convey the allegedly irrational, impulsive thoughts, feelings, and physical movements of Indian orators. The well-educated and highly rational, on the other hand, struggled to convey the full meaning of Indian speech. As Clinton explained, "the Reverend Mr. Kirkland, a missionary among the Oneidas, and sometimes a public interpreter, was indeed a man of liberal education; but those who have seen him officiate at public treaties must recollect how incompetent he was to infuse the fire of Indian oratory into his expressions; how he labored for words, and how feeble and inelegant his language."[55] A speaker like Kirkland grew flustered because he had been conditioned to having precise terms with which to express all his thoughts. An uncivil frontiersman, on the other hand, had developed a range of skills that allowed him to compensate for a limited vocabulary.

For the same reasons that education and social refinement were liabilities for translators, so one of their crucial abilities, in the minds of some, was the capacity to replicate the nonrational, or nonverbal, elements of Native American speech. The early-eighteenth-century colonial official and historian of the Iroquois, Cadwallader Colden, for example, recalled one occasion when "after the [Indian] speaker had employ'd a considerable time in haranguing with much elocution, the interpreter often explained the whole by one single sentence." The danger of this was that a "hesitating tongue" may leave an Indian oration appearing "mean" and faint but "a skillful interpreter may strongly move our passions by their lively images."[56] Colden was saying that, more than simply conveying verbiage, a skilled interpreter conveyed emotion; that is, like an artful orator or a gifted actor, a master interpreter was able to leave listeners with a deep and heartfelt sense of the authenticity and accuracy of his words—and that sense came not simply from utterances but also from manner, tone, and gesture. Significantly, this view was consistent with the widely held eighteenth-century belief that the uneducated or the deficient—children, the deaf, the insane, and "primitive" peoples—compensated for linguistic and mental inferiority with gesture and movement. Such people, lacking the capacity for precise speech, were forced to express themselves through the emotional prisms of bodily movement and facial expression.[57]

There is one final point that should be made about the presumed authenticity of Logan's speech. A well known eighteenth-century literary ideal was that of "sincerity," or, in the words of Lionel Trilling, a perfect "congruence between feeling and avowal."[58] When Rousseau, Ferguson, and Logan's admirers characterized unrefined or primitive speech, they did so in the context of this familiar eighteenth-century quest for a voice that defied the unnatural manipulations of transcribers and translators—that is, a voice freed from the layers of social convention that intervened between speakers and their feelings. If understood as a speaker of "sincere" speech, Logan would be unable to inspire in audiences emotions and sentiments he himself did not feel. What he communicated, indeed the very language he spoke, would be, in a certain sense, transparent: unencumbered by the refinements of polite society, it would be incapable of concealing the speaker's truest feelings—incapable of being duplicitous, Machiavellian rhetoric.

Perhaps in the minds of Jefferson and others Logan's marriage of true feeling to expression, and the frontiersman Gibson's lack of social refinement, amounted to a frontier literary economy unencumbered by verbal artifice and therefore unable to conceal the basic impulses and sentiments of speakers. Translation on the frontier, according to this doctrine, would have been less an act of literary intervention than a crude act of dictation made possible by the universality of basic human feelings.

* * * *

As HIS EUROPEAN ADMIRERS came to know him, Logan was shaped by an array of eighteenth-century assumptions about oratory, language, and translation. Chief among these was the notion that a talent for affecting speech was a natural attribute of leaders in undeveloped societies. And the power of that speech, what allowed it to defy the manipulation of transcribers and interpreters, was that it was inspired not by abstract rational thought but by the most natural and universal of human feelings. Not surprisingly, this transcendent idiom had lasting appeal. Editors included Logan's oration in McGuffey's *Fourth* and *Fifth Reader*; and one mid-nineteenth-century commentator wrote, "no piece of composition ever did more, if so much, as the speech of Logan ... to form the mind and develop the latent energies of the youthful American orator. Its influence has extended even into the halls of Congress, and has been felt upon the bench and in the bar of this nation; nay more, the American pulpit has been graced by energies which that speech has, in its warmest simplicity, called forth."[59]

The orator himself seems to have met a much less noble end. In late 1780, after retreating as far west as Detroit and serving in the Revolutionary War on the side of the British, Logan was killed, allegedly by a member of his own Iroquois band.[60]

Notes

1. See the excellent discussion in Colin G. Calloway, *The American Revolution in Indian Country: Crisis and Diversity in Native American Communities* (Cambridge, England, 1995), prologue and *passim*.
2. See for instance, the comments collected in Julian P. Boyd, ed., *Indian Treaties Printed by Benjamin Franklin, 1736–1762* (Philadelphia, 1938).
3. This is the version in Jefferson's *Notes on the State of Virginia* ([paperback ed., New York, 1954], 63) and it seems to be the most widely quoted one. Edward D. Seeber, "Critical Views on Logan's Speech," *Journal of American Folklore* 60, no. 236 (April–June, 1947): 143–46.
4. Jefferson to Governor Henry, 31 Dec. 1797, in Jefferson, *Notes*, 227.
5. Madison to Bradford, 20 Jan. 1775, and Bradford to Madison, 3–6? March 1775, in William T. Hutchinson and William M.E. Rachal, eds., *The Papers of James Madison* (Chicago, 1962), 1:135, 138.
6. Newspapers that published the speech were: *Pennsylvania Journal* (1 Feb. 1775), *Pennsylvania Ledger* (11 Feb. 1775), *New-York Gazette* (13 Feb. 1775), Rivington's *New York Gazetteer* (16 Feb. 1775), *Virginia Gazette* (4 Feb. 1775), *Gazette de France* (21 April 1775), and *Journal historique et littéraire* (May, 1775). Among the philosophical works that reprinted versions are, Abbé Raynal, *Histoire ... des deux Indes* (Geneva, 1780), IX:76–77; Abbé Robin, *Nouveaux Voyage dans l'Amerique septentrionale* (Philadelphia et Paris, 1782), 146–47; Joseph Mandrillon, *Précis sur l'Amérique septentrionale* (Amsterdam, 1783), 229–30. On the printing history of the speech, see Seeber's "Critical Views," 130–46, and his "Chief Logan's Speech in France," *Modern Language Notes* 61, no. 6 (1946): 412–16.
7. Jefferson, *Notes*, 62.
8. The eighteenth-century debate over the American environment is treated in Gilbert Chinard, "Eighteenth Century Theories of America as a Human

Habitat," *Proceedings of the American Philosophical Society* 91, no. 1 (Feb., 1947): 27–57; Ralph N. Miller, "American Nationalism as a Theory of Nature," *The William and Mary Quarterly*, 3d ser., vol. 12, no. 1 (1955): 74–95; and Antonello Gerbi, *The Dispute of the New World: The History of a Polemic, 1750–1900*, trans. Jeremy Moyle (Pittsburgh, 1973).
9. Jefferson, *Notes*, 63.
10. Ibid., 62.
11. Jedediah Morse, *The American Geography* ... (Elizabethtown, NJ, 1789), 18. See also De Witt Clinton, "Address before the New York Historical Society on the Iroquois or Six Nations," in *The Life and Writings of De Witt Clinton*, ed. William W. Campbell (New York, 1849), 237–38.
12. William Smith, *Some Account of the North American Indians* ... (London, 1754), 40.
13. Reuben G. Thwaites, ed., *The Jesuit Relations and Allied Documents* (Cleveland, 1897), 6: 243. Also, William Smith, *The History of the Province of New York* ... (London, 1767), 40; and Benjamin Franklin, "The Savages of North America," in *The Works of Benjamin Franklin*, ed., John Bigelow (New York, 1904), 10:386.
14. Cicero, *De Inventione*, trans., H.M. Hubbell (Cambridge, MA, 1949), 7.
15. For Logan's family background, I have relied mostly on James H. Merrell, "Shickellamy, 'A Person of Consequence,'" in *Northeastern Indian Lives, 1632–1816*, ed. Robert. S. Grumet (Amherst, 1996), 227–57. Earlier biographical accounts—which attribute to Logan more power than he had—include, Reuben Gold Thwaites and Louise Phelps Kellog, eds., *Documentary History of Dunmore's War, 1774* (Madison, 1905), 305–306, n. 21; and Franklin B. Sawvel, *Logan The Mingo* (Boston, 1921),12–14.
16. On Dunmore's War, Thwaites and Kellog, *Documentary History of Dunmore's War*; and Eric Hinderaker, *Elusive Empires: Constructing Colonialism in the Ohio Valley, 1673–1800* (Cambridge, England, 1997), ch. 5.
17. Jefferson, *Notes*, 234.
18. Ibid., 63.
19. Ibid., 234. Richard White has written that "Kayashuta and White Mingo were the Mingo Chiefs. Logan was merely a war leader, the Indian equivalent of Cresap." *The Middle Ground: Indians, Empires, and Republics in the Great Lakes Region, 1650–1815* (Cambridge, England, 1991), 358.
20. Daniel K. Richter, *The Ordeal of the Longhouse: The Peoples of the Iroquois League in the Era of European Colonization* (Chapel Hill, 1992), 46.
21. Father Joseph François Lafitau, *Customs of the American Indians Compared with the Customs of Primitive Times* (Toronto, 1974), 1:298.
22. Conrad Weiser, "An Account of the First Confederacy of the SIX NATIONS, their present Tributaries ...," in *The Treaty Held with the Indians of the Six Nations, At Lancaster, in Pennsylvania, in June 1744* ... (Williamsburg, n.d.), ix, repr. in *Iroquois Indians: A Documentary History of the Diplomacy of the Six Nations and Their League*, ed. Francis Jennings et al. (Woodbridge, CT, 1985, microfilm), reel 12.
23. Lafitau, *Customs of the American Indians*, 1:298.
24. Richter, *Ordeal of the Long House*, 47. Also see, Nancy L. Hagedorn, "'A Friend To Go between Them': The Interpreter as Cultural Broker during the Anglo-Iroquois Councils, 1740–70," *Ethnohistory* 35, no. 1 (Winter, 1988): 60–80.
25. William Wood, *New England's Prospect*, ed. Alden T. Vaughan (Amherst, 1977), 91–92.
26. Lafitau, *Customs of the American Indians*, 1:297.

27. *A Treaty between Pennsylvania, Virginia, and Maryland and the Six Nations at Lancaster* (Philadelphia, 1744), 6, in *Indian Treaties Printed by Benjamin Franklin, 1736–1762*, ed. Boyd, 46.
28. John Bartram, *Observations on the Inhabitants, Soil, Rivers, Productions, Animals* ... (1751; repr., Rochester, 1895), 58–59.
29. On the socio-politics of oratory, see Maurice Bloch's "Introduction" to *Political Language and Oratory in Traditional Society*, ed. Maurice Bloch (London, 1975), esp. 12–22. Though it focuses on a different region in a much later time period, Keith Basso's work on Apache silence is highly suggestive. See especially, "'To Give up on Words': Silence in Western Apache Culture," in *Language and Social Context*, ed. Pier Paolo Giglioli (London, 1972), 67–86. This function of silence is also touched on in Peter Burke, "Notes for a Social History of Silence," in his *The Art of Conversation* (Ithaca, 1993), esp., 134–35 and *passim*; and George Steiner, "Silence and the Poet," in his *Language and Silence: Essays on Language, Literature, and the Inhuman* (1967; paperback ed., New York, 1974), 36–54. Also see Christopher Looby, *Voicing America: Language, Literary Form, and the Origins of the United States* (Chicago, 1996), 86–96. For a more general treatment of the politics of speaking and not speaking, see Greg Dening, *Mr. Bligh's Bad Language: Passion, Power and Theatre on the Bounty* (Cambridge, England, 1992), 55–87.
30. On the controversy surrounding the speech, see Jefferson, *Notes*, n. 1, 298–300. The partisan political attacks on Jefferson's *Notes* are discussed in Linda K. Kerber, *Federalists in Dissent: Imagery and Ideology in Jeffersonian America* (Ithaca, 1970), 68–71.
31. On the likelihood that Logan spoke English, "Narrative of Captive John Slover," in *A Selection of Some of the Most Interesting Narratives of Outrages Committed by the Indians in Their Wars with the White People*, ed. Archibald Loudon (1808; repr., New York, 1971), 22. Slover reports being taken to Wachatomakak, a town of Mingos and Shawnees who spoke English "easily, having been often at Fort Pitt." In addition, William Robinson, taken prisoner by Logan, claimed Logan spoke English well; Jefferson, *Notes*, 242.
32. Witham Marshe, "Journal of the Treaty ... at Lancaster, Pennsylvania, June, 1744," in *Collections of the Massachusetts Historical Society*, 1st ser., vol. 7 (1800): 180; Jefferson, *Notes*, 282. James H. Merrell touches on this in *The Indians' New World: Catawbas and Their Neighbors from European Contact through the Era of Removal* (Chapel Hill, 1989), 147–148. Michael K. Foster's work on diplomatic speech is also suggestive. See, e.g., "On Who Spoke First at Iroquois-White Councils: An Exercise in the Method of Upstreaming," in *Extending the Rafters: Interdisciplinary Approaches to Iroquoian Studies*, ed. M.K. Foster, J. Campisi, and M. Mithun (Albany, 1984), 183–207. On linguistic prejudice among native peoples themselves, see also Lafitau, *Customs of the American Indians*, 2:264.
33. John Lawson, *A New Voyage to Carolina* (1709, reprint ed., Chapel Hill, 1967), 233.
34. Jefferson, *Notes*, 102.
35. Ibid., 282.
36. Arthur P. Sorenson, "Multilingualism in the Northwest Amazon," *American Anthropologist* 69, no. 6 (1967): 678. Also, Jean Jackson, "Language Identity of the Columbian Vaupés Indians," in *Explorations in the Ethnography of Speaking*, ed. Richard Bauman and Joel Sherzer (Cambridge, England, 1974), 50–64. Useful introductions to the matters of language choice, diglossia, and multilingualism can be found in Suzanne Romaine, *Language in Society: An Introduction to Sociolinguistics* (Oxford, 1994), ch. 2; and John Edwards, *Multilingualism*

(London, 1994), 83–88. For some compelling general remarks on the politics of language choice, see Clifford Geertz, *The Interpretation of Cultures* (New York, 1973), 241–43.
37. Some of the ways this process has shaped later Native American speeches are explored in Harry Robie, "Red Jacket's Reply: Problems in the Verification of a Native American Speech Text," *New York Folklore* 7, nos. 3–4 (1986): 99–117; and Rudolph Kaiser, "Chief Seattle's Speech(es): American Origins and European Conceptions," in *Recovering the Word: Essays in Native American Literature*, ed. Brian Swann and Arnold Krupat (Berkeley, 1987), 497–536.
38. Madison to Bradford, 20 Jan. 1775, in Hutchinson and Rachal, *The Papers of James Madison*, 1:136; Jefferson, *Notes*, 228.
39. Seeber, "Critical Views," 142.
40. Foster, "On Who Spoke First," 203, n. 5.
41. There is much recent scholarship on the relation between Indian speakers and European critics, translators, and transcribers. Particularly suggestive is Hertha Wong's work on late-nineteenth and early-twentieth-century Indian autobiographies. See her, *Sending My Heart Back Across the Years: Tradition and Innovation in Native-American Autobiography* (New York, 1992), 88–91. Mary Louise Pratt argues for a similar collaborative literature of the "contact zone"; see her, "Arts of the Contact Zone," in *Profession* (1991): 33–40; and "Criticism of the Contact Zone: Decentering Community and Nation," in *Critical Theory, Cultural Politics, and Latin American Narrative* (Notre Dame, 1993), 83–102. This work represents an adjustment of Arnold Krupat's earlier emphasis on the overwhelming Euro-American dominance and manipulation of "as told to" autobiographies to the point that any authentic Native-American voice is all but eliminated. Krupat, *For Those Who Come After: A Study of Native American Autobiography* (Berkeley, 1985).
42. Bradford to Madison, 3–6? March 1775, in Hutchinson and Rachal, *The Papers of James Madison*, 1:138.
43. Adam Smith, "Considerations Concerning the First Formation of Language," in *Adam Smith: Lectures on Rhetoric and Belles Lettres*, ed. J.C. Bryce and Andrew Skinner (Oxford, 1983), 220.
44. Adam Ferguson, *An Essay on the History of Civil Society* (1767; repr., Edinburgh, 1966), 173–74. On the broader implications of this theory for eighteenth-century poetry, see W. Jackson Bate, *The Burden of the Past and the English Poet* (Cambridge, MA, 1970), ch. 2.
45. John Heckewelder, "An Account of the History, Manners and Customs of the Indian Nations Who Once Inhabited Pennsylvania and Neighbouring States," *Transactions of the Historical and Literary Committee of the American Philosophical Society* 1 (1819): 119.
46. William Smith, *Some Account of the North American Indians*, viii, 40.
47. The impulse to distinguish between cultures that regard words as "signs" and those that view them as "symbols" corresponded with the emergence in the late-seventeenth and early-eighteenth centuries of the idea that, instead of resting on a natural or divine connection between words and objects, language was a social convention, indicative more of the habits of speakers than of material reality. This theme is explored in Michel Foucault, *The Order of Things: An Archaeology of the Human Sciences* (New York, 1970), ch. 4 and *passim*; Murray Cohen, *Sensible Words: Linguistic Practice in England 1640–1785* (Baltimore, 1977), and Richard Sennett, *The Fall of Public Man: On the Social Psychology of Capitalism* (New York, 1977), 73–87.

48. Amos Stoddard, *Sketches, Historical and Descriptive of Louisiana* (Philadelphia, 1812), 431–32.
49. Jean-Jacques Rousseau, "Essay on the Origin of Language," in *Two Essays on the Origin of Language: Jean-Jacques Rousseau and Johann Gottfried Herder*, trans. John H. Moran and Alexander Gode (Chicago, 1966), 12, 15, 16.
50. It is almost certain that the Ossian poems were not what Macpherson claimed them to be. The current status of the controversy is discussed in Howard Gaskill's "Introduction" to *Ossian Revisited*, ed. Howard Gaskill (Edinburgh, 1991), 1–18.
51. Benjamin Smith Barton, "Logan, Cresap, and Rogers," *Philadelphia Medical and Physical Journal* vol. 2 (1806), 151.
52. Stoddard, *Sketches, Historical and Descriptive of Louisiana*, 432.
53. Gilbert Chinard, "Jefferson and Ossian," *Modern Language Notes* 38, no. 4 (April, 1923): 202.
54. Ferguson, *An Essay on the History of Civil Society*, 173.
55. Clinton, "Address Before the New York Historical Society," 238–39.
56. Cadwallader Colden, *The History of the Five Indian Nations Depending on the Province of New York* (Ithaca, 1958), xi.
57. The eighteenth-century analogy between indigenous speech, children's speech, and that of the disabled is effectively explored in Rüdiger Schreyer, "Deaf Mutes, Feral Children, and Savages: Of Analogical Evidence in 18th Century Theoretical History of Language," in *Anglistentag 1993 Eichstätt: Proceedings*, ed. Günther Blaicher and Brigitte Glaser (Tübingen, 1994), 70–86. Also see, Nocholas Mirzoeff, *Silent Poetry: Deafness, Sign, and Visual Culture in Modern France* (Princeton, 1995), esp. 30–40.
58. Lionel Trilling, *Sincerity and Authenticity* (Cambridge, MA, 1972), 4 and *passim*. Other discussions of this theme are Herbert Read, *The Cult of Sincerity* (New York, 1969), ch. 1, and Leon Guilhamet, *The Sincere Ideal: Studies in Eighteenth-Century English Literature* (Montreal, 1974). Also see, Jay Fliegelman, *Declaring Independence: Jefferson, Natural Language, and the Culture of Performance* (Stanford, 1993), esp. 79–94; David Marshall, *The Surprising Effects of Sympathy: Marivaux, Diderot, Rousseau and Mary Shelly* (Chicago, 1988), 1–5; 84–177; and Nina Auerbach, *Private Theatricals: The Lives of the Victorians* (Cambridge, MA, 1990), esp. 3–12. American fears of "Machiavellian Duplicity" in political rhetoric are discussed in Gordon S. Wood, "Democratization of Mind in the American Revolution," in *Leadership in the American Revolution* (Washington, DC, 1974), esp. 75.
59. *The American Pioneer* 1 (1842): 7.
60. "Logan—The Mingo Chief," *Ohio Archaeological and Historical Publications* 20 (1911): 166–67.

Part V

Theory

– *Chapter 12* –

Spanish Colonization and the Indigenous Languages of America

൙ൟ

Isaías Lerner

Interest in learning the languages spoken by the inhabitants of America was immediate, from the very moment of the European "discovery" of the new continent. In the case of the Spaniards, this interest passed through the natural stages of total lack of knowledge, with recourse to gestures, and later the use of interpreters. The initial stage is recorded already by Columbus, as quoted by Fray Bartolomé de las Casas from the manuscript of the discoverer's log: "Saturday 13 October ... By signs I was able to understand that, by going south or sailing around the island to the south, there was a king who possessed large drinking vessels [of gold] and very many of them."[1]

Beyond the simple interest in communication for purposes of information, or of establishing some sort of dialogue in an unstable and frontier situation, a "scientific" interest in the languages of the peoples of the newly discovered lands simultaneously began to take shape.[2] This linguistic interest had a complex origin that responded to several of the intellectual, theological, and missionary concerns of humanistic Europe. In fact, the totally new reality of the American continent not only permitted ecological and commercial exchanges entailing complex consequences and requiring vast political readjustments, it also forced reconsideration of traditional Western ideas about history and culture, ideas that obviously had not taken American cultures into account.[3] Concern about the origin of things, already present in Greco-Roman thought, acquired new momentum during the Renaissance,[4] and the indigenous languages of America, previously totally unknown to Europeans (which was not the case with Asian and African languages), made it necessary to rethink the theory of an original language common to all humankind.[5]

It is no coincidence that the first Renaissance miscellany written in a modern language, Pedro Mexía's *Silva de varia lección* of 1540, devotes chapter XXV of its first part to theories about the first language in the world. The Sevillian humanist Mexía (1497–1551), cosmographer of the Casa de Contratación in Seville from 1537 onward and the Emperor's official chronicler in Spanish from 1548, tried to include in his miscellany, "for those who do not understand Latin books," as he says in his "Prohemio," "matters that were not very common, or did not circulate among ordinary folk, or which were important and useful in themselves, at least in my opinion."[6] Among these important and useful matters, Mexía apparently thought that the question of the first language used by humanity was of general interest for readers of his time. The inclusion of this subject probably was in response to questions raised about the primordial nature of Hebrew as the first universal language.[7]

Recognition of the multitude of unknown languages that the Spaniards found in America certainly was of no little importance in renewed European attention to this matter. The discovery of the American continents, of which the Jewish and Christian concepts of history had not even dreamed, forced new consideration of the problem of the original language common to all humankind before the Flood and the subsequent existence of many different languages. For the Church Fathers, naturally, the account in the eleventh chapter of Genesis was a sufficient explanation and an incontrovertible truth. The next step was the belief that Hebrew was that primordial language, and Mexía followed this official interpretation of the biblical text.

The chapter of the *Silva* just mentioned was based on the classical *locus* of St. Augustine's *City of God* and on St. Isidore's *Etymologies*, among other authorities.[8] It attracted the attention of the "chronicler of things of the Indies," Gonzalo Fernández de Oviedo, in his *Historia general y natural de las Indias*.[9] The *Historia*'s first part was published in 1535, and Oviedo continued to work on it until his death in 1557, adding new elements and rewriting what he had already published in order to complete the fifty chapters of his original plan.[10] It is obvious that Oviedo wrote chapter 43 of book VI of his first part after reading Mexía's miscellany, for he quotes it specifically. Here, Oviedo not only doubts the existence of a mere seventy-two languages derived from the confusion of tongues described in Genesis, but based on the new American evidence, he proposed the need to accept the theory of linguistic polygenesis to explain the variety of languages in America.

Ever since the publication of Vespucci's letters, Europeans had been aware of the large number of distinct languages in America.[11] For his part, Oviedo notes insistently that the multitude of tongues and their very great variation is one of the most characteristic traits of the New World: "What can we say about the very different tongues, so unlike one another, that exist in these our Indies, where the Indians from one province to another do not understand each other better, or even as well, as a Biscayan understands a German or an Arab?"[12] Oviedo even argued that this diversity partly explains the rapidity and ease of the conquest: "Owing to the very many tribes of Indians, these differences in their languages have been the chief weapons with which the Spaniards have taken control of these regions, together with the discord that constantly existed among their inhabitants."[13] Throughout his long work, Oviedo stressed this variety, and in his prologue addressed to the emperor—an extraordinary panegyric that acclaims the absolute novelty of these lands—he begins by mentioning this linguistic richness: "What mortal intellect could understand so great a diversity of tongues, of habits, of customs, in the men of these Indies?"[14]

But Oviedo goes beyond constant mention of this remarkable diversity; he notes the difficulties created by the need to employ interpreters and the possibility of errors and inaccurate interpretations, thus anticipating the necessity and advantages of direct knowledge of the newly conquered peoples' languages.[15] In book XVI, chapter 21, where he recounts the conquest of what came to be called "the New Kingdom of Granada," he refers to the difficulty of understanding the Indians of Bogotá and Tunja, at the time in a permanent state of war because "the enmity between them has been perpetuated for a long time by their predecessors." Oviedo laments ignorance of the two factions' languages, for knowing them would have facilitated the conquest:

> For on the one hand the Spaniards having the advantage, all would have been well done and without difficulty; but the Christians were as if muzzled, asking questions by signs; and being answered with signs, they gathered meaning only by chance. It is true that the interpreter whom they brought from Oppon and the mountains, as has been told,

knew something of our language, but very little. I feel convinced that this lack of adequate interpreters everywhere in these regions is the greatest danger for everyone, and the cause of prolonging and drawing out wars and failing to make peace; because when things are understood topsy-turvy, or not as they should be understood, disagreement is inevitable, especially because the Indians are very unreliable and still less truthful, and the devil gets between the Christians' covetousness and the Indians' greed and vice. So things turn out as we see they do, and this is well known in these parts.[16]

Indeed, the need for such knowledge became apparent with the first discoveries. It had two steps. The first and simplest was the compilation of vocabularies; the next step was the writing of grammars and the translation of catechisms and confessionals. In the compilation of vocabularies, first place must be given to Peter Martyr, who in his early Latin works *De Orbe Novo* (the first of them written between 1493 and 1510), lists some Amerindian words that he must have learned from the natives brought to Spain by Columbus and which he tried to transcribe with special care.[17] Also, the edition by Antonio de Nebrija of the first three "Decades" of Peter Martyr's book, published in Alcalá in 1516, contains a glossary that has Antillean words mixed with proper names and Hispanisms.[18] Another early vocabulary appears in Antonio Pigafetta's *Relación del primer viaje alrededor del mundo*, probably written around 1524. It contains some eighty words from the language of the Patagonian Indians that Pigafetta learned from a Patagonian who had been kidnapped by Magellan's sailors.[19]

For the seventeenth century we should mention small glossaries, not necessarily all made up of indigenous words, in texts such as *Descripción de la provincia de los Quixos en lo natural* (1608) by Pedro Fernández de Castro y Andrade, Count of Lemos, containing only eighteen words;[20] the "Table for understanding certain words in this History," with 156 words, which appears as an appendix in *Noticias historiales de las conquistas de Tierra Firme en las Indias Occidentales*, written by Fray Pedro Simón in 1627;[21] and the "Index" explaining words in Pablo José de Arriaga's *Extirpación de la idolatria del Pirú* in 1621.[22]

Contemporaneously with these glossaries, vocabularies also began to appear in literary texts. Thus in 1569 Alonso de Ercilla, at the beginning of the first part of his poem *La Araucana* on the Spanish conquest of Araucanian Indian lands, in which he was both a participant and the narrator, published a "Declaration of some things in this work ... that because they are of the Indies cannot be well understood ... so that they may be more easily understood." This small vocabulary was gradually expanded in later editions. In the edition with three parts (1589–90) he explained that a vocabulary was needed because "some words or names ... though from the Indians, are so accepted and used in that land, that they have not been changed in our language," thus identifying the naming process that was already conferring a special character on the Spanish language of America.

In his list of Americanisms, Ercilla included twenty-two words, some of which were geographical names and names of persons or gods, not all of them indigenous. In this long poem I have identified only a dozen or so truly indigenous words, some of them already so established in the ordinary Castilian vocabulary as to be absent from Ercilla's special list. The words used by Ercilla also reflect broader Spanish-American linguistic exchanges, for as it happens, none of the indigenous words is Araucanian: seven are from Quechua and Aymara and the others are from Antillean, Central American, and Mexican languages. All this reveals, on the one hand, the absorption of vocabulary acquired during the initial contact period with America and, on the other, the particular influence of the languages of Peru (Quechua and Aymara) on speakers of Spanish. In any case, other epic poems with American subjects would imitate this feature of Ercilla's poem and would include their own vocabularies.

The richest initial documentation concerning contact with American languages is found not in these few lists and glossaries, however, but in the prose of the historians of the Indies, beginning with Oviedo's *Sumario* of 1526. The historians, typically, used indigenous words in their writings and attempted to explain their meaning and synonyms, but without collecting these words into special, independent lists.

The next stage was the compilation of grammars and dictionaries of the indigenous languages, a task undertaken primarily by the clergy. It began very early, as soon as it became apparent that, in view of the large indigenous population, the scanty number of missionary friars could not take on the enormous job of teaching Spanish in addition to catechizing and teaching agriculture and new artisanal techniques.[23] In this process the ordinances of the Council of Trent (1545–1564) were of no little importance. They expressly favored the use of vernacular languages (*vulgares linguas*) for religious instruction of the people and ordered publication of catechisms in them. This policy indirectly encouraged evangelization in the Native American languages that were deemed most important numerically.[24] At the same time, Spanish slowly became the general language, as it is to this day, available for communication between indigenous communities that speak different languages.

The arrival of printing in America was part of this process. It first came to Mexico at the particular insistence of the Franciscan Fray Juan de Zumárraga (1468–1548), first bishop of Mexico, and Don Antonio de Mendoza, first viceroy of New Spain.[25] The exact date of its establishment there has given rise to considerable controversy and to a very complete bibliography.[26] In any case, the date of 1539 for the printing of the first book known in Mexico, the *Breve y más compendiosa Doctrina Christiana en lengua castellana y mexicana*, now seems incontrovertible. Soon after, in 1555, the first Spanish-Nahuatl dictionary appeared, compiled by the Franciscan Alonso de Molina.[27]

The establishment of printing in Peru is connected to its appearance in Mexico. Antonio Ricardo, of Piedmontese origin (his surname is a Hispanization of Ricciardi), emigrated to Mexico in 1570. Early in 1580 he left Mexico and established a printing shop in Lima, the first such enterprise in South America, as he states on the title page of his edition of Pedro de Oña's *Arauco domado* (Lima, 1596).[28]

Ricardo must have seen commercial possibilities in the ever more urgent need for texts for the burgeoning work of evangelization. The first provincial council in Lima, in 1551, had already established the obligation to use vernacular languages; hence, as had happened ten years before in Mexico, and again in the council of 1555, collections of sermons, doctrines, and confessionals in Quechua and Aymara soon proliferated in Peru. In fact, the Second Council of Lima, in 1567, banned the use of interpreters, thus legitimizing the use of Quechua as the language of religion; and the Third Council of Lima, in 1582–83, decreed the creation of a commission to unify and edit the text of a collection of sermons, a catechism, and a book of confessions. The result was the first book printed in Peru, the *Doctrina Christiana y catecismo para instrucción del los Indios* ... (1584). A trilingual text in Spanish, Quechua, and Aymara, the work is of extraordinary importance for our knowledge of language contacts in the Andean region during the second half of the sixteenth century.[29]

At the same time, work was being done on grammatical and lexical systematization and codification. Indeed, there are indications of the existence of manuscript grammars and vocabularies of Quechua as early as 1540.[30] But the first printed grammar "of the general language of the Indians of the realms of Peru" is that of the Dominican Fray Domingo de Santo Thomás, published in Valladolid in 1560, which also contains an extensive vocabulary.

This movement toward religious instruction in vernacular languages was not unanimously accepted by the royal bureaucracy, however, and in 1596 the Council of the Indies recommended to Philip II that instruction of the Indians be in the Castilian tongue in order to accelerate the disappearance of the indigenous languages, which the council considered to be sources of idolatry and superstition.[31] Philip II rejected the proposal, because he did not think it appropriate to force the Indians to abandon "their natural language," and gave orders that priests involved in proselytizing should "know the Indians' language."[32] In fact, there was an attempt to do both things at the same time. The Third Council of Lima, like the Second Council, insisted on the missionaries' obligation to study indigenous languages but also issued orders that prayers be taught in both Spanish and the indigenous tongues.[33]

Despite this kind of compromise, efforts continued, though with little success, to induce the natives to forget their mother tongues and adopt Spanish. The crown never completely abandoned its more or less utopian plan to Hispanize the people of America; but it is important to realize simply that colonial linguistic policy went through a number of different stages, which helps to explain the publication of grammars and the creation even of chairs for the study of the so-called "general languages." Thus in the Royal Cédula of Badajoz in 1580, Philip II authorized instruction in the general language in Lima for "those who have to teach doctrine to the Indians and must know the language in which they must preach and hear confession."[34]

Nevertheless, circumstances were developing that made it inevitable the clergy would gradually abandon study of American languages. In the eighteenth century the policies of the Bourbons, and particularly those of Charles III, intensified the forced acceptance of Spanish. Two political events of great importance for the history of America no doubt contributed to this policy: first, the expulsion of the Jesuits from America in 1767, since the Jesuits' teaching and religious instruction in their colleges and "reductions" were mostly given in the indigenous languages; and second, the native uprisings at the end of the eighteenth century. In 1770 in his famous Cédula of Aranjuez, Charles III ordered the imposition of Spanish, a decision that Rosenblat has called "the triumph of jurists over theologians."[35]

Although the social and political aim of the Cédula of Aranjuez was to cause the slow disappearance of the native languages spoken in the Spanish dominions, scientific interest in American languages did not diminish. One proof of this interest is that, in response to a Royal Order of 13 November 1787, the archbishop-viceroy Antonio Cavallero sent the royal library documentation on the languages of America consisting of twenty-one titles collected by José Celestino Mutis. Eight of these manuscripts were first published more than one hundred years later in Madrid, in 1928, under the title *Lenguas de América: Manuscritos de la Real Biblioteca*, in an edition of fewer than six hundred copies. All of these manuscripts were collected in the second half of the eighteenth century. Ample witness to the uninterrupted work of compiling vocabularies, carried out from the eighteenth century to the present, is provided also by the major work of Cipriano Muñoz y Manzano, Count of La Viñaza, *Bibliografía española de lenguas indígenas de América* (Madrid, 1892).

It is no coincidence that it was precisely in the eighteenth century that what we may properly call the first dictionaries of Americanisms began to appear, beginning with "Diccionario de voces americanas," probably written between 1751 and 1777 and only recently published for the first time. Its modern editor, Miguel Angel Quesada Pacheco, found this manuscript in the Library of the Royal Palace in Madrid and through internal evidence has been able tentatively to identify its author. He was the Panamanian Manuel José de Ayala, a compiler of the laws of the Indies and archivist of both the Secretariat of State and the "foreign desk" of the Indies.[36] Although, as its modern editor observes, this work was included in the catalogue entitled "Manuscritos de América" under the title "Diccionario de América," its existence was overlooked by linguists. *Diccionario de voces americanas* is a work of the utmost importance, consisting of approximately 2,800 entries, of which, according to Quesada Pacheco, 630 are native words. It also includes words of Spanish origin, belonging primarily to the vocabulary of flora, fauna, mining, and daily life, that acquired different meanings in America. This latter category of words is particularly interesting, because it is evidence of the accord reached by groups that on the Iberian Peninsula lived socially far apart, but who in America were forced to find a common language.[37] "Not all the vassals of the royal crown of Spain are of identical customs or similar languages," Gonzalo Fernández de Oviedo had observed.[38]

The other text that properly can be called a dictionary of Americanisms is the "vocabulary of the provincial words of America" in the *Diccionario geográfico histórico de las Indias occidentales* (1786–1789) compiled by the Ecuadorian Antonio de Alcedo.[39] Here, undoubtedly, we are in the presence of a more ambitious work, and one of much more encyclopedic scope than Ayala's, and it was received with enthusiasm and admiration by both scholars and politicians. It was quickly translated into English although the crown, concerned with the strategic value of its ample information, decreed its prohibition and confiscation. Both of these *diccionarios* are faithful to Enlightenment ideals and bear witness to the desire for independence and differentiation from the mother country that was to take shape in the national movements of the nineteenth century.[40] Hence they have more to do with the uses of Castilian in America than with concern for the fate and recovery of the linguistic stock of the continent's aboriginal inhabitants. Inescapably, however, they record a substantial part of the Native American heritage.

A detailed discussion of the mutual influences of Castilian and native languages upon each other lies outside the scope of this study. However, I would like to point out at least two aspects of the matter. In the first place, there is the Spaniards' role in the expansion of what came to be called "general languages" within what José de Acosta called "a veritable jungle of tongues."[41] In reference to the difficulties of evangelization without knowledge of the native languages, Acosta writes:

> Others speak more reasonably and say that since there is no longer an obligation [for missionaries] to learn and use a foreign language, at least they should not be allowed to be ignorant of what is called a general language; which does not seem so difficult to them, since the Incas by very wise legislation succeeded in making all the widely scattered areas of this realm speak the language of Cuzco, called Quechua, so that within the space of three thousand miles and more it is still in use even today.[42]

In general, then, the Spaniards used geographical coverage as a test for the adoption—from among a remarkable variety of languages, dialects and, in the case of the Incas, displaced languages—of one language that they thought of as the general language, or lingua franca, of a particular region.[43] In the New Kingdom of Granada, for example, it was Chibcha;[44] in Mexico, Nahuatl; for the Jesuits of the missions, Guaraní. This choice of geographical extent at the expense of diversity could hardly be helped, but it resulted in irremediable losses of our knowledge of native tongues.

Finally, the transformation of Spanish in America must be briefly noted.[45] The introduction of indigenous words—which persists today throughout Spanish-speaking territory and has found an echo in every register of the language—and the presence still in large areas of the Americas of speakers of indigenous languages along with Spanish speakers are part of this transformation. Indigenous words played, and still play, a fundamental role in the process of naming, and their penetration, permanence, or loss has a separate history that has not yet been studied in all its dimensions. In any case their presence in literary texts, from Ercilla to Góngora, from Cervantes to the picaresque novel, and from Lope de Vega to Tirso de Molina, bears witness to this influence. The different postures assumed by modern and contemporary linguists on the influence of the indigenous languages on phonetics, morphology, and the lexicon of American Spanish sometimes seem tinged with more or less obvious ideological factors. In this sense, the history of contacts between Spanish and the languages of Spanish America has not yet been fully written, and we may well say that it is being rewritten at this very moment.

Translation by Frances López-Morillas

Notes

1. Christopher Columbus, "Diario del Primer Viaje (1492–1493)," in Cristóbal Colón, *Los cuatro viajes: Testamiento*, ed. Consuelo Varela (Madrid: Alianza), 1986, 64.
2. Francisco de Solano, ed., *Documentos sobre política lingüística en Hispanoamérica 1492–1800* (Madrid: CSIC, 1991), xxiii–xxv, 1. In this otherwise very useful preliminary study, de Solano establishes a debatable comparison with the situation on the Hispano-Muslim frontiers.
3. Alfred W. Crosby, *Ecological Imperialism: The Biological Expansion of Europe 900–1900* (Cambridge, Eng.: Cambridge University Press, 1986).
4. Isaías Lerner, "La visión humanística de América: Gonzalo Fernández de Oviedo," in *Las Indias (América) en la literatura del Siglo de Oro*, ed. I. Arellano (Kassel: Edition Reichenberger, 1992), 16.
5. Claude-Gilbert Dubois, *Mythe et Langage au Seizième Siècle* (Bordeaux: Ducros, 1970), 98ff.
6. Pedro Mexía, *Silva de varia lección* (Madrid: Cátedra, 1989) I: 163–64.
7. Umberto Eco, *The Search for the Perfect Language* (Cambridge, Eng.: Blackwell, 1995), 74.
8. St. Augustine, *De civitate Dei*, xvi; St. Isidore, *Etymologiarum*, 1:xv.
9. Rómulo D. Carbia, *La crónica oficial de las Indias Occidentales* (Buenos Aires: Ediciones Buenos Aires, 1940), 94.
10. Lerner, "La visión humanística."
11. Antonello Gerbi, *La naturaleza de las Indias nuevas* (Mexico: FCE, 1978), 58.

12. Gonzalo Fernández de Oviedo, *Historia general y natural de las Indias* (Madrid: Atlas [Biblioteca de Autores Españoles], 1959), I : 202b.
13. Fernández de Oviedo, I: 203a.
14. Fernández de Oviedo, I: 8a.
15. For the function of interpreters during the early years of colonial life, along with other texts, see Solano, *Documentos sobre política lingüística*, xxxiv–xlvi.
16. Fernández de Oviedo, III: 107b.
17. Alberto M. Salas, *Tres cronistas de Indias* (Mexico: FCE, 1959), 47.
18. Rufino J. Cuervo, *Apuntaciones críticas sobre el lenguaje bogotano* (Paris: Garnier, 1914), par. 981; Enrique Carrión Ordóñez, *La lengua en un texto de la Ilustración* (Lima: Pontificia Universidad Católica del Perú, 1983), 160.
19. Antonio Pigafetta, *Relación del primer viaje alrededor del mundo* (Madrid: Aguilar, 1957), Bibliotheca Indiana, I: 31.
20. Ciro Bayo, "Vocabulario de provincialismos argentinos y bolivianos," *Rhi* (1906), xiv: 241–564; Miguel Ugarte Chamorro, "Las descripciones geográficas de Indias y un diccionario de americanismos," *Letras* (Lima, 1966), 76–77, 89–103.
21. Luis Carlos Mantilla, *Fray Pedro Simón y su Vocabulario de americanismos*, facsimile ed. of the "Tabla para la inteligencia de algunos vocablos" from Simon, *Noticias historiales* (Bogotá: Instituto Caro y Cuervo, 1986), 46.
22. Carrión Ordóñez, *La lengua*, 162.
23. José G. Moreno de Alba, *El español de América* (Mexico: FCE, 1993), 53.
24. Bruce Mannheim, "La memoria y el olvido en la política lingüística colonial," *Lexis* (Lima, 1989), xiii: 1, 19.
25. Emilio Valton, *Impresos mexicanos del siglo XVI* (México: Imprenta Universitaria, 1935), 6ff; Lawrence S. Thompson, *Printing in Colonial Spanish America* (Hamden: The Shoe String Press, 1962), 11ff.
26. Guadalupe Curiel and Arturo Gómez Camacho, "450 años de imprenta en México," *Universidad de México* (1989), XLIV, 467, 36–42; Antonio Pompa y Pompa, *450 años de la imprenta tipográfica en México* (México: Asociación Nacional de Libreros, 1988).
27. For the development of lexicography in Mesoamerica and the influence of Nebrija's *Diccionario*, esp. the edition of 1516, see Frances Karttunen, "The Roots of Sixteenth-Century Mesoamerican Lexicography," in *Cultures, Ideologies, and the Dictionary*, ed. Braj B. Kachru and Henry Kahane (Tubingen: Max Niemeyer Verlag, 1995), 77–78.
28. José Torre Revello, *Los orígenes de la imprenta en la América española* (Madrid: Francisco Beltrán, 1927), 15ff; Torre Revello, *Orígenes de la imprenta en España y su desarrollo en América Española* (Buenos Aires: Institución Cultural Española, 1940), 104ff; Valton, *Impresos mexicanos*, 187ff.
29. See the *Epístola* of the clergy who were on the council, in *Doctrina christiana...*, in *Documentos*, ed. Francisco de Solano, 85–86.
30. Fray Domingo de Santo Thomás, *Gramática o arte de la lengua general de los indios de los reynos del Perú*, study and transliteration by Rodolfo Cerrón-Palomino (Madrid: Ediciones de Cultura Hispánica, 1994), xi.
31. José Luis Rivarola, "Aproximación histórica a los contactos de lenguas en el Perú," in *Lenguas en contacto en Hispanoamérica*, ed. Klaus Zimmerman (Frankfurt: Vervuert, 1995), 145; Francisco de Solano, ed., *Documentos*, 112–15.
32. Silvio Zavala, *El castellano lengua obligatoria?* (Mexico: CEHM, 1977), 38.
33. Ana Gimeno Gómez, "Notas sobre la implantación de la lengua castellana en América," in *El español de América. Actas*, III Congreso Internacional de El

español de América, ed. C. Hernández *et al.* (Valladolid: Junta de Castilla y León, 1991), I: 231–39.
34. Francisco de Solano, *Documentos*, 77–78.
35. José G. Moreno de Alba, *El español de América* (Mexico: FCE, 1993), 55; Francisco de Solano, *Documentos*, 257–61.
36. Manuel José de Ayala, *Diccionario de voces americanas*, ed. Miguel Angel Quesada Pacheco (Madrid: Arco Libros, 1995), xiii.
37. For the adoption of indigenous words relating to the vocabulary of nature in America, see Manuel Galeote, *Léxico indígena de flora y fauna en tratados sobre las Indias Occidentales de autores andaluces* (Granada: Universidad de Granada, 1997).
38. Fernández de Oviedo, *Historia general*, I: 52b. Referring to initial disagreements in the newly discovered lands, Oviedo writes: "This is all the more true because different sorts of people have come here; for though all those who came were vassals of the kings of Spain, who can compare the Biscayan with the Catalan, who are from such different provinces and languages? How compare the Andalusian with the Valencian, and the man from Perpignan with the Cordobese, and the Aragonese with the Guipuzcoan, and the Galician with the Castilian (believing him to be Portuguese), and the Asturian and the man from La Montána with the Navarrese, etc.?"
39. Isaías Lerner, "Sobre dialectología en las letras coloniales: el *Vocabulario* de Antonio de Alcedo," *Sur* (Buenos Aires, 1982), 117–29, 350–51.
40. Isaías Lerner, "The *Diccionario* of Antonio de Alcedo as a Source of Enlightened Ideas," in *The Ibero–American Enlightenment*, ed. A. Owen Aldridge (Urbana: University of Illinois Press, 1978).
41. Fr. Joseph de Acosta, *De procuranda indorum salute*, in *Obras*, ed. Francisco Mateos (Madrid: Atlas, 1954; Biblioteca de Autores Españoles, vol. LXXIII) book IV, ch. 8, p. 517a.
42. Acosta, *De procuranda*, book IV, ch. 8, pp. 516–17.
43. Domingo de Santo Thomás, *Gramática o arte*, VIff; Moreno de Alba, *El español*, 51.
44. Manuel Alvar, *Resurrección de una lengua*. Introduction to the facsimile edition of Fr. Fray Bernardo de Lugo's *Chibcha Grammar* [1619] (Madrid: Ediciones de Cultura Hispánica, 1978).
45. José Luis Rivarola, *La formación lingüística de Hispanoamérica* (Lima: Pontificia Universidad Católica del Perú, 1990), 14ff.

– Chapter 13 –

DESCRIPTIONS OF AMERICAN INDIAN WORD FORMS IN COLONIAL MISSIONARY GRAMMARS

ை

Lieve Jooken

Introduction

SINCE THE 1970s and the academic revival of interest in the history of linguistic ideas, there has been a steadily increasing effort to bring the linguistic achievements of missionaries to the attention of modern linguists, who for years discarded this work as prescientific. In 1969, Victor E. Hanzeli could still call the linguistic discovery of the New World one of the major areas of pre-nineteenth-century linguistics "that remain to be scrutinized."[1] At the second International Conference of the History of the Language Sciences in 1981, the linguistic study of Native American languages was one of the "novelties."[2] More recently, in October 1995, an international colloquium on the study of Amerindian languages in the colonial period (La descripcion de las lenguas amerindas en la época colonial) was held at the Ibero-amerikanisches Institut in Berlin, where the overall conclusion of the papers was that "many missionary linguists approached the analysis with an open mind and tried various approaches."[3] Finally, the publication of ... *and the Word was God: Missionary Linguistics and Missionary Grammar* (1996)[4] clearly attests to the increased scholarly interest we witness today.

Most pertinently, colonial reports of American Indian speech are a topic of study in linguistic historiography because of the way they assimilated the grammar of new structures, which involved types of communication that classical grammar models did not encompass. European reactions to these new structures were, on the whole, ambiguous; they ranged from epithets like "confusing" to appreciations of the grammar's "richness." Examples of missionary grammars that go beyond the perspective of traditional Latin grammar show "that man's ability to think independently about linguistic matter and analyze linguistic problems may be more important than generally assumed."[5] They are steps toward a science of language and languages that studies the diversity of linguistic forms for its own sake and, hence, they reduce the claims of universal grammar, which prevailed in European language theory until well into the eighteenth century.

This article presents a case study of three eighteenth-century grammatical accounts, dealing with the South American languages Galibi and Mapuche and the Eskimo language Greenlandic. The authors of the descriptions were missionaries—or, in the case of Galibi, a political figure drawing on information from missionaries. They devised their works to assist fellow missionaries or compatriots in their religious and political ambitions.

Besides the linguistic description of these three accounts, this article also looks at the impact they had on contemporary European language theory. In Scotland, notably, the intellectuals of the time integrated a (conjectural) discussion of linguistic development into their theories on the progress of human society or into their analysis of how the human intellect operated.[6] In those hypotheses of linguistic development, missionary reports of exotic tongues became the commonplace reference to illustrate what were assumed to be early stages of human language.

One Scottish scholar, James Burnett, better known as Lord Monboddo, wrote the Enlightenment's major contribution to a broadly conceived classification of languages. Monboddo's *Of the Origin and Progress of Language* (6 vols., 1773–1792) incorporates descriptions of fourteen American Indian languages. The author places Galibi, Mapuche, and Greenlandic among the "more advanced" languages spoken in the New World, because in his view they are higher on the scale of grammatical complexity than, for example, Huron or Algonquian. Since Monboddo, like most of his contemporaries, had almost no critical reservation about his sources, an analysis of the picture that these sources offered is all the more relevant. Therefore the discussion that follows has two angles: first, the descriptions of grammatical complexity in the source texts, and, second, the reception of those descriptions in the work of Lord Monboddo.

Source Material

Word lists of the Carib language Galibi that had been circulating since the seventeenth century were compiled into a dictionary by the French agriculturist Simon-Philibert de La Salle de l'Étang (ca. 1700–1765) in 1763: *Dictionnaire Galibi ... Précédé d'un essai de Grammaire* (Paris, 1763). The grammatical description of this language takes up the first twenty-four pages. The author intended to provide future settlers with a practical grammar and dictionary, and he incorporated in this work all earlier French descriptions of Galibi, adding his own comments. He mainly drew on documents of the Jesuits Antoine Biet (ca. 1620–?)—author of *Les Galibis: Tableau véritable de les mœurs avec un vocabulaire de leur langue* (1661)—who spent a year in French Guyana from 1652 to 1653, and Pierre Pelleprat (1609–1667)—author of *Introduction à la langue des Galibis* (Paris, 1655)—who was a missionary to the Galibis of Venezuela at Guarapiche from 1653 to 1654.

Galibi belongs to the Cariban language family. It originally was spoken in Venezuela and French Guyana. Today there are approximately 20,000 Indian speakers of Carib languages left, all of whom are living in north-eastern Brazil.[7]

The Eskimo missionary David Cranz (1723–1777) was a Moravian brother of the Unitas Fratrum who spent a year in Greenland as a missionary between August 1761 and August 1762. The English translation of his two-volume work *The History of Greenland* was published in London in 1767. Volume I includes "A Brief theoretical Sketch of the Greenland Language, with a few Translations annexed" (pp. 217–27). Cranz's discussion of Greenlandic Eskimo may have been inspired by the earlier work of Norwegian minister Paul Egede, *Grammatica Grönlandico-Danico-Latina* (Copenhagen, 1760). Greenlandic, or Kalaallisut, is a member of the Eskimo Aleut family. About 46,000 speakers remain today.[8]

Chilean Mapuche, finally, is described by the Jesuit Thomas Falkner (1707–1784), who spent thirty-eight years in South America as a missionary, first in Chaco (Paraguay) and Tucumán (the Pampas), and from 1740 among the native tribes between Rio de la Plata and the Strait of Magellan. He was deported with the general expulsion of the Jesuits in 1767. Various names for the language and its dialects continue to be used today, the most general being Mapuche, Mapudungun, or Araucano; Moluche, Huilliche, and Picunche are its main dialects. The language is part of the Penutian language stock. The present number of Mapuche speakers may be estimated between 200,000 and 500,000.[9]

Falkner was the first Englishman to discuss Mapuche, which had been described before by the Spanish Jesuit P. Luis de Valdivia in his *Arte y Gramatica General de la Lengva que corre en todo el Reyno de Chile* (Lima, 1606). Falkner's *A Description of Patagonia and the Adjoining Parts of South America* was published in Hereford in 1774 and later translated into German (1775), French (1787), and Spanish (1835–1837). The final chapter of the book gives "An Account of the Language of the Inhabitants of these Countries" (1774: 132–44), that is, of the Moluche, who spoke a dialect of Mapuche (see Figs. 13.1 and 13.2). We may safely assume that it was the work of the Englishman rather than that of Valdivia, whose book appeared in a European edition only in 1887 (Leipzig), that informed eighteenth-century and early nineteenth-century European readers about the language of Chile.[10]

Analyzing the Grammatical Complexity of Galibi, Greenlandic, and Mapuche Words

My discussion focuses on that part of each grammatical account in which the European author analyzes the structure and meaning of indigenous *word forms*. Besides difficulties of pronunciation and orthography, one of the most challenging problems missionaries confronted was understanding how Indian languages communicate meaning and where the boundaries between words were.

The main reason for this was that all indigenous American languages share the phenomenon of *polysynthesis*. This means that their words may be very complex, to the extent of expressing whole utterances by a string of morphemes; in other words, a word consists mostly of a combination of a verbal and/or nominal stem and various particles that are affixed. As such, much of the syntax of these languages is actually established within a single word. One famous missionary grammar, the Recollet Gabriel Sagard's *Dictionaire de la langue Huronne* (Paris, 1632), observes that the Hurons have such "word-sentences." He does not analyze the meaningful elements of their words, however, and hence fails to spell out any structural rules in their complexity: "They have a

> ## CHAPTER VI.
> *An Account of the Language of the Inhabitants of these Countries.*
>
> THE languages of these Indians differ from each other. I only learned that of the Moluches; it being the most polished, and the most generally understood. A considerable absence from these countries has rendered the recollection very difficult: however, I shall give the best account of it I am able, to satisfy the curious and inquisitive.
>
> This language is much more copious and elegant, than could have been expected from an uncivilized people.
>
> The nouns have only one declination, and are all of the common gender. The dative, accusative, and ablative cases, have all the same termination, with their suffix or postposition. There are but two numbers, singular and plural; the dual being expressed by placing the word epu (which signifies two) before the word: but the pronouns have all the three numbers. The adjectives are put before the substantives, and do not vary their terminations, either in case or number: as,
>
> | Cume | good, |
> |---|---|
> | Cume huentu | a good man, |
> | Cume huentu eng'n | good men. |
>
> The

FIGURE 13.1 An account of the Mapuche language (of which Moluche is a dialect) spoken by Indians in southern Chile, in Thomas Falkner, *A Description of Patagonia and the Adjoining Parts of South America* (Hereford, 1774). (Courtesy of the John Carter Brown Library at Brown University)

great number of words, which are as much as sentences (...), like *Taoxritan*, give me some fish."[11]

At the same time, this "deviant" form of constructing words with a syntactic function had to fit into a concept of linguistic uniformity. Since the Middle Ages, Europeans shared a belief in the isomorphic relationship between language and reality; reality was one and universal, constituted identically for all people at all times and in all places. The parts of speech or word classes of Greek and Latin—traditionally noun, pronoun, article (Greek), verb, participle, adverb, conjunction, preposition, and interjection (Latin)— were believed to be the linguistic representations of universal logical categories. As there was one (divine) truth, so there was

(133)

The Declination of the Nouns.

Singular.	Plural.
N. Huentu, *the man,*	N. Pu huentu or ⎱ *the men,*
G. Huentuni, *of the man, &c.*	huentu eng'n ⎰
D. Huentumo,	G. Pu huentu, *of the men.*
A. Huentumo,	and so on, as in the singular.
V. Huentu,	
A. Huentumo,	
or Huentu engu,	

The Pronouns.

Inche,	*I,*	Quisu,	⎧ *he alone or*
Eimi,	*thou,*		⎩ *himself,*
Vei,	*he,*	Inche quisu,	*I myself,*
T'va or T'vachi,	*this,*	Inchiu,	*we two,*
Velli,	*that,*	Inchin,	*we many.*
Inei,	*whom,*		

And in the same manner,

| Eimi, | *thou,* | Eim'n | *you many.* |
| Eimu, | *you two,* | | |

For pronouns possessive is used the genitive, or sign of the genitive, of the pronouns; ni, *mine;* mi, *thine.* Likewise m'ten, *only;* used sometimes as an adjective or pronoun, and at other times as an adverb.

The verbs have only one conjugation, and are never irregular or defective. They are formed from any part of speech, either by giving it the termination of a verb, or adding to it the verb substantive gen, or, as it is pronounced, 'ngen, which answers to the Latin verb sum, es, fui, &c.

M m   EXAMPLES.

FIGURE 13.2 A grammatical analysis of the Mapuche language, in Falkner, *A Description of Patagonia and the Adjoining Parts of South America* (Hereford, 1774). (Courtesy of the John Carter Brown Library at Brown University)

one logical structure by which reality could be understood and, as a result, one grammar on which any particular language relied. All forms of expression could essentially be reduced to one fundamental structure, as the influential Port-Royal *Grammaire générale et raisonnée* (1660) intended to demonstrate.

For the missionaries, their Latin education obviously provided them with the most practical tool in their attempt to study and describe the language of their converts. Also since the first grammars of European vernaculars, dating from the sixteenth century, were modelled mostly after Latin grammar, it was hardly surprising that the Latin framework was used to describe New World languages. In terms of word structure, the drawback of this model was its restrictive hypothesis about the scope of complexity that could reasonably be expected in a language. The classical tongues largely defined what linguistic art could encompass in terms of inflections and declensions. A statement on the economy of Greek inflection by Lord Monboddo is significant in that respect: "its [Greek's] flections save the multiplication of words unnecessarily, expressing all that can be *conveniently* expressed in that way, and nothing more."[12] Consequently, the European criteria of *universality* and *appropriateness*, relying on the model of classical languages, in many cases impeded a truthful description of Indian speech, that is, a description that did not define the boundaries of grammatical complexity in terms of the grammar of Greek and Latin.

The French eighteenth-century grammar of Galibi by La Salle de l'Étang flatly denies that the Indian language can be rich in lexical and grammatical expression. The culture of its speakers, the author says, precludes it:

> Another proof of the richness of a language shows in the abundance of expressions, and the number of ways to express tenses, modes, or the means to express definite or indefinite signification. It will be easy to show that the Galibi language is lacking in that kind of proof... It suffices to cast a glance at their way of life, their customs, their occupations, and at the little knowledge that they have or can have.[13]

On the other hand, La Salle also stresses the imperfection of the knowledge he has been able to obtain about Galibi, a failure he imputes to the inconsistent spelling used by Europeans and their inability to distinguish between regional dialects and to recognize loanwords: "It is true," La Salle writes, "that we know only a part of the Galibi language" ("Il est vraisemblable qu'on ne connoît qu'une partie de La Langue des Galibis," 1763: xiii). In fact, it appears that the missionary Biet, one of La Salle's sources, thought he was describing Galibi when, in reality, he was describing forms in the process of pidginization.[14]

La Salle is very clear on the method to be used for compiling a grammar of Galibi, namely, understand the unknown by means of the known: "What can be easier? We will briefly explain the principles of the French language, and afterwards apply them to the language of the Galibis."[15] On the word level, he distinguishes between the "arbitrary" usage of certain particles that have no significance in themselves but merely serve "l'élégance" (1763: xii), that is, euphony, and other particles that are significant and stand for a particular concept, such as the nominal affix *ké*. Still, the analysis remains superficial, for *ké* may express "with," the author says, but also "sometimes because of," which is not further explained.

For all its extensiveness—the "essai de Grammaire" takes up twenty-seven pages and is followed by a dictionary in two parts, French-Galibi (sixty-nine pages) and Galibi-French (fifty-three pages)—the work nowhere gives a proper analysis of the linguistic features of Galibi that differ from Latin or French.

In his discussion of verbal inflection, La Salle, like the missionaries Pelleprat and Biet before him, fails to recognize the Galibi usage of a prefix added to each transitive verb to refer to both agent and patient. The form *sicaboüi*, for example, stands for "I have done it," where the prefix -s- realizes a combined reference to both the first person agent "I" and to the third person patient "it." This verbal form, however, is translated as "j'ai fait" (I have done) in the French text (1763: 10), that is, without the object "it." Likewise, because of the difficulty he has in determining which verbs are inflected and which are not, La Salle states that verbs are "irregular": "The majority of these verbs appear to be irregular, and often there is even no connection between the tenses, because none is derived from another."[16] As a result, his dictionary often lists inflected forms, such as "He has gone to look for water." ("Il est allé chercher de l'eau. *Tounaïé*," 1763: 40), without analyzing their formal complexity.

La Salle's overall judgement regarding Galibi construction is that it resembles the language of young children ("c'est celle qu'employe un Enfant," 1763: xiv), who do nothing but connect words referring to persons with words expressing sentiments or desires without applying any linguistic art, that is, without the use of conjugations or declensions: "Instead of saying, *I would like some bread*, a child and the Galibi will say, *me want bread*."[17] From that point of view, Galibi speakers apparently "suppress" articles, pronouns, prepositions, genders, and cases, which—from a universalist perspective—"should" amount to six, as in Latin: "The Galibis have nothing in their language that makes distinctions of gender, of number, and of case, for which there should be six in the declension of each word."[18]

* * * *

UNLIKE LA SALLE, David Cranz's account of Greenlandic does not insist on what should be expected in the art of any language. For a start, Cranz does not embed his observations on Greenlandic morphology or word structure in the categories the reader knows from European languages or the classical tongues. He has the following remark on the Greenlandic method of compounding words: "They also coin many denominatives and verbals; nay they compound a piece of a verb with a noun, in order to make new nouns for greater clearness."[19] Pronouns "are not placed before the word, but one or two of its letters are tacked to it behind" (1767: 220), he observes; and prepositions are affixed to nouns, which themselves are declined, for example, for possession: "*nunamit*, from the land; *nunaunit*, from my land" (1767: 221).

Cranz repeatedly points to the conciseness of Greenlandic expression and the intricacy of Greenlandic utterances, even though he sometimes mistakes combining elements into a single word for combining "words" themselves: "they join many words together, so that, like the North-Americans, they can express themselves very concise [sic] and yet significant [sic]" (1767: 218).

Moreover, Cranz's text even provides an analysis of a polysynthetic string: "A Greenlander that is master of his language, can express, with one tenfold-compounded word, the following whole sentence: 'He says, that thou also wilt go away quickly in like manner and buy a pretty knife'; Knife-pretty-buy-go away-haste-wilt-in like manner-thou-also-he says *Sauig-ik-sini-ariartok-asuar-omar-y-otit-tog-og*."[20] Analyses like these are not frequent in his work, and they are not accompanied by a comprehensive discussion of grammatical elements, but Cranz manages to convince his reader that the different speech of the Greenlanders is as organized grammatically as any European tongue.

* * * *

SIMILAR OBSERVATIONS concerning the difference in productivity and internal structure that distinguishes Indian word forms from those in European languages occur in Thomas Falkner's grammar of Mapuche. Falkner's twelve-page account of the Moluche dialect of the language comprises a grammatical analysis (1774: 132–40), a word list of numerals and adverbs (1774: 141), a translation of the Sign of the Cross, the beginning of the Lord's Prayer and the Creed (1774: 142–43)—"intermixed with a few Spanish words, where the Indian idiom is insufficient" (1774: 143)—and a short vocabulary of eighty-seven words (1774: 144).[21] The grammar confirms some of the features of verb conjugation in Mapuche, which has remained fairly unchanged over nearly three hundred years.[22]

Although Falkner uses Latin verbal conjugation as a point of reference, and starts with a discussion of how Mapuche verbs show the typical categories or "accidents" (number, mood, person, tense, and voice) of Latin, he also observes that Mapuche uses inflections in a different manner.

In contrast to Cranz, Falkner is aware that not all elements in the string that is a Mapuche utterance are "words" that have meaning in isolation; some are what he calls "particles" (1774: 134). Tenses, for example, of which in Mapuche, he says, there are "as many ... as in the Greek tongue" (1774: 134), are formed by "interposing" (1774: 134) the following particles between the stem and the finite suffixes (1774: 134–35):

Present	(none)
Imperfect	*bu*
Perfect	*yee*
Preterperfect	*yeebu*
First aorist	*abu*
Second aorist	*yeabu*
First future	*a*
Second future	*yea*

Hence, unlike Latin, Mapuche does not "fuse" several grammatical meanings (such as person, tense, number) into one inflectional ending. The first person singular indicative of the verb *elun* (root *elu*), "to give," looks as follows in the several tenses:

Present	*Elun*
Imperfect	*Elubun*
Perfect	*Eluyeen*
Preterperfect	*Eluyeebun*
First aorist	*Eluabun*
Second aorist	*Eluyeabun*
First future	*Eluan*
Second future	*Eluyean*

Besides a classical pattern of categories, Falkner's description also takes into account verbal forms that have no parallel in Latin and Greek. Although like many of his predecessors and contemporaries he considers polysemy—one form having two or more different meanings—a linguistic "impropriety" (1774: 139) and refers to, for example, the "equivocation in their tongue which is found especially in the prepositions; where one having many significations, the meaning is oftentimes very much confused" (1774: 139),

Falkner gives a truthful analysis of some of the typical inflectional structures in the words of the language.

He recognizes the productive derivation of verbs "from any part of speech" (1774: 133), which is done either by adding the finite verbal suffixes to the stem or by adding the inflected substantive verb *'nge*. For example (1774: 134):

Ata	evil or bad
Atan or *Atangen*	to be bad
Atal'n or *Atalcan*	to corrupt or make bad

Apart from derivation, Falkner observes the "mode" of "compounding verbs, altering their significations" (1774: 140). He roughly puts several changes of meaning together, for example, those "signifying and expressing how and in what manner the thing is done, by the interposition of prepositions, adverbs, adjectives, &c" (1774: 140). Having analyzed the elements of verbal conjugation, he is able to analyze a number of polysynthetic units, such as (1774: 135):

Chasimota iloavinquin,   Let me eat it with salt

Now iloavin is the first future, with the particle vi interposed, to signify *it*. I do not know whether quin is anything more than a particle of ornament; as in the word chasimota; where the concluding syllable ta is useless, but for the sake of sound; as chasimo, without any addition, is the ablative case of chasi, *salt*.

And (1774: 140):

Pevemgelavin,   I saw him not on this manner

Pen signifies *to see*; pevin is *I saw him*; vemge, *on this manner*; and la is the negative.

Most importantly, Falkner's text describes another, optional, verbal property, typical of many South American languages. Falkner calls it the phenomenon of "transition: whereby they signify, as well the person that acts, as him on whom the action passes, by the interposition or addition of certain determinate particles to express it" (1774: 137). This verbal property implies that in verbs that express an action involving two or more referents, one "portmanteau" morpheme is added to the verbal stem, which refers both to the referent who performs the action or who generates it and to the receiver or patient of the action. Significantly, La Salle de l'Étang's grammar does not analyze a similar case in Galibi—*sicaboüi* ("I have done it")—in which the prefix *-s-* refers both to the first person subject "I" and the third person object "it."

Falkner identifies six different types of transition, which formed part of a larger set he says he does not remember completely. The first three types are realized by "particles" that are contracted with the finite suffixes, varying according to mood and to number of the patient. In the fourth type the morphemes of transition vary according to number and mood and are added to the inflected verbal forms. The fifth and sixth types are expressed in morphemes placed between stem and finite suffixes (1774: 138–40). The following sets of elements can be deduced from the account:

TRANSITION MORPHEMES

1. From me to thee or you   *ei/y*
2. From you to me   *en*
3. From him to me   *mo*
4. From him to thee   *eneu* (sg.), *eymu mo* (dual), *eim'n mo* (pl.)
5. From me or you to him   *vi*
6. mutual   *huu*, or 'as it is pronounced' *wu*

TRANSITION MORPHEMES CONTRACTED WITH FINITE SUFFIXES IN THE INDICATIVE

	sg	dual	pl
1.	*eymi*	*eymu*	*eim'n*
2.	*en*	*eiu*	*ein*
3.	*mon*	*moiu*	*moin*

4. (no contraction paradigms mentioned)
5. (no contraction paradigms mentioned)
6. (no contraction paradigms mentioned)

Applied to the verb *elu* ("to give"), this yields the following structures:

1. *Elueymu* — I give to you two
2. *Eluen* — You give to me
3. *Elumoin* — He gives to us many
4. *Eluneu* — He gives to thee
5. *Eluviyu/vimu* — We or you two give to him
6. *Ayuwimi* — Thou lovest thyself

Forms of *transition* have been discussed in modern studies in terms of "focal" and "satellite person" by Salas,[23] in terms of "suffixes of interaction" by Contreras and Alvarez-Santullano,[24] and in terms of topic inflection, reflecting a person-oriented hierarchy of discourse participants by Grimes.[25] They show that Falkner's analyses, taking into account the contemporary context, are remarkably accurate from a descriptive point of view. Compare this example by Grimes (1985: 150, no. 18) with one of Falkner's analyses:

pe-a-E-n
see-future-PARTICIPANT=MINIMAL-indicative=speaker=singular
you will see me.

This is an instance of Falkner's second type of transition. It shows that he isolated the *"e"* correctly but mistook the finite suffix *"n"* for part of the element that expressed transition.

Lord Monboddo's Interpretation of La Salle de l'Étang, Cranz, and Falkner

In the three roughly contemporary works we have considered, two very different attitudes toward the complexity of American Indian word forms prevail. The author La Salle de l'Étang perceives almost total irregularity in the Galibi language and does not suggest any analysis of forms to understand its grammar. Cranz and Falkner, however, point out the significance of the concise, polysynthetic word forms of Greenlandic and Mapuche. Falkner even draws up paradigms of grammatical elements that make up the inflection of verbs and puts Mapuche on a par with Greek in terms of linguistic art.

These disparate types of description led to equally disparate views in language theory of the era, in which the assumed grammatical perfection of languages was a criterion for classification. The following remark from one of Lord Monboddo's manuscripts indicates what the Scottish author derived from La Salle de l'Étang's work, a work he counted among accounts of Indian languages "that can be depended upon":[26] "all the words of their language ... tho mostly very long words, some of them of many Syllables, & very few of them Monosyllables, are all Primitive words, & unconnected one with another."[27] Because of this "parcel of Indeclinable words" (MS.24505.v.f.102) that is the Galibi language, Monboddo believes that discourse must be defective in Galibi and rely on what he believes are characteristics of the early stages of speech in human beings, such as tones of the voice or gestures.

In contrast, Monboddo concludes Greenlandic is more perfect than could be expected from an "unrefined" people: "One might rather entertain the conjecture, that they must have had some judicious clear heads, to reduce their tongue to such an artful and pretty rule."[28] Yet, although he observes that the language is very rich in words, Monboddo does not make mention of the more original analyses of word structure that Cranz introduces. He singles out Cranz's remarks that deal with separate parts of speech (nouns, pronouns, adjectives) only as far as these parts resemble those of European languages, but he says nothing about Cranz's analysis of "word sentences."

In the case of Mapuche, however, Monboddo acclaims the art of the phenomenon Falkner described as "transitions": "And it has not only reciprocating verbs, like the Greek middle verbs, but also verbs which distinguish by Flection, not only the pronoun, which is the Agent of the Action, but the pronoun which is the Subject of it whether it be I, thou, we, Ye, he or they."[29] Still, the fact that Monboddo speaks of a "pronoun," instead of a "particle," like Falkner, and does not use the specific term "transition" reveals that he still tries to identify a completely different linguistic structure in terms of traditional grammatical categories.

The "very great art" of an Indian language like Mapuche ultimately did not shake Monboddo's original perspective on the connection between language and culture. Instead of distinguishing a language from its role as a cultural icon, and instead of regarding its grammar as a complex expression of meaning that has its own structural worth, his final point is that a grammatically complex language cannot have been an inherent part of the history of a people that he supposed to be culturally primitive. As a matter of fact, Falkner's analysis convinced the Scottish judge that "some time or other" the Mapuches must have been "connected with some more civilized nation, from whom they have learned to speak."[30]

Thomas Falkner introduced his description of Mapuche by saying that the language was "more copious and elegant, than could have been expected from an uncivilized people."[31] The concessive tone of his words hints at the fact that the discovery of "regular" structures in American Indian languages to some extent puzzled eighteenth-century Europeans. If the general course of the history of civilization was from *rudeness* to *refinement*, then Indian tribes could teach Europeans about European cultural prehistory, and so Indian languages were expected to do so likewise. If these languages had grammatical rules instead of the expected random combinations of words, then Monboddo's notion that they were not really the languages of their Indian speakers provided one way to maintain the assumption that Indian culture was less refined than European culture.

Conclusion

In our comparison of three eighteenth-century European descriptions of indigenous Amerindian languages with complex word structures, we have highlighted differences in descriptive accuracy. We have not traced the factors that may explain the discrepancies, such as the amount of time an observer was exposed to the language, the sources he could rely on in composing his grammatical analysis, or his capacity as an analyst of language. Our aim has been to illustrate the disparate character of the linguistic information that was available to Europeans of this era who tried to gain an insight into the languages of the New World.

Our conclusion on eighteenth-century understanding of the patterns of Amerindian word forms ends on a point of unresolved conflict. On the one hand, we have shown that using labels like "pre-scientific" does not do justice to some missionaries' independent analyses of what to them were new grammatical structures. On the other hand, the availability of empirically independent descriptions did not yet induce scholars to interpret the new forms of linguistic expression as alternative, rather than more primitive, forms of expression; and even if scholars did so, this did not yet yield a theoretical separation between the structure of a language and its connection with evaluative cultural categories. In that sense, an interpretative gap still separates Enlightenment linguistic theory from the broadened linguistic horizon at the start of the nineteenth century, when that next step would be taken. A comment by nineteenth-century linguist Wilhelm von Humboldt on his own attitude toward the study of languages, from an 1836 treatise, is significant in that respect: "We have everywhere set out at first from the *structure* of languages alone, and in forming a judgement about it have also confined ourselves solely to this."[32] Enlightenment language theory is a far cry from this position of linguistic autonomy, but it bears elements of transition that were the immediate condition for this development.

Notes

1. Victor E. Hanzeli, *Missionary Linguistics in New France: A Study of Seventeenth- and Eighteenth-Century Descriptions of American Indian Languages* (The Hague, 1969), 14.
2. Sylvain Auroux, et al., eds., *Matériaux pour une histoire des théories linguistiques* (Lille, 1984), XIV.
3. Even Hovdhaugen, "Early Grammars of Amerindian Languages of Latin America," *Beiträge zur Geschichte der Sprachwissenschaft* 6, no. 1 (1996): 131.
4. Even Hovdhaugen, ed., *... and the Word Was God: Missionary Linguistics and Missionary Grammar* (Münster, 1996).
5. Even Hovdhaugen, "A Grammar without a Tradition? Fernando de la Carrera's *Arte de la lenga yunga* (1644)," in *Diversions of Galway: Papers on the History of Linguistics*, ed. Anders Ahlqvist (Amsterdam & Philadelphia, 1992), 121.
6. See, e.g., Henry Home (Lord Kames), *Sketches of the History of Man* (Edinburgh, 1774); Thomas Reid, *An Inquiry into the Human Mind on the Principles of Common Sense* (Edinburgh, 1764). For an introduction to Enlightenment views of the Americas, see P.J. Marshall and Glyndwr Williams, *The Great Map of Mankind: Perceptions of New Worlds in the Age of Enlightenment* (Cambridge, MA, 1982).
7. These are data from *The Encyclopaedia of Language and Linguistics*, ed. R.E. Asher (Oxford, 1994).
8. Ibid.
9. See Robert A. Croese, "Mapuche Dialect Survey," in *South American Indian Languages: Retrospect and Prospect*, ed. Harriet E. Klein and Louisa R. Stark (Austin, 1985), 784–801. Asher, *The Encyclopaedia of Language and Linguistics*, indicates 440,000 speakers were reported in 1982, with around 400,000 in Chile between the Itata and Toltén rivers and 40,000 or more in Argentina.
10. Research on these and other missionary grammars and dictionaries was carried out at The John Carter Brown Library in spring 1995, sponsored by a JCB Research Fellowship. I want to thank the library staff for its generous assistance and hospitality.
11. Gabriel Sagard, *Dictionaire de la langue Huronne* (Paris, 1632), preface, 8: "Ils ont un grand nombre de mots, qui sont autant de sentences ..., comme Taoxritan, donne-moy du poisson." Note that French quotations are in the original spelling.
12. Lord Monboddo, *Of the Origin and Progress of Language*, vol. II (Edinburgh & London, 1774), 421, my emphasis.
13. Simon-Philibert de La Salle de l'Étang, *Dictionnaire Galibi* (Paris, 1763), xiv–xv: "Une autre preuve de la richesse d'une Langue, se tire & [sic] de l'abondance des tours de phrases, & de la quantité de moyens d'exprimer les temps, les modes ou les manieres de signifier d'une façon déterminée ou indéfinie. Il sera aisé de démontrer que cette preuve manque à la Langue des Galibis ... Il suffiroit de jetter un coup d'œil sur leur genre de vie, sur leurs mœurs, sur leurs occupations, sur le peu de connoissances qu'ils ont ou qu'ils peuvent avoir."
14. See Odile Renault-Lescure, "À propos des premières descriptions d'une langue Caribe, le Galibi," *Amérindia: Revue d'Ethnolinguistique Amérindienne*, special no. 6 (1984): 201. See also the essay by Ives Goddard in this volume.
15. La Salle de l'Étang, *Dictionnaire Galibi*, iii: "Quoi de plus simple? On exposera en abrégé les principes de la langue françoise, & on en fera l'application à la langue des Galibis."

16. Ibid., 8: "La plûpart de ces verbes paroissent irréguliers, il n'y a même souvent aucun rapport entre les tems, qui ne dérivent point les uns des autres."
17. Ibid., xv: "Au lieu de dire, Je voudrois du pain; l'Enfant & le Galibi diront, Moi vouloir pain. Aou icé meyou."
18. Ibid., 1–2: "Les Galibis n'ont rien dans leur langue qui fasse la distinction du genre, du nombre & des cas qui sont au nombre de six pour la déclinaison de chaque mot."
19. David Cranz, *The History of Greenland* (London, 1767), 220.
20. Ibid., 224–25. For a list of other eighteenth-century descriptions of Greenlandic, see Elke Nowak, "How to 'Improve' a Language: The Case of Eighteenth Century Descriptions of Greenlandic," in Ahlqvist, *Diversions of Galway*, 157–67.
21. The text has remained unnoticed in the history of linguistics. For a more elaborate discussion of this work, see Lieve Jooken, "The Grammar of Moluche in Thomas Falkner's *A Description of Patagonia* (1774)," to appear in *Proceedings of the Berkeley Linguistics Society 22, Special Session: Historical Issues in American Indian Languages* (Berkeley).
22. See modern studies by Constantin Contreras and Pilar Alvarez-Santullano, "Los Huiliches y su sistema verbal," *RLA: Revista de Lingüística Teórica y Aplicada* 27 (1989): 39–65; and Adalberto Salas, "The Minimal Finite Verbal Paradigm in Mapuche or Araucanian at the End of the Sixteenth Century," in *Language Change in South American Indian Languages*, ed. Mary Ritchie Key (Philadelphia, 1991), 166–77.
23. Adalberto Salas, "Terminaciones transiciones en el verbo mapuche: Crítica y bases para una nueva interpretacíon," *RLA: Revista de Lingüística Teórica y Aplicada* 16 (1978): 167–79.
24. Contreras and Alvarez-Santullano (1989).
25. Joseph E. Grimes, "Topic Inflection in Mapudungun Verbs," *International Journal of American Linguistics* 51, no. 2 (1985): 141–63.
26. Lord Monboddo, *Of the Origin and Progress of Language*, vol. I, 2d rev. ed. (Edinburgh & London, 1774), 532.
27. Lord Monboddo, "Observations on the Galibi and Caribbee Languages," unpublished manuscript (c. 1766), Monboddo Papers, National Library of Scotland, Edinburgh, MS.24505.v.f.101.
28. Lord Monboddo, *Of the Origin and Progress of Language*, vol. I, 2d rev. ed. (1774), 556–57.
29. Ibid., 551–52.
30. Ibid., 549.
31. Thomas Falkner, *A Description of Patagonia and the Adjoining Parts of South America* (Hereford, 1774), 132.
32. Wilhelm von Humboldt, *Über die Verschiedenheit des menschlichen Sprachbaues und ihren Einfluss auf die geistige Entwicklung des Menschengeschlechts* (Berlin, 1836). English translation by Peter Heath, *The Diversity of Human Language Structures and Its Influence on the Mental Development of Mankind* (Cambridge, England, 1988), 217.

– *Chapter 14* –

"SAVAGE" LANGUAGES IN EIGHTEENTH-CENTURY THEORETICAL HISTORY OF LANGUAGE

༺༻

Rüdiger Schreyer

The Orthodox View of Linguistic Relationships

FOREIGNERS SPEAK FOREIGN LANGUAGES.[1] The diversity of languages is a commonplace fact. It becomes a problem whenever people begin to wonder why the languages on this Earth are so many and so different. For Christians, the diversity of languages was a problem, but until the eighteenth century it was a problem with a biblical solution: All human beings stem from one human couple, from Adam and Eve. Language had been bestowed on Adam by God Almighty, even though the method of transmission was somewhat obscure. Later the Flood had drowned the whole of humankind with the exception of Noah and his family; therefore all humans ultimately derive from him. Why, then, do they not all speak one language? Again the Bible provides the answer. Linguistic diversity is the result of the confusion of tongues at Babel, a punishment visited upon humanity by the Creator. This linguistic and social catastrophe dispersed humankind all over the globe. The original languages of Babel—with the possible exception of Hebrew—began to change.[2] In time many minute changes transformed them, sometimes perhaps beyond recognition. Wars, disasters, migrations, conquests, and commerce led to their inexorable corruption. And thus the linguistic curse of Babel lingers to the present day.

The Christian view of history was informed by the idea of the Fall—a change from pristine divine perfection to diabolical corruption. Humanity's linguistic fall from grace had begun with Babel, and no one knew where or when it might end. This dark view of linguistic (and cultural) diversity survived well into the eighteenth century. It proved flexible enough and vague enough to accommodate the vernaculars of the newly discovered peoples of Asia and Africa; thousands of years of wandering might have taken their remote ancestors to the most distant corners of the earth.[3] Was it not reasonable to assume that they, too, were children of Noah?

The Biblical preoccupation with genealogy may have suggested a compatible genealogy of languages. To Christian writers, similarities between remote languages pointed to migrations of their speakers from a common homeland with a common mother tongue. To trace the meanderings of the tribes of Israel or to provide a suitable ancestry for their own tongue, early etymologists and comparativists collected words of many languages. Vocabularies were scanned for words similar in sound and meaning. If found—and some could always be found—such words were interpreted as cognates, as evidence for a genealogical link between the compared languages.[4] If Hebrew cognates were found, all the better! Did this not prove that the language under scrutiny was related to, or even descended from, the most venerable language of them all? To us these etymologies appear weird and wonderful. But to early comparativists they were satisfactory, and more important, they were in tune with God's revelation.

The Amerindian Challenge

The discovery of the New World challenged the comfortable world view that had, over centuries, evolved from Christian lore. Even the mere existence of the Americans constituted a threat. How did they fit into the Great Chain of Being, God's grand scheme of things? They were so different and so savage that they barely seemed human. Indeed, there were rumours of Indian tribes that lacked the tell-tale signs of humanity—sociability, reason, and language. Most American savages, however, appeared to be sociable, rational, and even talking animals. Had not the Pope himself pronounced them human beings?

The discovery of wild—but nonetheless human—creatures gave rise to an "inquiry that merits attention," as the historian William Robertson (1721–1793) put it with Scottish understatement. Robertson knew "with infallible certainty," as only the Bible could give, "that all the human race spring from the same source." But "how was America peopled? By what course did mankind migrate from one continent to the other? and in what quarter is it most probable that a communication was opened between them?"[5]

That America was peopled from the other continents was a foregone conclusion. Migration was the only solution in line with the Bible. Unfortunately, in the case of the Americans, there were unprecedented difficulties. What route could their migrating ancestors have taken? They could hardly have sailed across the uncharted depths of the Ocean Sea. And a pedestrian migration from Asia presupposed the unlikely existence of a landbridge between America and Asia in the uncharted, icy wastes of the North.

Perhaps the inhabitants of the New World could be connected to those of the Old World by a linguistic link. Similar customs point to related peoples, and so do similar languages. Many scholars were, therefore, "seized by the strong desire of getting to know the languages of these people. For there are some who think if they found traces of the languages of our continent in the Americans, they could find out from this which way the first inhabitants arrived in America."[6]

The familiar comparative method was the ultima ratio. Hundreds of word-lists compiled by missionaries, travellers, explorers, and merchants were collected, scrutinised, and compared in the fond hope of finding American cognates of some—preferably ancient—Old World language.[7] A late exponent of this method was François Lafitau (1681–1746), a learned Jesuit missionary and comparativist.[8] Lafitau maintains that the American idioms could not possibly be an American invention. He finds order and economy even in the languages of the most uncivilised American tribes. The natives themselves are perfectly unaware of this and therefore truly amazed when the subtle linguistic rules and artifices of their language are expounded to them.[9] In view of the linguistic ignorance of modern savages, Lafitau argues, it makes little sense to credit their rude ancestors with the invention of such methodical grammars. Consequently the Amerindian languages cannot but derive from a non–American mother tongue.

Lafitau readily admits that this postulated mother tongue is hard to trace. The Amerindian languages are radically different not only from Hebrew, Greek, and Latin, but also from the oriental languages or, indeed, any other known language.[10] Therefore, Lafitau concludes with impeccable logic, they must derive from an Old World language unknown to us. He concludes that "a great part of the American peoples and, perhaps, the Huron and Iroquois in particular, are descended from the barbarous peoples who first occupied Greece," peoples who according to Herodotus (c. 485–425 B.C.) spoke "languages of a structure totally different from that of the later Greeks."[11] Fortunately, Herodotus and other ancient authors list a few words from these extinct barbarous tongues. Many of these would have been deformed by ignorance and mispronunciation, but some "are purely Huron and Iroquois."[12] Finding illustrative examples was easy for someone as versed in the Iroquoian languages as Lafitau.

Lafitau was not the only one to forge an etymological link between the Old and the New world. But even the uninhibited *furor etymologicus* of the times could not make a strong case for a European or Asian descent of the Americans. The alleged similarities between Amerindian and Eurasian languages were few and far between. Furthermore, in the course of the eighteenth century, the old and crude comparative-etymological approach itself came under attack. As early as 1713 Adrian Reland (1676–1718) scolded etymologists such as Becanus (Jan van Gorp,1518–1572) or Schriekius (Adrian van Schriek, 1560–1623) for indiscriminately collecting and comparing words from different languages in the naive belief that the mere existence of phonetically and semantically similar words would be sufficient proof of a genealogical link.[13] Words coincident in sound and meaning might, after all, be the result of onomatopoeia or pure chance.[14] With the old comparative method, says Reland, anything can be derived from anything.[15] To improve it, he suggested that words of rare use be excluded. Furthermore, prospective cognates should be short and common, such as *sun, moon, water, earth, good, bad* or numbers, "whose names are found in all languages."[16]

During the eighteenth century the unrestrained and unprincipled etymologising of former times was losing credibility, and so were the genealogical relationships alleged between the languages of the Old and the New World. Robertson dismissed proposals that the Americans were the offspring of colonising Jews, Canaanites, Phoenicians, Carthaginians, Greeks, Scyths, Chinese, Swedes, Norwegians, Welsh, or Spaniards as pure speculation, resting on no more than "the casual resemblance of some customs, or the supposed affinity between a few words in their different languages."[17]

But how could one account for the Amerindian languages without deriving them from an Old World language? Some argued that the languages were "really" related to each other but in time had undergone so many changes that all similarities had vanished. It was common knowledge that no American nation had the use of writing.[18] And was change not particularly rampant in languages unfixed by an alphabetic script?

However, decreeing a connection without a shred of evidence could not satisfy the emerging empirical bent of mind. Novel and sometimes unorthodox theories were proposed and rejected in due course.[19] To most Europeans the suggestion that Americans derived from Adamic tribes that had survived the Flood was preposterous. Even more so was the notion they were the children of an American Adam, an ancestor that the Bible had omitted to mention.

Lord Kames (1698–1782) toyed with the idea that God had created several human pairs and placed them strategically in different parts of the world. He conjectured that their descendants, "having no assistance but their natural talents, were left to gather knowledge from experience, and in particular were left (each tribe), to form a language for itself; that signs were sufficient for the original pairs, without any language but what nature suggests; and that a language was formed gradually, as a tribe increased in numbers and in different occupations, to make speech necessary."[20]

This, Kames declared, was the most plausible scenario. Sadly, however, Revelation "contradicts every one of the facts mentioned above," and—good Christian that he was—Kames discarded the hypothesis of a polygenesis of peoples but not of languages.[21] Like most theoretical historians of the Enlightenment, he opted for a solution that allowed him to have his Bible and ignore it too. Ingeniously wedding the Christian idea of Fall and degeneration to the Enlightenment idea of progress, he reconciled "sacred and profane history" by postulating that the confusion of tongues was followed by a return to savagery. That deplorable event dramatically reversed all nature by scattering humans "abroad upon the face of all the earth," depriving them of society and rendering them savages, a state of degeneracy from which they gradually re-emerged at different rates of progress.[22]

If you may not begin with savages, re-interpret Scripture to make humanity's lapse into savagery plausible and then blithely follow the lead of Lucretius (96–55 B.C.), Diodorus Siculus (died ca. 20 B.C.), and Horace (65–8 B.C.). Start with *mutum et turpe pecus*, start with a wild speechless couple and let man invent language and himself.[23]

The Eighteenth-Century "Science of Man"[24]

Eighteenth-century Europe met the Amerindian challenge by restructuring its view of man, by creating a new philosophy of man on scientific principles. Emulating natural philosophy, the new science was to be based on experience and observation. It was to employ the method of analysis and synthesis mapped out by Bacon and practised so successfully by Newton: the new scientist had to observe the phenomena, establish their underlying principles (analysis), and reconstruct them from these principles in a causal chain (synthesis).

The new science of man, or moral philosophy, also had to provide an explanation for the diversities and similarities of peoples and cultures distant in time and space. Moral philosophers regarded all societal achievements, institutions, arts, and sciences as "inventions" of society, resulting from the dialectic interaction of the God-given, innate principles of human nature with the geographical and social circumstances of a people. All societal phenomena were the result of a complex historical process of directed change from chaos to order, unruliness to rule, simplicity to complexity, or—to use a dichotomy dear to the eighteenth century—from nature to art. It was the task of the moral philosopher to create a plausible, genetic reconstruction of the cultural and societal progress of mankind. This grand undertaking was variously known as natural, conjectural, philosophical, or theoretical history.

Theoretical history rested on the dogma that people in similar circumstances develop similar social institutions. It depicted societal progress as a "natural" sequence of stages, each the effect of the immutable principles of human nature and the societal and natural environment of the previous stage. It was based on the assumption that an isolated society undisturbed by external disruptions eventually would go through a fixed sequence of stages, from nuclear family through savagery, barbarity to civilised society. To (re-)construct this sequence the moral philosopher would arrange all cultures along a progressivity scale, which he would then temporalise by declaring it the "natural" history of societal evolution. The resulting quasi-historical construct was recognised as an idealisation, a conjectural history of the "natural" ascent of man.

The theory of societal progress offered a new explanation of the once puzzling cultural similarities between peoples separated by long stretches of space or time, an explanation more plausible than the gratuitous and unlikely assumption of historical contact or genealogical relationship. According to the new theory, the societal characteristics of a people are the natural effect of environmental factors on an immutable human nature. It must, therefore, be expected that peoples at the same stage of progress will exhibit more similarities, while peoples at different stages will exhibit more differences.

Unfortunately, the doctrine of progress left a major question unanswered: why were not all peoples in this world at the same stage of progress? Were they not all human? Were they not all Noah's children? Did they not all have the same time to improve themselves? The short answer was this: they may have had the same time, but not necessarily the same opportunities. Circumstances in different parts of the world are not equally favourable for progress, so all societies will not progress at the same rate. Indeed, some may barely progress beyond the first stage.[25]

This ingenious theory of stunted societal growth explains why all stages of human progress were present on this earth simultaneously—for the scientific pretensions of the theoretical historian a real godsend. At one stroke it converts all peoples of this earth into living and observable evidence for some stage of progress or other. Any particular societal, linguistic, or cultural trait observed in a people at a certain stage of progress turns into legitimate evidence for that stage. Contemporary savage and barbarian peoples turn into vestiges of former times, experiments of history, whose careful observation will shed light on the undocumented pre-historic stages of the civilised nations of Europe. And of course, it will bring us closer to natural man. Lord Monboddo (1714–1799) speaks for many of his contemporaries: "Whoever would trace human nature up to its source, must study very diligently the manners of barbarous nations, instead of forming theories of *man* from what he observes among civilized nations."[26] They are our window to the past. In them we can observe the way we were.

The Theoretical History of Language

As John Locke (1632–1704) had once said—and everyone believed—language is the common bond and the great instrument of society. It is the means for the communication of individual experience. It is the means for the transmission of knowledge from one person to another and from one generation to the next, thus enabling the gradual accumulation of knowledge. Language therefore is essential for the transformation and progress of society. But at the same time it is the product of society, created or invented like the other arts and sciences in response to its ever changing needs. Language is a tool gradually sharpened and improved by the society it is helping to change.

Theoretical historians, then, recognise a feedback loop between language, mind, and society, a loop responsible for their mutual improvement or progress. Since language plays a key role in this progress, any theoretical history of society must include a theory of linguistic evolution.[27] Central to such a theory is the question of why and how man, left to the principles of his own nature, would, or could, or must, have "invented" and improved his language. The Scottish philosopher Dugald Stewart (1753–1828) gives a concise analysis of the purpose, scope, and method of this endeavour:

> In examining the history of mankind, as well as in examining the phenomena of the natural world, when we cannot trace the process by which an event has been produced, it is often of importance to be able to show how it may have been produced by natural causes. Thus ... although it is impossible to determine with certainty what the steps were by which any particular language was formed, yet if we can shew, from the known principles of human nature, how all its various parts might gradually have arisen, the mind is not only to a certain degree satisfied, but a check is given to that indolent philosophy which refers to a miracle, whatever appearances, both in the natural and moral worlds, it is unable to explain.[28]

Language is not innate: children must learn it from their parents. It is "by art," a product of society, following a regular path of progress. It develops *pari passu* with the other arts and sciences in a dialectic process. Of necessity, a language mirrors the culture of its speakers: Cultural poverty is mirrored by linguistic poverty; cultural richness by linguistic richness. A primitive people must have a primitive language, and a polished people must have a polished language.

One of the first and most influential Enlightenment thinkers to adumbrate a theoretical history of language was Bernard Mandeville (1670–1733).[29] His *Fable of the Bees* (1729) had a great impact on the theoretical historians of the eighteenth century. At the time the book was considered subversive enough to be burned publicly by the hangman in Paris. Perhaps its worst threat to Christian doctrine was not its spectacular and misunderstood thesis "private vices, public benefits" but its secular theory of societal evolution. Skirting Biblical truth Mandeville suggested that savages and their languages might well be the result of historical accidents. During migrations, wars, and other upheavals, might not infants have been abandoned by their parents? Might they not have survived in a favourable environment? Might they not have developed a rudimentary means of communication? And would this not be improved and built upon by successive generations?[30]

Mandeville begins his theory of the progress of language and civilisation with the *fictio philosophica* of a primordial couple.[31] He maps out a sequence of evolutionary stages without much elaborating the details. Man is a social animal by nature and necessity, and even the most rudimentary society is not imaginable without a means of communication, however primitive. Giving clear recognition to the functional link between society and communication, Mandeville sees linguistic and societal evolution as a dialectic invisible-hand process, an evolutionary process driven by the needs common to all the individuals in a community, but without any conscious planning on their part.[32] In the progress of language as in that of the arts and sciences, individuals following their own private interests nevertheless work in a concerted, albeit unpremeditated, manner for the common good.

If man in the state of nature had all the faculties needed to develop language and society, the story of Adam and Eve and the story of Babel could be discarded as pious but unscientific myths. The formation of society, far from being a unique, divinely guided event, could be seen as a process that might occur and reoccur any time and any place. And so might the origin and progress of language. In Mandeville's polygenetic theory, genetically unrelated languages no longer pose a problem. There is no reason why they should not have sprung up independently in different parts of the world, finally arriving at their present state driven by nothing but the varying needs of their speakers.

Christian doctrine viewed linguistic change as a deterioration from the God-given and perfect language of Paradise. The new view of linguistic progress from primitive chaos to a sophisticated structure was the very opposite. It offered a theory of the linguistic rise of man as a scientific alternative to the pious theory of the linguistic fall. And it offered a scientific explanation for the similarities and differences of all the languages of the earth.

Evidence for a Theoretical History of Language

Theoretical historians often resorted to conjectures, and they knew it. But, to be plausible, even conjectures had to refer to facts. As Stewart and others often pointed out, there is no point in forging a long, causal chain of human progress if all its links are mere fictions. The Enlightenment had proclaimed a new science based on experiment and observation. However, what evidence was there for the origin of language? What evidence for a reconstruction of the undocumented prehistoric stages of civilised languages? The origin of language was reconstructed from facts collected about infants, deaf-mutes, and feral children; the history of later stages drew on facts about the languages of primitive, that is, savage societies. Indeed, these languages became a veritable goldmine of linguistic data. The savages of this world represented the early stages of cultural progress and—language reflecting the cultural progress of its speakers—of linguistic progress, too. The prehistoric "earlier" stages of language could be recovered by studying the speech of the "earlier" societies of the New World, and—because of the regular march of progress—this study would shed light on the undocumented stages of our own civilised languages. Savage languages were mentioned, described, analysed, and discussed in reports by Jesuit, Franciscan, Protestant, and Moravian missionaries, in accounts of travellers, voyagers, adventurers, and pirates. They were accessible in the numerous collections, selections, anthologies, and translations published in many volumes by Richard Eden (1521–1576), Richard Hakluyt (1552–1616), Samuel Purchas (1677–1626), Charles de Brosses (1709–1777), and others.

Theoretical history thus had created a conceptual framework in which Amerindian languages could find their place. At the same time, it had turned all the languages of this globe into evidence for students of linguistic progress. Naturally, the idea of linguistic progress was not welcomed by everyone. In fact, in the eighteenth century there were two major theories of linguistic development. The orthodox Christian theory clung to the concept of a monogenetic, divine, and perfect language, confused at Babel and deteriorating ever since. The (r)evolutionary new theory argued for linguistic progress from unstructured simplicity to structured complexity. These theories were in obvious conflict, and so were their advocates. To prove each other wrong they needed evidence, and to find this evidence they increasingly looked to the wild languages (as Herder called them), especially those of the savage Americans.[33]

In the eighteenth-century debate on the origin of language, these linguistic data were gaining in importance. But not all theoretical historians made the same use of the facts available or exploited them with the same fullness or detail.[34] Reference to particular wild languages was virtually absent in the arguments of Mandeville and

Condillac (1715–1780); it increased with Rousseau (1712–1778) and Herder (1744–1803) and carried an enormous weight in Lord Monboddo's history of the origin and progress of language. Even orthodox advocates of a divine origin of language, such as Süßmilch, exploited the purported evidence of savage languages without ever doubting their relevance. Thus, increasingly, proponents of and opponents to a human development of language attempted to bolster their arguments with linguistic observations. Observations on Amerindian languages, in particular, were unquestioningly proffered and accepted as evidence.

Theoretical historians would hunt for primitive societies with primitive languages, that is, languages exhibiting features their philosophy branded as primitive: poverty of vocabulary, dearth of abstract terms, lack of grammatical structure, usually taken to mean lack of inflections. Christian apologists would hunt for primitive societies with full-fledged languages exhibiting all the features expected from a civilised tongue: richness of vocabulary, wealth of abstract terms, grammatical structure. The discovery of sophisticated languages among savages would weaken the link progressivists tried to forge between the evolution of language and society and thus discredit their hypothesis.

This line of argument can be illustrated by reviewing the work of two thinkers who made extensive use of evidence from pre- and post-linguistic savagery, but with one difference: James Burnett, Lord Monboddo (1714–1799), a Scottish judge, argued for the humanity of language; Johann Peter Süßmilch (1707–1776), a physician, chaplain in the army of Frederick the Great of Prussia, and author of a work on mortality statistics, argued for its divinity.

In 1754 Süßmilch read his *Attempt of a proof that the first language had its origin not from man, but solely from the Creator* before the Prussian Academy of Sciences, of which he was a member.[35] The first language, Süßmilch wrote, comes either from man or from God; and the evidence of savage languages militates against a human origin of language.[36] Linguistic signs are arbitrary, the result of either random or reasonable choice on the part of their creator. Random choice, however, will never produce order. Any complex, symmetrical, ordered, perfect, and purposeful structure therefore must be the product of an intelligent, reasonable, and purposive mind.[37] In all languages Süßmilch finds perfection, order, and rules, even beauty and harmony: "Such is language and such are all languages, take and examine whichever you will. Even the languages of the most uncultivated nations have their rules of perfection and order."[38] The universal and very abstract categories represented by the parts of speech—substantives for substances, verbs for actions, adjectives for qualities, and numerals for numbers—show that the makers of languages must have been very subtle thinkers rather than dumb savages.

Süßmilch finds his evidence in exotic vernaculars, even those of the most primitive tribes: "The miserable Greenlanders, the dirty Hottentots, the polysyllabic Oronocks, the nomadic Tartars, the sophisticated Chinese, the Japanese and his antipode, the Carib, they all speak an orderly language."[39] Süßmilch's favourite primitives are "the miserable Greenlanders": "This poor people, veiled in cold, ice, darkness, and filth, nonetheless has a perfect language, which may be difficult for a European to learn, but still has everything that makes up a language."[40] How can any one believe that people "who seem barely more intelligent than bears and seals" would ever have had the wits or energy to create such an artful and regular language?[41] And, that hypothetical savage, man in the state of nature, must have been more ignorant than the most ignorant savage. Without language, he did not have the full use of reason, and without the full use of reason, how could he have devised a complex, sophisticated linguistic structure? If natural man could not have done it, if his savage descendants could not do it, why do primitive tribes speak sophisticated languages? The conclusion is inescapable: human language must have been bestowed on their—and our—ancestors by a greater artificer.[42] Language is divine by default.[43]

For Monboddo, on the other hand, language is human. In his conjectures he strives to demonstrate an advancement toward linguistic order on both the material (phonetic) and the formal (grammatical and lexical) levels of language. As Herder noted approvingly, Monboddo took great pains to collect linguistic information and support his arguments with linguistic illustrations. Monboddo interviewed linguistic experts, such as Roubaud, a Jesuit missionary, on Huron, or Joseph Banks (1743–1820) and Daniel Solander (1745–1782) on the languages of the South Seas. He also collected grammatical and lexical information on exotic and savage languages from a wide range of written sources. Of Amerindian vernaculars, he mentions Eskimo, various Algonquian languages, Huron, Carib, Galibi, Tupi, Guarani, and Quechua. Of non-Amerindian vernaculars he mentions Chinese and Tahitian, as well as some more familiar oriental and occidental languages. Yet Monboddo's linguistic knowledge was neither first-hand nor particularly deep.

Take the example of Huron, for Monboddo one of the most primitive languages on earth: small vocabulary, no abstract terms, no grammar, no clear articulation—a good candidate for the earliest post-linguistic stage. Monboddo's knowledge of Huron stems mainly from Brother Gabriel Sagard's *Grand voyage du pays des Hurons* (1632) and its appended dictionary. Indeed, Sagard (?–1650) was the first inspiration for Monboddo's monumental six-volume opus on the origin of language. Why prefer Sagard to the more accessible and linguistically superior observations by the Jesuits Brébeuf (1593–1649), Lafitau, or Charlevoix (1682–1761), according to whom Huron was anything but primitive? Monboddo did not know them or did not want to know them. For, clearly, Sagard's insistence on the imperfections of Huron lends stronger support to Monboddo's division of human languages into first languages and formed languages, a division fundamental to his theory of progress.[44] Formed languages are languages of art, a term implying regularity, order, structure. Examples of such languages were easy to find. What Monboddo needed was a very, very primitive language, a first language, and Sagard's Huron fitted the conjectural bill.

Conclusion on Conclusions

All participants in the debate on the origin of language seem to agree on the existence of primitive societies. They agree that there ought to be a parallel linguistic and societal development. They also agree that primitive cultures therefore ought to speak primitive languages. But they disagree about the existence of primitive languages.

The basic structure of the arguments for and against the human origin of language is simple. Theoretical historians list and discuss a range of more or less primitive languages spoken by more or less primitive peoples. To their mind, this proves that language is—or at least could be—invented by man and evolved by society. The defenders of the faith, however, assert that no primitive peoples speak primitive languages. To their mind, this paradoxical state of affairs permits only one explanation: Language is God-given, its origin divine.

The modern historian of linguistics notes a curious perversity. Christian traditionalists claimed that there are no primitive languages. This is the reigning view of modern linguistics. Enlightenment theoretical historians claimed that language is a product of social man. This, too, is the reigning view of modern linguistics. Thus traditionalists came to the wrong conclusion—the divinity of language—for the right reasons, while progressivists came to the right conclusion—the humanity of language—for the wrong reasons. Let me therefore conclude, with the benefit of hindsight, that sometimes in the history of linguistics arguments are more important than conclusions.

> *This essay is dedicated to the memory of Paul Salmon (1921–1997), scholar and gentle man.*

Notes

1. And so did our ancestors. Over the years the meaning of many words has changed, although their spelling may still be the same. Understanding therefore is a major problem for historians of ideas. But even if they understand the meaning of earlier writers, can they retain their terms in their own analysis? If they do, they run the risk of being misunderstood. If they do not, they run the risk of their authors being misunderstood. Modern terms often fail to capture the full meaning, and even more often, the emotive value, of historical terms. In this paper, to describe indigenous cultures I adopt seventeenth and eighteenth century terms such as wild, savage, primitive, etc. Then as now, these terms were pejorative when applied to autochthonous cultures, albeit in different ways. Modern readers should be aware of this, if only to understand the natural superiority Europeans arrogated to themselves over most non–Europeans. For the connotations of historical terms I refer word-lovers to the second edition of the *Oxford English Dictionary*.
2. For a while the old belief that Hebrew was the language of Paradise was still alive. Many authors derived the European languages from this mother tongue. Engelbert Kämpfer (1651–1716), *A History of Japan and Siam* (London, 1727), traced Japanese back to Hebrew, obligingly mapping out for us the route taken by the children of Israel. Adrian Reland derived the Romance languages from Hebrew via Phoenician, Greek, and Latin. Other authors spun out elaborate etymological yarns to prove that their favourite vernacular was closest to the original language.
3. According to the lights of the eighteenth century, Chinese showed little resemblance to any other language. The difficulty was discussed and removed by making Chinese an exception, a language artificially and consciously created by wise men. Thus the Chinese were brought back into Noah's fold by scholars who did not have the slightest knowledge of the Chinese language.
4. See Elke Nowak, "How to 'Improve' a Language: The Case of Eighteenth Century Descriptions of Greenlandic," *Diversions of Galway: Papers on the History of Linguistics,* ed. Anders Ahlqvist. (Amsterdam 1992), 157–67.

5. William Robertson, *The History of America*, 2d ed., 2 vols. (London/Edinburgh, 1778), 1: 264–65.
6. "Multos Eruditos incessit vehemens desiderium linguas illorum hominum cognoscendi. Erant enim, qui putabant si vestigia linguarum nostrae Continentis deprehenderentur in Americanis, hinc colligi posse, qua via in Americam primi incolae pervenissent: quod hactenum plane dubium est." Adrian Reland [Hadrianus Relandus], "Dissertatio de Linguis Americanis," *Dissertationum miscellanearum pars tertia, et ultima* (Bibliopolae, 1708), 3: 143–229 at 145.
7. For historians of linguistics it would be beneficial to have a bibliography of these word-lists, which were copied, rearranged, reassembled, and reprinted so often, that their sources are sometimes hard to find.
8. Joseph François Lafitau, S.J. (1681–1746), *Moeurs des sauvages amériquains comparées aux moeurs des premiers tem* (Paris, 1724.) This influential work thoroughly compares the customs of the "wild" Americans with those of the ancient peoples of Europe, the Greeks in particular. My references are to the English translation by William N. Fenton and Elizabeth L. Moore, *Customs of the American Indians Compared with the Customs of Primitive Times*, 2 vols. (Toronto, 1974).
9. Ibid., 253.
10. Ibid., 260. The few Greek, Latin, and French words found in Huron and Iroquois are considered to be loans, as are the Basque words found in Eskimo.
11. Ibid., 255–56.
12. Ibid., 258.
13. Goropius Becanus (Jan van Gorp van Hilvarenbeek) used etymology to prove that Hebrew derived from Dutch.
14. Reland, "Dissertatio," 148.
15. Ibid., 151.
16. Ibid., 145, 150. This sharpening of the comparative method unfortunately reduces the number of cognates in American and non-American languages. Reland therefore presents word-lists of American languages to enable the reader to make a judgement on this issue.
17. William Robertson (1721–1793), *The History of America*. 2 vols., 2d. ed. (London/Edinburgh, 1778), 1: 266.
18. This is Reland's solution. He argues for an Asian origin of the Americans, mainly on the basis of alleged cultural and religious similarities. The only linguistic criterion is the purported absence of alphabetic writing in all the peoples of Asia and America. The lack of similarities between languages can be explained: In the course of centuries, languages may have been lost, or—like Chinese—newly created, or changed beyond recognition. If the languages of Europe could change, so could the less stable American languages (Reland, "Dissertatio," 153).
19. See Robertson, *History of America*, 264–66.
20. Henry Home, Lord Kames, *Sketches of the History of Man. Considerably improved in a second edition in four vols.*, Facsimile reprint (Hildesheim, 1968), 1:76.
21. Ibid., 1:76–77.
22. Ibid., 1:78–79.
23. Cf. my remarks on Mandeville below.
24. Perhaps it needs to be pointed out that throughout the history of the English language "man" as in "mankind" or in the term "Science of Man," "natural man" could be used to refer to the whole of humankind. It seems to me that in reviewing the ideas of times past we should retain at least some of the key

terms. By (ex-)pressing old ideas in new moulds historians run the risk of falsifying history.
25. The Inca resembled the Romans because they were at the same stage of progress. If the Romans had reached that stage 1500 years before the Inca, it was because their circumstances had favoured swifter progress.
26. James Burnett, Lord Monboddo (1714–1799), *Of the Origin and Progress of Language*, 6 vols. (Menston, 1967 [1773–1792]), 1:133, 141.
27. We find the seeds of such a philosophical investigation in the seventeenth-century works of Hobbes (1588–1679), Pufendorf (1632–1694), Locke, and others, but it was not until the eighteenth century that the urgency of this problem was felt. This is why the question of the origin of language usually was addressed within the wider context of theories of societal development by such authors as Mandeville, Condillac, Rousseau, Adam Smith, Herder, or Monboddo.
28. Dugald Stewart, *The Collected Works of Dugald Stewart*, ed. Sir William Hamilton (Edinburgh, 1877), 4:39.
29. For a detailed analysis of Mandeville's theoretical history of language see Rüdiger Schreyer, "Condillac, Mandeville and the Origin of Language," *Historiographia Linguistica* 5 (1978): 15–43.
30. As we have seen, the idea later was taken up by Lord Kames.
31. The idea is borrowed from natural law theory, where it was employed as an exploratory device by Pufendorf and others.
32. The term was coined by Adam Smith (1723–1790), while the concept was elaborated by Adam Ferguson (1723–1816), *An Essay on the History of Civil Society*. With a new introduction by Louis Schneider (New Brunswick/London, 1980 [1767]).
33. There are many open questions concerning the use of "savage" languages in Enlightenment glottogonic theories. Which languages were they? Which linguistic features did theoretical historians fasten upon? How did they interpret their information? Who were their informants? What data were available or accessible? What data were actually used? How were they used?
34. Victor Hanzeli, "De la connaissance des langues indiennes de la Nouvelle France aux dix-septième et dix-huitième siècles," *Amérindia Spécial* 6 (1984): 223, notes that in the debate between Maupertuis (1698–1754) and Turgot (1727–1781) both stress the importance of the study of savage languages, but neither cites one single linguistic "fact." He concludes that the real issue was the "the origin of knowledge and not the origin and development of languages." But, as most theoretical historians of language would have claimed, no development of mind is possible without a development of language.
35. Johann Peter Süßmilch (1707–1767), *Versuch eines Beweises, daß die erste Sprache ihren Ursprung nicht vom Menschen, sondern allein vom Schöpfer erhalten habe* ... (Berlin, 1766). For a more detailed, albeit rather decontextualised, interpretation of Süßmilch's book cf., Jutta Steinmetz,"Vollkommenheit und Ordnung bei Johann Peter Süßmilch. Eine Pilotstudie."*Beiträge zur Geschichte der Sprachwissenschaft* 7 (1997): 265–76.
36. Süßmilch, *Versuch eines Beweises*, 3–4.
37. Süßmilch applies to glottogenesis the familiar proof of God's existence from the "artificiality" (i.e., the complex structure) of his creation. Invisible-hand processes are not within Süßmilch's mental scope, it seems.
38. Süßmilch, *Versuch eines Beweises*, 17, 19. "So ist aber die Sprache und so sind alle Sprachen beschaffen, wir mögen nehmen und prüfen welche wir wollen.

Auch die Sprachen der uncultivirtesten Völker haben ihre Regeln der Vollkommenheit und Ordnung" (Süßmilch, ibid.,16).
39. "Die elenden Grönländer, die schmutzigen Hottentotten, die vielsylbigen Oronocks, die umschweifenden Tartarn, die feinen Chinesen, der Japaner und sein Antipode, der Caraibe, alles redet eine ordentliche Sprache." (Süßmilch, ibid., 71).
40. "Dieses arme Volk, das in Kälte, Eis, Finsterniß und Schmutz verhüllet, hat gleichwohl eine vollkommene Sprache, die zwar einem Europäer schwer zu erlernen ist, die aber doch alles hat was zu einer Sprache gehöret." (Süßmilch, ibid., 27). Cf. also: "Die elenden Grönländer haben, wie schon angeführt, eine schwere und vollkommene Sprache, die ganz besondere Kunststücke besitzet, die wir in keiner unserer bekanten Sprachen antreffen, allein mit dem Rechnen sieht es bey ihnen schlecht aus"(Süßmilch, ibid., 29).
41. Süßmilch, ibid., 81.
42. Süßmilch, *Versuch eines Beweises*, 31. He will not consider how God might have proceeded, "since my proof is merely philosophical."(Süßmilch, ibid., Vorwort, 5).
43. There are, of course, other arguments for a divine origin of language. Süßmilch (ibid., 31, 82–83) also maintains that all languages share the same universal grammar and the same eight parts of speech. He claims that comparison will confirm the family relationship of all languages, another argument for the monogenesis of language in God (Süßmilch, ibid., Inhalt). Why should different inventors independently hit upon the same solution? Given the infinite grammatical possibilities, why should they choose the same universal grammar? Why is the same solution encountered even among "the very wildest and most stupid peoples, who even at this moment barely have the human shape, albeit a perfect language similar to that of the other more intelligent peoples"?
44. Hanzeli, "De la connaissance des langues indiennes," 22.

Select Bibliography

We have limited the following list to titles that focus on language and language use in the early-modern Americas. Additional works treating related themes are cited in the notes.

Adorno, Rolena. *Guaman Poma: Writing and Resistance in Colonial Peru*. Austin, 1986.
Amate Blanco, Juan J. "La filologia indigenista en los misioneros del siglo XVI." *Cuadernos Hispanoamericanos: Revista Mensual de Cultura Hispanica* 500 (1992): 53–70.
Anderson, Arthur J.O., Frances Berdan, and James Lockhart. *Beyond the Codices*. Berkeley, 1976.
Andresen, Julie Tetel. "Images des langues amérindiennes au XVIIIe siécle." In Daniel Droixhe and P.P. Gossiaux, eds., *L'homme des Lumières et la découverte de l'autre*, Brussels, 198: 135–45.
Axtell, James. "The Power of Print in the Eastern Woodlands." In *After Columbus: Essays in the Ethnohistory of Colonial North America*, New York, 1988: 86–99.
Bakker, Peter. "'The Language of the Coast Tribes is Half Basque': A Basque-American Indian Pidgin in Use between Europeans and Native Americans in North America, ca. 1540—ca. 1640." *Anthropological Linguistics* 31 (1989): 117–47.
Bauman, Richard, and Joel Sherzer, eds. *Explorations in the Ethnography of Speaking*. Cambridge, England, 1974.
Bayarin, Jonathan, ed. *The Ethnography of Reading*. Berkeley, 1993.
Benson, Elizabeth P., ed. *Mesoamerican Writing Systems*. Washington, DC, 1973.
Berlo, Janet C., ed. *Text and Image in Pre-Columbian Art: Essays on the Interrelationships of Verbal and Visual Arts*. Oxford, 1983.
Boone, Elizabeth Hill. "Pictorial Documents and Visual Thinking in Postconquest Mexico." In Elizabeth Hill Boone and Tom Cummins, eds., *Native Traditions in the Postconquest World*, Washington, DC, 1998.
———. *Stories in Black and Red: Mexican Pictorial Histories*. Austin, forthcoming.
Boone, Elizabeth H., and Walter D. Mignolo, eds. *Writing Without Words: Alternative Literacies in Mesoamerica and the Andes*. Durham, NC, 1994.
Bragdon, Kathleen. "'Another Tongue Brought In': An Ethnohistorical Study of Native Writings in Massachusett." Ph.D. Thesis, Brown University, 1981.
———. "Linguistic Acculturation in Massachusett in the 17th and 18th Centuries." In *Papers of the Twelfth Algonquian Conference* (Ottawa, 1981): 12 1–32.
———. "'Emphatical Speech and Great Action': An Analysis of Native Speech Events Described in Seventeenth-Century Sources." *Man in the Northeast* 33(1988): 88–101.

Campbell, Lyle. *American Indian Languages: The Historical Linguistics of Native America*. New York, 1997.
Cummins, Thomas. "From Lies to Truth: Colonial Ekphrasis and the Act of Crosscultural Translation." In Claire Farago, ed., *Reframing the Renaissance: Visual Culture in Europe and Latin America 1450-1650*, New Haven, 1995.
Drechsel, Emanuel J. *Mobilian Jargon: Linguistic and Sociohistorical Aspects of a Native American Pidgin*. Oxford, 1997.
Durand-Forest, Jacqueline de. "L'Indien de la Nouvelle Espagne vu par les missionnaires franciscains (XVIe-XVIIe siecles)." In Redondo Augustin, ed., *Les Representations de l'autre dans l'espace iberique et ibero-americain, II: Perspective diachronique*, Paris, 1993: 101–105.
Ebacher, Colleen M. "The Old and the New World: Incorporating American Indian Forms of Discourse and Modes of Communication into Colonial Missionary Texts." *Anthropological Linguistics* 33, no. 2 (1991): 135–65.
———. "The Colonial Missionary Text and Communicating Across Cultures." *Cincinnati Romance Review* 12 (1993): 1–14.
Fabian, Johannes. *Language and Colonial Power: The Appropriation of Swahili in the Former Belgian Congo*. Cambridge, England, 1986.
Farago, Claire, ed. *Reframing the Renaissance: Visual Culture in Europe and Latin America 1450-1650*. New Haven, CT, 1995.
Fausz, J. Frederick. "Middlemen in Peace and War: Virginia's Earliest Indian Interpreters, 1608–1632." *Virginia Magazine of History and Biography* 95 (Jan. 1987): 41–64.
Feister, Lois M. "Linguistic Communication between the Dutch and Indians in New Netherland, 1609–1664." *Ethnohistory* 20 (1973): 25–38.
Foster, Michael K. "On Who Spoke First at Iroquois-White Councils: An Exercise in the Method of Upstreaming." In M.K. Foster, J. Campisi, and M. Mithun, eds., *Extending the Rafters: Interdisciplinary Approaches to Iroquoian Studies*, Albany, 1984: 183–207.
Galeote, Manuel. *Léxico indigena de flora y fauna en tratados sobre las Indias Occidentales de autores andaluces*. Granada, 1997.
Galloway, Patricia. "Talking with Indians: Interpreters and Diplomacy in French Louisiana." In Winthrop D. Jordan and Sheila L. Skemp, eds., *Race and Family in the Colonial South*, Jackson, MS, 1987: 109–29, 161–64.
Garibay Kintana, Angel María. *Historia de la literatura náhuatl*. 2 vols. Mexico City, 1953–54.
Gimeno Gómez, Ana. "Notas sobre la implantación de la lengua castellana en América." In C. Hernández et al., eds., *El español de América*, Valladolid, 1991: vol. 1, 231–39.
Goddard, Ives. "Some Early Examples of American Indian Pidgin English from New England." *International Journal of Linguistics* 43, no. 1 (1977): 37–41.
———. "Eastern Algonquian Languages." In Bruce Trigger, ed., *The Handbook of North American Indians*, vol. 15, *Northeast*, Washington, DC, 1978: 70-77.
———, ed. *Handbook of North American Indians*, vol. 17, *Languages*, Washington, DC, 1996.
Gray, Edward G. *New World Babel: Languages and Nations in Early America*. Princeton, 1999.
Greenblatt, Stephen. "Learning to Curse: Aspects of Linguistic Colonialism in the Sixteenth Century." In Fredi Chiappelli, ed., *First Images of America*, Berkeley, 1977: vol. 1, 561–80.

Gruzinski, Serge. "Colonial Indian Maps in Sixteenth-Century Mexico." *Res* 13 (1987): 46–61.

———. *Painting and Conquest: The Mexican Indians and the European Renaissance.* Paris, 1992.

———. *The Conquest of Mexico: The Incorporation of Indian Societies into the Western World, 16th-18th Centuries.* Cambridge, England, 1993.

Hagedorn, Nancy L. "A Friend to Go between Them: The Interpreter as Cultural Broker during the Anglo-Iroquois Councils, 1740-1770." *Ethnohistory* 35, no. 1 (1988): 60-80.

———. "Brokers of Understanding: Interpreters as Agents of Cultural Exchange in Colonial New York." *New York History* 76 (1995): 379–408.

Hanzeli, Victor. *Missionary Linguistics in New France: A Study of Seventeenth- and Eighteenth-Century Descriptions of American Indian Languages.* The Hague, 1969.

Hart, William B. "For the Good of Our Souls: Mohawk Authority, Accommodation, and Resistance to Protestant Evangelism, 1700-1780." Ph.D. Thesis, Brown University, 1998.

Hefner, Robert. W., ed. *Conversion to Christianity: Historical and Anthropological Perspectives on a Great Transformation.* Berkeley, 1993.

Hovdhaugen, Even, ed. *... and the Word was God: Missionary Linguistics and Missionary Grammar.* Münster, 1996.

Jahr, Ernst Håkon, and Ingvild Broch. *Language Contact in the Arctic: Northern Pidgins and Contact Languages.* Berlin, 1996.

Jooken, Lieve. *The Linguistic Conceptions of Lord Monboddo (1714–1799).* Leuven, 2000.

Kachru, Braj B. and Henry Kahane, eds. *Cultures, Ideologies, and the Dictionary.* Tübingen, 1995.

Karttunen, Frances, and James Lockhart. *Nahuatl in the Middle Years: Language Contact Phenomena in Texts of the Colonial Period.* Berkeley, 1976.

———. "Nahuatl Literacy." In George Collier, Renato Rosaldo, and John Wirth, eds., *The Inca and Aztec States*, New York, 1982: 395–417.

———. *Between Worlds: Interpreters, Guides, and Survivors.* New Brunswick, NJ, 1994.

———. "The Roots of Sixteenth-Century Mesoamerican Lexicography." In Braj B. Kachru and Henry Kahane, eds., *Cultures, Ideologies, and the Dictionary: Studies in Honor of Ladislav Zgusta*, Tübingen, 1995: 75–88.

———. "Rethinking Malinche." In Susan Schroeder, Stephanie Wood, and Robert Haskett, eds., *Indian Women of Early Mexico*, Norman, OK, 1997: 290-312.

———. "Indigenous Writing as a Vehicle of Postconquest Continuity and Change in Mesoamerica." In Elizabeth Hill Boone and Tom Cummins, eds., *Native Traditions in the Postconquest World*, Washington, DC, 1998: 421–447.

Key, Mary Ritchie, ed. *Language Change in South American Indian Languages.* Philadelphia, 1991.

Klein, Harriet E., and Louisa R. Stark, eds. *South American Indian Languages: Retrospect and Prospect.* Austin, 1985.

Klor de Alva, Jorge. "Language, Politics, and Translation: Colonial Discourse and Classical Nahuatl in New Spain." In Rosanna Warren, ed., *The Art of Translation: Voices from the Field*, Boston, 1989.

Krieger, Carlo. "Ethnogenesis or Cultural Interference? Catholic Missionaries and the Micmac." In William Cowan, ed., *Actes du vingtième congrès des algonquinistes*, Ottawa, 1989: 193–200.

Lauzon, Matthew. "Savage Eloquence in America and the Linguistic Construction of a British Identity in the 18th Century." *Historiographia Linguistica* 23, no. 1/2 (1996): 123–58.

Leahey, Margaret. "'Comment peut un muet prescher l'évangile?' Jesuit Missionaries and the Native Languages of New France." *French Historical Studies* 19, no. 1 (Spring, 1995): 105–31.

Leibsohn, Dana. "Primers for Memory: Cartographic Histories and Nahua Identity." In Elizabeth H. Boone and Walter D. Mignolo, eds. *Writing without Words: Alternative Literacies in Mesoamerica and the Andes*, Durham, NC, 1994: 161–87.

——. *Contingent Cartographies: Indigenous Paintings, Maps, and the Colonial Fabric of Mexico*. Forthcoming.

Lerner, Isaías. "The *Diccionario* of Antonio de Alcedo as a Source of Enlightened Ideas." In A. Owen Aldridge, ed., *The Ibero-American Enlightenment*, Urbana, IL, 1978.

Lockhart, James. *The Nahuas after the Conquest: A Social and Cultural History of the Indians of Central Mexico, Sixteenth through Eighteenth Centuries*. Stanford, 1992.

Mallery, Garrick. *Picture Writing of the American Indians*. 2 vols. 1893; reprint edition, New York, 1972.

Mannheim, Bruce. *The Language of the Inka since the European Invasion*. Austin, 1991.

Marcus, Joyce. *Mesoamerican Writing Systems: Propaganda, Myth, and History in Four Ancient Civilizations*. Princeton, 1992.

Mazzotti, José Antonio. "Betanzos: de la 'epica' incaica a la escritura coral: Aportes para la formulacion del sujeto colonial en la historiografa andina." *Revista de Critica Literaria Latinoamericana* 40 (1994): 239–58.

——. *Coros Mestizos del Inca Garcilaso: Resonancias Andinas*. Lima, 1996.

Mazzotti, José and U. Juan Zevallos-Aguilar, eds. *Asedios a la Heterogeneidad Cultural. Libro de Homenaje a Antonio Cornejo Polar*. Philadelphia, 1996.

Mignolo, Walter. "Literacy and Colonization: The New World Experience." In René Jara and Nicholas Spadaccini, eds., *1492/1992: Re/Discovering Colonial Writing*, Minneapolis, 1989: 51–96.

——. "On the Colonization of Amerindian Languages and Memories: Renaissance Theories of Writing and the Discontinuity of the Classical Tradition." *Comparative Studies in Society and History* 34, no. 2 (1992): 301–30.

——. *The Darker Side of the Renaissance: Literacy, Territoriality, and Colonization*. Ann Arbor, 1995.

Morrison, K.M. "Discourse and the Accommodation of Values: Toward a Revision of Mission History." *Journal of the American Academy of Religion* 53, no. 3 (1985): 365–82.

Murray, David. *Forked Tongues: Speech, Writing, and Representation in North American Indian Texts*. Bloomington, IN, 1991.

Nowak, Elke. "How to 'Improve' a Language: The Case of Eighteenth-Century Descriptions of Greenlandic." In Anders Alqvist, ed., *Diversions of Galway: Papers on the History of Linguistics*, Amsterdam, 1992: 157–67.

Puccinelli Orlandi, Eni. "Les Ameriques et les Europeans: Un Clivage de sens ou la danse des grammaires." *Cahiers de Praxematique* 17 (1991): 73–92.

Rafael, Vicente L. *Contracting Colonialism: Translation and Christian Conversion in Tagalog Society under Early Spanish Rule*. Ithaca, 1988.

Rama, Angel. *The Lettered City*. J.C. Chasteen, trans. Durham, NC, 1996.

Riley, Carroll L. "Early Spanish-Indian Communication in the Greater Southwest." *New Mexico Historical Review* 46 (1971): 285–314.

Rivarola, José Luis. *La formación lingüística de Hispanoamérica*. Lima, 1990.

———. "Approximación histórica a los contactos de lenguas en el Perú." In Klaus Zimmerman, ed., *Lenguas en contacto en Hispanoamérica*, Frankfurt, 1995.

Salmon, Vivian. "Missionary Linguistics in Seventeenth-Century Ireland and a North American Analogy." *Historiographia Linguistica* 12, no. 3 (1985): 321–49.

Schreyer, Rüdiger. "Linguistics Meets Caliban or the Uses of Savagery in Eighteenth Century Theoretical History of Language." In Hans Aarsleff, Louis Kelly, and Hans-Joseph Niederehe, eds., *Papers in the History of Linguistics*, Amsterdam, 1987: 301–14.

———. *The European Discovery of Chinese (1550-1615), or The Mystery of Chinese Unveiled*. Amsterdam, 1992.

———. "Deaf Mutes, Feral Children and Savages: Of Analogical Evidence in Eighteenth Century Theoretical History of Language." In Günther Blaicher and Brigitte Glaser, eds., *Anglistentag 1993 Eichstätt*, Tübingen, 1994: 70-86.

———. "Take Your Pen and Write: A Documented Sketch of the Beginnings of Huron Linguistics." In Even Hovdhaugen, ed.,… *and the Word was God: Missionary Linguistics and Missionary Grammar*, Münster, 1996: 77–121.

Silverstein, Michael. "Dynamics of Linguistic Contact." In Ives Goddard, ed., *Handbook of North American Indians*, vol. 17, *Languages*, Washington, DC, 1996: 117–36.

Szasz, Margaret Connell. *Indian Education in the American Colonies, 1607–1783*. Albuquerque, 1988.

———. *Between Indian and White Worlds: The Cultural Broker*. Norman, OK, 1994.

Trexler, Richard. "We Think, They Act: Clerical Readings of Missionary Theatre in 16th Century New Spain." In Steven L. Kaplan, ed., *Understanding Popular Culture: Europe from the Middle Ages to the Nineteenth Century*, Berlin, 1984: 189–227.

Watts, Pauline Moffitt. "Hieroglyphs of Conversion: Alien Discourses in Diego Valadés's *Rhetorica Christiana*." *Memorie Domenicane*, new series, no. 22 (1991): 405–33.

———. "Languages of Gesture in Sixteenth-Century Mexico: Antecedents and Transmutations." In Claire Farago, ed. *Reframing the Renaissance: Visual Culture in Europe and Latin America 1450-1650*, New Haven, 1995: 140-51.

Wogan, Peter. "Perceptions of European Literacy in Early Christian Contact Situations." *Ethnohistory* 41, no. 3 (1994): 407–29.

Wolfart, Hans Christoph. "Notes on the Early History of American Indian Linguistics." *Folia Linguistica* 1 (1967): 153–71.

Wurtzburg, Susan, and Lyle Campbell, "North American Indian Sign Language: Evidence of Its Existence before European Contact," *International Journal of American Linguistics* 61, no. 2 (April 1995): 153–67.

Yoneda, Keiko. *Los mapas de Cuauhtinchan y la historia cartográfica prehispánica*. Mexico City, 1981.

Contributors

James Axtell is Kenan Professor of Humanities at the College of William and Mary.

Kathleen J. Bragdon is Associate Professor of Anthropology at the College of William and Mary.

Norman Fiering is Director and Librarian of the John Carter Brown Library at Brown University.

Ives Goddard is Curator and Head of the Division of Ethnology, Department of Anthropology, at the National Museum of Natural History in Washington, D.C.

Edward G. Gray is Assistant Professor of History at Florida State University.

Bruce Greenfield is Associate Professor of English at Dalhousie University.

William B. Hart is Assistant Professor of History at Middlebury College.

Lieve Jooken is lecturer in English at the Economische Hogeschool St. Aloysius, Brussels, Belgium.

Frances Karttunen is Senior University Research Scientist at the Linguistics Research Center, University of Texas at Austin.

Margaret J. Leahey is Associate Professor of Humanities and Dean of the School of Arts and Sciences at Gwynedd-Mercy College.

Dana Leibsohn is Assistant Professor in the Art Department at Smith College.

Isaías Lerner is Professor of Hispanic Literature at the Graduate School of the City University of New York.

José Antonio Mazzotti is Assistant Professor in the Department of Romance Languages at Harvard University.

Rüdiger Schreyer is Akademischer Oberrat at the Institut für Anglistik, Aachen University of Technology, Germany.

Pauline Moffitt Watts is a member of the European History faculty at Sarah Lawrence College.

INDEX

Abenaki Indians
    pidgin and, 34, 35, 72, 73
    writing by, 202
acculturation versus continuity, 155–72
Acosta, José de
    on Chinese writing and education, 8
    on Nahua pictograph painters, 5
    on native languages, 289
Aguilar, Jerónimo de, 219
Alcedo, Antonio de, 289
Algonquian language, 31, 67. *See also* Pidgin Algonquin
    Basque pidgin mixed with, 63
    different forms of, 17
    Eliot's translations of, John, 178
    French interpreters travelling with, 46
    Montagnais and, 16
    name origin of, 16
    Norwood and, Henry, 28
    pidgin and, 33, 34, 35, 36, 39, 63, 71–75
    polysynthesis of, 3
    Portuguese and, 16
    subgroups from, 174
Allouez, Claude, 21, 104
American Indian languages, 2, 15–60
    number of, 16
American Indians
    calumet and, 20, 21
    communicating with, 15–60
    gestures and, 17–18
    greetings methods of, 19–20
    offerings by, 20
    tobacco and, 20–21
    traders and, 19
    wampum and, 20
    word forms descriptions in colonial missionary grammars of, 293–309
Amerindian
    challenge of, 311–14
    discursive traditions maintenance of, 156
    languages, 82, 163, 293, 307
    mapmakers, 119–21, 123, 124
    writing upon images by, 132

Andrade, Pedro Fernández de Castro y, 284
André, Louis, 105
Andrews, William, 231, 232
Archer, Gabriel
    beaverskin trading and, 26
    gestures and, 22
    Powhatan and, 24–25
Arnold as interpreter, Benedict, 49
Arriaga, Pablo José de, 284
Atahualpa, 217, 220, 224
Ayala, Manuel José de, 288, 289
Aztec
    alphabetic literacy cases and, 155–72
    conquest of as documented in Nahuatl, 157
    doña Marina and language knowledge of, 226
    history of, writing of, 157–58
    pictographic writing of, 5, 155

Babel
    and origin of language, 310–11, 319
    as scientific myth, 318
    of tongues, 15–60
Bacon, Nathaniel, 38
Bakker, Peter, 63
Banks, Joseph, 321
Barclay, Henry, 231, 236–37, 238, 240, 247
Barlowe, Arthur, 19
Barton, Benjamin Smith, 270
Bartram, John, 265
Basque language, 30–32
    Algonquin pidgin mixed with, 63
Biard, Pierre, 2
    on gestures, 4
    on rote learning, 195
Biet, Antoine, 295, 299, 300
Bigot, Jacques, 105, 107
body language, 18
Bonnefoy, Antoine, 40
Boyle, Robert, 181
Bradford, William and Logan's speech, 259, 267, 268
Brant, Joseph, 237
Brant, Milly, 237

Brébeuf, Jean de, 102, 103, 108, 322
  on dance as disease cure, 111
  on dreams, 110
  on tobacco, 110
Brosses, Charles de, 319
Brulé, Étienne, 46
Buffon, Le Comte de, 260
Burnett, James. *See* Monboddo, Lord

calumet, 20
Campanius, Johannes
  pidgin and, 37
  Pidgin Delaware and, 64, 65, 70, 71
Cartier, Jacques
  Indian welcome to, 19
  interpreters and, 219
  kidnapping people to become
    interpreters by, 216
  Stadaconans and, 24
  training of interpreters and, 41, 45–46
  voyage up the St. Lawrence by, 25
cartography and graphology in New
    Spain, indigenous, 119–51
Castilian in America, 287, 289
Castro, Lope Garcia de, 159, 162
Caunauhstansey, Old Abraham, 235, 236,
    238–39
  on angels, 245
  death of, 247
  hiring of, 231
  Johnson on, William, 240
  Ogilvie on, John, 247, 249
  rote learning of students of, 242
  salary of, 254n. 29
Cavallero, Antonio, 288
Charbonneau, Toussaint, 218
Cherokees, 40
Chi, Gaspar Antonio, 220, 227
Chickasaw Indians, 39, 40
Chicora, Francisco de, 217, 223
Chinese writing as universal language, 8
Christian versus Iroquois version of
    creation, 244
Cicero, 85, 260
  on eloquence of speech, 261
  hieroglyphics and, 93
Claus as interpreter, Daniel, 48, 248, 249
Clinton, DeWitt, 238, 271
Cockenoe, 220, 229n. 30
Cocom, Nachi, 220
Colden, Cadwallader
  on interpreters, 271–72
  on trust, 49
Colón, Diego, 222
Collapiña, 159
Columbus, Christopher
  flight of his captive interpreters,
    222–23
  gestures usage and, 22–23, 281
  kidnapping people to become
    interpreters by, 216, 218, 284

  language problems of, 23, 215, 281
  mortality of his captives, 222
  signing and, 22–23
  women captives and, 226
continuity versus acculturation, 155–72
Coronado, Francisco Vásquez, 123–24
Corte-Real kidnapping people to become
    interpreters, Gaspar, 216
Cortés, Hernán, 218
  Aztec writing about, 158
  conquest of Montezuma's empire
    by, 84
  doña Marina as interpreter for, 216,
    224–25, 226
  flight of captive interpreter of, 223
  interpreters and, 219
  kidnapping people to become
    interpreters by, 216
  spiritual conquest of Mexico starts
    with, 87
Cotton and learning of real Indian language by, John and Josiah, 74
Cranz, David, 295, 300–301, 302, 305, 306
Creoles, 62, 63
Cresap, Michael, 259, 262, 265
cultural brokering, 49

Dablon, Claude, 104
Davis, John
  Eskimo welcome to, 19
  fire and, 21
Delaware Indians. *See also* Pidgin
    Delaware
  book on jargon of, 37–38
  grammatical categories of language
    of, 66–68
  interpreter of, 50
  pidgin and, 36–37, 63–71
Díaz del Castillo, Bernal, 223, 226
doña Marina, 226
  age and, 227n. 7
  death of, 222
  Diaz del Castillo on, Bernal, 229n. 28
  as interpreter to Cortés, 216, 224–25
  skills of, 226
  survival strategy of, 225
Donnacona, 24, 25, 41, 45, 46
Dunmore's War, 262
Dunster, Henry, 176
Durán, Diego, 157

Eden, Richard, 319
Edwards, Jonathan, 74, 238, 239
Egede, Paul, 295
Eliot, John, 240
  Algonquin genders in speech and,
    67, 178
  informants of, 226
  learning of real Indian language by,
    74, 220
  Logick Primer by, 179

Eliot, John (*cont.*)
   Massachusett Bible and, viii, 5, 185
   Massachusett literacy and, 180–81
   translations of English religious texts by, 176–78
Elliot, Sir John H., 7
Erasmus, Desiderius, 233
Ercilla, Alonso de, 284–85, 290
Eskimo language Greenlandic, 294
   analyzing grammatical complexity of words of, 296–305
   Cranz on, David, 300–301
   Monboddo on, Lord, 305–6
   writings about, 295
etymology, 311, 313
evolution, societal, 317, 318

Falkner, Thomas, 295–96, 297, 298, 301–5, 306
Felipe as interpreter, 224, 226
Ferguson, Adam, 269, 270, 272
Fleet as interpreter, Henry, 57n. 72
Florentine Codex, 5, 225
Focher, Juan, 84
Fontaine, John, 38–39
Foulger, Peter, 220, 221
Franciscan(s)
   grammar teaching by, 93
   image usage for teaching of reading by, 92
   images woven into tapestries by, 89
   influence on language existing today by, 95
   languages of gesture and gesticulation used by, 85, 87
   manipulation of hybrid languages by, 86
   Nahuatl dances and response by, 88
   standardization attempt by, 91, 92
   writings of, 84
French dialects, 17

Galibi language, 294
   analyzing grammatical complexity of words of, 296–305
   dictionary of, 295
   La Salle de l'Etang on, Simon-Philibert de, 299–300
   origin of, 295
   pidginization of, 299
Garcilaso de la Vega, El Inca, 163–66
   on Felipe as interpreter, 224
   on learning Quechua, 220
   on reciprocal language learning, 219
Garnier, Charles, 106
gesture(s), 4, 17–18
   ancient rhetoric and, 85–86
   Archer and, Gabriel, 22
   charades as, 22
   Columbus and, Christopher, 22–23, 281
   Franciscan usage of, 85
   liabilities of, 18
   in sixteenth-century Mexico, 82, 84–89
   through time, 85–86
Gibson, John, 262, 263, 267, 272
Gomes, Estevão, 216
Gookin, Daniel, 178
Gosnold, Bartholomew, 26, 32
Granganimeo, 19
Greenlandic Eskimo language, 294
   analyzing grammatical complexity of words of, 296–305
   Cranz on, David, 300–301
   Monboddo on, Lord, 305–6
   writings about, 295
greetings methods, 19–20
Guerrero, Gonzalo de, 219
Gyles as interpreter, John, 44

hand signals. *See* gesture(s)
Hawley, Gideon, 45
healing rituals, 110–12
Hebrew language, ix, 310, 313
   American Indians language and, 176
   as first universal language, 282, 311, 323n. 2
Heckewelder, John, 269
Herder, Johann Gottfried von, 319, 320, 321
Hiacoomes, 221
hieroglyphs usage in sixteenth-century Mexico, 92–93
Hill (Kanonraron), Aaron, 249
Hilton, William, 32
Hunt, Thomas, 218
Hurons, 103
   dance as disease cure by, 111
   European disease and, 109
   healing rituals of, 110–12
   images to appease, 106
   language connection to ancient Greece of, 313
   language of, 2
   masks and, 112
   Monboddo on language of, Lord, 322
   tobacco and, 110, 112
   word-sentences of, 296, 297

Iberville, Pierre La Moyne d', 19–20, 21
   sign language and, 26
Inca
   cases of alphabetic literacy and, 155–72
   history of, 159
   khipu of, 155, 159, 160, 161, 162
   language of, 3, 81, 160, 170n. 19
   Quechua language usage by, 289
Inca language
   epic form of narration and, 160, 170n. 19
   polysynthesis of, 3
   writings of, 81
Incan quipus, 82

indigenous languages of America and
    Spanish colonization, 281–92
interpreters, 41–53, 215–29
    castaways and exchanges of, 218–19
    Clinton on, Dewitt, 271
    Colden on, Cadwallader, 271–72
    competence of, 224–25
    European training as, 43
    flight of, 222–23
    Indian reliance on, 266
    kidnapping individuals to become,
        44–46, 215, 216–18, 221
    missionaries and, 219–21
    mortality of, 222
    Oviedo y Valdés on, Gonzalo
        Fernández de, 283, 284
    religion and, 52
    rewarding of, 51
    ritual kin and, 221
    traders as, 48
    training of, 41
    trust and, 49–51
    women as, 226
    youth as, 225–26
Iroquoian and Mohawk schoolmasters
    and catechists in mid-eighteenth
    century, 230–57
    baptism and, 244–45, 247
    Christian versus Iroquois version
        of creation and, 244
    communion and, 244, 245–46
    drunkenness and, 247, 249
    fostering literacy and religious
        change and, 236–46
    headmen (sachems) in Iroquois
        society and, 234–36
    Iroquois creation myth and, 243–44
    Iroquois multi-God beliefs and, 241
    reasons for religious change and
        practice and, 233
    value of literacy and, 247
Iroquoian language, 2
    connection to ancient Greece of, 313
    different forms of, 17
    interpreter for, 44, 50
    name origin of, 16
    pidgin and, 36, 39, 72
    polysynthesis of, 3
    teaching children of, 45
Ixtililxochitl, Fernando de Alva, 157,
    158–59, 164

James, Thomas, 178
Jamestown, 217
    communicating by signs in, 24–25
    interpreters in, 47
jargon. *See* pidgin
Jefferson, Thomas
    authenticity of Logan's speech and,
        265–66
    on eloquence of speech, 260–61, 265
    on Indian usage of language, 266
    on Logan's speech, 259, 260, 261,
        262, 267, 272
    portrayal of Logan by, 263, 264
Jesuit(s), 92
    attitude toward women of, 107,
        115n. 35
    dreams of Hurons and, 110, 117nn.
        63, 66
    expulsion from America of, 287
    French versus English and language
        skills by, 108
    gestures and, 4
    image usage by, 102–3
    interpreters and, 41–42
    language skills in New France of, 108
Joncaire as interpreter for New France,
    Louis-Thomas Chabert de, 44
Johnson (Brother Waronghyage),
    William, 52, 232, 238, 246, 2
    48–49
    on Caunauhstansey, Old Abraham,
        236, 240
    on constant flux of Mohawk beliefs,
        246–47
    on Mohawks learning English, 237
Jonathan, Philip, 246
Joutel, Henri, 4, 27

Kames, Lord, 314
Kauder, Christian
    on Mi'kmaq as lay priests, 203–4
    Mi'kmaq hieroglyphs and, 192,
        193, 206
Kellog as interpreters, Joseph and
    Rebecca, 44–45, 221, 226
kidnapped people as interpreters,
    44–46, 215, 216–18, 221–27
    flight of, 222–23
    refusal of cooperation of, 221
    mortality of, 222
    survival strategies for, 225
    thin line between and domestic-
        ity, 217
Kiowa language, 3
Kodiak Island, 6

Laet, Johannes de, 64, 69
Lafitau, Joseph François, 263, 264, 312–
    13, 322
Lahontan, Baron de, 16
Landa, Diego de, 220
language(s). *See also* individual
        languages
    American Indian, 2
    Chinese, 8, 323n. 3
    definition of, 1
    genealogy, 310–11
    Hebrew. *See* Hebrew language
    Huron, 2
    interpreters of, 41–52, 215–29

language(s) (cont.)
  Kiowa, 3
  Mohawk, 3
  New World, 319
  origin, 310–11, 319
  perfection, 7–8
  pidgin, 29–40
  primitive, 322
  progress, 319
  religious instruction and, 286, 287
  Tlön, 3
  universal, 7–8, 282
language studies and establishment of colonial rule, 178–80
La Salle de l'Étang, Simon-Philibert de, 295, 299, 300, 304–5
La Salle, René-Robert Cavelier, 4, 27
Lawson, John, 17, 266
Lechford, Thomas, 176
LeClercq, Chrestien
  on coming up with idea for Mi'kmaq hieroglyphs, 201–2
  Mi'kmaq hieroglyphs and, 190, 192, 194, 203
  teaching Mi'kmaq to memorize prayers, 195–96
  teaching Mi'kmaq to read, 196, 197, 200
Lee, Arthur, 246
LeJeune, Paul, 31, 261
  coining of words by, 108
  images in New France and, 103–4, 106–7
LeMercier and European disease in New France, 109, 110–11
León-Portilla, Miguel, 1, 167
Léry, Jean de, 2, 205
Lescarbot, Marc, 31
Levett and pidgin, Christopher, 35
Lewis and Clark Expedition and Sacajawea, 218, 222
Lindeström, Peter, 64
linguistic refinement, eighteenth-century theories of, 310–11
literacy and impact on Massachusett speakers, 180–82
literacy and religious change fostering experiment, 230–57
literate and nonliterate, 96n. 5, 153–211
Locke, John, 316
Logan (Mingo/Soyechtowa), 258–77
  biographical sketch of, 261–62
  Bradford and speech of, William, 259, 267, 268
  challenge to authenticity of speech by, 265, 272
  death of, 273
  importance of speech of, 260
  Jefferson on speech of, Thomas, 259, 260, 261, 262, 267
  making of, 258–77
  Ossian's writing compared to, 270
  printing of speech of, 259–60
  reputation of, start of, 259
  speech of, 259–60
Luis de Quirós, 223

Macpherson, Charles, 270
Macpherson, James, 270
Madison on Logan's speech, James, 259, 267
Maillard, Pierre Antonine-Simon, 197–99
  choice of Mi'kmaq hieroglyphs over Roman alphabet usage, 197–98
  Mi'kmaq hieroglyphs and, 190, 192, 194
  on Mi'kmaq notetaking, 202–03
  teaching Mi'kmaq memorization, 197
man, science of, 315–16, 324–25n. 24
Mandeville, Bernard, 317–18, 319
Manzano, Cipriano Muñoz y, 288
maps/mapmaking in New Spain, 119–51
  color and, 127, 147–48n. 10
  conscripted terrain and, 142–44
  features of, 124–26
  as history, 123
  makers of, 124
  number of, 146n. 4
  paper used for, 145n. 1
  reading of, 141
  reason for, 122–23
  samples of, 12, 125, 130, 135, 138, 140
  seepage of ink and paint on, 134, 150n. 18
  writing on, 128–41, 143, 148–49n. 12
Mapuche language, 294
  analyzing grammatical complexity of words in, 296–305
  Falkner on, Thomas, 301–5
  first description of, 295–96, 297
  grammatical analysis sample of, 298
  Monboddo on, Lord, 306
  other names for, 296
Marsh, Witham, 266
Marsolet as interpreter, Nicolas, 46
Martin and Logan's speech, Luther, 265
Martyr, Peter, 284
Masks and healing ceremonies, 112–13, 117nn. 72, 77, 118n. 78
Massachusett
  literary impact on speakers of, 180–82, 183
  silence and, 264
  translations into, 176–78, 179, 183
Massachusett Bible, viii, 5, 185
Massachusett Pidgin, 71, 72, 73
Mayan, 129
  Chi and, Gaspar Antonio, 220, 227
  doña Marina and, 224, 226
  kidnapping for purpose of interpreters of, 216, 222
  Lande among, Diego de, 220

language of, 3
pictographs and hieroglyphs of, 83
writing of, 6, 129
Mayflower, 218
Mayhew, Experience, 74, 177, 187–88n. 19
Mayhew, Thomas, 176, 220, 221
McGuffey's Reader, 273
Megapolensis and pidgin, Johannes, 36
Melchor, 223
Mendieta, Gerónimo de, 84
Mendoza, Antonio de, 123, 286
Mercer, Hugh, 50
Mexía, Pedro, 282, 283
Mexico
   Nahuatl as language of, 289
   pictures, gestures, and hieroglyphs in sixteenth century in 81–101
   preservation of books in, 84
   printing arrival in, 286
Michaëlius and pidgin, Jonas, 35–36, 66, 70, 72
Micmac people, 2, 19, 108
   Basque-Algonquin pidgin and, 63
   Gyles as interpreter of, John, 44
   oldest pidgin in eastern North America and, 30–31
   Rand on, Silas T., 205
Mignolo, Walter, 81–82, 83
Mi'kmaq hieroglyphs, 189–211
   content of, 198–99
   description of, 191–92
   development of, 201–2
   as evangelization tool, 199–200
   Kauder and, Christian, 192, 193, 203–4, 206
   lasting nature of, 207
   LeClercq and, Chrestien. See LeClercq, Chrestien
   literacy and, 200
   Maillard and, Pierre Antonine-Simon. See Maillard, Pierre Antonine-Simon
   Pacifique and, Father, 192, 205–6
   rote learning and, 195
   samples of, 193, 194
missionary grammars and descriptions of American Indian word forms, 293–309
Mohawk language, 3
   Christian texts published into, 233–34
   pidgin and, 30, 36, 72
Mohawk schoolmasters and catechists in mid-eighteenth-century Iroquoia, 230–57
   baptism and, 244–45, 247
   Christian versus Iroquois version of creation and, 244
   communion and, 244, 245–46
   drunkenness and, 247, 249

   fostering literacy and religious change and, 236–46
   headmen (sachems) in Iroquois society and, 234–36
   Iroquois creation myth and, 243–44
   Iroquois multi-God beliefs and, 241
   reasons for religious change and practice and, 233
   value of literacy and, 247
Molina, Alonso de, 286
Monboddo, Lord, 305–7, 316, 320, 321–22
   on Greek inflection, 299
   on Huron language, 322
   on language in New World, 294–95, 320
Montagnais language
   Algonquin and, 16
   Basque-Algonquin pidgin and, 63
   French interpreters travelling with, 46
   Jesuits in New France and, 108
   multilingual jargon of, 31
   Pastedechouen and, Pierre-Antoine, 42
   pidgin and, 30
Montezuma, 84, 157, 158
   doña Marina interpreting, 224–25
Montour, Andrew, 50
Montreal
   founding of, 220
   Ogilvie in, John, 232
   Sahonwadi and Mohawks relocating to, Paulus, 249
Morse, Jedediah, 261
mortality of snatched indigenes, 222
Morton, Thomas, 176
Motolinia, Toribio de, 89, 91, 92
multilingualism
   interpreter usage rather than usage of, 266–67
   Mohawks desire for, 239
   Sahonwadi and, Paulus, 237
Munsee language, 63, 64, 71
Muskogean language
   different forms of, 17
   name origin of, 16
   pidgin and, 39
Mutis, José Celestino, 288

Nahua pictographs, 5, 6, 82
   to phonetic European system, 6
Nahuas
   European's assumptions about, 87–88
   gestures and, 86, 87
   images, objects, and gesture usage to instruct, 89
   language and, 2, 3, 5, 6, 81, 95
   pictographs and hieroglyphs used by, 82
   song, dance, and drama usage by, 88–89
   tecpillahtolli and, 224, 225

Nahuatl
    documentation of conquest
        in, 157
    dances of, 88
    doña Marina and language of, 224
    first grammar of, 93
    Roman Latin and, 94
    writings in, 129
Nahuatl language, 2
    dictionary of, first, 287
    doña Marina's skill in, 226
    Florentine Codex and, 5
    Mexico and usage of, 289
    polysynthesis of, 3
    Sahagún and, Bernardino de, 219–20
    writing example of, 6
native language spoken and written in
        Southern New England, 173–88
    creation of shared communicative
        practice and, 174–75
    description of, early, 175–78
    introduction to, 173
    language studies and establishment
        of colonial rule and, 178–80
    linguistic map of, 173–74
    literacy and impact on Massachusett
        speakers and, 180–82
    politics of language description
        and literacy and, 184, 185–86
    questioning the texts and, 183–84, 185
nature, human, 316
Nauirans and Jamestown, 24–25
Nebrija, Antonio de, 284
New France, 27
    European diseases in, 109
    interpreters for, 44, 219, 220
    Iroquois as tormenter in images
        used in, 107
    language of images in seventeenth
        century in, 102–18
    paintings and engravings sent to, 106
    printing press in, 198
    Ursuline order establishment in,
        115n. 23
New Spain. See also maps/mapmaking
        in New Spain
    alphabetic writing in, 132, 149n. 13
    conscripted terrain in, 142–44
    doña Marina as interpreter in, 216
    graphology and indigenous cartog-
        raphy in, 119–51
    learning language in, 83
    printing in, 286
New Sweden, 64
Nicollet, Jean, 46
Nipmuck Indians, 17, 174, 178
North American usage of pidgins and
        jargons, east coast, 61–78
Norton, John, 244
Norwood, Henry, 28–29

Occaneechi Indians and pidgin, 38, 39
Oel, Jacob, 246
Ogilvie, John, 231, 232, 240
    on Caunauhstansey, Old Abraham,
        236, 247, 249
    on Mohawks and Christianity, 239
    on Sahonwadi, Paulus, 237
Old Abraham. See Caunauhstansey,
        Old Abraham
Olmos, Alonso de, 223
Olmos, Andres de, 93
Oña, Pedro de, 286
Ortiz as interpreter, Juan, 43–44
Ossian, 270
Oviedo y Valdés, Gonzalo Fernández
        de, 223, 283–84, 288
    published works containing some
        American languages of,
        282–83, 285

Pacifique (Henri Buisson de
        Valigny), Père
    Mi'kmaq hieroglyphs and, 190, 192,
        205–6
    views of Mi'kmaq hieroglyphs, 206
Pamptico Indians, 17
Pascagoulas Indians, 20
Pastedechouen, Pierre-Antoine, 42
Peachey, James, 248
Pelleprat, Pierre, 295, 300
Penn and pidgin, William, 37, 64, 66
Perrot, Nicolas, 21
Peru, 159–168. See also Quechua
    alphabetic literacy in, 159
    Incan history writing in, 159
    khipu usage in, 159, 160, 161, 162
    kidnapped interpreters usage in, 217
    printing in, establishment of, 287
philosophy, moral, 315–16
Pidgin Algonquin, 73
    historical significance of, 74–75
Pidgin Delaware, 30, 63–71, 72, 73
    Delaware language versus, 6, 68–69
    Munsee language and, 63, 64
    pronouns in, 67–68, 70
    pronunciations of, 77n. 22
    sources of, 64
    Unami language and, 63, 64, 71
pidgin language, 29–40
    Algonquin-based, 71–75
    attractive features of, 30
    Basque form of, 30–32
    Chinook usage of, 61
    east coast of North America usage
        of, 61–78
    English form of, 33–34
    jargon versus, 62–63
    oldest in eastern North American,
        30–31
    Spanish form of, 32–33
Pidgin Massachusett, 71, 72

Pierron, Jean, 105–6
Pigafetta, Antonio, 284
pipes. *See* calumet
Plymouth, 33, 174, 218, 222
politics of language description and literacy, 184, 185–86
polysynthesis, 3, 108, 296, 301, 303, 305
Poma de Ayala, Guamán, 166–67, 217, 220
Powhatan Indians, 24, 41
  interpreters and, 47
  pidgin and, 30, 38, 39, 72
  uprising of 1622 of, 42
Pratz, Antoine Le Page du, 39
printing arrival in America, 286
Purchas, Samuel, 319

Quechua, 2, 159–60
  language of, 163, 285, 289
  as language of religion, 286
  poetry of, 164
  reciprocal language learning and, 219, 220
  writing of, 166
Quinnipiak Indians, 17
quipus
  description of, 6
  Incan, 82

Rand and Mi'kmaq hieroglyphs, Silas T., 190, 204–5
Raynal, Abbé, 260
Reland, Adrian, 313, 324n. 18
Ricardo, Antonio, 286
Ricci and Chinese writing, Matteo, 8
Richer, Jean, 46
Richter, Daniel K., 264
Robertson, William, 312, 313
Rolfe, John, 217
Rousseau, Jean-Jacques, 269–70, 272, 320
Ru, Paul du, 21

Sacajawea, 218, 222, 223, 227
sachems in Iroquois society, 234–36
Sagard, Gabriel, 111, 296, 322
Sagouarrab as interpreter, Laurence, 51
Sahagún, Bernardino de, 157, 224
  Florentine Codex and, 5
  informants of, 226
  Nahuas and, 6, 219–20, 225
  Nahuatl dance ceremony account by, 88
Sahonwadi, Cornelius and Daniel, 231, 235, 236–37, 238, 240, 247
Sahonwadi, Paulus, 232, 235, 240, 247
  drawing of, 248
  hiring of, 231
  multilingualism of, 237
  replacement for, 246
  Revolutionary War and moving of, 249
  rote learning of students of, 242

Samoset and pidgin, 34
Sapir, Edward, 3
Sauvole, Antoine de, 20
Savage as interpreter, Thomas, 47
savage languages in eighteenth-century theoretical history of language, 310–26
  Amerindian challenge and, 311–14
  evidence for, 318–22
  orthodox view of linguistic relationships and, 310–11
  science of man and, 315–16
science of man in eighteenth century, 315–16
Shawnee Indians and beaverskin trading, 26
Shelikhov, Grigorii, 6–7
Shikellamy (Mingo), 261
sign language. *See also* gesture(s)
  French failure with, 28
  Norwood and, Henry, 28–29
  sticky situations and usage of, 26
signs and symbols, 79–151
silence, 264–65
Simón, Fray Pedro, 284
Siouan language
  different forms of, 17
  name origin of, 16
  pidgin and, 39
Slany, John, 218
Smith, Adam, 268
Smith, John, 38
  history of Virginia by, 28
  interpreters and, 47
  pidgin and, 72, 73
Solander, Daniel, 321
Soto and interpreter usage, Hernando de, 43–44
Southern New England and native language spoken and written, 173–88
  creation of shared communicative practice and, 174–75
  description of, early, 175–78
  introduction to, 173
  language studies and establishment of colonial rule and, 178–80
  linguistic map of, 173–74
  literacy and impact on Massachusett speakers and, 180–82
  politics of language description and literacy and, 184, 185–86
  questioning the texts and, 183–84, 185
Spanish colonization and indigenous language of America, 281–92
  Charles III's decision to use Spanish only, 287
  printing and, 286
Spanish dialects, 17
  jargon inspired by, 32–33

Spelman as interpreter, Henry, 47
Squanto, 218
　death of, 222
　kidnapping of, 33
　pidgin and, 34
Stadaconans, 19, 24
Standish, Miles and pidgin, 34
Stanton, Thomas, 49
Stewart, Dugald, 317, 318
Strachey and pidgin dictionary, William, 38, 72, 73, 77n. 35
Stuart, John, 232, 249
Süßmilch, Johann Peter, 320–21
Supno, 159

Tachnechdorus, 261
tapestries usage for teaching Christian doctrine, 89, 90, 99n. 28
Testera, Jacopo de, 83–84, 91, 92, 93
texts, questioning the, 183–84, 185
Tezozomoc, Fernando Alvarado, 157, 158, 164
theoretical history of language, savage languages in eighteenth century, 310–26
　Amerindian challenge to, 311–14
　evidence of, 318–22
　orthodox view of linguistic relationships and, 310–11
　science of man and, 315–16
Thomás, Domingo de Santo, 287
Thomas and his book on Indian jargon, Gabriel, 37, 64
Thorowgood, Thomas, 175
Tisquantum (Squanto), 218
　death of, 222
　kidnapping of, 33
　pidgin and, 34
Tlön language, 3
tobacco, 20–21, 26
　as cure for disease, 110–11, 112
　Huron beliefs about, 110
　as offerings, 110
　Virginia settlers and, 38
Torquemada, Fray Juan de, 88
Torres, Luis de, 23
Tower of Babel, ix
　rise of numerous languages after fall of, 9
Trilling, Lionel, 272
Tupinamba people, 2
Tuscarora Indians, 17

Unami language, 63, 64, 71

Vaca, Alvar Nuñez Cabeza de, 25–26
Valadés, Diego, 84, 89, 90
　on hieroglyphic writing as teaching aid, 92–93
Valdivia, P. Luis de, 296
Valverde, Vicente, de, 224

van der Volgen as interpreter, Lawrence Claessen, 44
van Eps as interpreter, Jan Baptist, 44
Vasquez de Ayllón, don Lucas
　flight of captive interpreter of, 223
　kidnapping people to become interpreters by, 217
Velasco, Luis de, 217
Verrazzano, Giovanni da, 21–22, 23–24
Vespucci, Amerigo, 283
Virginia
　Indian school in, 42
　pidgin and, 38
　pidgin usage in, 72

wampum
　belts of, 6
　as medium of alliance and peace, 20
　as offering at church, 110
　as offering to guests, 20
　pidgin and, 71
Waymouth, George, 19, 26
Weiser as interpreter, Conrad, 48, 59n. 90
Wequash, 221
Wheelock and teaching of Indians, Eleazar, 42
Williams, Eunice, 221, 225, 226
Williams, Roger, 73, 179
　on Algonquin language, 17, 74
　Key into the Language of America by, 59n. 89, 175–76, 220–21
　as interpreter for Narragansetts, 49
Wilson, Thomas, 240–41, 245
Winslow, Edward, 34, 71–72, 180
Woccon Indians, 17
Wood, William
　on dual forms of pidgin usage, 73
　on Massachusett usage of silence, 264
　on southern New England languages, 175
word forms, descriptions of in colonial missionary grammars, American Indian, 293–309
writing
　alphabetical type in Mexico and Peru after 1492, 81
　first appearance of New World languages in books, 284
　on maps, 128–41, 143
　native attitudes toward, 191
writing and Christianity in maritime Canada in 1675–1921. See Mi'kmaq hieroglyphs

Yupanqu, Titu Kusi, 162–63

Zeisberger as trusted interpreter, David, 50
Zumárraga, Juan de, 286